THE AIMS OF JESUS

BEN F. MEYER

The Aims of Jesus

SCM PRESS LTD

232

334 00027 0

First published 1979
by SCM Press Ltd
58 Bloomsbury Street, London WC1

Filmset by Input Typesetting Ltd
and printed in Great Britain by
REDWOOD BURN LIMITED
Trowbridge & Esher

George H. Dunne
amicitiae sacrum

CONTENTS

PREFACE

Passages from the Bible cited in the following pages are finally my own translations, but made under the guidance of the *Revised Standard Version* (London and New York: Nelson 1952), *The Holy Scriptures* (Philadelphia: Jewish Publication Society of America 1955), *The New American Bible* (New York: Kenedy 1970), and Edgar J. Goodspeed's *The New Testament: An American Translation* (Chicago: University of Chicago Press 1923). In rendering passages from the synoptic gospels I have tried to take account of the Aramaic substratum. In citing synoptic texts I have taken Mark as a base, usually signifying a parallel passage in Matthew or Luke by 'par.' and parallel passages in both by 'parr.'. Thus, I am supposing that whoever wishes to look up the texts will use a synopsis (such as those edited by Kurt Aland in Greek and English).

Having profited from the suggestions of both, I would like to thank Professor F. E. Crowe of Regis College, Toronto, for reading an early draft of the first chapters and my friend and colleague Professor E. P. Sanders of McMaster University, Hamilton, Ontario, for reading the whole of the manuscript.

I would like to thank the officers of McMaster University for their support of scholarship not in word only but in deed and truth (I John 3.18) by seeing to it that the faculty have time and opportunity for research. Finally, I thank Mr Philip Davis for verifying a series of references for me, Miss Alice Korporaal for typing the manuscript, and the librarians of Mills Memorial Library, McMaster University, la bibliothèque de la faculté de théologie, Université de Neuchâtel, and la bibliothèque des Pasteurs de Neuchâtel for their amiable service.

Burlington
Ontario
December 1977

ABBREVIATIONS

ASTI	*Annual of the Swedish Theological Institute*, Leiden
Billerbeck	H. L. Strack and P. Billerbeck, *Kommentar zum Neuen Testament aus Talmud und Midrasch*, Munich: Beck, 1922–28; vols. V and VI, 1956, 1961
BuK	*Bibel und Kirche*, Stuttgart
BuL	*Bibel und Leben*, Düsseldorf
BJRL	*Bulletin of the John Rylands Library*, Manchester
BTB	*Biblical Theology Bulletin*, Albany
BZ	*Biblische Zeitschrift*, Paderborn
BZNW	Beihefte zur *ZNW*
CBQ	*Catholic Biblical Quarterly*, Washington
ED	*Euntes Docete*, Rome
ET	English translation
EvTh	*Evangelische Theologie*, Munich
EVV	English versions
FRLANT	Forschungen zur Religion und Literatur des Alten und Neuen Testaments, Göttingen: Vandenhoeck und Ruprecht
Greg	*Gregorianum*, Rome
GuL	*Geist und Leben*, Würzburg
HJ	*Historisches Jahrbuch*, Munich
HTR	*Harvard Theological Review*, Cambridge, Mass.
HUCA	*Hebrew Union College Annual*, Cincinnati
Int	*Interpretation*, Richmond, Va.
JBL	*Journal of Biblical Literature*, Missoula, Mont.
JJS	*Journal of Jewish Studies*, London
JTS	*Journal of Theological Studies*, Oxford
Jud	*Judaica*, Zürich
KuD	*Kerygma und Dogma*, Göttingen
McCQ	*McCormick Quarterly*, Chicago

NovT	*Novum Testamentum*, Leiden
NTS	*New Testament Studies*, Cambridge
Or	*Orientierung*, Zürich
RB	*Revue biblique*, Paris
RevSR	*Revue des sciences religieuses*, Strasbourg
RGG	*Die Religion in Geschichte und Gegenwart*, Tübingen: Mohr, [3]1957–62
RivB	*Rivista Biblica*, Rome
RSPT	*Revue des sciences philosophiques et théologiques*, Paris
RSR	*Recherches de science religieuse*, Paris
RSV	Revised Standard Version of the Bible
SBBerlin	*Sitzungsberichte der Preussischen* [since 1944 *Deutschen*] *Akademie der Wissenschaften zu Berlin*, Berlin
SBHeidel	*Sitzungsberichte der Heidelberger Akademie der Wissenschaften*, Heidelberg
SBLeipzig	*Sitzungsberichte der sächsischen Akademie der Wissenschaften zu Leipzig*, Leipzig
SBU	Symbolae biblicae upsalienses, Lund
SBT	Studies in Biblical Theology, London: SCM Press, and Naperville: Allenson
SDB	*Supplément au Dictionnaire de la Bible*, Paris: 1928ff.
SNVAO	Skrifter utgitt av Det Norske Videnskaps-Akademie i Oslo
StTh	*Studia Theologica*, Lund
SvExA	*Svensk Exegetisk Årsbok*, Lund
TDNT	*Theological Dictionary of the New Testament*, tr. G. W. Bromiley, Grand Rapids: Eerdmans 1964–74
ThBl	*Theologische Blätter*, Leipzig
ThZ	*Theologische Zeitschrift*, Basel
TQ	*Theologische Literaturzeitung*, Leipzig
TLZ	*Theologische Quartalschrift*, Tübingen
TS	*Theological Studies*, Woodstock, Md.
TSK	*Theologische Studien und Kritiken*, Hamburg
TWNT	*Theologisches Wörterbuch zum Neuen Testament*, ed. G. Kittel and G. Friedrich, Stuttgart: Kohlhammer 1933–73
ZDPV	*Zeitschrift des Deutschen Palästinavereins*, Wiesbaden
ZkTh	*Zeitschrift für katholische Theologie*, Vienna
ZNW	*Zeitschrift für die neutestamentliche Wissenschaft und die Kunde der älteren Kirche*, Berlin
ZRG	*Zeitschrift für Religions- und Geistesgeschichte*, Cologne
ZThK	*Zeitschrift für Theologie und Kirche*, Tübingen

I

INTRODUCTION

After two hundred years of historical-Jesus research, the bulk of which by common consent has proved a failure, it would seem reasonable to ask the writer of yet another book on the topic not to make the old mistakes. If he must err, let the error consist in something other than the exploration of painfully familiar blind alleys. For if the project has really learned from the past, hope might flicker in the reader's heart that it will prove not to be a blind alley at all but an avenue to insight.

What, then, was the old mistake, or better, the root of the old mistakes?

The question has been variously answered. For more than a half-century following the publication of David Friedrich Strauss's *Life of Jesus*[1], critics urged that the old mistake was the lack of exact source-criticism. The time came, however, when the scholarly community began to acknowledge that Strauss had been more right than his critics, that the key question was not the order of the sources but their nature. For convenience's sake we might date the rise of this view at 1901, when Wrede published his book on the messianic secret.[2] From that time to this, the basic dilemma of historical-Jesus research has been attributed, shorthand fashion, to 'the nature of the sources', that is, primarily, to the nature of the gospel literature.

The phrase 'the nature of the sources' has a tantalizing ambiguity about it. It has carried a considerable variety of connotations and nuances in the studies of the past generation. But in the context presently to be defined these differences have only secondary importance. The more important question is: 'Does "the nature of the sources" pose a dilemma fundamentally technical in nature? Is the basic dilemma of historical-Jesus research this, that the historian's techniques are not yet quite up to the task of finding answers to his questions? Is it possible that progress in the development of historical techniques – the honing of techniques precisely adapted to the nature of the sources – might resolve the dilemmas of historical-Jesus research?'

The answer, in my opinion, is 'No'. But this 'no' should be understood. The question is not whether progress in technique can generate knowledge. It evidently can and does. But such progress continues to lie under the sign of a basic and baffling dilemma, not a technical but a cultural dilemma, and one having important repercussions on every effort to appropriate the Christian heritage. It is a dilemma formulated by Van Austin Harvey as the incompatibility between intellectual honesty and traditional Christian belief.[3]

Harvey's view has some *prima facie* support. The determination to find a viable alternative to traditional Christian belief was among the key forces powering historical-Jesus research from Reimarus to Schweitzer. This enormous effort was not an undiluted success. But in so far as it came to grief this was not for merely technical reasons. The seeds of failure were sown at a deeper level, in the presuppositions of the historians. The 'old mistake' lay in these presuppositions. Furthermore, it remains a question whether 'the old mistake' was not continued in the presuppositions of what came to be called 'the new quest'. The fruitful area of discussion and debate, then, is the area of presuppositions, and specifically, of two kinds of presupposition.

History is the asking and the answering of certain kinds of questions. To consider first the asking of a question: 'Who murdered Dunaway?' supposes as known that Dunaway is dead; that his death was neither natural nor accidental; that somebody murdered him. The unknown is the identity of the somebody. Here the knowns have been selected out of a reservoir of knowns concerning the death of Dunaway, and selected with the precise purpose of specifying the unknown to be known. The same is true of every deliberately formulated question. These knowns are selected to specify this unknown, and this unknown is fastened on for the sake of some yield, some gain, envisaged in the conversion of the unknown into a known. The key to the selection of the unknown to be known – the key, therefore, to the whole enterprise – is purpose. Purpose may be of any kind, and in the history of inquiry bearing on the historical Jesus it has widely varied. For Reimarus, the purpose was to commend the religion of reason and to discredit that of revelation; for Strauss, to translate Christianity into Hegelian wisdom; for the post-Bultmannian 'new quest', to reintroduce Jesus into theology as more than a merely factual presupposition. Relative to the asking of historical questions, all such purposes are presuppositions.

Second, we might consider the answering of questions. This takes place by the formulation of hypotheses, i.e., possible answers. The range of hypotheses is established and limited by what the historian conceives as possible. These judgments of possibility are presuppositions.

There are still other kinds of presupposition. But the kinds meant to fix attention for the moment are these two: the purposes governing the choice of questions and the judgments determining the range of hypotheses.

Such presuppositions are not merely private. In considerable part they reflect a culture, and it is no surprise to the historically conscious critic that a certain cultural continuum is observable in the presuppositions of the quest not only from Reimarus to Schweitzer but from Reimarus to the post-Bultmannians. In this two-hundred-year period the purposes governing the choice of questions have been extremely diverse. But the assessments of possibility governing the range of historical hypotheses have been remarkably consistent. This is the point at which the cultural continuum has most decisively imposed itself, thereby defining the modern Christian dilemma in general: the incompatibility between intellectual honesty and traditional Christian belief. For the heritage of Christian belief affirms as indispensable what the heritage of modern culture excludes as impossible. Theological effort – for example, the Bultmannian demythologizing programme – has therefore been concentrated on mediating between these two sets of claims.

Before proceeding further, two observations on the dilemma 'honesty versus traditional belief' are in order. First, if this formula is accepted as it stands, not only historical-Jesus research but the entire positive phase of Christian theology generally is condemned to the status of salvage operations. This has become ever clearer over the past hundred years, the period from liberalism to 'the new hermeneutic'. All those movements, to quote Professor Harvey, 'may be regarded as a series of salvage operations, attempts to show how one can still believe in Jesus Christ, and not violate an ideal of intellectual integrity'.[4]

But the second observation is that the formula as it stands is essentially provisional. The incompatibility of intellectual integrity with traditional Christian belief is without any doubt a lived experience of countless modern Christians. Nevertheless, intellectual integrity, absolute as personal moral norm, is also inevitably relative to antecedent judgments of the truth of things. This is why, in the concrete, intellectual integrity is always revised in accord with concrete revisions in the grasp of knowledge and of truth. One might argue that honesty is honesty everywhere and always and, in a formal sense, this is true. But the honest convictions of a medieval man are not one and the same as the honest convictions of a son of the Enlightenment. Again, the modern Christian dilemma is modern, not medieval. It dates from the late seventeenth century and is objectified in the accounts of knowledge that grew up with the Enlightenment. In so far as these accounts of knowledge are themselves in turn found to be inadequate and are revised, intellectual integrity is again open to concrete redefinition. Such redefinition modifies the culture at its foundations and subtly alters its total contour. It follows that with a *basic breakthrough* in the account of knowledge the modern Christian dilemma might be radically resolved, cracked open, and the way cleared for constructive projects irreducible to theological salvage operations.

This, in fact, is what is happening in our time, as may be observed in the work of Bernard Lonergan.[5] But no single aspect or trait of Lonergan's work epitomizes this breakthrough. His phenomenology of knowledge, a fundamental and detailed theory of human cognition, describes the dynamism of cognitional structure: the structure itself and the distinct moments concretely constituting it. It describes that dynamism as conscious; as intentional;[6] as characterized by successive increments. Thus, the dynamism of human knowing begins with sense knowledge. But inasmuch as there supervenes on sense knowledge a wondering which transcends sense, sense knowledge is revealed as data for knowing activities of a higher order. The single dynamism or drive of conscious human intentionality converts wondering to questioning and questioning to question-answering; it solicits reflection on the answers and climaxes in the act of judging them to be certainly or probably true or false. This defines the point at which the human knower grasps the real, for reality becomes known by our knowing what is true (*ens per verum innotescit*).

Cognitional structure itself and the detailed description thereof may be named 'generalized empirical method'. Now, it is the fecundity of Lonergan's generalized empirical method – first, its grounding of a rigorously critical epistemological realism; second, its grounding of the critical technique which reduces conflicting views of reality to differences on knowledge and objectivity and these, in turn, to differences in cognitional theory; third, its grounding of an entirely non-reductionistic account of the methods of science, scholarship, philosophy, and theology – which constitutes Lonergan's 'basic breakthrough'.

It should be noted at once that this breakthrough is the supposition, not the object, of the present study. I would not wish the reader to expect the present study to be borne along on a flood of insight inspired by Lonergan's achievement. So mistaken – and so high – an expectation could not but be disappointed. In referring to Lonergan and to the breakthrough status of his work as cognitional theorist and methodologist, I wish mainly to indicate the principal resource on which I draw in rejecting the many reductionistic philosophies which, whether or not they have won the historians' conscious agreements, have exercised a decisive remote control over historical-Jesus work and, while throwing some aspects of the historical Jesus into high relief, have tended to reduce the 'quest' to a sequence of painfully limited and distorted research projects.

Thus, two characteristic views of the post-Enlightenment era have had a decisive impact on this research: first, the view that the universe is a closed system; and second, the view that the only way to judge the past is by the present. Strauss and Bultmann may be taken as typical witnesses to the first view, each expressing himself in characteristic idiom. 'The chain of secondary causes', says Strauss, 'cannot be disturbed by arbitrary acts of interposition';[7] or, as Bultmann puts it, 'The historical method includes the presupposition that history is … a closed continuum of effects'.[8] Kähler and Troeltsch offer representative statements of the second view. For a critical history of Jesus, according to Kähler, the assumption that he was a mere man is a *conditio sine qua non*.[9] Troeltsch states the more general principle: It is essential for the historian to assume that the experience of the past cannot have been fundamentally dissimilar to his own.[10]

These two views – that the universe is a closed system, and that judgment of the past is limited by present experience – are finally based on epistemological assessments, the first having to do with the nature of empirical science, the second, with the conditions of historical interpretation.

Now, at both these points Lonergan has shown that the underlying epistemological assessments are defective. The originators of the first view correctly recognized the possibility of a transition from common-sense knowledge to empirical scientific knowledge. But the view itself (usually but not necessarily worked out in deterministic terms) mistakenly overlooks the abstract character of the invariant formulations which empirical science aims at.[11] The conclusion that the universe is an impenetrably closed system rests finally on this oversight. It is an old mistake, one dating from the seventeenth century, and the mistake is not corrected merely by abandoning the mechanistic determinism of Galileo. Nor can we rely on the scientific community to correct it. This is rather a project for cognitional theory, since cognitional theory, not empirical science, is equipped to answer such questions as 'What is the nature of empirical science?' It follows that only in so far as one functions as cognitional theorist is one equipped to pronounce on views, including world-views, that are grounded in a given understanding of empirical science.[12]

The second view, Troeltsch's principle of analogy, rightly recognizes that the resources for interpretation are immanent in the knowing operations of the interpreter; but the view itself, as Collingwood pointed out a generation ago, and as Lonergan has pointed out in more detailed and definitive fashion, is simplistic. That the Greeks and Romans controlled overpopulation by the exposure of infants, observed Collingwood, remains no less true for lacking any referent in the experience of the writers of the *Cambridge Ancient History*.[13] Historical interpretation, Lonergan has insisted, involves an extrapolation of the interpreter's own resources to the meaning of another man at a different point in history – an operation the success of which is rigorously conditioned by the interpreter's self-knowledge.[14]

The self-knowledge in question here touches at least non-reflexively, but at best reflexively, the whole range of acts which engage cognitional theory. The principle of analogy, connoting likeness and diversity, and solving the problem of diversity through an extrapolation controlled by self-knowledge, is vitiated when made to mean not a process, but a body, of knowledge, and not a body of knowledge but only a pool of assumptions. This is how the principle has functioned in nineteenth-century and much twentieth-century theory and practice. Though Kähler and Troeltsch arrived at different stances regarding 'Jesus and critical history', they conceived the problem in terms of like assumptions about critical history, and the assumptions were insufficiently tested. For a critical history of Jesus, the principle of analogy is invoked on the basis that Jesus was a man; it has nothing to say about his being 'a mere man'. In the nineteenth century the principle was often and easily and unconsciously corrupted into Pope's theorem of perennially valid common sense: 'Whatever is very good sense must have been common sense in all times.'[15]

With respect to 'old mistakes' in historical-Jesus research (for example, the mistake of the closed universe world-view or the mistake of the Troeltschean principle of analogy) Lonergan's contributions to cognitional theory thus appear to be relevant. As in the nineteenth century, the purposes governing the choice of questions in serious[16] historical-Jesus research today are explicitly theological or consciously open-ended toward theology.[17] But so long as the integrity of the historian and theologian is felt to be incompatible with the integrity of the Christian heritage, this research is reduced to salvage operations; that is, common cultural assumptions are affirmed and then that much of the Christian heritage which is not in clear discord with them is cautiously salvaged – a delicate operation assuredly testing the intellectual integrity of the salvager. Thus, men accepting the dilemma and working within it may define a single dimension of Jesus' history as the viable heritage, and claim that the tension between honesty and Christianity has thereby been resolved. But such salvage solutions leave a residue of nagging dissatisfaction. They neither tackle the root problem of knowledge nor cohere with New Testament faith.

In the light of important progress in cognitional theory, however, the dilemma 'honesty versus traditional belief' can itself be resolved. We should not forget that men can be honestly mistaken, honestly befuddled about basic issues; that many have honestly appropriated relatively inauthentic ideals and traditions; that honest men have oiled the wheels of chaos. The question we are evoking is not, then, a question about honesty but about the convictions to which honesty is relational. We are asking to what extent Christians who feel compelled not merely to effect an *aggiornamento* of traditional belief but to find basic alternatives to it, are compelled by common but uncriticized cultural assumptions. At any rate, the precept that no man can use electric lights and take miracles seriously[18] solves nothing; it leaves the basic questions raised by this not only un-answered but unasked, – which is why, today, we intend to go another way.

The immediate aim of the present work (which, happily, cannot be limited to avoiding old mistakes) is to understand the Jesus of ancient Palestine. It is remarkable that such key figures in the history of the question as Strauss, Wrede, and Bultmann were not deeply interested in this aim. And many of those who were (e.g. liberals driven to history to justify a Christianity without Christian doctrine) seemed only in rare instances (e.g. Harnack) to delight in history as such. Often their inquiries were too immediately and abruptly functional to the academic religious interests which, alone, engaged them. They accordingly tended to over-look the larger history which Jesus himself inherited and in which he lived and moved, each presenting only so much 'background' as was necessary to make his idea of Jesus intelligible.

But this is not history. Nor is a survey of the teaching of Jesus history in the proper sense. Nor is history merely the minute examination of gospel data with a view to passing judgments of historicity on them. History is reconstruction through hypothesis and verification. Its topic is 'aims and consequences', for history involves, first of all, the grasp of aims in relation to the dynamics of the time, i.e., the springs of actually advancing move-ments. These are more than 'background'. They say where the action is and supply the terms of its explanation. Moreover, they are themselves constituted by concretely incarnated and variously interacting aims. On the other hand, the movements actually advanced thereby are *de facto* consequences: massive, continuously ongoing, unforeseeable, and irrevoc-able. They generally correspond quite imperfectly to the intentions of anyone in particular; indeed, they seem to mock all pretension to predict or control them. Nevertheless, the question about the aims of historical figures has pivotal importance for the understanding of the events decid-ing and constituting the course of history. Unless historical events and directions are grasped in terms of interacting intentions, the understand-ing of them is shallow, external, barren.

In this respect historical-Jesus research got off to a good start in the latter eighteenth century. It was conceived in terms of the question about Jesus' aims (H. S. Reimarus). A century later the question was taken up again by liberal theologians (e.g., Albrecht Ritschl). Reimarus defined Jesus' aim as political sovereignty for Israel; the liberals defined it as moral progress for the world. Both definitions reflect the ulterior aims of the definers. Reimarus's aim was to strip the figure of Jesus of transcen-dental meaning; the liberals aimed at putting Jesus in immediate touch with nineteenth-century ideals. True, neither definition has worn well. But if the answers have by and large failed to satisfy, the question remains as good as ever.

It is a question which, to be sure, can stand on its own, and so remain within the framework of biography. But, as observed above, it can also have great importance for the understanding of public events. What events? The events that engulfed Jesus personally and issued in his death? No doubt. But equally beyond doubt the question of Jesus' aims has a yet greater significance with respect to the *de facto* historical outcome of his career. Positively, this was the coming to be of the Christian *ekklēsia*; negatively, it was the historically definitive break between Jesus and Judaism. How do aims and outcome correlate here?

Such questions obviously transcend the narrowly conceived limits of the 'new quest'. The latter movement was an effort by a school of theologians to meet problems in some measure peculiar to the school and to do so partly in accord with, partly in violation of, the school's inherited canons of theological legitimacy. I hope that, by contrast, the present inquiry will be seen to belong to 'the newest questioning', as Heinz Schürmann has named it, – a questioning and questing which springs from and seeks to commend 'a more open hermeneutic'.[19]

My interest in theory – in a hermeneutic open to human action's social and historical impact as well as to its illumination of possibilities of human existence – is entirely practical, geared to practice and to debate about practice. I would like not only to disagree with much of the work previously and currently done in historical-Jesus research but to allow the disagreements to be traced to their roots and the roots to be exposed. That is why the present study is in two parts. Part One offers a grounding of the practice in Part Two. This grounding pertains partly to historical methodology, partly to philosophy, partly to theology. True, not all disagreements in historical reconstruction are reducible to differences in method and in basic stance. Many differences in reconstruction derive from differences in attention to data, in resources for the construing of data, in flair for finding patterns or in readiness to acknowledge complexities. But the great, gross differences *are* methodological, and method is founded on fundamental options. Part One offers an account of such options, specifying the necessary and useful (though not sufficient) conditions of the historical reconstruction in Part Two.

Part Two, it should be emphasized, is a *historical* reconstruction. Its historical character is neither enhanced nor – historicist ideology to the contrary notwithstanding – corrupted by its being explicitly placed in a theological context. That context is the shift from one mode of theology to another, namely, from the classicist to the historical appropriation of the earthly Jesus.[20] Historical understanding is in no sense diminished by rejecting Troeltschean relativism or the panoply of biases epitomized in the claim to be dogma-free.

The reconstruction in Part Two is centred on a single theme: the goal informing Jesus' career. Was there a radical unity in this career? If so, what set of aims did it spring from? The importance of this question for any historical reconstruction is underlined by the circle of the whole and the parts. One understands the whole in function of understanding the parts and the parts in function of understanding the whole. To focus all effort on defining the aims of Jesus is to try and break the circle open, i.e., to locate the whole in terms of which the parts of the story of Jesus become finally intelligible. The result is not, it was never meant to be, startling, stunning, novel. What novelty the present study has lies in its rejection of a large number of current clichés dealing with history or the history of Jesus. Some of them are false ('To a historian nothing is unique'[21]) but most are just simplistic ('Jesus proclaimed the message; the Church proclaims *him*'[22]). As the clichés fall by the wayside, however, some earlier observations – like Dalman's ' . . . the "kingly sovereignty" of God appears as the decisive element in the salvation of the community of revelation'[23] or Ernst Fuchs's 'The starting point of Jesus' proclamation . . . is [his] full authority to gather a people for God under the banner of the rule of God . . . '[24] – are recharged with meaning.

PART ONE

HERMENEUTICAL ISSUES

INTRODUCTION

To do 'hermeneutics' in the strict and technical sense is to formulate problems of interpretation philosophically and to solve the problems so formulated. With reference to cognitional theory (the account of understanding as such) hermeneutics bears on a sub-question (the understanding of written texts). In the strict and technical sense it belongs to the theory defining how the possibility of effective interpretation is conditioned.

In current usage, however, the phrase 'hermeneutical issues' carries broader and more concrete connotations. It refers to the entire set of questions men commonly turn to last of all and out of a sort of desperation; that is, when, determined to understand and unable to do so spontaneously, they have first had recourse to expert guidance only to find themselves bewildered and frustrated by competing and irreconcilable interpretations. Then come the hermeneutical issues. They invite a step backward, a reflective return to fundamentals, and this in the hope of again confronting the log-jam of conflicting interpretations but equipped now to break it, to break through to truth.

The pages that follow are concerned with such a log-jam and so with hermeneutical issues in the broad and concrete sense. The intention is not only to provide a rationale for the historical investigation in Part Two but to do so dialectically, i.e., by locating and sorting out the conflict-generating issues.

There are, of course, many areas of conflict and many ways of dealing with them. I propose two points of immediate interest to history; the historicity of data and the effort to reconstruct. The two are related, for success in the effort to reconstruct depends on the availability of historical

data. Now, the effective appropriation of data for inquiry into the historical Jesus[1] is no easy matter. I argue that currently conventional judgments of possibility make *a priori* misvaluations of historicity inevitable
and that, like methodical credulity, methodical scepticism (the systematic
presumption of non-historicity until proved otherwise) does the same.
Second, the ideal of getting beyond atomistic judgments of historicity to
historical reconstruction has for the most part been either ignored or
abused. Critical history has been unambitious and ambitious history,
uncritical. Scholars of the Straussian cast, like Wrede or Bultmann, make
no effort to reconstruct history, whereas the fearless hypotheses of a
Reimarus or a Schweitzer collapse like playing cards.

These are the main matters of discussion in the next three chapters. The
fifth chapter, 'History and Faith', is an attempt to get to at least one
ultimate root of conflict. This chapter, then, is an effort at dialectics in the
strict sense.[2]

II

A REVIEW OF THE QUEST

For two centuries the figure of Jesus has tested the ambitions of historians.

The historians were unaware of being tested. They came to the gospels as critics, set on peeling away the layers of subjectivity – dogma, fraud, myth, naiveté, bias – that had misled Christendom and kept 'the real Jesus' concealed. Yet each generation's portraits of him seemed regularly to pale and vanish, and the bulk of the literature is unreadable today. Most of it was conceived and born in cultural eras (from the Enlightenment to the first world war) that have gone dead on us. We know that we ourselves have come out of these eras and cannot but depend on them in a thousand ways. Nevertheless, this crowded and relatively recent past has come to seem depleted and remote. For meaning, especially for religious meaning, we look to other resources, older and more recent.

Dogma, fraud, myth, naiveté, bias. The gospels are, in fact, dogmatic, richly and variously objectifying the faith that gave them being. 'Bias' may not be the term to describe them, but neither their authors nor their intended readerships were disinterested parties. The mythical (so named in a technical sense) lay at their heart and centre. But was the scandal of the critics a judgment on the gospels? Gospel literature was in many ways naive, but naive literature can be great and a literature without subjectivity is dead. Fraud might justify scandal but the charge of fraud was mistaken.

What made the critics scandal-prone was an evolving epistemological ideal. As dogmatic, the gospels seemed to contradict this ideal and the critics disapproved. Their options were to regard dogma as fraud and reject it (Reimarus), to neutralize it by interpretation (Strauss), to locate and skirt round it (Holtzmann and the liberals), to confront it squarely and consign it to the superseded past (Schweitzer). The epistemological ideal was the realization of ultimately grounded knowledge, which Reimarus sought in *Vernunft* (reason), Strauss in *Begriff* (idea), Holtzmann in *Historie* (factual history), and so forth. The evolving forms of this ideal exercised a sometimes remote but finally decisive control over the critics. This holds for the entire history of research and it holds, first of all, for Reimarus and Strauss and the liberals. Thus, Reimarus reflected that:

> God, if it had been his intention through the Bible to give mankind a super-natural instruction for its salvation, would have had to give this as efficiently as possible; namely, as an ordered and complete whole, so that everyone could clearly see what was required in the way of fidelity and good conduct – and not scattered all across the Bible, often expressed, indeed, in an extremely unclear way.[1]

Strauss for his part recalls:

> In its very source my critique of the life of Jesus stood in an inner relationship to Hegelian philosophy. Even in my university years it seemed to me and to my friends that for theology the most important point of this system was the distinction in religion between representation (*Vorstellung*) and idea (*Begriff*), which, though different in form, can have the same content .... The most crucial question soon became: What is the relationship of the historical compo-nents of the Bible, especially the gospels, to the idea? Does historicity belong to the content, which, being the same for representation and for idea, would demand acknowledgment from the latter? Or is historicity to be reduced to the mere form, so that conceptual thought is independent of it? As we looked for counsel in the writings of Hegel and his leading followers, we found precisely this point, on which above all we wanted light, most left in the dark.[2]

The liberals were eclectics, the positivist ideal of history as strict science alternating with the Kantian ideal of 'interpretation' determined by the people's moral needs. This unlikely combination explains, for example, the ambiguities of the second edition of Johannes Weiss's book on the Kingdom of God.

> The first edition of this essay [wrote Weiss] was the product of a pressing personal conflict. With the Albrecht Ritschl school I was convinced of the uncommon significance of the kingdom of God for systematic thought, this being the organic centre of Ritschl's own theology. Even today I am of the opinion that his system and specifically this central concept represents the doctrinal form best suited to bring the Christian religion home to our genera-tion .... But at an early date I was unsettled by the clear impression that Ritschl's idea of the kingdom of God and the idea carried by the same words in the proclamation of Jesus were two very different things. The essay appearing in the year 1892 was an attempt to accent this distinction sharply and energeti-cally. The pointed form in which it appeared offended and frightened many. But I believe I am not mistaken in estimating that its basic notion is to all intents and purposes acknowledged today [i.e., 1900].[3]

Evidently, systematic theology in Germany had been unable to assimilate the all-commanding eschatological dimension of the New Testament. Hence the split mentality characterizing the interim situation and exemplified by Weiss himself: The positivist reasserts the discovery of eschatology; the neo-Kantian sticks with Ritschl.

The mirroring of current cognitional theory has been so typical of research and writing on Jesus that without attention to it the course of this research is only superficially intelligible. That Reimarus was a deist, Strauss a Hegelian, Holtzmann a liberal, Bultmann an existentialist, that all of them were children of the Enlightenment, and that their enabling hermeneutical resources were also in every case inhibiting and reductionist, would seem basic to the understanding of the quest.

1. REIMARUS AND STRAUSS

Reimarus's essay 'On the Aim of Jesus and of his Disciples'[4] belonged to the twilight of the Age of Reason.

Europe had long since been shaken by 'the new philosophy'. Like a time-bomb, the idea of the heliocentric universe, recovered from antiquity in the 1500s, exploded early in the seventeenth century. New systems of ideas, values, and preferences were to be part of the fall-out. Kepler, Galileo, and Newton triggered a mutation in human consciousness that has no parallel in the history of the Christian era. The marvel of the Newtonian synthesis in particular crowded the old system of *auctores* off the stage. Prior to Newton

> the truth about religion was revealed in the Scriptures; the truth about geometry in Euclid, the truth about physics in Aristotle .... [The ancients] had left nothing but a few stray stalks in the way of tidying up. Since there was only one answer to every question, and the ancients had filled in all the answers, the edifice of knowledge was completed.[5]

But with the violation of limits by a venturesome minority, the familiar assurances, allowing the European Christian a sense of at-homeness in his world, began to sag and collapse.

'The new philosophy', however, was creative. The debates of late scholasticism, the competition of closed orthodoxies, the cult of the ancients, yielded painfully to pressures of growth. The pain was felt by the vested interests; for the discoverers discovery was heady wine. Moreover, continuity with the past was strained, not severed. The *auctores* were still questioned, though not so much by deferential pupils as by ambitious younger colleagues.

The immediate principle of discovery was method; its radical principle, 'Reason'.

> By the time of the Peace of Westphalia (1648) men were ready to turn an ear to what Reason had to report of God, man, and the world alike, for the devastating wars of religion seemed to declare the bankruptcy of those world-views that

had hitherto ruled Europe. The medieval scheme of things – a finite universe contingent to its roots, ever open to divine intervention; a static, gradated ontological order and a divinely sanctioned hierarchy of authority; the primacy of faith in the life of man, the acknowledgment of God's mysteries, belief in the better world of the after-life; the absolute character of Christian society and culture – had been questioned by the Renaissance and modified by the Reformation, but had not been radically revised. Now Europe was offered a different vision: an infinite, self-sufficient, dynamic universe closed to divine intervention but open to rational inquiry; the primacy of reason for the understanding of nature and man; the relativity of cultures; the possibility of progress. These new perspectives emerged gradually, elicited by sciences founded on observation and experiment and expressed mathematically, by the attempt to digest scientific achievement philosophically, by a new reading of the ancient classics, by explorations, travel books, and missionaries' fascinating reports from the Orient. At first tentatively, then with confidence, all past values were questioned.[6]

Still, the giants of the scientific revolution from Copernicus to Newton were all religious men. In Kepler, Galileo, and Newton, moreover, the itch to theologize was irresistible. Newton found a place for God, first, as Creator of the colossal clock of the universe; second, as its maintenance engineer. The latter function was derided by his own contemporaries, witness Leibnitz:

> According to their [Newton's and his followers'] doctrine, God Almighty wants to wind up his watch from time to time, otherwise it would cease to move . . . . Nay, the machine of God's making is so imperfect according to these gentlemen, that he is obliged to clean it now and then by an extraordinary concourse, and even to mend it as a clockwork-maker mends his work.[7]

To Leibnitz it was evident that if God had the sense to set the universe in perpetual motion, no further interventions were required.

The dispute illustrates the failure of seventeenth-century and subsequent thinking to differentiate between scientific and philosophical principles. Force and velocity competed with potency and act. Buried under the ruins of Aristotelian physics lay also all past achievement in the analysis of knowledge. But the new cosmologies were hardly to blame. The various religious and philosophical orthodoxies that felt threatened by 'the new philosophy' were as unequipped as Galileo or Newton to make positive sense of the knowledge-explosion. A war was on and in its hubbub the fine discrimination that might have salvaged principles of discrimination from ancient and medieval resources was left uncultivated.

Deism was motored by the new temper of the times. Though the movement was limited in both numbers and life-span and died without lineal descendants, it can still be taken to represent schematically a half-way house between the religious world of the seventeenth century and the secular humanism of the nineteenth and twentieth. With its allegiance to

Reason, its admiration for the ethical systems of antiquity, its awe before unalterable nature, deism might seem to swim in the mainstream of the Enlightenment current. But deism had a pervasive, distinctive, subsurface mood: a smouldering and obsessive hatred for revealed religion with its priests and mysteries, its pomps and superstitions. 'Even the sane among the deists', writes Peter Gay, 'had a paranoid view of history and politics: they saw conspiracies everywhere . . . .'[8]

Such was Reimarus's judgment of the New Testament gospel: a conspiracy hatched by the disciples of Jesus to assure themselves a livelihood after the death of their master and the defeat of his goals.

Reimarus did not announce this harsh view of the origins of Christianity at the outset of his essay. He began didactically, with a definition of the essence of religion: 'the doctrine of the immortality and blessedness of the soul'. Unlike predecessors such as Tindal, however, Reimarus did not set out to show that the gospel, if only correctly interpreted, perfectly enshrined the essence of religion. The driving purpose of the essay was to discredit Christianity through a complete, internally coherent explanation of its origins.

Never before had the gospels been looked at so hard and so long from so limited an angle of vision. The angle of vision was that of historical explanation. What makes Reimarus significant is that he conceived the history of Jesus as an unknown that remained to be known. To this task he brought philological erudition and, above all, historical imagination, diseased but alive. His theory of development (the 'two systems' of which the 'first' was Jesus' own aim and the 'second' the reinterpretation devised by the apostles) made his critique the most incisive in deist literature. Toland and Chubb had already claimed to discover the original Jesus: an inspired proponent of natural religion, swiftly obscured by early Christianity. But Reimarus climaxed this side of the deist movement, first, by his better informed and more concentrated attention to the texts, but especially by devising a single theory with complementary prongs. Over and above describing the original Jesus, the theory said exactly how and why he had been concealed.

The initial assumption of Reimarus's critique was that 'the four evangelists comport themselves as historians who have drawn up the record of the essentials of what Jesus said and did'.[9] This did not square with the later conclusion that the gospel narratives were written from the standpoint of a 'system', and one so affecting 'the character and articulation of the history' as to leave only vestiges of 'the earlier system' as clues to the real story. Reimarus never resolved this contradiction, and the incoherence was only one defect among many. He also had the fatal tendency to fill in gaps in the evidence by imaginative psychological drama.[10] Again, insensitivity to religious themes[11] accompanied the fetish for conceptual neatness. Reimarus's mind-set had been acquired early through journeys to Holland and England. Socinians and deists had their impact. So did the logical-mathematical methodology of Christian Wolff. But the essay on Jesus is as much the fruit of obsession as of Enlightenment philosophy. The explosions of what Schweitzer called Reimarus's 'lofty scorn' are likely to strike the reader today as merely paranoid. But hate, whether finally a plus-factor or a minus-factor in historical inquiry,[12] at least kept the critic's eye on target. Reimarus did not doubt that what gave real edge to inquiry into the history of Jesus was its significance for Christian faith:

> The essential elements of Christianity are the articles of faith by the doubt or disavowal of which I would cease to be a Christian. And to these belong especially Christ's spiritual redemption through his passion and death; the resurrection from the dead as a confirmation of the plenary value of the passion; and the return to reward or to punish, as a fruit and consequence of the redemption. So whoever takes up these fundamentals to establish or to attack them goes to the heart of the matter. In contradistinction, there are secondary elements relating to Christianity, which to be sure can coexist with it but do not constitute articles of faith. Nor are they so closely bound up with faith that without them the articles could not possibly stand and with them could not possibly fall. To this class first of all I relegate the miracles, on which people put so much stress. For it cannot be denied that the miracles of themselves do not constitute a single article of faith. Supposing, moreover, that the articles of faith carried with them an intrinsic credibility, evidence, or certainty, why should we hanker after miracles, so as to believe? With regard to faith, accordingly, Christ himself would have the miracles accounted as accessory elements. Thus, he taxes as an evil and perverse generation those who do not believe unless they see signs and wonders.[13]

The point of view sets Reimarus apart from the Rationalists who followed him. The centre of Christianity was the kerygma, including the parousia. The question of miracles was kept in perspective. Reimarus was unpersuaded that Jesus worked true miracles but the question did not rivet his attention. The one miracle that counted was the resurrection, and analysis of the Matthean text showed that this was a fraud. 'What was common talk among the Jews remains highly probable; namely, that the disciples came by night and stole the corpse, and then said he was risen.'[14]

Reimarus anticipated in remarkable fashion views that would become commonplace in nineteenth- and twentieth-century criticism: Jesus stood wholly within Judaism; the apostles were the founders of Christianity; Paul, who called for belief, is set over against Jesus, who called for trust; the Jesus of history substantially differed from the Christ of faith. But his shrewdest and most important move was nothing other than the structuring of his total project: to fix attention on the gospels' own centre ('the articles of faith') and to test this centre against a historical inquiry into Jesus' aims.

In the fading light of the Age of Reason, Reimarus hoped for the dawn of the religion of reason (*Vernunftreligion*) to shape the future. It never came. History went the way of Rousseau and Romanticism, of Feuerbach and atheist Humanism. For sober Reason, methodically reductionist, wary of vision, imagination, and enthusiasm, self-enclosed and self-satisfied, the day was over and done.

In Reimarus's Germany the commanding philosophical orientation derived from Christian Wolff (d. 1754). In the interim between Reimarus and Strauss the period of Wolffian dominance was closed by Immanuel Kant (1724–1804), whose cognitional theory offered an alternative to the scepticism that marked the end of the Age of Reason and, still more significantly, established a new career for philosophy: the turn to the subject. Hegel (1770–1831) dominated the following generation by the sweep, power, and daring of his thought. The self-appropriation of human intelligence lay in its discovery of itself as the locus at which the Absolute, coming to self-consciousness, became Spirit. In history Absolute Spirit manifested itself, first, as art, in the objective form of sensuous manifestation; second, as religion, in the subjective form of representation (*Vorstellung*); lastly, as philosophy, in the absolute form of pure idea or thought (*Begriff*), wherein the opposition of subject and object was resolved. The content of religion and philosophy was the same, but the form was different. In the imperfect form that was religion, man posited God as other than, and so in opposition to, himself. Hence, the stage of religion represented an as yet unresolved estrangement which itself had a three-phase history: the Oriental religions, in which God was an objective power in nature, the religions of the Jews, Greeks, and Romans, in which he was a subjective individuality, and Christianity or 'absolute religion' in which God was Spirit.

In 1833 the twenty-five year old philosopher and theologian, David Friedrich Strauss (1808–1874), filled with Hegel yet confidently independent,[15] set himself a sizable double task: to submit the gospels to the most rigorous and exhaustive historical critique and to show that, nevertheless, the dogmatic significance of Jesus remained inviolate. No single book in the history of the quest was to have the impact of his *Leben Jesu* (vol. I, 1835; vol. II, 1836).

Its first seventy-five pages supplied an admirably articulated statement of purposes, presuppositions, and method. The book, he said, championed a method which, though not altogether original (De Wette among others had already applied it to the Old Testament) was here brought to bear for the first time in thoroughgoing fashion on the gospels: the 'mythical interpretation'. The competing views, systematically attacked, were 'the antiquated systems' of supernaturalism and naturalism, the latter being still more antiquated than the former. For naturalism subverted the narrative itself, our one means of acquaintance with the history in question. The supernatural approach, on the other hand, was ruled out on philosophical grounds. Revelations, apparitions, miracles, prophecies, angels, and devils were excluded as impossible, for they would imply a disturbance of 'the chain of secondary causes' by 'arbitrary acts of interposition'.[16]

The positive solution had first of all to be philosophically viable. The philosophical error of the supernaturalists had been to introduce change and time into the divine action by simultaneously attributing to God mediate action on the world as a whole and immediate action in individual cases. Thus, Strauss made his own the position typically assumed by philosophers since the Enlightenment, but the argument supporting the position was distinctive. The error of the deists had been, reductively, to deny the reality of God. Only an atheist could consistently suppose a world impenetrable by 'immediate divine agency'. The solution must be that 'God acts upon the world as a whole immediately, but on each part only by means of his action on every other part, that is to say, by the laws of nature'.[17] 'World', then, was conceived as a single, integral, dynamic entity, like a living body.

By steering between what he took to be the reefs of supernaturalism and atheism, Strauss was induced to turn his attention away from the explanation of events to the narrative that represented them. The posing of a new question – the question of the nature of the gospel literature – suddenly made the dispute between naturalists and supernaturalists appear irrelevant. The naturalist explanation of events was hopeless; the supernaturalist, impossible. But the impasse was avoided if the reality of the event to be explained was itself a false assumption. Thus parting company with contemporary tradition both in Hegelianism and in exegesis, Strauss changed the state of the question on both fronts. On the philosophical front he provoked a bitter split among the industrious Hegelians of Berlin. On the exegetical front he delivered the *coup de grâce* to the school of Rationalism. In the larger world of Christian conservatism (which included the conservatives of the universities) Strauss became a byword. The storm unleashed by his *Leben Jesu* cost him his academic career.

Radical developments generally take place not by someone's seeing something new but by his seeing everything in a new way. The Straussian development is no exception. The great achievement of Strauss's book was the shift from event to account. His interest in the account, however, was not centred on the sequence and interrelationships of the gospels but on the very nature of the gospel literature.

The next two generations of critics missed the thrust of this revision. They especially found fault with Strauss's failure to deal with the synoptic question and source criticism,[18] thus betraying a tenaciously held illusion; namely, that 'the earliest sources' (by the mid-1860s Mark and Q) were the key to historical reconstruction. Only at the turn of the century with Wrede, and still later with the form critics, did it register on the world of scholarship generally that the central question was not the order of the sources but their nature. If Mark could no more be classed as 'pure history' than Matthew, what startling, central advantage for the quest did 'the primacy of Mark' finally have? Strauss's priorities in the placement of the question were generations in advance of his time.

Many of Strauss's long discussions of historicity would have been cut short had he carried his concern with the nature of the gospel literature a step further; that is, to the definition of specific literary genres. In retrospect, Strauss framed his project in too narrow terms. 'To investigate the internal grounds of credibility in relation to each detail given in the gospels', he says, ' . . . is the sole object of the present work.'[19] The goal once set, the alternatives were limited to the mythical versus the historical. The lacuna was attention to specific literary genres, which might have specified variations in the sense of 'myth' as applied to texts as diverse as the infancy narratives, the baptism scene, the temptation, the transfiguration and the resurrection accounts. It might also have successfully mediated between the strictly and literally historical and the wholly unhistorical. Finally, it might have turned Strauss's attention to the immediate religious content of the gospel text.

His earliest critics pointed out the disinterest in positive historicity. Besides neglecting to survey the sources as such before plunging into historical critique, they complained, Strauss failed to ask what the residue surviving the onslaught added up to, if anything. Positive results simply escaped his horizon. The reader of today is struck by the equally cool indifference to the religious concerns of gospel texts both in themselves and in redactional context. Again and again Strauss noted variations of motive in parallel and quasi-parallel passages, but these motives were named and dismissed; they were left unexplored and unrelated – not only unrelated to Jesus, but unrelated among themselves as early Christian theology. Strauss's critics were themselves too obsessed with historicity in the most narrow sense and the slashing attack on it mounted by their adversary to note this other blind spot. Indeed, they shared it.[20]

Strauss considered it naive in the extreme to suppose that interpretation should be no more than a straightforward mediation of the intended sense of the text to be interpreted. Cultural change taking place between the composition of writing and its later interpretation demanded the unequivocal akcnowledgment 'that the matters narrated in these books must be viewed in a light altogether different from that in which they were regarded by the authors themselves'. Calling this 'impartial' interpretation, he thus evoked a critical theme, the way to objectivity, and indicated his own posture with respect to it. The condition of 'impartial interpretation' was maximum consciousness of the *differences* between then and now, between the writer and the interpreter, between diverse cultures and contexts, suppositions and foci of interest.[21]

The crucial difference between then and now he conceived as the gulf between two ways of grasping reality, the mythical and the philosophical.

> If religion be defined as the perception of truth, not in the form of an idea, which is the philosophic perception, but invested with imagery, it is easy to see that the mythical element can be wanting only when religion either falls short of or goes beyond its peculiar province, and that in the proper religious sphere it must necessarily exist.[22]

Here, at the outset, the general character of the gospels was less a literary discovery than a deduction from Hegel, just as in his concluding dissertation Strauss would explicitly find the 'truth' of the gospel history 'deduced from the truth of those conceptions'; i.e., from a Hegelian reinterpretation of church dogmas.[23]

The process of mythicizing 'has no analogy in the present mode of thinking'.[24] It was instinctive; and it excluded the intent to deceive.[25] Myths originated popularly (the myth-maker was simply the spokesman of a people), were transmitted orally, and added to progressively. Long before Jesus the main body of the Christian myth had emerged as an expression of hope. The Messiah was to be such-and-such and to do thus-and-so.[26] In the gospel literature myth sometimes provided the substance of a narrative and sometimes was merely an accidental adjunct to a historical account; the first was 'pure', the second 'historical' myth.[27] In both cases the myth had a double source. It arose from messianic conceptions antedating Jesus, and it reflected the impact on the disciples of Jesus himself.[28] Besides myth (and reminiscence) there was legend, a catch-all rubric for the indefinite and pictorial which, unlike myth, could not be traced back to an 'idea', such as messianism. Finally, there were the editorial additions of the evangelists 'designed merely to give clarity, connection, and climax to the representation'.[29]

The rationalists had favoured the hypothesis that biblical narratives were close in time to the events they described. Otherwise it would have been difficult to guarantee the 'fact' which the narrative recorded and from which the critic distinguished the 'opinion' ascribing events to supernatural causes.[30] On this basis Eichhorn supposed that the Pentateuch was written in the desert.[31] For similarly methodical reasons Strauss was led to the exactly contrary view. Absence of eyewitness testimony was a condition of the mythical interpretation.[32] Indeed, he explicitly conceived his book as a test of the eyewitness theory.[33] But it seems to have been the necessity of time needed for tradition to bring its offspring to term that ruled out an early composition of the gospels.[34]

Characteristically, Strauss presented criteria not for historicity but for non-historicity.[35] He was aware, however, that the boundary line between the historical and the unhistorical was 'unsusceptible of precise attainment', and he ended his discussion of method with a remark worth citing (though Strauss himself did not live up to the implied ideal): 'The author of this work wishes especially to guard himself in those places where he declares he knows not what happened from the imputation of asserting that he knows that nothing happened.'[36]

Throughout his work Strauss sytematically recorded the opinions competing with the mythological interpretation. As the supernatural mode of explanation was excluded *a priori*, the axe fell heavier on Rationalistic exegesis, the details of which, together with Strauss's gift for ridicule, make for entertaining reading. But the Rationalist school was never the real enemy. As Schweitzer clearly saw, Strauss's target was 'the supernatural nimbus' surrounding the figure of Jesus. Here he and the Rationalists were partners. It is instructive to see him at work where evidence relative to a given question was admittedly not compelling. An example, chosen almost at random, is the question of 'the brothers of the Lord'.

Strauss fully appreciates the complexity of the data: There is no decisive evidence that Mary bore children other than Jesus. He takes it as settled that, according to Matthew, Joseph and Mary had conjugal relations after Jesus' birth (Matt. 1.25).[37] But he acknowledges that *prōtotokos* ('first-born') in Luke does not necessarily imply younger brothers; that *adelphos* ('brother' in Greek), like *'āḥ*, ('brother' in Hebrew), may signify a more distant relative; that James, *ton adelphon tou kyriou* ('the brother of the Lord') in Gal. 1.19, is not a brother but a cousin of Jesus; that the total state of the evidence leaves 'perplexity on every side' which can be resolved only, 'and then, indeed, but negatively and without historical result', by admitting obscurity and confusion in the sources. What, then, is his final conclusion?

> We have consequently no ground for denying that the mother of Jesus bore her husband several other children besides Jesus, younger, and perhaps also older; the latter, because the representation in the New Testament that Jesus was the first-born may belong no less to the myth than the representation of the Fathers that he was an only son.[38]

Some of Strauss's positions have passed into common possession. The priority of concentrating on the gospel literature itself, the need of criteria for specific judgments of historicity, the non-historicity of the bulk of the Johannine sayings-material,[39] the hopelessness of explaining the miraculous naturally, grasp of the need to measure the distance between the New Testament and the modern world – these were Strauss's successes. Again, much of his work, particularly the Hegelian options, failed to take root. As an effort to persuade his contemporaries to reinterpret the whole of Christian doctrine in a Hegelian mode, the book was a failure. The schema relating religion and philosophy, the metaphysical style of demythologizing which issued in the single Straussian dogma (man is both human and divine), the refutation of supernaturalism on grounds that it introduced time and change into God's action – none of this survived. For the rest, the book remains a model of attention to material detail and an index to the state of knowledge of the gospels at the time of its appearance, as well as a monument to ideology and the passion to reduce all things to thought. Finally, one issue lives on unresolved by consensus: whether 'the matters narrated in these books must be viewed in a light altogether different from that in which they were regarded by the authors themselves'. This question and its tie with 'the mythological interpretation' still haunts Christian theology and calls for resolution.

2. FROM HOLTZMANN TO THE FIRST WORLD WAR

The period from 1860 to the first world war was marked by the activity of three critical movements: liberal theology and exegesis, the school of comparative religion (*religionsgeschichtliche Schule*) and the system of 'thoroughgoing eschatology'. Related by numerous presuppositions, they nevertheless differed in aim and interest. The liberals searched the New Testament for a reflection of their own idea of religion as interior experience and ethical ideal. The *religionsgeschichtliche Schule*, approaching primitive Christianity as a purely historical phenomenon, sought to situate it in the religious milieu of Judaism and non-Judaic Hellenism. Finally, 'thoroughgoing eschatology' proposed itself as the definitive solution to a specific but central New Testament problem, the proclamation and expectation of the reign of God. The three movements reshaped historical-Jesus research.

The problem confronted by the liberal school in the late nineteenth century was the development of Christianity from Jesus to the ancient church. The liberals aimed at an interpretation of the teaching of Jesus, of Paul, and of the Catholicism initially represented in Clement and Ignatius, together with a reconstruction of the continuities and discontinuities between these points.

They had been schooled in method by Ferdinand Christian Baur and his critics. Baur's contribution lay in the insistence that the intelligibility of the New Testament depended on a chronological ordering of its parts to show the line of development. The critique of Baur pressed the point that this order had to be established *a posteriori*, in the light of positive data.

Perhaps no single figure exercised a more important influence on liberal exegesis than Heinrich Julius Holtzmann (1832–1910), though the transition from Strauss to Holtzmann might be disparaged as a passing from ill-starred genius to professorial industry. His *Die synoptischen Evangelien: Ihr Ursprung und geschichtlicher Charakter* (1863), still conditioned, like all such literature of the time, by the wake of the Straussian hurricane, supplied the two elements most felt to be wanting in Strauss's work: a thoroughgoing examination of the sources and a concluding sketch of the career of Jesus (*Lebensbild Jesu*).

Holtzmann abominated Strauss for having 'drawn the blood from the veins of the most vitally depicted, most distinctive memories' of Jesus '. . . so as then to banish the wan, drained phantoms, one by one, to the Hades of abstract thought'. Baur and the tendency criticism (*Tendenz-kritik*) of the Tübingen school fared better, but not by much. In any case Holtzmann contested Strauss's claim that, just as Feuerbach had dotted the 'i' of Straussian dogmatics, so Baur had furnished *post factum* the critical underpinnings of the *Leben Jesu*. No; 'the only way' to arrive at 'the authentic, true-to-life representation of [Jesus'] being' was to undertake an exhaustive, impartial investigation of the sources even at the risk of appearing to offer 'calculating tables' seemingly removed from all religious interest. Otherwise, the field would be surrendered to the scepticism of Strauss and the circular argumentation of piety, or – an alternative as yet barely thinkable – 'we have to renounce once and for all the achievement of this kind of goal'.[40]

To Holtzmann the key problem was the order of the sources. On this topic the contemporary state of the question authorized one positive conclusion; namely, that the synoptic affinities pointed to a common source ('A'). On this basic supposition the relations of the synoptics were determined by six analyses: the composition of Matthew, the composition of Luke, doublets, Old Testament citations, stylistic traits, and redactional modifications. In every case, according to Holtzmann, the evidence finally compelled acceptance of the following solution: the synoptics depend on A (*Urmarcus*); Matthew and Luke on a second source, L(ogia: *Urmatthäus*), as well as on Mark and diverse oral and written traditions. Indeed, the evidence converged so perfectly on this conclusion that the critic invited the reader to make any of the above lines of evidence his point of departure.

The present writer took him at his word, examining the argument from Old Testament citations, only to discover that the analysis was unreliable and misleading,[41] – and worse, irrelevant.

Irrelevance is the book's mortal flaw. Of themselves, the 'calculating tables', such as the characteristic vocabularies of the synoptics and the notations on their individual styles, were a useful contribution. But all this work was rigorously oriented towards the solution of the synoptic problem. Why? Because Holtzmann harboured two expectations: first, that 'the earliest sources' would be plain and undogmatic; second, that, as such, they would offer direct access to the Jesus of history.

Holtzmann, his school and his generation, remained mesmerized by a siren-song: the lure of early sources, the critical importance of reducing to a minimum the time-lag between event and account. By comparison with the second century, its ecclesiastical evolutions, its apocrypha, its gnostic literature, the age of the evangelists seemed sober and *sachlich*. The earlier one went back, the better things got. Of our gospels the earliest was Mark, and nothing commended Mark more than his distinctive insistence on the disciples' 'steady progress' from misunderstanding toward acknowledgment of Jesus' messiahship.[42] Baur had found this aspect of Mark too 'dark' to build an argument on.[43] To Holtzmann, on the contrary, it was the hallmark of the historical. In simple, straightforward Mark Jesus' sayings are 'exteriorly motivated, short, decisive utterances which interpret the fact itself that occasions them, or which interpretatively point to the factual, for the most part without the least digression into the dogmatic.'[44] It was the simplistic equation of 'early sources' with guileless history that led both to the exaggeration of the importance of the synoptic problem and to the style of interpretation Holtzmann inflicted on Mark. Indeed, time and reflection have shown that all Holtzmann's equations were simplistic. First, the chronological order of the synoptic redactions did not say which synoptic traditions were the oldest. Second, no synoptic redaction and no body of synoptic tradition was untouched by 'dogmatic' concerns and conceptions. Third, the hankering for 'objective' sources was a positivist prejudice grounded in the illusion that access to history should not be mediated by the intelligence of the historian himself but rather should be 'objectively' guaranteed by sources equipped to do his job for him.

Comparison between Holtzmann and Strauss on a specific question illustrates the difference of mentality and method in the two critics. Their discussions of the texts on the anointing of Jesus by a woman (Mark 14.3–9; Matt. 26.6–13; Luke 7.36–50; John 12.1–8) can serve the purpose. Strauss's approach is as follows: First, he notes the material detail ranging Luke against the other synoptics and John (chronology, the character of the woman, and the point of the story). These details had led the majority of commentators to distinguish two anointings. To be consistent, argues Strauss, they should allow three, for there are striking divergences of detail between Matthew and Mark on the one hand, and John on the other (chronology, house and host, identity of the woman, kind of anointing, identity of the spectators who react to the scene).

Second, he develops his own opinion, reducing the three basic accounts to variants of one tradition. But at this point he refutes all attempts so to harmonize the variations as to allow the more or less exact identification of an actual historical event. Third, he argues for the antiquity of the Matthew/Mark tradition *vis-à-vis* the other, more developed versions, and explains the divergence between John and Luke in terms of a single detail (the anointing of the feet), exploited in different senses by the two evangelists. In short, he conceives the whole problem in terms of the study of the transmission of tradition (*Traditionsgeschichte*).[45]

Holtzmann, by-passing consideration of John, proceeds differently. On undivulged grounds he affirms the historicity of the Bethany event. Without differentiating between event and account, he sets the scene in historical context between the Sanhedrin's formulation of policy (Mark 14.12 par.) and the willingness of Judas to serve as its tool. In fact, for Judas the Bethany scene triggers 'a psychological crisis'.[46] (Besides psychologizing the scene, the critic is apparently looking at the fourth gospel out of the corner of his eye.) What about Luke's account?

> The kernel of this story, coming to Luke from later, somewhat tangled tradition, is historical. The décor belongs to Luke, and in the form of the narrative a mingling at least has come about with the story of a later anointing which took place in Bethany. But most probably the two accounts refer to the same fact, and the report of Luke derives from eyewitnesses more removed from the Lord and the family of Simon. Our story is therefore to be conceived neither as a tendentious restructuring nor as allegorical fiction. Furthermore, the Simon of v. 40 is identical with Simon the leper (A) Mark 14.3. That Jesus had cured him of his leprosy was at once the basis of the invitation on Simon's side and the basis of the parable in vv. 41f on Jesus' side.[47]

Such differences of detail as that in Luke the woman is a 'sinner' and that this is central to the point of the story do not fix the critic's attention. On the other hand, only Holtzmann, not the evangelists, reports the cure of Simon.

The *Jesusbild* that concludes the book furnished from Mark the main lines of the liberal 'life of Jesus': the baptism scene as the origin of his messianic ideas, the preaching of the ideal kingdom in the Galilean period and its failure, and the turning-point at Caesarea Philippi after which Jesus resolutely accepts and moves toward his tragic destiny. The reader who pauses to consider the labour that preceded this result may be tempted to wonder *ut quid perditio ista?*

The centre of gravity in liberal theology was a timeless ethic. Jesus was the creative genius of a new teaching, 'the highest expression of the human spirit'. It was a moral teaching, never better expressed than in the Sermon on the Mount and the parables. For here, as Baur put it in 1860, 'the inner power of the truth immediately penetrating to the hearts of men reveals itself in its world-historical significance'.[48]

The liberals grumbled that Strauss had failed (in Otto Pfleiderer's words)

> to bring out the peculiarity and originality of his religious genius and in this way to discover in the original personality and reforming activity of Jesus the originating cause of the rise of the community of his disciples and their faith in him as the Messiah and [in] his divine mission.[49]

To reach this core of personality required the hermeneutics of empathy. In Pfleiderer's estimation, the 'most brilliant' part of Theodor Keim's life of Jesus was

> his delineation of the religious personality of Jesus, – how in it were combined in a unique degree strength and harmony, complete openness towards the world with perfect inwardness towards God so as to become the source of a new religion, in which self-surrender and liberty, humility and energy, enthusiasm and lucidity, are blended and the chasm of previous ages between God and man filled up. His description of the psychological development of the messianic consciousness of Jesus out of inward experiences and outward impressions and impulses is also drawn with great delicacy of touch; at all events, it is an able and suggestive effort to penetrate, as far as the state of the sources admits, by means of sympathetic and reproductive divination, to the personal experiences and mental states of the religious genius from whom a new epoch in the world's religious history proceeded.[50]

At the same time, it was an ideal of liberal research to isolate the kernel of Jesus' thought. This was done by noting that the effort of his public career was to deepen the traditional notions of messianism, so that finally the veritable kingdom could be recognized as 'an inner kingdom of conversion'. 'The kingdom of God is within you' (Luke 17.21) was a favourite text.

The sterility of liberal theology and the factitious character of its historical criticism were evident to some well before the movement had run its course. In reaction to the dogmatic liberalism and overly narrow base of Albrecht Ritschl's reconstruction of New Testament history, a new school of research was born in Göttingen in the early 1890's. The founding fathers of the *religionsgeschichtliche Schule*, Eichhorn, Gunkel, Bousset, Weiss, and Wrede, addressed themselves to the milieu of early Christianity. Ranke and Mommsen represented in their eyes the ideal of painstaking research, and the social thought of the last quarter of the nineteenth century, which stressed the role of the anonymous masses in historic movements, seemed to offer the germ of a solution to the enigma of Christian origins. In sharp contradistinction to the liberals, this school tended to reject the effort to find modern philosophical conceptions and psychological processes in the New Testament. Just the opposite. They were bent on uncovering the primitive, the strange, the disconcerting, all that was unmodern: ecstasy and enthusiasm and a supernatural kingdom of God.

In 1892 Johannes Weiss published his slim volume, *Die Predigt Jesu vom Reiche Gottes*.[51] Weiss contested the initial options of current exegesis and systematic theology on the most critical point, Jesus' essential message. The kingdom was not, as Ritschl had maintained, 'the moral organization of mankind', but an exterior, future, supernatural reality. Moreover, there could be no question of 'founding' it. Jesus merely proclaimed it and awaited its outbreak. Thus, the serene man of wisdom, an image promoted not only in the still-born literature of nineteenth-century piety but even in the work of independent critics like Julius Wellhausen,[52] was replaced by the prophet whose ecstatic experiences led him to announce the shattering of all foundations, the judgment and the end of the world.

Weiss pronounced in favour of the two-source hypothesis (in a sense which supposes *Urmarkus*), but warned against 'the touching trust' which the critics had placed in Mark's chronology and descriptions. The material has been permeated through and through by the religious conceptions and redactional art of the evangelist. He noted, too, that Matthew has conserved material belonging to the most primitive layer of tradition. He was impressed by Dalman's work on the Semitic substratum, but cautious about the flood of 'mistaken translations' presupposed by some as a methodical point of departure. Attention to the redactional traits of the synoptics allowed him to determine, more or less probably according to the case, the secondary character of certain material (e.g., the explanation of the parable of the Tares Amid the Wheat).[53] He analysed the rhetoric of Jesus, briefly but compellingly, as the gauge of the eschatological crisis.[54]

The measure of Weiss's achievement in the main body of his book is the extent to which subsequent scholarship, while amplifying, correcting, and nuancing, has fundamentally confirmed it. Weiss, says his disciple Schweitzer,

> establishes the third Either-Or in *Leben-Jesu-Forschung*. Strauss had established the first: either wholly historical or wholly supernatural. The Tübingen school and Holtzmann had fought through the second: either Synoptic or Johannine. Now the third: either eschatological or uneschatological![55]

The third Either-Or, as it represented true contradictories, was a real one, and the honour of establishing it does belong to Weiss. It is somewhat daunting, then, to find his *Jesusbild* so inferior to his analysis of the kingdom theme.

Weiss takes the baptism scene as a report on the origin of Jesus' messianic consciousness.

The import of the original conception of the narrative seems to be that Jesus now for the first time is really called by God to the status of sonship. . . . From now on he feels within himself the powers of the divine Spirit.[56]

Weiss, too, was a captive of the psychological reconstruction of Jesus' history pioneered by Reimarus and cultivated by the liberals. To Holtzmann the baptism event had meant 'a unique enhancement in the self-awareness of Jesus'.[57] It struck 'his spirit's eye like a beam of light from heaven, his spirit's ear like a divine voice'.[58] Driven into the desert, his life was borne as by a storm wind. The first moment of consecration to his mission must have been a convulsive experience which left trembling echoes, etc.[59] Weiss was not to be outdone:

> The same Spirit that had given him the certainty of his calling drives him with vehement force into the desert. Translated into our language and mode of thought: The mighty exultation, the happy joy, which he senses under the downpour of divine love and heavenly power suddenly gives way to a deep agitation. Doubt and care crowd in upon him, from all sides possibilities open to him which he experiences as temptations and false routes. In short, in place of the first happy certainty and enthusiasm come convulsive inner battles. . . .[60]

The outcome of these inner battles was a distinctive self-understanding. He was aware of having a status superior to that of John. 'What then is left, but that he is the Messiah?' On the other hand, messiahship in its fulness was future and 'the question of how he is to be able to attain it' was Jesus' 'enigma'.[61] Meantime, messiahship, like the kingdom of God, remained a personal faith. The confession of Peter was meant only 'in a proleptic sense', as was Jesus' own profession before the high priest.[62]

> A turning-point is reached no earlier than the resurrection and exaltation of Jesus. There for the first time God *made* him, whom the Jews crucified, Lord and Messiah (Acts 2.36). That is the only possible form in which the messiahship of Jesus could count on being understood.[63]

In John's gospel alone, according to Weiss, was messiahship retrojected into the public ministry.[64]

> If he had the certainty of being the chosen one of his Father, and if on the other hand the Messiah was to appear in glory, it is self-evident that he is *not* the Messiah, the Son of man in the sense of Daniel, already in the present, but only that he could *become* so.[65]

Therefore

> no one who shares our view that the messiahship of Jesus must have been a faith based on altogether personal religious experiences will marvel that he spoke clearly of this secret of his soul only with reluctance, and rarely, and above all not to all comers.[66]

Psychological reconstruction is again at work in Weiss's treatment of the turning-point of Jesus' career, the shift from buoyant optimism to the pessimistic realization that 'many indeed are called but few chosen'. Such was 'the painful outcome' of his work.[67] Condemnation began to dominate his public utterances. But what was to be the solution to the stiff-necked lack of response? 'According to Mark 10.45 we may surmise that he discerned in his own death the specific means for the redemption of his own people.'[68] Nothing less could do, for Israel was held fast in the grip of the Pharisaic leadership.

> With steady gaze he sees this denouement ahead. As soon as he grasps the human necessity of his death it becomes for him a divine necessity, too ... a means for the ushering in of the kingdom of God.[69]

On the sequence leading up to this turning-point Weiss's star pupil, Schweitzer, is more specific. Jesus had sent the disciples on their mission with the firm word that before they finished their journey through the towns of Israel, the Son of man would come (cf. Matt. 10.23). But the disciples did finish their mission! Their return, no Son of man having come, prompted in Jesus a compelling need to be alone with his disciples expressed in the words 'Come away by yourselves to a lonely place and rest awhile' (Mark 6.31).[70]

How frequently the critics discover personal crises among the hardy *dramatis personae* of the gospels! Weiss was more circumspect than Schweitzer, but both regularly called on *The Strategy of the Fearless Detective*, which has four operative principles:

(1) Any given sentence in the gospels may be taken to reflect fact.
(2) The fact is separable from its sense in the gospel's own context.
(3) It acquires a new sense from a context established by the detective, who fearlessly correlates a selection of such facts.
(4) Nothing in the gospels that contradicts the new correlation may be taken to reflect fact.

According to Principle One the evangelists, as Reimarus put it, 'comport themselves as historians'. But according to Principle Four, they do not do so with perfect consistency. The deftness of the detective is measured by how nimbly he closes the gap between the two principles. Reimarus, the trail-blazer, is awkward at this point, but his successors proved to be resourceful. Thus, Holtzmann and Weiss apply Principle One primarily to Mark (or *Urmarkus*), Principle Four to the later gospels. To the guileless reader the words 'Come away by yourselves to a lonely place and rest awhile' might as well have been cast in the narrative mode: 'The apostles rejoined Jesus and reported to him all they had done and taught. Then they went with him by themselves to a lonely place to rest awhile.' The same guileless reader is apt to suppose that the words have no other sense than to introduce a change of locale, preparing the following scene of the multiplication of loaves in the wilderness. But according to Principle Two, the elements that constitute context and mediate meaning are like building-blocks; dismantled without loss, they can (according to Principle Three) be selectively reassembled to constitute a new context and mediate a new meaning. Thus, 'My God, my God, why hast thou forsaken me?' can become 'Why hast thou not pushed my political programme?' and 'Come away by yourselves to a lonely place and rest awhile' can be made to mean 'so that I can get hold of myself again'.

This is not to attack historical imagination and construction as such. First, the evangelists themselves have demonstrably recombined words of Jesus, setting them in new contexts. A striking example is the word which so impressed Schweitzer: 'But when they persecute you in one town, flee to the next; for truly I say to you, you will not have gone through all the towns of Israel before the Son of man comes' (Matt. 10.23). Matthew has placed this word in the missionary discourse preliminary to the sending out of the disciples. The placement makes sense, once the notion that 'the evangelists comport themselves as historians' is revised and the sense of the discourse is grasped in terms of the Matthean redaction. In Matthean terms, 10.23 with its persecution motif is connected with 10.19f. (cf. Luke 12.11) and paralleled by 23.34b (cf. Luke 11.49). However, the original context of the word, as Heinz Schürmann showed some years ago,[71] is not the discourse of Jesus prior to the sending out of the disciples. (So Schweitzer built on sand from the start.) The image of flight relates the text to Matt. 24.16-27 and reveals its character as a word of consolation: The climactic eschatological crisis will be 'shortened for the sake of the elect' by the coming of the Son of man. Such constructive activity, characteristic of pre-redactional transmission as well as of the redactions, necessitates a reconstructive activity on the part of any historian wishing to control his data. Moreover, critical history controls data in large part through a different and still more ambitious reconstructive activity. History begins with the historian's own questions, questions not limited to the concerns of his sources, and it proceeds by the way of 'historical imagination' (the projecting of hypotheses). The criticism levelled against the Fearless Detectives is simple insistence on data-control as part and parcel of imaginative reconstruction. Strauss had made this point against the naturalists' reconstructions of events standing behind miracle accounts and Wrede was to make it against the psychologizing of the liberals.[72]

William Wrede's book,[73] like Strauss's *Leben Jesu*, was a study in the nature of the gospel literature. When Strauss deals with the data of the messianic secret, wrote Wrede,

the customary traits of his criticism are in evidence; great acuteness, German thoroughness, and absolute honesty; but so are his typical weaknesses: the atomistic character of the treatment, the dominance of the dogmatic (if anti-dogmatic) concern (the miracles-question), the restriction to the negative or, what amounts to the same thing, the lack of feel for the history of the tradi-tion.[74]

Inasmuch as Wrede conceived his own contribution to the understanding of the gospel literature specifically in terms of the Markan redaction, he saw his true predecessor, rather, in Gustav Volkmar.[75] Volkmar, so far as he could determine, was the first to relate Jesus' commands of secrecy to the theme of the resurrection. He saw the key to Mark in the word of Jesus following the transfiguration: 'And as they were coming down the moun-tain, he charged them to tell no one what they had seen, until the Son of man should have risen from the dead' (Mark 9.9). Volkmar commented:

Here Mark, in terms that are almost explicit, gives the key to the understanding of this didactic scene [the transfiguration] as of his whole gospel: All the glory therein revealed is a *mysterion* which prior to the crucifixion was not understood – nor conceived of.[76]

This, too, was the seminal intuition of Wrede, who developed it in detail.

In a preliminary note on 'desiderata for Life-of-Jesus research', Wrede reproached the critics for their bad habit of too quickly abandoning the realm of the gospels for the sake of reconstruction. The observation bore on method. The whole community of critics, said Wrede, acknowledged in the abstract that a gospel was a later writer's conception of the life of Jesus, not that life itself. But this acknowledgment, he insisted, had too little effect in the concrete. It was generally remembered only when the critic felt pressed; that is, when confronted with the miraculous or a contradiction. Otherwise the abstract acknowledgment was forgotten and the critic assumed he was on bedrock.

Wrede's study begins with a sketch of the standard *Jesusbild* found in the literature since the proposal and acceptance of the primacy of Mark (Weisse, Wilke, Ritschl, Holtzmann, Weizsäcker, Wendt, Baldensperger, Schürer, Wernle, Wellhausen). His objection to their common charac-teristic (the gradual revelation of messiahship and the gradual evolution of the disciples' understanding of it) was based on Markan texts. This hurt, for the critics had thought that in taking their stand on the antiquity of these same texts, they had carved out a citadel of rock.

Page after page Wrede measured the theses both of the liberal 'lives' and of the transitional work of Weiss against a new understanding of Mark. His method and fundamental contribution consisted in a resolute effort to deal with details of the Markan redaction in terms of its total conception. This emerged from a correlation of data: the recognition of Jesus by the demons, the commands of silence, the 'riddle' character of the parables, Jesus' private teaching of the disciples, and their chronic 'misunderstanding'. Together these data constituted the messianic secret. Wrede took the sense of the secret to be the identity of Jesus as supernatural Son of God, his words as a supernatural teaching, his life and death as a supernaturally preordained destiny. In function of this acquisition, he argued that the approach to individual texts should move from general conception to particular detail. If the supernatural was a stumbling block to historical criticism, Wrede urged that the solution was not to whittle away at a particular event (e.g., the recognition of Jesus by a demon) in search of a historically explicable nucleus (e.g., a supposed religious hypersensitivity of the mentally-ill toward Jesus), but to make the historicity of the particular event stand or fall with the historicity of the general conception. Inasmuch as the general conception was supernatural and the supernatural by definition unhistorical, the problem was in principle resolved. The critical moment lay in the reduction of individual event to general conception; a sign of such reducibility was the patterned recurrence of an event (e.g., the numerous recognitions of Jesus by demons). The critical task was completed by explaining the origin of the conception. Wrede's own tentative explanation of the phenomenon of the demons was as follows:

> First it was recounted how the demons were stricken with fear at the approach of their enemy Jesus. That was a given idea. But now, because the notion obtained that the messiahship of Jesus was unknown, the thought occurred that the demons were an exception. This idea then became significant and gained a determinate shape.[77]

Weiss had exemplified the futile whittling away of data by his translation of the messianic secret into the idiom of natural explanation. Jesus spoke of this highly personal 'secret of his soul . . . only with reluctance, and rarely, and above all not to all comers'. Wrede ridiculed such compromise formulas, as he ridiculed the whole notion of deriving special personal experience from the baptism account.[78] To Wrede it was clear that the prohibitions of the revelation of Jesus' messiahship were unintelligible as historical reality. They could be vindicated neither by reference to a step-by-step pedagogy nor through a distinction between popular 'political' messiahship and messiahship as Jesus conceived it. According to the gospel accounts, Jesus accepted messiahship without reservation at the entry into Jerusalem and before Pilate. As for the possibility of finding in 'suffering messiahship' a historical motive for the secret, Wrede refused to allow the supposition that Jesus could know in advance of his passion. He maintained furthermore the reducibility of the 'suffering messiahship' idea to the already rejected 'refusal of political messiahship'.[79]

What of the prohibitions against speaking of miracles? To begin with, Wrede said, miracles could not be treated as history.[80] But even apart from this, Jesus meant miracles to be interpreted either in a messianic sense or in a non-messianic sense. If in a messianic sense, then the prohibitions against speaking of them in precisely this sense were unintelligible; if in a non-messianic sense, the prohibitions were again unintelligible for two reasons, framed as rhetorical questions: '(1) How is it that in precisely these individual cases [Jesus] hits upon the idea of imposing silence, an idea which he otherwise does not have? and (2) How can he hope through his prohibitions to make the far-reaching public character of his activity innocuous?'[81]

Set in the context of early Christian thought, the secret is seen as a theological idea worked out after the time of Jesus to fill a lacuna in the earliest traditions of the ministry: the lack of messianic claims. Historically, Jesus did not claim to be the Messiah. In the earliest Christian thought, as Weiss had had the merit of emphasizing, his messiahship was considered to date from the resurrection. The 'secret' was designed to resolve the tension between the memory of the ministry, in which messianic claims were lacking, and the development of christological thought, which spontaneously retrojected messiahship from the resurrection to the public life.

Inasmuch as Wrede revealed the thoroughgoing dogmatic supernaturalism of Mark, his book signalled the defeat of the conception of the gospel as a historical presentation of the life of Jesus.[82] But Wrede himself missed the peculiar intent of gospel-writing almost as badly as the liberals had. The difference was that they took Mark to be a reliable historian; he took Mark to be an unreliable (dogmatic) historian. Thus, Holtzmann rejoiced that the Markan Jesus spoke 'for the most part without the least digression into the dogmatic', whereas Wrede observed that the Markan Jesus was dogmatic through and through; indeed, that 'the gospel of Mark belongs to the history of dogma'.[83] This, however, yielded no new estimate of the Markan genius. To Wrede it merely showed that Mark was a naive, artless, and unconscious writer, little gifted for the task of 'setting himself in the historical situation'.[84] It did not occur to Wrede that Mark might not only have harboured dogmatic conceptions, but further, might have conceived the project of gospel-writing in terms so distinctive as to make the reproach of naiveté on the level of 'story-line' totally beside the point. Wrede's estimate of Mark's capacities as a writer only indicates that the critics were *still* missing the Markan point.

Wrede recognized that 'the writer's own thinking' was concentrated on the 'dogmatic aspects' of the story. This meant that 'the gospel no longer offers a historical view of the real life of Jesus. Only pallid remnants of such a view have passed over into a supra-historical faith-concept'.[85] The flaw here is the lack of evidence and total improbability that there was ever a pre-dogmatic version of the life of Jesus, an original story of which only 'pallid remnants' have survived. Wrede's insight still fell short, inasmuch as the bearers and shapers of the tradition from its most remote origins apparently supposed that the 'dogmatic' account of Jesus was the only kind that could be authentic and true.

The duel between Wrede and the liberals recapitulated that between Strauss and the Rationalists. The liberals were, in fact, sobered Rationalists and Wrede a minor Strauss. The trait common to all four parties was the *a priori* rejection of the supernatural. Within this context Strauss remains the champion critic for his clarity on the issues and for the coherence of his criticism. What Wrede considered a weakness in Strauss ('the restriction to the negative') is in reality evidence of superior consistency.

3. FROM BULTMANN TO THE PRESENT DAY

Technical progress has been a steady characteristic of New Testament studies in the twentieth century. One need only recall the linguistic and environmental research of Gustav Dalman, the application of form criticism to the gospels by Martin Dibelius and Rudolf Bultmann, the increased availability of rabbinic sources through Paul Billerbeck, the great collaborative effort represented by the *Theological Dictionary* of Gerhard Kittel and Gerhard Friedrich. All these instances of technical progress have naturally come under critique,[86] but the field of basic debate, of radical disagreement and impasse, lies elsewhere, in cognitional theory. This has been widely recognized in theological circles, particularly under the impulse of Bultmann. Hermeneutics, understood since Schleiermacher as the doctrine of *Verstehen* (the 'understanding' proper to human studies) has explicitly imposed itself over the past decades as the controlling question for exegesis, history, and theology.

From the first books and articles on the New Testament to appear in Europe after the first world war it was clear that the self-reliant optimism which the liberals had found among the evangelical counsels had been tempered. Liberal theology was, in fact, a war casualty. Karl Barth broke cleanly with the rationalistic thought and scholarship of the pre-war years, passionately repudiating the effort to know Christ 'according to the flesh' (cf. II Cor. 5.16). The Barthian break was not without antecedents. In 1892 the systematic theologian Martin Kähler had reacted to the liberal 'lives of Jesus' with a biting reassertion of biblical faith.[87] Contrary to a common impression, Kähler never regarded the historical reality of Jesus' life as dispensable in favour of 'the Christ of faith'. His concern was indeed with the Christ of faith, but precisely as contrasted to the nebulous, non-dogmatic Jesus of liberal research. In the period after the war, when his force was most felt, it sometimes seemed deflected to support a kerygmatic docetism Kähler would never have acknowledged.

Among the new alternatives to liberalism was the kerygma theology of Rudolf Bultmann. It was a theology which, in contradistinction to all efforts to excogitate a plausible 'essence of Christianity', settled on the New Testament's own definition of the vital centre. This was the proclamation of salvation in the death and resurrection of Christ.

The rise of kerygma theology was complicated by its association with Bultmann's negative attitude toward the usefulness of Jesus' history. Indeed, the theology has sometimes been misinterpreted as an escape from historical scepticism. Actually the theology came first, legitimizing historical disinterest and cultivating it as a theological plus. Theology positively called for the collapse of the quest.

Bultmann's *Jesus*[88] testified to the collapse. Since the author considered virtually nothing of the 'life' of Jesus knowable, discussion of it was limited to approximately a page. Jesus was baptized by John. His own 'sect' derived from John's as a splinter-group. Both were set in the context of contemporary messianic movements. As the unpolitical character of neither was readily obvious, and as both appealed to a popular following, the two leaders were inevitably executed. It is likely that for the sake of political peace the Jewish leaders worked hand in hand with the Romans in the execution of Jesus.[89]

If the concern of the book is not a 'life', what is it? Bultmann answers in an Introduction sketching a new orientation to history. Nature, he says, can be examined with impersonal objectivity; if history is examined this way, its essence escapes the examiner. In history man recognizes something of himself. He does not face mute nature; rather he enters into dialogue. This dialogue should be distinguished from a mere 'evaluation' after the facts are in. It is the opening up of oneself in conscious readiness to be questioned and challenged by historical reality. There is, says Bultmann, a way of treating history which seeks to achieve objectivity through method. By that very fact the inquirer cuts himself off from contact with whatever surpasses or contradicts the set of anticipations which the method embodies. This happens, for example, when the historian fixes on the goal of making a historical personality 'psychologically intelligible'. The very expression supposes that it is the historian who determines what the possibilities of psychic life are to be. Whatever contradicts these possibilities must be systematically labelled 'unhistorical'.[90] 'Whoever is of the belief that he first learns through history the possibilities of his own existence, will therefore reject this psychological style of inquiry. . . .'[91]

The renunciation of a seeming objectivity is actually the condition of a real objectivity. Bultmann is uninterested in giving Jesus good marks for insight or courage. He is exclusively interested in what can become actual now. This is what Jesus himself is interested in. For what can become actual now is response to the challenge Jesus poses as proclaimer of the reign of God.[92] The question of Jesus' personality, and specifically the question whether he understood himself as the Messiah, becomes altogether immaterial. (The sources do not, in any case, allow certainty on the matter.) The focus of interest is Jesus' words, which 'encounter us as questions, how we ourselves wish to interpret our existence. That we ourselves are agitated by the question of our existence is, to be sure, the presupposition. But then the questioning of history will lead not to the enrichment of timeless knowledge, but to an encounter-with-history which is itself a temporal process. . . .'[93]

Jesus is beyond doubt the source of the proclamation which the New Testament attributes to him. But to what extent the primitive community has conserved the authentic picture of Jesus and his proclamation is another, and ultimately irresolvable, question. 'For those whose interest is in the personality of Jesus, this state of affairs is distressing or devastating; for our purpose it is of no crucial significance.'[94] In fact, says Bultmann, the reader if he wishes can uniformly supply the name 'Jesus' with quotation marks, understanding it as a siglum for the oldest stratum of the tradition.[95]

Bultmann is saying, in effect, that the questions debated by the liberals were superficial and irrelevant and that one should rather approach the gospels as Augustine or Luther did, looking for light on the puzzle of one's own existence. The ideal is unconditional openness to value.

This is the power of Bultmann's proposal and performance: the openness to be invited, challenged, changed. Hence the metaphors of 'meeting' and 'listening'. The value of history lies in vital contact with new possibilities of becoming. This vital contact Bultmann describes as a 'listening' to history,[96] to its questioning 'how we wish to grasp our own existence',[97] it is 'a maximally personal encounter'.[98]

Two things, however, should be remembered. First, this vital contact is preceded by historical criticism as systematic and impartial as the dissection of a frog. Second, it is rigorously circumscribed by a reductionist principle: Whatever lies outside the sphere of the existentially communicable is pulverized. Thus, the particulars of Jesus' history are irrelevant to faith, and messiahship is reduced to the liberals' interest in 'personality'. These views would later be refined and complemented: Eschatological claims cannot in any sense, measure, or manner be validated; past events cannot be salvific; the content and modalities, the 'what' (*Was*) and the 'how', (*Wie*) of Jesus' history are unknowable and irrelevant; the 'mythological' conceptions of eschatology, of redeemer and of redemption, are over and done with.[99]

Bultmann attacked the liberal critic for coming to the gospels armed with methods for evaluating Jesus. What he found wrong in this was that it extinguished light in advance. The question raised by his own systematic exclusions is whether they have not inadvertently done the same.

Since the 1950s, in any case, a challenge has arisen within the Bultmann school itself to the notion that the Christian kerygma can dispense with the realities of Jesus' history. James M. Robinson's programmatic essay on a 'new' quest of the historical Jesus[100] outlined the theological state of the question. The nineteenth-century quest, inasmuch as it proposed historical reconstructions as equivalently an alternative to faith, was theologically illegitimate; and inasmuch as it misconceived the nature of the sources as furnishing data for a 'biography' of Jesus, it set itself an impossible task. The new quest was new to the extent that it acknowledged the kerygmatically conditioned nature of the sources, abandoned the quest of Jesus' biography, and in no sense aimed to substitute a historical construct for faith in the biblical Christ. Its aim rather was to define the continuity between Jesus and kerygma. Günther Bornkamm's *Jesus von Nazareth*[101] was among the first expressions of this 'post-Bultmannian' movement.

Bornkamm shared neither the widespread historical scepticism that grew up in the wake of Bultmann nor the theological conviction that faith for the sake of its own integrity must renounce the quest of history. The purpose of the book was 'to seek the history in the kerygma of the gospels and the kerygma in this history'.[102] In numerous significant particulars, such as the origin of the institution of the twelve in the ministry of Jesus, Bultmannian views were abandoned,[103] though such changes were often left isolated and their significance unexploited. The fully acknowledged kerygmatic character of the sources led to no global rejection of the historicity of detail and in some cases the historicity of synoptic tradition was surprisingly assumed.

Despite the break in principle with the theological mentality of the research which preceded the first world war, the book had significant ties with the past, reflecting, as Bultmann's own work always had, the Enlightenment critique of the miraculous. Thus, prophetic knowledge was nowhere attributed to Jesus. His decision to go to Jerusalem, 'unquestionably the decisive turning-point in the history of Jesus',[104] had for its purpose the proclamation of the coming kingdom in 'the city of the great king'. Like Wrede, Bornkamm considered the synoptics' view (namely, that this was a journey into prophetically certain death and glorification) as 'later tradition', while conceding that Jesus must have reckoned with 'the distinct possibility of a violent end'.[105]

In accord with the tradition of Wrede and Bultmann, Bornkamm denied the use of messianic titles by the Jesus of history. He was unimpressed by the effort to attribute to Jesus or to the gospels the alleged Judaic scheme of 'hidden' and 'revealed' Son of man. But he emphasized the 'implied' or 'indirect' christology which Bultmannians generally acknowledge in the sayings and actions of Jesus: the 'messianic' thrust contained in the historical immediacy of every word and act.[106] In accord with this accent, the eschatological consciousness of Jesus was distinguished by a 'realized' element. This again stood in contrast to the futurist, unfulfilled eschatology of Weiss, Schweitzer, and Bultmann. Bornkamm located the shift from eschatological promise to fulfilment in the present of Jesus rather than exclusively in the post-paschal Christian community.[107]

In 1971 Joachim Jeremias, aptly described as the principal custodian in our time of 'the heritage of detailed and exacting philological, environmental research about Jesus',[108] published *Die Verkündigung Jesu (New Testament Theology* I: *The Proclamation of Jesus*).[109] The work crowned a career of nearly a half-century's publication in the field of historical-Jesus studies. Jeremias's first important book directly centred on Jesus had been a ground-breaking investigation of his symbolic imagery.[110] In the course of time two monographs appeared, one on Jesus' eucharistic words,[111] the other on his parables,[112] to instruct a generation of scholars on how to make philological expertise, environmental erudition, and interpretative technique serve the historian's craft. *The Proclamation of Jesus* continued this tradition, drawing a lifetime's exegetical and historical achievement into a final synthesis. Among the new elements were an incisive study of Jesus' personal idiom and especially of the 'reign of God' language he minted for the end of time and a striking reconstruction of the original Son of man thematic.

The sheer technical mastery of Jeremias's contributions allowed them to stand on their own. No distinguishing, all-commanding theological rationale appeared to inform them. Let the monograph *Jesus' Promise to the Nations*[113] illustrate. The historical question which this work addressed (Did Jesus conceive the entry of the Gentiles into salvation and, if so, how?) did not spontaneously arise out of any systematic theological exigence; rather, it arose out of the discovery that gospel texts grounding the world mission in the words of Jesus were secondary developments in the tradition. The question, in other words, indicated no distinctive philosophical or theological problematic or commitment. (Contrast the Bultmannian 'new quest'!) Moreover, Jeremias's answer to the question, though it accorded well with the historic Lutheran emphasis on justification by faith, might conceivably have been worked out in exactly the same terms by an American Baptist or an Italian Catholic.

This freedom from narrowly conceived canons of theological relevance did not, however, amount to theological indifference or neutrality. In the Foreword to his epoch-making *The Parables of Jesus*, Jeremias enucleated his view of the theological significance of historical-Jesus research: 'Only the Son of Man and his word can invest our message with full authority.'[114] This appeared to designate the historical Jesus not only as the ultimate but as the exclusive source of the authority of Christian preaching – a view numerous critics attacked as incompatible with the thought and practice of the New Testament church and specifically with the mentality of the evangelists (who seem to believe that for all their transposing, recasting, and adding, they are presenting nothing other than the *ipsissima vox Jesu*). Jeremias nuanced his view in an address delivered in 1956 at the 500th anniversary of the University of Greifswald.[115] Here he balanced the danger of kerygmatic docetism against that of non-kerygmatic ebionitism; that is, he affirmed the theological necessity of the kerygma of the Easter church as preservative of the transcendental significance of Jesus' words and deeds.

In Jeremias's estimate the central importance of historical-Jesus research was theologically justified by two themes: 'Incarnation' and 'Jesus as the Call of God'.

In this context the thrust of the word 'Incarnation' lay in the concrete humanity of Christ. It signified, first, that Jesus was fully man; second, that this was by the will of God for our salvation. That Jesus was a man fulfilled the condition of the possibility of historical inquiry bearing on him. That this concrete humanity was divinely and unreservedly willed for our salvation grounded the theological appropriateness of such inquiry. This second point is where the accent fell in Jeremias's thought. Attention precisely to the Jesus of ancient Palestine was in every Christian era the theologically appropriate consequence of 'Incarnation'; in the modern era critical history was a peculiarly apt and fruitful – and so, finally, indispensable – form for this attention to take.

Again, in the context of the debate on the historical Jesus and the kerygma of the church, Jeremias posited the indissoluble unity of 'God's call' and 'man's response'. He expressly recognized that access to God's call was mediated by the faith-response of the New Testament church. He nevertheless insisted that call and response, though inseparable, were distinct, and that the ultimate and decisive norm of Christian theology was the call rather than the response.[116] This theological stance, no doubt calculated in the first instance to expose and reinforce the central importance of focusing on Jesus, did so on grounds likewise calculated to relativize the theological diversities of the New Testament church. The insistence on differentiating between call and response implied the impossibility that any response, be it ever so rich and accurate, should adequately comprehend or exhaust the call. Thus, by reference to 'Jesus as the Call of God', Jeremias not only offered theological justification for historical-Jesus research, he also underlined the common reference and, indeed, ultimate coherence of the New Testament canon.

Jeremias's book on the proclamation of Jesus made no effort, however, to define in greater detail the relation of critical history to theology. One should not, perhaps, complain of this in the face of the book's concrete contributions to historical and theological knowledge, e.g., the elegantly precise and compendious treatments of Jesus' speech (fields of meaning, rhetorical range, style, rhythm, variety of tone, conscious allusions, omissions, and ambiguities, new coinages, distinctive idiom, etc.) which punctuate the work at strategic points and illuminate it from end to end. Nevertheless, it is today being recognized ever more widely and explicitly that progress in dealing with theoretical questions is indispensable and, in particular, that the conditions of the possibility of effective historical-Jesus research must find not only performative but thematic definition.

The need to define both the to-be-related and their relations – historical-critical method(s), historical knowledge, theology in its diverse forms and phases – has begun to command current discussion of historical-Jesus questions in newly fundamental form. The discussion has never been more basic and open. The past generation saw Bultmann's strict prohibition of any inquiry 'behind the kerygma' give way (in the 'new quest') to selective inquiry designed to cure kerygma theology of its docetism and to modify its isolation from 'cosmos', 'history', and 'society'.[117] This movement has now been followed in Germany by an increasingly powerful protest against the legacy of Troeltschean historicism (e.g., Pannenberg,[118] Stuhlmacher,[119] Roloff,[120] Hengel,[121] Schürmann,[122] Goppelt[123]) and by the call both for a radical critique of current methodology and for the development of a fuller, broader-based, multidimensional methodology.[124] It may be that the era of 'blame the sources' is being succeeded by an era of 'blame the methods', whereas the deep and crucial lack at the root of the failures of the quest has lain neither in the New Testament sources nor in historical-critical methods but rather in the philosophical baggage needlessly inhibiting and encumbering exegetes and historians. To be sure, the current call for a re-examination of methods explicitly includes the reconsideration of basic presuppositions (e.g., the general conception of history,[125] judgments of what in principle is possible,[126] etc.). Indeed, the breadth and open-endedness of this 'newest questioning' are among its most promising and inviting traits.

4. THE QUEST AS A HISTORICAL PHENOMENON

As a phenomenon in intellectual history, the quest of the historical Jesus records the changes of religious horizon effected by the evolution of modern European philosophy and specifically of the philosophy of knowledge. From its Enlightenment origins this philosophical tradition had been ill-disposed toward the classical religious heritage of the West. The dogmatic substance of the gospels had accordingly become a wishbone in the throat of avant-garde Protestantism. The alternative to swallowing it, it seemed, was to explain it and, as Basil Willey remarked of seventeenth-century thinking, something was 'explained' . . . when its history had been traced and described.[127]

The final reason for the gulf between the gospels themselves and this literature of explanation lay in a hermeneutical law: Before data can generate new knowledge they must be understood in their own terms. The gospels, designed to evoke a faith-response, could present evidence serviceable to historical explanation only on condition that they were already understood in their own right. But to men who instinctively found religious dogma alien, New Testament perspectives were not easily identifiable. Consequently, the record of the quest offers a rich repertory of self-parody in the guise of historical comment. Of the jeering at the apostles on the day of Pentecost Reimarus remarks: 'If [they] had spoken with one another rationally, distinctly, and decently, like reasonable, well-conducted, sober men, this mockery could not have taken place.'[128] The random example might be easily multiplied.

Why was there no quest of the historical Jesus in Roman Catholicism? In part, no doubt, for the same reasons that the wholehearted adoption of critical biblical scholarship generally was postponed in Catholicism for over two hundred years. 'The father of modern biblical studies' was a French Oratorian priest, Richard Simon (d. 1712), whose express purpose was to serve the truth and so be useful to the Catholic Church.[129] But Simon's pioneer venture into the ambiguities of history coincided with a time at which Catholic theology was in full retreat to the fortress of uniform orthodoxy, and the theologians (as Bernard Lonergan has put it) 'began to reassure one another about their certainties'.[130] Bossuet and the Jesuits combined to nip this critical effort in the bud, and Simon had no Catholic successors. The second Catholic experience with critical scriptural scholarship, toward the turn of the twentieth century, was still less happy. Alfred Loisy's eclectic synthesis of 1902, *L'Évangile et l'Église*, sparked a crisis, or at least what the Roman curia took to be a crisis, for Catholicism. The book's immediate purpose was to take issue with Harnack's notion that the growth of dogma was a corruption of the religion of Jesus. In dogma and its evolution Loisy saw, rather, the fulfilment of the vital necessity of evolution, for which the point of departure was the eschaton announced by Jesus but unforeseeably delayed. Jesus had not consciously anticipated the church. But his gospel had in fact prepared the way for the church and was prolonged in it as church and dogma evolved through the centuries in continued expectation of the kingdom. From the standpoint of traditional Catholic theology the condemnation of Loisy's book was doubtless justified; but it also signalled the victory of reactionary

Roman circles over the nascent resurgence of Catholic critical scholarship.

The period of official Catholic suspicion of critical biblical studies was closed in 1943 with the publication of Pius XII's *Divino Afflante Spiritu*. In the long interim between Simon and Pius XII, the church's hardy refusal to relinquish a jot or a tittle of its dogmatic heritage was combined with an instinctive unease regarding any methodology for an ecclesiastical discipline, such as exegesis, in which the official magisterium was not an intrinsically conditioning factor. Official controls did not, however, prevent the appearance of numerous conservative 'lives' (such as those of Léonce de Grandmaison[131] and Jules Lebreton[132]) produced in the context of apologetics. But, in general, the controlling anti-dogmatic bias of the German quest guaranteed the non-participation of Catholics in the movement.

The quest has had its human side. One thinks of Reimarus dutifully marching off to church every Sunday for a service he considered a hoax; of Strauss, fired from his post between the publication of the first and second volumes of his *Leben Jesu*; of the twenty-three-year-old Schweitzer, catching fire at the discovery of the key to the story of Jesus while on army manoeuvres in Alsace;[133] of the modernist drama and Loisy's *mot*, at once serious and cynical, to the effect that it was the kingdom that was awaited and, alas, the church which arrived.[134]

Still the practitioners of the quest, however they understood religion, conceived their project in religious terms. The positive aim of Reimarus, remote but real, was to commend natural religion. Strauss aimed to save Christianity by making it intelligible in post-Enlightenment terms. The same can be said for the neo-Kantian liberals and contemporary existentialists. Yet measured in the scales of the gospels themselves, the quest for most of its history has been fundamentally if unintentionally un-Christian. How is it that this monument to the spirit of German theology, as Schweitzer hailed it, reflected so little of the world of Luther and Melancthon? The answer turns on the radically revisionist character of the Enlightenment and its interpretation of the scientific revolution. Bayle's *Encyclopedia* was the certificate of divorce between Europe and its religious past. In the early seventeenth century the battle had been waged in the name of science against Aristotle and Ptolemy, but in the name of religion, too, against Renaissance naturalism. As Herbert Butterfield has pointed out,

> Christians helped the cause of modern rationalism by their jealous determination to sweep out of the world all miracles and magic except their own. Some of this generation of scientists argued that Christian miracles themselves could not be vindicated unless it could be assumed that the normal workings of the universe were regular and subject to law.[135]

But, as he notes later,

if earlier in the century religious men had hankered after a mathematically interlocking universe to justify the .rationality and self-consistency of God, before the end of the century their successors were beginning to be nervous because they saw the mechanism becoming possibly too self-complete.[136]

Unwittingly they had opened the way for 'a colossal secularization of thought in every possible realm of ideas at the same time'.[137] This is what Paul Hazard called 'the crisis of the European mind', and Peter Gay, 'the rise of modern paganism'.[138]

It would be simplistic to suppose that the scientific revolution of itself produced this outcome. The first half of the seventeenth century showed once again how ugly and brutal religious passion could be. *Odium theologicum* poisoned Europe for a hundred years prior to the Peace of Westphalia. As in Restoration England and Regency France, nature took delayed revenge. Evidently without resources to meet the challenge creatively, Catholic theology retired into a dogmatic corner,[139] while avant-garde Protestant theology allied itself with the spirit of the time. In eighteenth-century Germany, orthodoxy in the Wolffian mode gave way to rationalism or its opposite, pietism.

The key issue was the claims of reason. To practically all participants in the quest, much of what Luther or Melancthon considered essential to Christianity ran counter to reason; i.e., it violated the conception of reality as an impermeable system of finite causes. Bultmann is the spokesman of a two-hundred-year tradition when he says that 'for modern man' the conceptions of spirits and miracles, redeemer and redemption, are 'over and done with'. To hold the contrary would involve a *sacrificium intellectus* 'in order to accept what we cannot sincerely consider true'.[140] Spoken in the tradition of Goethe and Schiller, of Kant, Schelling, and Hegel,[141] of the post-Enlightenment mainstream. Here Christian and agnostic, rationalist and idealist, liberal and existentialist find common ground.

But the present situation in cognitional theory represents breakthrough progress on a revolutionary scale. The goal of *Insight*[142] was to guide the process of consistently intelligent and rational self-appropriation. The objectification of the operations constituting scientific knowing was but a moment in this process. But it was a moment heavy with consequence, for it subverted both the popular slogans and the elaborate epistemologies which had long frustrated appropriation of the pre-Enlightenment past. But *Insight* did not invite the reader to install himself in this past. It consciously depended on Kant and, indeed, on the entire modern tradition, which it illuminated by setting it in a fully articulated cognitional context. This context was the naturally structured unfolding of intelligence, which included recognition of its own dynamism: the pure or unrestricted desire to know. Intricately calibrated yet simple as sunlight, *Insight* thematized the spontaneously boundless and untrammelled openness of intelligence as the secret of man's historic advance through ongoing differentiations of consciousness. Thematization of the dynamism powering this process has opened some new vistas as well as resolved some old antinomies.

The appropriate result in the present context (i.e., against the historical backdrop of the mentality ruling the quest of the historical Jesus) is to recognize that, whereas the achievements of empirical science are the common property of agnostic and theist, positivist, existentialist, and Thomist, the philosophical world-view of the Enlightenment may be indifferently accepted or abandoned. Indeed, its validity, never self-evident, is now seen to be illusory. Might one hope that there is no longer need to insist on the total irrelevance of pointing, in support of it, to the achievements of modern medicine and technology?

The Enlightenment world-view took shape in a period of theological collapse. But with the current recovery of resources for appropriating the vast, pre-Enlightenment heritage of the human spirit, the cheerful jettisoning of excess Enlightenment baggage can begin. There should be no doubt as to what this means for a final estimate of the quest of the historical Jesus. It means that most of the efforts constituting the quest failed not only in the sense and for the reasons conventionally alleged[143] but because for the questers Enlightenment propaganda had become cultural assumption. The assumption drastically contracted the range of divine and human possibilities. The error was a massive scotoma gratuitously distorting the quest through the whole of its history.

The progress in cognitional theory we have referred to establishes the historicity of nothing whatsoever and in no way lightens the proper task of history. On the contrary, it disposes of certain shortcuts such as the *a priori* dismissal of the prophetic and miraculous as unhistorical. On the other hand, there is an enormous harvest undamaged by the contemporary epistemological breakthrough, the fruit of laboriously cultivated environmental, philological and, in the widest sense, literary research which has been accumulating especially over the past hundred years. This, together with the definitively settled fact that the proclamation and ministry of Jesus were totally eschatological, belongs to the authentic legacy of the quest.

Though most of its monuments were failures, the quest remains an ongoing movement because the modern West is irreversibly historically minded. For us the goal of the quest – the understanding of Jesus in his own terms – is not optional. It is indispensable. The error of the quest has been its confusion of ends and means. The end was the understanding of Jesus in his own terms, which, the questers clearly saw, were not those of any other time and place and therefore not those of any later moment in the stream of Christian history. They inferred from this that tradition was irrelevant to the process of arriving at the goal. But historians must be interpreters, and it is a condition of effective interpreting that the consciousness of the interpreter be informed by the tradition which the to-be-interpreted has generated (*wirkungsgeschichtliches Bewusstsein*).[144] Collectively, the failures of the quest may well constitute Western thought's single most imposing dramatization of this hermeneutical law. In its gains and successes, however, the quest also marks an era in the history of Christian contemplation, its course inscribing only the most recent chapter in the history of the theology of the life of Jesus.[145] It is in this large latter context that the works of an Adolf Schlatter or of a Romano Guardini belong. And it is with reference to this context, finally, that even a modest review of the quest can hope to be more than tinkling brass: not *phōnē* (sound) only, but *logos* (word).

III

THE GOSPEL LITERATURE: DATA ON JESUS?

Our purpose in this chapter is not to survey the gospels with a view to salvaging what is 'factual' in them. Our purpose, rather, is to contest a proposition which, if true, would thwart our project in advance. The project is to define the aims of Jesus; the proposition which would thwart it is that the gospels do not supply data on him.[1]

On the face of it this proposition seems outlandish. It presents itself, however, as the conclusion of an elaborate inquiry and it is grounded in an important insight: The gospels are confessional, the product of faith-formulation, and have their most distinctive qualities from faith itself. Making this insight a point of departure, critics and theologians in our time have argued that the kerygmatic character of New Testament faith-formulation disqualifies it as historical: First, it does not intend past events; second and consequently, it does not provide data on Jesus. Our question is correspondingly twofold: Did early Christian faith-formulation intend past events? And do we have in it data on Jesus? We begin with the first question and we pose it, first of all, with reference to the pre-gospel formulations of faith.

1. EARLY FAITH-FORMULATION

The transformation of Jesus' disciples into a religious body presenting itself to Israel as the seed of messianic restoration is a stunning phenomenon. That it was the Easter experience which effected this transformation is beyond reasonable doubt. The resurrection is the key to all Christian witness to Jesus.

Early in the life of the Christian movement such witness was epitomized and stylized. Lapidary form functioned as a preservative with the result that numerous expressions of primitive christological faith are still accessible to us. They are found mainly in the letters of Paul and the missionary discourses of Acts.

There is this difference between the two sources. Sometimes Paul indicates a citation by asserting the traditional character of a given faith-formula (e.g. I Cor. 11.23; 15.3). The missionary speeches in Acts, on the other hand, are 'citations' in a sense corresponding to ancient historiographical convention. Furthermore, Paul's sources are identifiable as liturgical or catechetical tradition, whereas a concrete counterpart explaining the transmission of the discourses in Acts is not readily discoverable.[2] The resultant difficulty of estimating the relative antiquity of the public proclamation to non-believers in Acts touches a number of significant points. How, for example, assess historically the lack of references in the discourses to the expiatory value of the death of Jesus? Here there is a wide spectrum of opinion.[3] A swift and selective survey of both sources (Paul and Acts) will, however, allow us to learn enough of the church's initial life of faith to situate major New Testament testimonies to Jesus in the context of their origins.

I Corinthians 15.3–5

In I Cor. 15.3–5 we have a confessional formula which Paul declares he himself had received and in turn handed on[4] to the Corinthians, namely:

> that Christ died for our sins in accordance with the scriptures
> and that he was buried
> and that he was raised on the third day in accordance with the scriptures
> and that he appeared to Cephas, then to the twelve.

This handsomely sculpted kerygmatic formula, probably first composed in Aramaic,[5] dating at least from the forties of the first century,[6] attesting the common faith of the churches of the Levant and of the Mediterranean basin,[7] doubtless served catechetical purposes as a summary in its own right[8] and perhaps as a recapitulation of points to be developed.[9]

Comparable, though less elaborate and probably more primitive, formulas occur elsewhere in Paul, alluding to Jesus

> who was delivered up for our transgressions
> and raised for our acquittal (Rom. 4.25).

or again

> who died,
> but more, was raised,
> who is at the right hand of God,
> who makes intercession for us (Rom. 8.34).

These kerygmatic texts[10] share three characteristics with the formula of I Cor. 15.3-5: (1) the schematic juxtaposition of death and resurrection, (2) the ascending accent on the resurrection as climactic,[11] and (3) the scriptural background (specifically Aramaic and Hebrew texts) on the suffering and glorified Servant.[12]

The confession of I Cor. 15.3–5, in accord with these comparable texts and with its own rhetorical structure,[13] makes its central affirmation in the parallel lines one and three. Lines two and four function each as the warrant of the preceding statement.[14] Owing to the role of these latter lines, the total formula affirms: He really died and he really rose.[15] But while this affirmation is conscious and emphatic, it is wholly relative to the heart of the confession: Christ died for our sins, as scripture prophetically attests he would, and God raised him on the third day, as scripture prophetically attests he would. (As this paraphrase attempts to indicate, the motif of scriptural testimony is not the primary theme but a qualifier; the primary thematic accent falls on 'he died for our sins' and 'he was raised on the third day'.)

As in Rom. 4.25 ('delivered up for our transgressions'), the motif of expiatory death finds conscious expression: Christ died *for our sins*. Inasmuch as the phrase 'for our sins' derives its very wording from Isa. 53.5,[16] the following 'in accordance with the scriptures', – which specifically modifies 'for our sins'[17] – must refer to the great Deutero-Isaian passage on the Servant, and perhaps to other texts as well, in the light of Isa. 53.[18] If the formula's most problematic aspect is the scope of 'on the third day',[19] its most distinctive aspect lies in the last line: 'he appeared to Cephas, then to the twelve'.[20] While this is designed to authenticate the reality of Jesus' resurrection, it does not do so by substituting 'proof' for faith; rather, it locates the testimony which specifies faith, thus attesting primitive Christianity's commitment to apostolic tradition as the basis and rule of faith.[21]

In its simplicity and density the formula expresses the distinctive intention of primitive Christianity's defining confession: salvation through the paschal mysteries of Jesus. It inescapably follows that the faith of the church was not grounded on a strained hope for an imminent parousia,[22] but on the tradition, originating with Cephas and the twelve,[23] which proclaimed salvation already realized in principle. This mentality conditioned the whole of early Christianity's eschatological consciousness and set it apart from that of contemporary eschatological communities such as Qumran.[24]

We have thus far attempted to catch the intention of the formula, to understand it in its own terms, to take full account of its kerygmatic and confessional function. In so doing we have implicitly answered our own question, namely, whether the formula intends past events. It inescapably does. Is there any way in which this confession of Christ's death as expiatory and prophetically attested could be purified of the intending of the past event of the death? No way. Nor is there any plausible way to purify the resurrection-confession of the intending of the resurrection as past event. Even were the statements 'Christ died' and 'he was raised' in themselves ambiguous, the 'warrants' of burial and apparition would resolve the ambiguity.

But there is more here than simply the settling of an isolated point. The formula of I Cor. 15.3-5 illuminates the structure of early Christian faith as a faith that intends and interprets events: present meaning hinges on past happening. Past happening is attached to present proclaiming and confessing, not extrinsically, but precisely as the object of the proclaiming and confessing: Christ died for our sins!

In this light it becomes clear that 'Jesus is Lord!' and 'Lord, come!' presuppose 'he was raised on the third day'. That is, Christian faith-formulation not only intends past events but is so founded on such intending as to be otherwise unintelligible. This, in fact, is Paul's point in the passage opened by his citation of the present formula: 'If Christ has not been raised, then our preaching is in vain and your faith is in vain' (I Cor. 15.14).

Nor will it do merely to concede with Bultmann that 'the preaching which proclaimed the risen Lord had also to speak in some way of the earthly Jesus and his death',[25] for so to adopt the concessive mood is to underplay a massive fact, namely, that the synoptic tradition was born of resurrection faith. The massive fact of this development should guide our understanding of its first phase. Though the resurrection could never cease to be an object of confession and reflection in itself, it swiftly became, above all, the focus for a concentrated (re)consideration not only of Jesus' death but of his entire pre-paschal career.

I Corinthians 11.23–25 and Philippians 2.6–11

The text of I Cor. 11.23–25 cites a liturgical formula:

> For I received from the Lord what I also delivered to you:
> that the Lord Jesus on the night he was betrayed
> took bread, and having spoken a blessing, broke it and said,
> 'This is my body which is for you.
> Do this in remembrance of me.'
> In the same way also the cup after supper, saying
> 'This cup is the new covenant in my blood.
> Do this, as often as you drink it, in remembrance of me.'

The formula affirms in faith the Last Supper, passion, and death; it interprets them: Jesus offers his life 'for you'; and it gives the origin of this interpretation: Jesus himself.[26] Liturgical in function (therefore repeatedly renewed with cultic force in the present), the text is also an affirmation from the past and about the past. It specifies the time as 'the night he was betrayed'. Thus, the Judas tradition is incidentally alluded to. The participle *eucharistēsas*, 'having spoken a blessing', if taken in conjunction with the later phrase *meta to deipnēsai*, 'after (the) supper', indicates the context of the meal. Finally, by the eucharistic words Jesus is represented as interpreting the meal as a symbolic action binding its participants in covenant-communion with him. Evoking the prophetic themes of the Servant (Isa. 53) and the new covenant (Jer. 31.31), he moreover expresses the intent to make his death both an expiation (*'yper 'ymōn*) and a covenant sacrifice (cf. *diathēkē*).

Our present point is not that this liturgical text establishes the historicity of the Last Supper but simply that we have here a text whose faith-affirmations bear circumstantially on the past. There is little room for doubt that the primitive Christian community understood its own central cultic act as rooted in words Jesus spoke 'on the night he was betrayed'.

The pre-Pauline hymn of Phil. 2.6–11 is another precious testimony of early Christian faith:

> who being in the form of God
> did not count equality with God a thing to be grasped
> but emptied himself
> taking the form of servant.
>
> Having become like men
> and appearing as a man
> he humbled himself
> becoming obedient to death.
>
> This is why God raised him high
> and gave him the name over every name
> that at Jesus' name every knee should bend
> and every tongue confess
> that Jesus Christ is LORD![27]

The hymn celebrates the universal lordship of Christ, but in a special way. Elsewhere in early Christian formulation the contrasting sequence of death/resurrection or of humiliation/exaltation is viewed from the standpoint of '*pro nobis*' (Rom. 4.25) or of testimony (I Cor. 15.3–5) or of scriptural fulfilment (I Cor. 15.3–5; Acts 4.11) or of problem and solution (Acts 2.23f.) or of man's work and God's work (Acts 2.23f.; 3.15; 4.10f.; 5.30; 10.39f.).

Such formulas accordingly express (and are designed to evoke) a diversity of responses to the thematic reversal of death/resurrection or humiliation/exaltation: thanksgiving (Rom. 4.25), firmness in the commitment of faith (I Cor. 15.3–5), and so forth. The Philippians hymn is different. It contemplates the depth of Christ's humiliation and the height of his exaltation, moving from an initial wonder to a final and climactic acclamation.

The world of men does not appear in the field of vision (although if we consider the hymn as performance, the confessing community is present to summon every knee and tongue to the acknowledgment of the Kyrios). Attention is exclusively focused on Jesus in relation to God: on an obedience which awesomely braves every humiliation and then, in catharsis, on a dazzling exaltation. Humiliation and exaltation are related as obedience and recompense. He 'emptied himself' and 'humbled himself'; therefore, God exalted him. The pivotal 'therefore' derives from Isaiah 53, which is likewise a literary source of the general scheme 'obedient lowliness/exalted lordship'.[28]

The Servant theme might thus appear to anchor the text in a familiar context. But on closer examination the hymn's uniqueness among the formalized expressions of early Christian faith becomes increasingly evident. Certain of its words (e.g., *morphē*, 'form') smack of 'terminology'; more important, the inescapable motifs of pre-existence and incarnation[29] and the terms in which the divinity of Christ is described create the impression of a lyric flowering from the soil of speculation.

The notion that the hymn's conceptual model was the gnostic redeemer myth has now, we hope, been laid to rest.[30] Our most solid clue to the conceptual background is the pre-existence motif which, as elsewhere in the New Testament, has something of a parallel in the Wisdom mysticism of Hellenistic Judaism.[31] The relevant data (the motifs of pre-existence and divinity, the 'terminology', the indications of familiarity with the scriptures in both Hebrew and Greek[32]) point to a milieu of Jewish-Hellenistic Christians (in Antioch, for example) among whom the impact of Christ's resurrection from the dead produced the church's first speculative (or, better, 'contemplative') christology. The hymn's focus is on Christ's exaltation as the fruit and recompense of his obedient humiliation. Lordship – a new reciprocal relation between Christ and the world of men – differentiates Christ's exaltation from his pre-existent equality with God. But if the intended focus is on lordship as the fruit of obedience, the hymn's most *distinctive* testimony, nevertheless, must be its affirmation of incarnation, which is here assimilated to the humiliation theme.[33] Thus the humiliation has two phases or moments: the incarnation (strophe 1) and the obedience unto death (strophe 2). This extraordinary vision echoes a constellation of Jewish-Hellenistic Wisdom themes set in a new key by meditation on the glorified Son of man.[34] In 'explaining' the glorification by reference to Jesus' voluntary and obedient self-humbling, the hymn epitomizes Jesus' historic existence in a single decision. In its own way this faith-lyric attests our point (on the New Testament faith-formulas' intending of the past) as incontestably and impressively as do the texts of I Cor. 11.23–25 and 15.3–5.

Formulas in the speeches of Acts

Unlike the numerous definably pre-Pauline confessions of faith in the letters of Paul, the missionary discourses of Acts (2.14–36, 38–40; 3.12–26; 4.9–12, 19–20; 5.29–32; 7.2–53, 56; 10.34–43; 13.17–41, 46–47; 17.22–31) pose, as we have already noted, a special historical question; namely, are these free compositions from the hand of Luke? Or were they drawn from source material? In either case, how well do they reflect the actual preaching of the primitive community two generations prior to the Lukan redaction?

The numerous and significant theological archaisms which mark the discourses orient us toward the acknowledgment of a primitive kerygma in Acts. On the other hand, there is no sizable stretch of text in the discourses from which the sign of the redactor is absent. These two data have directed the most reliable literary criticism to a nuanced position with reference to the respective roles of tradition and redaction in the discourses, distinguishing not only from one discourse to another, but from one to another part of the same discourse.[35] The result is this: Past criticism, whether conservative or radical, is shown to have been by and large incomplete in its assessment of the data and too cavalier in its conclusions. Second, it does not seem possible to isolate full kerygmatic passages which are verbatim primitive. Third, there are nevertheless solid indications of the antiquity of numerous kerygmatic procedures and christological, soteriological, and ecclesial themes.

To review the situation briefly, taking the paschal experience of the disciples as the point of departure: The resurrection, immediately interpreted as messianic event,[36] was seen as the divine vindication of Jesus. Consequently, it was related from the outset to the history whose climax it formed. For a variety of purposes[37] the earliest Christians promptly sought scriptural testimony both to the *vindicatio* (the resurrection) and to the *vindicandum* (the pre-paschal Jesus rejected by Israel and crucified). What were the main themes and scriptural sources of this initial effort of reflection, in so far as the discourses of Acts indicate?

A status of importance must be accorded the theme of the Isaian Servant's passion and glorification. In the missionary discourses this is variously reflected, though (as in the hymn of Phil. 2) without reference to the motif of expiation. See especially Acts 3.13, 'God ... glorified (*edoxasen*[38] cf. LXX Isa. 52.13) his servant (*ton paida autou*, cf. LXX Isa. 52.13) Jesus, whom you delivered (*paredōkate*, cf. LXX Isa. 53.6, 12; Targ. Isa. 53.5) ...; v. 14, 'But you denied the ... Righteous One (*ton dikaion*[39] Isa. 53. 11) ...; v. 26, 'God, having raised up his servant (*ton paida autou*, LXX Isa. 52.13) ...' Given this solid basis for comparison, cf. 2.23, 'this

Jesus, delivered up (*ekdoton*, cf. Targ. Isa. 53.5) according to the definite will and foreknowledge of God' (cf. Isa. 53.10). Cf. Acts 3.18; 4.28; 7.52; 10.43; 13.27, 29. A further plausible connection: Acts 2.33, 'Being therefore exalted (*yposōtheis*)...'; 5.31, 'God exalted (*ypsōsen*) him ...'; cf. LXX Isa. 52.13, *ypsōthēsetai*.[40]

Structurally similar to the Servant theme in the conjunction of humiliation/exaltation motifs is the text of Ps. 118.22 (Acts 4.11). The early use of this testimony is indicated by parallels (Mark 12.10f. parr.) deriving from pre-Markan tradition.[41] Just how ancient its Christian use was cannot be known with certainty, but it may already have been interpreted messianically in pre-Christian times.[42]

It is noteworthy that all six of the explicit citations bearing on the person of Jesus and figuring in the schematized missionary discourses are concerned with his resurrection and glorification. In the order of their appearance in the text of Acts they are (1) Ps. 16.10 (Acts 2.25–28; 13.35); (2) Ps. 132.11 (Acts 2.30); (3) Ps. 110.1 (Acts 2.34f.; 5.31); (4) Deut. 18.15f. (Acts 3.22); (5) Ps. 118.22 (Acts 4.11); (6) Ps. 2.7 (Acts 13.33). The Psalms, looked on as a treasury of messianic testimonies, were preferentially drawn on to particularize and celebrate the glorification of Jesus as messianic enthronement (Pss. 110; 132), vindication and victory (Ps. 110), sonship (Ps. 2), and the prerogative of preservation from corruption (Ps. 16). The antiquity of the use of these themes as well as of the theme of the 'the name' (Acts 2.38; 3.16; 4.10, 12; 10.43), of the prophet like Moses (Acts 3.22; 7.17–41), and of the judge of the living and dead (Acts 10.42) is indicated by a variety of data.[43]

The intense soteriological and christological reflection which the traditions of Acts attest was complemented by an ecclesial self-understanding richly nurtured on scriptural and especially eschatological themes. The multi-faceted life of the church – its proclamation to Israel and debates with the Jewish *élite*, its liturgical celebrations, its rapidly evolving community structures, the problems raised by external persecution and internal friction, the eventual launching of the world mission – contributed to the growth of this self-understanding and so registered its influence on the formation and development of the gospel tradition. Before dealing directly with the relationships between early kerygma and the growth of the gospel tradition, what can be said of the initial christological faith of the church as a phenomenon in itself?

The attempt to distinguish various originating *loci*[44] and distinct stages of development[45] within early Christianity is notoriously difficult. The most significant question turns on the point of departure; i.e., on how the resurrection's initial impact on the disciples is to be understood. More exactly: Is the element of realized eschatology, which is found in the oldest accessible kerygmatic themes and formulas, to be attributed to the church's accommodation of an originally futurist eschatology to 'the delay of the parousia' or other factors? Or is this realized element already given in the paschal experience of the disciples? The fact that the resurrection of the dead was understood in Judaism exclusively as eschatological fulfilment would seem to impose the latter view upon us.

This strictly eschatological understanding of resurrection was, of course, distinct from the idea of the revivification of the dead as met with in the Elijah and Elisha cycles or other miracle-stories. For there the *terminus ad quem* was the life of this world; it was a step back into the present. The *terminus ad quem* of the eschatological resurrection of the dead was 'the age to come'. Here lay the uniqueness of the resurrection of Christ: It was a step into the future. We can begin to understand the thrust of the paschal experience of the disciples only to the extent that we can grasp how the earliest church understood its already given participation in the future, i.e., today's share in 'the bread of tomorrow': in forgiveness (as a proleptic realization of acquittal at the judgment), in charism (proleptic realization of the outpouring of the Spirit in the reign of God) – both of which were bound up with baptism – and, finally, in the eucharist (proleptic realization of the eschalogical banquet). With respect to the risen Christ himself, the post-paschal community evidences no stage of consciousness in which the exaltation of Jesus was lacking or his lordship still future.[46] Regarded from the outset as the supreme eschatological event, the resurrection threw sudden light on the immediate past and future. As for the past, the crucified Jesus was vindicated as *'o dikaios*, the Righteous One; as for the future, the goal of Israel's salvation history was on the point of attainment, for Jesus was already installed in glory as the Lord and Saviour to come. Those who called on his name were accordingly the first fruits of messianic Israel, destined for acquittal at the outbreak of the judgment. The resurrection was their clarion-call, for it grounded their hopes.

The immediate instinct of those in 'the service of the word' was to find this stunning reversal attested in the scriptures. The result was a garland of testimonies which contoured the first Christians' understanding both of Jesus and of themselves. The crucifixion and the resurrection were set under the sign of prophetic necessity. The Psalms mainly witnessed to his glorification, and the Servant texts mainly to his suffering. But the Psalms also spoke of his suffering, and it was a Servant text (Heb. Isa. 53.12; Targ. Isa. 53.11–12) which revealed his exaltation as an interim of gracious intercession for the world. The conviction that Jesus had gone to his death in innocence for the sake of men was epitomized in catechetical formulas which drew on Isaiah 53 for two motifs: his 'handing over' or 'deliverance' (Gal. 2.20; Rom. 4.25; 8.32), and his death 'for our sins' (Rom. 4.25; I Cor. 15.3) or 'for us' (Rom. 8.32; Eph. 5.2; cf. I Cor. 11.24;

Gal 2.20; I Tim. 2.6). With their own pneumatic experience confirming them in the persuasion of salvation already accomplished in principle, the believers in Christ called for the consummation with the cry 'Lord, come!' (I Cor. 16.22; cf. Rev. 22.20).

2. THE DEVELOPMENT OF THE GOSPEL TRADITION

Was the rise of gospel traditions a natural outgrowth of Easter faith? Or was it an enigmatic development that might easily not have taken place?

The solution lies in recognizing the vindication-character, in primitive Christian faith, of the resurrection of Jesus. Because the resurrection was seen as vindication, it was by that very fact related to the historic drama of mission and rejection. This was no free option, but imposed on the Christian community. The kerygma to Israel culminated in the appeal to be converted and baptized, and so to inherit the messianic blessings (the forgiveness of sins and the gift of the Spirit, Acts 2.38; 5.3). Now, these were presented as the gifts of whom? Of a seemingly discredited prophet, crucified like other Galileans who had had their hour and then vanished without a trace. But if God had really vindicated Jesus by raising him from the dead and glorifying him, his whole career was suddenly laid bare as eschatological drama. Hence the search for scriptural testimony to this career, which was found above all in the latter part of Isaiah and applied to Jesus' baptism, (Isa. 61.1; Acts 10.38), to his preaching (Isa. 52.7; Acts 10.36), to his being 'handed over' (Targ Isa. 53.5; LXX Isa. 53.6, 12; Acts 2.23; 3.13), and to his suffering and death (Isa. 53.7–12; Acts 8.30–35). Salvation, that is, was seen to issue from the scripturally attested history of Jesus and the heralds of salvation presented themselves as witnesses to that history. It is not by chance, then, that we find in the kerygma of Acts a so-called 'historical section' (Acts 2.22; 10.37–39; 13.23–25),[47] nor is it merely owing to an idea of the redactor that Peter is made to claim 'We are witnesses of everything he did in the country of the Jews and in Jerusalem' (Acts 10.39). Nor, finally, is it in the least disconcerting that the requisite qualification of a candidate to take the place of Judas among the twelve is that he be 'one of the men who have accompanied us during all the time that the Lord Jesus went in and out among us' (Acts 1.21).[48] For in the acknowledgement of the risen Jesus we already have the seeds of the gospel tradition.

The overarching fact is that Palestinian Christianity was nourished on the memory of Jesus. The earliest kerygmatic, liturgical, and catechetical texts evidence a generic homogeneity with the fully developed gospel literature. This generic homogeneity may be described by the expression 'confessional witness', in which 'witness' includes reference to the past. The description should be nuanced and verified; but first we will propose, as plausible, a sketch of how the gospel tradition developed in successive phases.

The pre-Pauline formula of I Cor. 15.3–5 and the traditions conserved in the first half of the book of Acts indicate that the bearers of primitive Christian witness, first in time and importance, were 'Cephas and the twelve'. The forms of witness varied in accord with the audience: *kērygma* was addressed to outsiders, *didachē* to the Christian community. (The terminology, however, is not absolutely consistent.[49]) They were parallel activities, though from the standpoint of a convert to the Christian movement, they came in sequence: first, *kērygma*, then *didachē*. Owing to the influence of C.H. Dodd, the gospels are not infrequently described as 'expansions of the kerygma'.[50] The terminology is misleading. The kerygmatic or proclamatory note is forced and inappropriate when applied to the gospels. The element of truth in the misformulation is that the general scheme of *kērygma* in Acts was no doubt indistinguishable from the scheme of a principal type of Palestinian *didachē*, namely, the Jesus tradition.

Kērygma was the summoning of Israel to its messianic heritage, which necessarily involved the vindication of the crucified Messiah. But with the growth of the community, *didachē* gathered independent momentum. Here the figure of Jesus already reigned supreme. He had been revealed in the light of the resurrection as Servant of God and Prophet like Moses. Consequently, his words and acts alike[51] were invested with eschatological authority, the veritable Torah of Israel restored. Still, continuity with the ancient Israel was consciously cultivated here, too. The book of Deuteronomy, read in the light of the paschal mystery of Christ, was the Jerusalem church's messianic charter.[52]

Kērygma and catechesis instinctively took narrative form, for salvation was conceived as 'event' rather than as 'truth'. The question for preacher and catechist was not 'What is the first principle?' but 'Where does the story begin?' The question early found an answer attested in Acts (1.22; 10.37; 13.24–25): 'when the Baptist called Israel to repent and to be baptized.'[53]

The most prominent themes of primitive Palestinian catechesis were the passion and resurrection, the first as prologue to the second. As they finally figure in the gospels after a long and complex history, the resurrection narratives have been reduced to a kind of glorious epilogue to the whole. The passion narratives, which followed a simpler pattern of development by expansion, survive as among the oldest pre-redactional unities in the gospel literature. Here the sub-question 'Where does the story begin?' was answered, in accord with the Palestinian formula of Rom. 4.25 (cf. Mark 14.41 par.) by: 'when Jesus was taken captive.'

Catechetical traditions embodying the sayings of Jesus and anecdotal accounts of his ministry were in all probability as old or practically as old as the formation of passion and resurrection accounts.

The form critics have proposed a typology of this catechetical tradition which at least allows us to place the question of the foci of primitive catechesis and to identify restricted formal unities which took shape in the course of oral transmission and are conserved in the gospel redactions.[54] Besides pre-redactional units on the basis of form, the period of exclusively oral transmission produced units on thematic, topical, and chronological bases.[55] The original constituent elements of such pre-redactional unities were self-contained units. But they were not like playing cards in a shuffled deck. From the start they had a time structure in the sense that certain episodes distinctly marked a beginning and others an end. The passion and resurrection marked the end; at the beginning stood the baptism of Jesus and the call of the disciples who were to become the twelve. A certain geographical order was likewise understood from the start: Jesus came from Nazareth, his public career was itinerant, and he died in Jerusalem.[56]

Christian tradition attributed a literary fixation of oral tradition to the apostle Matthew. The earliest testimony to this effect (conserved in Eusebius, *Historia ecclesiastica* 2.15.2; 3.39.13) comes from Papias (fl. AD 70–125), bishop and chronicler of primitive Christianity, whose access to apostolic tradition was mediated (according to Irenaeus) by Polycarp, a member of the Johannine circle. It is uncertain that the so-called Q tradition (material common to Matthew and Luke alone) was ever independently fixed in writing but it did find written form in combination with numerous pre-Lukan materials prior to the Lukan redaction (Proto-Luke).[57] To the present writer it seems likely, despite noteworthy arguments to the contrary, that the oldest of the canonical redactions is Mark.[58] Apropos of Markan priority, however, we should insist on two points which, though occasionally acknowledged in theory, are repeatedly abandoned in practice. By Markan priority is meant the relative antiquity of Mark *vis-à-vis* the other canonical redactions. This does not systematically guarantee the relative antiquity of Markan traditions *vis-à-vis* traditions in Matthew, Luke, and John. It grounds no wholesale deductions, not even that wholesale deduction so regularly met in the critical practice of the past hundred years, namely, Markan priority till proved otherwise. Second, even when priority is established in the case of some particular tradition, this does not *ipso facto* establish a superior claim to historicity. To confuse relative antiquity *vis-à-vis* other traditions with superiority in the claim to historicity is to deny *a priori* that a tradition arising to correct or clarify an earlier tradition might do so in historically valid fashion. The fundamental distinction between a tradition's antiquity and its claim to

historicity accounts for why criteria for the historical ordering of traditions, though certainly relevant to historical-Jesus research, are less crucial than criteria for historicity itself. In some cases one can make historical judgments despite being unable to reconstruct the historical sequence
of traditions. In other cases a solidly probable reconstruction of the history
of traditions nevertheless leaves the question of historicity still unresolved.
William R. Farmer has accordingly made a valid and important point: 'In
seeking to understand Jesus the critic can no longer give to any particular
gospel the place of importance Baur gave to Matthew, or for that matter
the importance Schleiermacher gave to John, or that Emanuel Hirsch
now gives to Mark.'[59] It is not the order of the gospels that counts for
historical inquiry but their nature; which brings us back to our original
question: Do the gospels intend the past and do they supply 'data' on
Jesus?

The answer is 'yes', if the proposition to which we are saying yes is (*a*)
understood first to express a global expectation which, antecedent to
detailed examination, is on various grounds reasonable; (*b*) then converted into an accumulation of specific critical judgments of historicity; (*c*)
defensible, whether as antecedent expectation or as consequent and
specific confirmation, against reasonable objection. These three conditions are, in fact, fulfilled.

First, the scope of the proposition is initially global and its sense is
conditioned by the observation that the central intent of the gospels is the
nourishment of faith. Past event, then, figures in the gospel literature only
as relevant to revelation and response. Instinct with catechetical concern,
the gospels' intending of the past is popular, confessional, uncritical; creative as well as recognitive; sober rather than enthusiastic. Accordingly, the
proposition 'The gospels intend past events and supply us with "data" on
Jesus' asserts a positive expectation without deciding particular genres or
particular cases in advance. As an as yet undifferentiated expectation, it
cannot *a priori* exclude the possibility of legend, midrash, folklore, parable,
paradigm, and so forth, for any and all of these might be vehicles of
confessional witness (and, indeed, of confessional witness to the historic
past as such). General and undetailed, this expectation is none the less
reasonable. We see it grounded in the observations offered above on the
earliest Christian faith-formulations, for a certain fundamental continuity
between these past-intending faith-formulations and the later gospel
literature is to be expected and is *a posteriori* evident. To suppose from the
start (e.g. in the name of 'the paschal experience of the disciples') that the
substance of gospel narrative about Jesus is in reality a likely retrojection
onto him of independently generated religious concerns is to forget, first,
that the subjects of the paschal experience were for the most part the
pre-paschal disciples of Jesus; second, that no mission to Israel could have

been seriously projected or carried out by these disciples unless they could plausibly claim to be presenting, in the light of the scriptures, an eyewitness account of Jesus;[60] third, that to invoke the paschal experience of the disciples in order to account for the beginnings of christology and ecclesiology is to move to the unknown not from the known but from the still more unknown (*ignotum per ignotius*);[61] and fourth, that the reference back to Jesus – the account of the gospel tradition offered by the gospel tradition itself – is massively commended to us by the entire tradition-oriented world of antiquity and, in particular, by the tradition-oriented world of Palestinian Judaism (though only the gospel texts examined in detail allow us to understand the vitality and flexibility with which the reference back to Jesus is concretely realized). In sum, we are saying that even before we examine the gospel texts in detail, there is every reason to expect the gospels to be filled with the memory of Jesus. These general considerations are meant to provoke an initial insight into the situation of the primitive Christian community in the contexts of antiquity, of ancient Israel, and of Easter faith.

Second, the positive expectation of data on Jesus is specified and fulfilled *a posteriori* in three ways: by inferences of historicity (significant even when not compelling) attendant on historical reconstruction wherein given masses of data prove to be coherent and reciprocally reinforcing; by inferences of the historicity of individual and relatively isolated data on the basis of positive indices such as discontinuity, originality, etc.; and by the discovery of historical intentions at work in specific gospel texts.[62] These concrete inroads into the historical unknown are complemented by the discovery of a primitive Christian creativity. The motive force of this creativity was primarily catechetical purpose relative to a changing church. This is evident in the elaboration of discernibly post-paschal didactic and parenetic structures and in the shaping of written redactions, each stamped with a distinctive vision of Christ and his work. Creativity prompted the inclusion of folklore[63] and midrashic[64] motifs into the gospel tradition, the reformulation of eschatological material in the interests both of community parenesis and of a newly specified expectation of the eschatological consummation[65] and, not least of all, the transformation of traditional materials in token of missionary theology, together with the addition of an explicitly universalist missionary mandate.[66]

This creativity attests the collective consciousness on the part of the bearers and shapers of the tradition that they lived under the ascendancy of the Spirit and taught with the authority of the Spirit. The inadequacy of the parallel with rabbinic tradition lies chiefly here. The authority of catechetical activity in the various stages of the growth of the gospel tradition cannot have simply turned, in early Christian consciousness, on the accuracy of apostolic memory. Rather, it directly depended on the apostolic conviction of the possession of the Spirit. It is precisely *because* the word of Jesus was authoritative that it was recast and readdressed to a swiftly growing, historically conditioned church. In this recasting process the church asserted its pneumatic status *vis-à-vis* its authoritative traditions, be these the ancient scriptures or the memory of Jesus.[67] The mentality of primitive catechesis, then, was defined by an unreserved commitment to the authority of Christ; but this authority was mediated by a distinct consciousness of the Spirit's presence generating freedom and power. From the only point of view coherent with the faith-consciousness of primitive Christianity, there follows as the night the day the primacy for faith of the New Testament scriptures themselves over a narrowly conceived, historically ascertainable *ipsissima vox Jesu*. At the same time, it becomes one of the tasks of historical criticism to examine the all-permeating claim of Christian catechesis that in the gospel tradition, continuously and creatively recast, it is indeed the *ipsissima vox Jesu* which speaks. The material tradition of Jesus' words and acts was subject to omissions, transpositions, and additions, for this belongs to 'remembering'. Theologically conditioned contemporary criticism tends to be sensitive to the significance of omissions, transpositions, and additions; but the value of such sensitivity is too often undermined by the mistake of relegating the substance of the material tradition to Christian invention.

An important factor, historically, in the elaboration of this latter view and a motive, accordingly, for the adoption of a methodically sceptical stance toward the historical reliability of the gospel tradition has been the hypothesis that the early church 'made no attempt to distinguish between the words the earthly Jesus had spoken and those spoken by the risen Lord through a prophet in the community'.[68] The first form of this hypothesis was introduced in the last decade of the last century by Hermann von Soden;[69] it was adopted, reformulated, and popularized by Bultmann[70] and further developed within the Bultmann school.[71] In 1962 Bultmann's argumentation was subjected to close examination and found wanting;[72] and in 1974 the hypothesis suffered what may prove to have been a crippling blow from a trenchant review of its history and of the data it was supposed to account for.[73] It remains at the least unproved and, in view of Paul's differentiation of his own word from that 'of the Lord' (I Cor. 7), positively improbable that there was ever a class of Christian prophets who, speaking in the name of the risen Christ, supplied the church with sayings which could be and were put on the lips of Jesus and assimilated to the synoptic tradition.

Third and last, our proposition that the gospels intend the past and supply data on Jesus must be defensible against objection. The one objection which, if sustained, might be thought decisive is that Paul worked in complete independence of the gospel tradition, that he saw no point in it beyond the bare factuality of the death of Jesus, and that with his declaration 'though we once knew Christ according to the flesh, we regard him thus no longer' (II Cor. 5.16), he stands as a reproof to every kind of hankering for knowledge of the historical Jesus. But is not all this tendentious? Paul in fact offers literary testimony to the gospel tradition prior to the Markan redaction, but it is the testimony of a *ḥākām*, of one who enjoys a mastery of his resources and can draw on them with ease, flexibility, and imagination.[74]

Paul's letters abound with echoes of Palestinian catechesis. They do not greatly differ from the allusions to be found in the letters of James and of Peter (I Peter). For Paul the word of Jesus was decisive (I Cor. 7.10). It shaped his understanding of the apostolate[75] and affected nearly every aspect of his parenesis.[76] The gospel tradition may well have been a proximate source of his stock of agrarian imagery.[77] He was at home with Jesus' parables and drew freely on them.[78] His own prayer and doctrine of prayer derived, as did that of early Christianity generally, from Jesus.[79] The historicity of Jesus, born of woman (Gal. 4.4), belonging to the race of Abraham (Gal. 3.16; Rom. 9.5) and the lineage of David (Rom. 1.3), living under the law (Gal. 4.4; Rom. 15.8), exercising a ministry to Israel in fulfilment of the promises to the patriarchs (Rom. 15.8), and dying on a cross (*passim*), was as substantial to Pauline, as it was to Markan or Lukan, theology. Finally, his repudiation of the knowledge of Christ 'according to the flesh' was simply the repudiation of un-faith, and of his own previous un-faith as a persecutor of the church. It did not even peripherally touch Palestinian catechesis and in no way reflects negatively on the quest of the historical Jesus in a Christian sense.[80]

IV

JESUS AND CRITICAL HISTORY

Historians differ among themselves in presupposition, angle of interest, the theory and practice of methods, in interpretation and explanation. In the ongoing critique of past effort, old differences are ironed out, fresh differences emerge, a few blind alleys are abandoned and a few new ones explored, some hypotheses are revised, some discarded. At its best this critique is more than a changing climate of opinion. It is a painfully hard-won learning process.

This developing achievement has shaped our century and world as pervasively and incisively as 'the new philosophy', dissolving one vision of things and creating another, shaped the seventeenth and eighteenth centuries. The new consciousness in our era is the historical consciousness, the recognition that the collective and personal selfhood of man is fashioned by his own decisions. It is a 'historical' consciousness not only because man – and every man – is thus the product of his own history but because the rise of history as a distinctive mode of knowledge has revealed this to him. It has been a momentous revelation, confronting him (i.e., us) as never before with the question how to interpret autonomy: Has history ushered in the kingdom of man? Or is man, precisely by this self-fashioning, rooted in God? The history of Jesus is relevant to this question; but first, the understanding of history as a mode of knowledge is relevant to the history of Jesus. Our immediate concern, then, is to understand history not as event but as knowledge of event, insight into its actuality and meaning.

1. INTERPRETATION AND EXPLANATION

Interpretation is the grasp and mediation of meaning. Let 'meaning' refer to what the meaning subject deliberately intends to communicate. In principle this is readily intelligible but in special cases it may require mediation, as when an interpreter is called on to bridge a language-gap between the subject and a particular audience. If for a particular audience the subject is not only of a different language zone but of a different cultural zone and a different time zone, a more elaborate task is required of the interpreter, but his aim remains the same: to clarify what Plato or Polybius, Caesar or the Song of Songs, the message on the potsherd or the drawing in the catacomb means, intends, seeks to communicate. This kind of interpretation we call 'pure exegesis'.

It is not, however, the whole of interpretation. Consider Julius Caesar as chronicler of Roman military operations in Gaul. What Caesar intended his account to communicate is quite distinct from what Caesar, as soldier and statesman, ultimately intended. Indeed, Caesar's literary work is not a direct, but at best only an indirect, index to his ulterior intentions. To know these – to know the significant whole of what he intended – it is by no means enough to understand what he intended to communicate. The point is even clearer when the writer and the agent are not one and the same person. To understand Caesar it is not enough to understand what Suetonius meant to say about him.

Now, the grasp and mediation of what a writer had deliberately sought to communicate may require an imposing technical apparatus of detection and a wide range of detective skills: the control of languages and linguistic tools, a hold on initially unfamiliar literary genres, a flair for twigging unfamiliar symbolic patterns and for finding a way into horizons that are subtly strange for being now more, now less, differentiated than those habitual to the interpreter. But if this is imposed by the project of pure exegesis, then to discover the significant whole of what historic agents (be they writers or not) ultimately intended calls for still more elaborate techniques, a hardier and more differentiated scepticism, a larger experience of life and grasp of motives and values, a more creative and wide-ranging imagination. To understand sources in terms of their own intentions is merely to make contact with data more or less relevant to an ulterior task. This ulterior task, the discovery of what historical agents really intended and the effective mediation of this discovery to a given audience, we call 'historical interpretation'.

A social event like a cocktail party may turn out to correspond rather well to the intentions of all concerned; but, as social events are not produced under laboratory conditions, an element of unpredictability is built into them. A revolution may fail to correspond to what anyone intended. It is certainly not what the old regime intended and it may be only more or less, if at all, what the revolutionaries planned. Historians inquire not only into the intentions of all concerned but into the unpredictable interaction of these intentions and so into 'the meaning of the revolution'. Since the revolution is not itself a subject of intending acts, its 'meaning' lies in the interaction of the totality of intentions and in the impact of this interaction: the changes wrought in the field of social possibilities, the new situation with its new set of orientations. 'Meaning', then, is no longer an intention but the confluence of variously related intentions. These are not disembodied intentions; they inform instruments of action: words, gestures, bodies, ballistic missiles. The result is a constellation of new options, more numerous and promising or fewer and more desperate than before. Though disconcerting, revolutions are not unintelligible. The 'Why?' asked by the survivors of the old regime or a dazed population or a neighbouring people or a latter-day historian supposes that there are reasons, reasons why the revolution was wanted and planned, why its launching succeeded, why it went beyond or fell short of the revolutionaries' intentions (or both), why it ended the way it did. What we have called 'historical interpretation' does not answer this 'Why?'. Intentions do not account for the interaction and realization of intentions; and unrealized intentions, in particular, whether of the old regime or of the revolutionaries, are of secondary significance at this point. The aim of finding out why this went forward and that did not, though a project of no little interest, is also one of considerable dimension and difficulty. We call it 'historical explanation'.

Historical criticism was born of the realization that even pure exegesis required that the historical context of the work to be interpreted be defined. It matured with the further realization that historical interpretation was more than pure exegesis and more than the mere harmonizing of accounts. As it became clearer how much more, criticism became that much more complex. For the aim of criticism is arrival at interpretation and explanation, and this arrival is conditioned by the successful effort to control data and to establish facts – projects never definitively completed. So whole generations of skilled practitioners work at essentially preliminary tasks such as the establishing of critical texts, the preparation of adequate linguistic tools, the fixation of chronologies, the identification of literary genres and sources. If history is interpretation and explanation, the concrete job of historical criticism is to open a path to intending subjects and to the course of events. Intending subjects charge history with meaning. But it is 'the course of events' which in trenchant and peremptory fashion settles which subjects shall prove decisive and what meanings – reduced, enlarged, transformed – shall find flesh-and-blood realization.

The methodical enterprise which is history bears an analogy to science and the analogy has repeatedly proved fatal to historians jealous of scientific success. To note a single but crucial point of divergence: Scientists systematically omit consideration of particular times and places, since these contribute nothing to what they are after. (A free fall is a constant

acceleration be it in Pittsburgh or Pisa, in our day or Galileo's.) Historians, on the other hand, take enormous pains to fix particular times and
places: places, because they specify the field of contact or sphere of
influence; times, because historical criticism is ordered to explanation and
temporal sequence must be established for its causes and conditions to be
assigned.

Science sets it sights on invariant correlations. As empirical, it begins
with concrete data and ends by verifying its correlations in them; but, as
science, the correlations are abstract.[1] History, on the other hand, is
committed to the concrete variable. Its generalizations are not abstract
but concrete. They do not hold in every case but say how men generally
act. Their typological forms result from the accumulation of concrete
detail. Though one may speak of 'scientific' as distinguished from
'scissors-and-paste' history (editorial harmonizing), it remains that history, pre-critical, critical, or 'scientific',[2] lacks the distinctive note of science, the quest of invariants. The salient traits of history derive from the
concreteness of its objects: the intent of particular subjects (interpretation)
and the correlation of particular consequences with their concrete deter-
minants (explanation). Generalizations are guidelines, but, as they do not
express invariant correlations, particulars are not deduced or predicted
from them.

The terms interpretation[3] and explanation do not represent new proposals in answer to the question 'What should historians aim at?' They say,
rather, what historians have in fact been aiming at for some time. To
adopt them as technical terms is to make three related points: (1) that
history focuses on human action which, by contrast to natural process, is
original and unpredictable though potentially familiar, thanks to the historian's own rational consciousness; (2) that human purpose is regularly
an important determinant of human action; and (3) that what goes forward in time does so out of the interaction of purposes informing a
panoply of instruments.[4] Historical interpretation is accordingly functional to explanation; but the converse is likewise true, for actions and
interactions reveal intentions by putting them to the test. Interpretation
and explanation, then, designate distinct but inseparable aspects of the
historical unknown to be known. Criticism works toward the discovery of
aims and outcomes; if definition of the aims of the *dramatis personae* is
indispensable to definition of what was going forward and why, so the
latter effort is regularly relevant to the discovery of who wanted what, how
badly, and to what end.

The 'critical' phase of history, then, is nothing other than the structured
process of finding answers to questions aimed at interpretation and explanation. But history also has a metacritical phase: the historian's own
encounter with the answers. Here he is no longer a practitioner of histori-

cal criticism, though the claims on his alertness and judgment are as great. Here above all he is listener and learner. But this listening and learning, these dialogical reactions, insights, and judgments, transcend the principles of historical criticism. Historians in agreement on the intent of the Enlightenment *philosophes* may have quite different encounters with them; and the differences, which are apt to be cast finally in philosophical terms, reveal the relative richness or poverty of the historian as human knower and human being.

In due course we will return to the metacritical phase, the moment 'beyond criticism'; first we will discuss critical history, the strategically structured effort to interpret and explain.

This effort begins with the discovery that the way to knowledge is through the designation of particular unknowns. What were Caesar's general horizons and particular perspectives? How did he understand the situations he entered and his own role in them? What did he think possible and what did he aim to achieve? How did he plan to achieve it? In what measure did he succeed? Why did he fail? History consists in specifying unknowns (i.e., in asking questions) and in systematically converting them into knowns (constructing and cross-checking answers). The sequence, then, is: question, hypothesis, verification.[5] This sequence, already operative in pure exegesis, is recurrent at two levels of critical history, at the level of 'controlling the data' and at the level of 'establishing the facts'.

We have called these 'levels' but they are levels on a spiral. For in the process of question, hypothesis, verification, the inquirer moves back and forth between knowns and unknowns; and while the original unknowns are converted into knowns which generate still more unknowns, the original knowns are seen in a constantly changing light and so are re-valued upward and downward like currencies in crisis. Question, hypothesis, and verification represent a genuine sequence; 'controlling the data' and 'establishing the facts' represent a reciprocal transaction. The control of data does not take place at the outset as a first but final acquisition. Until the creative imagination has assembled its hypotheses – the first step toward establishing the facts – it is not clear what the data really are (i.e., where they come from and what they mean). To illustrate: The text of Matt. 5.17 (*mē nomisēte 'oti ēlthon katalysai ton nomon ē tous prophētas. ouk ēlthon katalysai alla plērōsai*) is a datum. To 'control' it I should like to know how to translate it in accord with what Matthew meant by it and how to translate it (or whatever of it, if anything, derived from Jesus) in accord with what Jesus meant by it. Now, I cannot simply settle these matters at the outset; I must have construed for myself something approaching a totality of meaning which I take to approximate Matthew's vision of things and a totality of meaning which I take to approximate Jesus' vision of things. There is, then, an upward-moving back-and-forth alternation between the understanding of this single datum and the positing for verification of two distinct if related worlds of meaning.

2. CONTROLLING THE DATA

Historia means inquiry, the quest of answers to questions. In a question hypothetical or real knowns are used to define an unknown. In an inquiry the process of choosing from hypothetical or real knowns to specify unknowns is continuously repeated until the targeted or ultimate unknown is converted into a known.

At every phase of inquiry progress derives from questioning but depends on data. Now, data are givens. They may also be knowns, either in the minimal sense of being known of, or, as may be, in the sense of being understood. Generally, however, data are not understood until the inquiry is finished. It remains to say in what sense data must be or become knowns for the inquiry to get started.

Concretely, the question for an inquiry into the Jesus of ancient Palestine is whether the data of the gospels are data on Jesus. For it is evident that, though we can pose whatever questions we like, without data on Jesus the inquiry is futile. I should say 'relatively futile' for the data of the gospels certainly relate to Jesus in some way. Anton Fridrichsen observed that the man of God in Eastern antiquity is never isolated but is always

> the centre of a circle taught by his words and example, in which his manner of life and teaching continues after his death. What is taught and written in this circle is ultimately derived from its founder and embodies his life and character.[6]

But history worked out on this strategy is necessarily quite general and limited. The question about the thrust of gospel data remains. It is not enough to arrive at the bare recognition that, as the peculiarity of the Christian confession is its historical dimension, so the peculiarity of the historical testimony of the gospels is its confessional dimension. Control of the data requires insight into how the gospel literature refers to the past of Jesus and this must be brought to bear on a mass of detail, repeatedly answering the question, 'Is this a potential datum on Jesus?'

Having discovered (e.g. by form-critical analysis of apophthegms) the complexity of this question, the critic may feel bound to make the conditions of an affirmative answer rigorous; namely, to state a supposition against historicity and to derive from it a working criterion by which the supposition is made operative and is itself tested. Concretely, the supposition is this: that the gospel literature was not only stamped by the confessional concerns of the church but was created by the church to express and serve those concerns. The working criterion is: The origin and character of particular gospel materials should be so understood unless this is positively implausible, i.e., unless the materials run counter both to the Judaism of the time (a possible source for the church) and to the certainly ascertained tendencies of the church.

The above supposition is initially no more than a supposition, and if the premises of an inference are suppositions, the conclusion can only be a supposition. Now, the aim of criticism is not to achieve coherence of supposition but to generate knowns. The sense of these elementary observations has been repeatedly overlooked or violated in twentieth-century criticism, partly, no doubt, under the powerful thrust of reaction against liberal theology and its pretension to make faith hinge wholly on historical knowledge. But however ill-advised or even un-Christian such a pretension might be, it is a question whether reaction to the liberals has been measured or extravagant. Concretely, the question is whether the above supposition ('The form of the gospel traditions is narrative about Jesus, but their substance is the earliest church's expression of its own self-understanding and concerns') is taken from the start as the equivalent of an irreversibly established known.

Jesus is represented in the gospels as being baptized by John the Baptist, as making the reign of God his central proclamation, as consorting with publicans and sinners. Are such representations historically accurate? Or are they simply indices to the concerns of the church? By common consent they are historically accurate. The common consent has emerged because the traditions are not otherwise plausibly explained. Jesus' being baptized by John crosses the grain of the church's transparent tendency to keep John subordinate to Jesus. Jesus' 'reign of God' language has its own sharp profile *vis-à-vis* both Judaism and the church. The consorting with publicans and sinners violates the fabric and pattern of Judaic piety. Though fragmentary evidence indicates that Palestinian church practice cohered with the traditions about Jesus (e.g. Peter, according to Acts 9.43, stayed in the home of Simon *the tanner*, one considered immoral by profession[7]), this has not prevented the critics from acknowledging the authenticity of the traditions about Jesus.

Now, what conclusion must be drawn regarding the initial supposition 'The form of the gospel traditions is narrative about Jesus but their substance is the earliest church's expression of its own self-understanding and concerns')? Does it remain privileged and inviolate? Hardly. The supposition has been relativized, for it has had to make room for the transmission of traditions discontinuous with Judaism and the church. What the fact of such transmission says is that 'the tendencies of the church' were complex. They included, for example, a touchiness about the status to be attributed to John the Baptist and a willingness to transmit traditions which run counter to that touchiness. In terms of the original supposition such willingness is inexplicable.

The criterion grounded in the supposition is no more absolute than the supposition itself. It was exclusively on the basis of the supposition that the criterion was conceived as the acid test which a tradition must pass to be acknowledged as historical. But inasmuch as certain traditions passed the test and so relativized the supposition, the criterion is inevitably relativized, as well. In a word, positive judgments made in accord with the criterion of methodical scepticism reveal the self-reversal of methodical scepticism.

Is this going too far? May we not simply adjust the supposition and say that most but not all gospel materials were created by the church? This would be, first, to forget that the supposition was never an established known but only a supposition; and second, to dodge the new issue that has arisen from the positive judgments of historicity, for what must now be explained is *why some authentic materials were conserved*. However one might answer this question, it must be inferred in any case that, if authentic materials contrary to church tendencies were conserved, authentic materials in accord with church tendencies were *a fortiori* conserved. The new unknown is the identity of these '*a fortiori* traditions', and this unknown is evaded rather than confronted by any attempt to rehabilitate the now evidently arbitrary global supposition of non-historicity.

Radical critics will understand the argument when it is turned not against them but against their adversaries. Make, then, the global supposition that the gospel accounts are historical. Ground a criterion in the supposition: The accounts are historical except when harmonization is positively implausible, i.e., when the accounts are flatly contradictory or so contrary as to shatter the presumption of Jesus' psychological unity. Now, the gospels represent Jesus as insisting on the observance of every last item of the law and as abolishing the dietary prescriptions *en bloc*; as reserving the revelation of secrets for his disciples and as proclaiming them to all comers; as excluding a ministry to the Gentiles and as practising one. Do these results imply the implausibility of the supposition, or not? Do they or do they not reverse it? Do they or do they not call for different as well as additional patterns of inference?

What follows is simply this: Both programmatic catch-phrases – 'Non-historicity until proved otherwise' and '*In dubio pro tradito*' – are inadequate and self-defeating.[8]

Our argument, however, should be understood as no more than a repudiation of schematic and self-reversing programmes. It remains that, of contradictory accounts, one at least must be non-historical; that distinctive, post-paschal concerns are evident throughout the gospel literature; that traditions in discontinuity with the tendencies of the church were certainly conserved; that traditions in continuity with church tendencies were *a fortiori* conserved; that methodical scepticism is as unself-suspecting in the face of this compelling inference as methodical credulity is in the face of transparent post-paschal concerns.

Two practical consequences are inescapable.

In the first place, there will be three columns for historicity judgments on the material: yes, no, and question mark. Perhaps considerable portions of the material will be methodically left in the question-mark column. For there will be no gap between actual knowns and unknowns on the one side, methodical decisions about historicity on the other. By contrast, the methodical sceptic is instructed by his method that the Last Supper accounts, for example, standing as they do in conspicuous continuity with the earliest church, are *ipso facto* non-historical. Now the methodical sceptic (unless he is a particularly dogmatic hard-liner) knows perfectly well that he does not know whether or not there really was a Last Supper, as this may be among the unidentified *a fortiori* traditions. No matter. For him no less than for his methodically credulous cousin, there are only two columns, yes and no. For both schools, method, founded on an *als ob*, its feet firmly planted in the air, makes up for the lack of knowledge. Supposition disposes of residues. 'I do not know' is eliminated.[9]

In the second place, the quest of evidence pertinent to historicity will necessarily be open, supple, and delicate, and judgments of historicity qualified by nuances over the scale of probability. Matters will not be settled by a single systematic question. No method will be admitted to which caution, nuance, and the admission of doubt are alien.

The effect of methodical scepticism has been to stifle historical investigation from the start. It seems only right, then, to begin by exposing the oversights involved in the methodical sceptic's style of deciding historicity questions, namely, in peremptory fashion by a single acid test and dealing with the data atomistically. Questions of historicity are not reasonably handled in this way. On the whole it is rare that a solid judgment of historicity can be made prior to and apart from a large frame of reference, i.e., the substance of a historical investigation. If a historical project is to get under way, the initial stance *vis-à-vis* particulars cannot be general mistrust. On the other hand, the course of investigation is likely to generate selective mistrust. Thus Collingwood:

> Suetonius tells me that Nero at one time intended to evacuate Britain. I reject his statement, not because any better authority flatly contradicts it, for of course none does; but because my reconstruction of Nero's policy based on Tacitus will not allow me to think that Suetonius is right. And if I am told that this is merely to say I prefer Tacitus to Suetonius, I confess that I do: but I do so just because I find myself able to incorporate what Tacitus tells me into a

coherent and continuous picture of my own, and cannot do this for Suetonius.[10]

But the judgments made in the course of investigation should, as far as possible, be independently verified. Independent verification follows either a direct or an oblique pattern of inference. The components of the direct pattern are intention, knowledgeability, and veracity. If the intention of the writer can be defined to include factuality and if the writer is plausibly knowledgeable on the matter and free of the suspicion of fraud, historicity may be inferred. These general considerations retain their validity despite having often been found guilty by association with precritical history and then with an obsolete positivism. Paul's use of the *apo*-formula in I Cor. 11.23a intends Jesus as the originator of the eucharistic tradition (I Cor. 11.23b–25).[11] Can Paul have been mistaken? Is it plausible that he has taken a Hellenistic cult-legend for a tradition originating with Jesus? Or, can it be that Paul knows a Hellenistic cult-legend when he sees one, but thinks it meet and just that the Corinthians receive it as a tradition originating with Jesus? These questions, undeniably relevant to the issue of historicity, call for an answer that favours it.

The usefulness of the direct pattern of inference, however, is limited in biblical criticism because of the frequent indefinability of the factor of intention. Form criticism has shown that scenes like those of the controversy dialogues are *per se* typical. Even supposing that the scenes were constructed from reminiscence, the intention that created the pericope was not *per se* to offer a one-to-one relation between pericope and particular event. If it were, pericopes would be simply recorded memories and so would regularly exhibit the inner coherence of the remembered event. But time and again in the analysis of pericopes such inner coherence is lacking. Moreover, what is true of pericopes is true of whole gospels. It was the achievement of form criticism to have demonstrated that the gospel literature was *composed*. In this process of composition the career of Jesus has been (to use Bultmann's term) 'precipitated' in the pericopes; but the evidence is against presuming that either the gospels as such or the individual pericopes as such are merely recorded memories. A first (but in many cases unmanageable) step is to determine how a given account of Jesus intends its object, for if the direct pattern of inference is to make any contribution at all to the resolution of a historicity question, its application will have to vary in accord with the diverse ways in which accounts intend their objects.

The frequent difficulty of defining exactly how an account intends its object has led the critics to concentrate on establishing oblique patterns of inference. (They are 'oblique' inasmuch as they approach the narrative indirectly, neither ambitioning nor depending on definition of its intention.) Of oblique patterns, a major one, regularly yielding compelling inferences of historicity, is the *index of discontinuity*: Historicity is inferred when a tradition about Jesus is discontinuous with the tendencies of the community which transmits it. It will be noted that this partly corresponds with the unique criterion of the methodical sceptic. It differs, however, in four ways. First, it is not proposed as unique, i.e., as the one and only way to historicity. Second, it is not proposed as a 'criterion' but as an 'index'. Third, it differentiates between the contradictory and the discontinuous. Fourth, it omits the requirement that the matter in question be unparalleled in Judaism. As we have already dealt with the first point,[12] let it suffice to comment briefly on the second, third, and fourth.

'Criterion', as the term has been used in discussion of this topic, specifies what is universally requisite that a gospel tradition be acknowledged as historical. But, in fact, no factor proposed by the critics as a 'criterion' is invariably requisite to the inference of historicity. That Jesus was crucified is historical, though the fact of the crucifixion accords with post-paschal faith. That Jesus had disciples is historical, though this accords with contemporary Jewish practice. Since what is really at stake in the so-called criterion is not what is uniquely sufficient and so invariably *necessary* to establish historicity but rather what tends to make historicity more likely than non-historicity, I would prefer to drop the term 'criterion' altogether in favour of the more modest term 'index'.

'Discontinuity' is a broader category than 'contradiction'. The discontinuous may be merely archaic, embracing pre-paschal situations and interests whether or not they positively contradict post-paschal church tendencies. Historicity is *a fortiori* inferred when the substance of an account goes positively against the grain of post-paschal practices and concerns.

It has often been observed that Judaism in general is a possible source for the Jesus tradition. What has not been observed, however, is that the requirement of simultaneous discontinuity with Judaism and the post-paschal church errs by excess. That the community should gratuitously adopt from Judaism elements in discontinuity with its own concerns, practices, and tendencies simply does not make sense. Discontinuity with the post-paschal church is sufficient by itself to establish historicity.

This, however, by no means diminishes the significance of discontinuity with Judaism. For, whereas such discontinuity is not requisite to historicity, it is a distinct and positive index to it. We will call this *the index of originality* and offer, as the prize example of a tradition established on this basis as historical, Jesus' consorting with publicans and sinners. Inasmuch as a given instance of originality may be of post-paschal provenance, the degree of probability attaching to inferences of historicity on this basis will vary in accord with the particulars of the case.

Another index to historicity is *irreducibly personal idiom*. (The best known examples are Jesus' use of *Abba* and *amen*.) Again, form is significant as a perservative of tradition. The gospel parables, thanks especially to their organic, self-contained structure (a factor making modifications more or less easily liable to detection), offer a royal road to authentic sayings-material and a particularly solid base from which to assess the historicity of parallels. Still another index is the recording of traditions in diverse forms (e.g., as narrative and as saying) and diverse strata (e.g., in proto-Lukan material and in Mark or John). Like Aramaic substratum, multiple attestation is not of itself decisive, but both are factors in judgments of historicity. Finally, it should be emphasized once more that all the indices to historicity (Discontinuity, Originality, Personal Idiom, Resistive Form, Multiple Attestation, Multiform Attestation, Aramaic Substratum) operate *in sensu aiente*: that is, their presence favours historicity but their absence does not of itself imply a verdict of non-historicity. Where no inference is possible one way or another, the material is ranged in the question-mark column rather than disposed of on the basis of an assumption.

3. ESTABLISHING THE FACTS

The logic of history is the organization of the effort to arrive at interpretation and explanation. It is a logic learned by discovering how and why good historians perform well. Apprentices learn this by imitation and osmosis; but all are inevitably affected by theory, too.

Now, theory offers this difficulty, that history is a matter of mind and, as Hume wryly observed, when the mind becomes the object of reflection it seems 'involved in obscurity'. Historians making their own operations the object of reflection and finding themselves in surprisingly unfamiliar surroundings may be tempted to fall back on whatever ready-made cognitional theories happen to be available to them.

Happily, there are exceptions. Collingwood, both a historian and a philosopher, blocked out an account of history that took the full measure of the advances in successful practice. At the centre of Collingwood's reflections lay a new understanding of fact.

This consisted in redefining the historical unknown. The unknown in history was 'the inside' of the event, i.e., the thought or purpose which charged it, making it an 'action' and giving it meaning and direction. Event in this plenary sense is 'a historical fact'. 'Facts', therefore, emerge at the *end* of inquiry, as its conclusion. They are inferred 'according to rational principles' from data 'discovered in the light of these principles'. Therefore, 'for the historian there is no difference between discovering what happened and discovering why it happened'.[13]

To adopt this view is not to deny the critical role played by data at the beginning of the inquiry and throughout to its conclusion. The role of data is initially to allow the specifying of unknowns and continuously thereafter to set the limits within which the process of converting unknowns into knowns advances. Data are indispensable, for without them the question about the inside of an event could not be so much as formulated.

It is a datum of history that Charles de Gaulle retired from the presidency of the Fifth Republic in the spring of 1969. The historian's interest is fixed, among other things, on the reasons which led him to let this happen. 'Why it happened' is not even a question except in dependence on the material datum that it did happen. But this datum remains opaque until the unknown, 'why it happened', is converted into a known, thus becoming what Collingwood means by 'a historical fact'.

Again, the detective would not have known that Dunaway's nephew murdered Dunaway unless he had anticipated this solution by supposing a motive on the nephew's part and had correlated this with a constellation of other data until the whole was converted into a compelling inference. Here 'what happened' is essentially an unknown to be known; 'why it happened' enters as a factor into the hypothesis of what happened. Now, it remains true that the question could neither be formulated nor answered except on the basis of a reservoir of data (beginning with the datum that Dunaway was murdered). But the fact of the matter, namely, that Dunaway's nephew was the culprit, emerged only at the end of the inquiry and the data critical to uncovering the fact came to light progressively and cumulatively as the inquiry wore on and especially as it drew to a conclusion.

In a single ongoing movement of inquiry data are criticized and facts are established. Before the first world war, no distinction was made between data and facts, and the historian's task was discharged by first criticizing them and then correlating those that passed muster. The point of departure for contemporary practice, on the other hand, has been the conception of a targeted unknown which would yield only to inference; and the strategy of the inference consisted in the projecting and selecting of hypotheses bearing on 'what happened'. The innovation lay in understanding this from the start as an unknown.

To summarize and complete the foregoing reflections on data and facts, there are principles of historical criticism.

The first principle: *History is knowledge.* That is, it is not belief. An activity of independent intelligence, its tools are the question and the hypothesis, not scissors and paste. Rather than accepting authority, it confers it.[14]

Is this a rejection of court practice, a prejudice against eyewitnesses in favour of circumstantial evidence? It is rather an insistence on court practice. Testimony, to the court, does not provide truth but data. The advantage of hearing testimony is the jump in the availability of factors to be weighed. First-hand knowledge is ideal, but this is precisely why the court prefers the way of investigation to the way of belief. Thus, what may be absolutely certain to the witness may become only more or less probable to the court, depending on how the particulars intended by the witness's testimony correlate with actual knowns. If the court cannot directly appropriate the witness's knowledge, it can nevertheless have the next best thing, which is not belief but inference. In its final state, moreover, the inferences of the court may be, not the next best thing to the knowledge of the witnesses, but superior in scope, perspective, accuracy, and certainty to the knowledge of any and all witnesses.

There is belief and belief. No physicist has performed all the experiments whose results he uses. But unless he were to suppose that there is a conspiracy organized to deceive him, he takes his beliefs to be reductively knowledge. If some of what he takes on faith is mistaken, he feels confident that the error will eventually turn up, perhaps as a problem in his own work or in the work of his colleagues or in the professional journals he reads, or, if not in his own lifetime, then following it. So, perhaps, we may substitute for 'belief' the term 'supposition under remote control'. It operates analogously in history.

Life is short and history long. Good questions are more easily available than satisfying answers. But the inquirer is often enough chagrined to sense that what he is looking for is not the bull's-eye answer but the bull's-eye question. There is, however, one thing the historian can always do, one thing he can always know. He can always know exactly what he is doing. So he can know when he is cheating, namely, when he pretends to know what he only supposes or believes. Again, he can know when he is not functioning as a historian, namely, when he supposes the unverifiable and is aware he is merely supposing, or when he believes, without pretending to do anything other than that.

The second principle: *Historical knowledge is inferential.* For history, unmediated knowledge is generally unavailable and in any case irrelevant. There remains inference, in which implicit generalization is operative. Thus, the indices to historicity are founded on generalizations so fundamental they are rarely made explicit, e.g., 'Men are not gratuitously self-contradictory.' If it were thought that this generalization holds only for modern man, not for antiquity, or not for Jewish antiquity, the most rigorous criterion of judgment would have to be abandoned as inadequate and Jewish antiquity classified as unknowable. But this is a self-reversing option. It would take extraordinary knowledge of Jewish antiquity to know that there, at least, men were gratuitously self-contradictory.

Inferences are not suppositions, not intuitions, not charismatic, mystical, private. They are communicable and the care to communicate the groundedness of conclusions is a characteristic of history. The critic's bare comment that he finds views contrary to his own to be *fantastisch* is not history.

How can the historian know that what he calls a known is more than a guess? The question is meant to elicit the recognition that we do have insights that meet questions squarely and definitively. This happens when no further questions on the point are pertinent, when the pertinent questions have all been answered.[15] There are, of course, irrelevant questions, which take their rise from the fertility of undisciplined imagination. They usually begin 'But, what if . . .' and head away from available evidence.

The value of the conditional syllogism ('If A, then B. But A. Therefore B.') is that it neatly expresses all the elements in the process of inferring. The major and the minor propositions warrant the conclusion. The major proposition isolates the warrant as warrant. The minor proposition affirms the warrant as datum. Moreover, the effort to analyse an inference is facilitated by casting it in terms of conditioned/conditions; for example, this may helpfully mediate the explicit recognition that the conditions of a true inference are limited; that truth depends on the knowledge not of all things but of some things, i.e., of specified conditions and their fulfilment. If both medieval and contemporary men value knowledge, courage, friendship, wealth, and power, then medieval and contemporary men have numerous traits in common. But . . . . Therefore. If we can know that contemporary and medieval men have numerous traits in common without knowing everything about all medieval and contemporary men, then historical relativism is not viable as a theory of knowledge. But . . . . Therefore.

The third principle: *The technique of history is the hypothesis*. As history is the formulation and resolution of questions, i.e., the naming and discovering of unknowns, its technique is evidently the hypothesis. The concrete significance of this emerges from contrast with the definition of the unknown in pure exegesis.

Exegesis aims at discovering Paul's questions, Paul's data, Paul's answers. This may be arduous, as indicated by the various hermeneutic circles. Thus, the process of coming to understand is piecemeal, cumulative, and sometimes dialectical. It may involve swiftly changing scaffoldings of hypothesis, reversal, new hypothesis, partial confirmation, adjustment, and so on. When the revised hypothesis, its presuppositions and ramifications, meet the text in substance and in detail, when particular insights cohere to reinforce one another, when Paul's question has been identified with *its* suppositions, and his data are seen to be luminously relevant to his conclusion, the meaning has been grasped; now it must be effectively mediated to others.

The unknown to be known has been fixed in advance: What does Paul mean to say? And the exegete has worked with an inestimable advantage. While he was trying to understand, Paul was trying to be understood. The letters are contoured to answer the question.

In history, on the contrary, there is a quantum jump in the unknown, for the historian's questions are simply his own. Paul, never having heard them, cannot be expected to offer a ready-made answer to them. From the historian's standpoint, the exact determination of the questions and answers of others provides him with no more than potential data from which he must choose what he needs. The premium on hypothesis comes with the freedom to fix on whatever unknowns he wishes, and until he exercises this freedom he has not begun to function as a historian in the contemporary sense. Until he poses his own question, his data remain unfocused, for data are dead until they become relevant to the uncovering of unknowns. But once a question is posed, an answer is called for, and unless the answer is instantaneously available, it must be mediated. This is done by evoking the range of possible answers and selectively narrowing it. Such is the way of hypothesis.

As actual data are knowns pertinent to questions and hypotheses, the quest of the historical Jesus has foundered in two ways. For Strauss, Wrede, and the Bultmannians, there were not enough knowns to support hypotheses. For Reimarus, Holtzmann, and Schweitzer, there were hypotheses galore, but without control of their presupposed knowns.

The fourth principle: *Hypotheses require verification.* The hypothesis answers a question for intelligence ('What?' or 'Why?'); its verification answers a question for reflection ('True or false?'). Through the whole of a learning process the learner shifts from the one question to the other. Hypotheses in process of refinement are blocked and reshaped by intervening judgments. Judgments, on the other hand, say yes or no to *something*, i.e., they have a content. Lonergan has distinguished between the proper and the borrowed content of judgment. Its proper content is the specific contribution of judgment to cognitional process: the answer of yes or no. The borrowed content is complex: a direct borrowed content is found in the question to which one answers yes or no; an indirect borrowed content issues from reflective insight, by which one grasps the link between the conditioned and its conditions and the fulfilment or non-fulfilment of the conditions.[16] The products or contents of intelligent and reflective insight are not, then, juxtaposed on the same level. Reflective insight at once takes up and transcends the intelligent response to 'Why?' Judgment accordingly climaxes the knowing process. As intelligent insights require judgments, so hypotheses require verification.

If the principle is evident, so are the questions which immediately arise: 'How verify hypotheses?' and 'At what point are they verified?'

To begin with an observation, it is the mark of successful performance that the historian knows what the strengths and the weaknesses of his argument are. He may, for example, point to secondary but relevant questions that remain unanswered. His assessment thus goes beyond the relevance of already adduced evidence. But the insight by which he grasps a relevant question to which nothing in the reservoir of knowns offers an answer is in principle the same insight which allowed him to grasp knowns as relevant. In principle; for it is always simpler to know what one knows than to know what one ought to know. It is easier to see that X, which is known, is relevant, than to diminish the indeterminacy of the relevant unknown, to name it Y, and so to be able at least to say, 'Y is a pertinent question that remains unanswered.'

This is a clue to the verification of hypotheses. The first step is to define their conditions as fully as possible, a project stimulated by asking why one is sure of the relevance of relevant knowns, for these are an avenue to the determination of relevant unknowns. Once they are determined, the historian can cudgel his wits to make them known or, alternatively, settle the matter of their probable or certain unknowability. When all its conditions are known and known to be fulfilled, the hypothesis is invulnerably verified.

The abstract definition may seem forbidding on two counts. First, there is a haunting chimaera, the relativist's demand for the impossible. Everything must be known for anything to be known. But, though flawless as supposition, this is mere supposition, and when tested against the facts of knowledge, it is self-reversing. The conditions of every hypothesis are limited. Second, the historian may suspect that even within the limits of his limited question, there are further pertinent questions which have not occured to him. If this is in fact the case, the contributions of others in the scholarly community may make the hypothesis invulnerable – or reverse it. In any case, verification is invulnerable when no further pertinent questions arise.

4. BEYOND CRITICISM

To differentiate, in knife-making, the ends of production and of the thing produced, these are respectively the knife and 'to cut'. Following this scheme, the end of historical production is a narrative interpreting and explaining the past and the end of the narrative is knowledge – even wisdom. For Collingwood the point of history is to know what man can do, thus to know what he is, and so, finally, to know oneself. Bultmann accents the first modality: what man can do. The value of history lies in contact with new possibilities of existence.

The contact with possibilities incarnated in Socrates or Caesar or Jesus is not simply 'evaluation'. In the rush to evaluate (Marc Bloch called it 'the mania for judgment') Bultmann saw the danger of forfeiting encounter. But what he commended was precisely openness to value. This was the point of listening, making contact, giving insight a chance. The issue would seem to be, not whether there is to be any evaluation, but whether it is to be merely external, quick, and cheap. I can learn nothing from Socrates or Caesar without evaluating what they incarnate as on the side of life or death, as insight or blindness, as wisdom or folly or madness.

The peculiar value of history, its wealth of invitations to understanding and decision, to growth, perhaps to reversal, relates to the metacritical moment. To attribute any value whatever to arrival at the intentions of subjects is to acknowledge metacritical goals. It is to say that the dynamism of critical history is in the service of ulterior ends. It is no escape to make interpretation functional to explanation, for as the question of value is recurrent, it is posed with respect to explanation, too.

Explanation, like interpretation, aspires to make intelligible not only the march of time but the life of man. It has thus mediated the understanding of the man-made world of meaning in which men live. It is history that has revealed this world of meaning as man-made. To the pre-historical mind the social organization of life was a massive and compelling fact. Without exception the great religions of antiquity ascribed the all-encompassing world of custom no less than the world of nature to the gods. History above all led men to discover that, unlike sunlight and mountains, the organization of life was not simply 'there', but was the product of effort; that it was problematic rather than self-evident; that its origins were open to investigation and its operations to critique; that it was a project requiring support, capable of redirection, subject to collapse, and a challenge to constructive genius. Historical explanation has meant release from imprisonment in routine and a cure for the mindless worship of contemporaneity.

Other values attach to historical interpretation and explanation and have been celebrated in the debate on the goals and uses of history. The one point I would like to make is that, given any value, interpretation and explanation are proximate and open goals, open to the ulterior purposes which account for why history is undertaken, but which themselves transcend historical criticism. Thus, Max Weber took value and the relation to present values to be the right criterion for choosing what to study. What principle of criticism could prove him right or wrong?

Since the positivist heyday it has become clear that the disclaimer of ulterior interest (like the supposition that facts spoke for themselves) was an elaborate illusion. One of the unacknowledged aims of the positivists was the aim of being acknowledged as practitioners of a science as scientific as the natural sciences. But whatever the basic postures and ulterior interests of historians, they are there. They have an impact on every aspect of the historical enterprise, including the understanding of method. Finally, the motives, values, uses, and ulterior purposes of history, be it ever so critical, are themselves metacritical presuppositions. They are not controlled by method but arise from the historian's intellectual and moral being, and in the end they account more fundamentally and adequately than anything else for the kind of history he produces. For a history of Jesus what counts is especially the stance toward religion and faith. This is why we turn now to questions arising from the confrontation of history and faith – with the intention of putting some theological cards on the table.

V

HISTORY AND FAITH

From Reimarus on, the historians of Jesus have been passionately convinced that they were contending for high stakes. When their question seemed to be dying out, it came to life again. The question persists and there is no doubt about why. It has always pivoted around a fixed centre, a specific conviction with roots so luxuriant, so vital, old, and deep that its demise is not to be predicted. It is the conviction of inalienable ties between Christian faith and the Jesus of ancient Palestine. The ties have been debated, narrowed and nuanced, weighed and found wanting, elaborately denied; but the conviction endures, massive, stolid, stubborn, taking its stand on creeds that have ridden out the ages. From the beginning Christian faith has been a confession of events in human history. The events were more than a point of departure. Faith was not only grounded in them, it included them in interpretative affirmations. So history with its claims on the man of faith has become the arena where his faith is affirmed, attacked, defended, reappropriated, redefined.

What importance do these debates have for faith? Considerable importance, for they determine the relative compatibility of faith and integrity. In the long course of these debates from the Enlightenment to the present some (e.g. early German pietists) have decided that faith required the renunciation of intelligence (*sacrificium intellectus*); others, far more numerous, that intelligence – better, intellectual integrity – required the renunciation of faith; others, that *malgré tout* and by the skin of one's teeth one could keep hold of both faith and integrity; and, finally, still others, that, when all was said and done, intellectual integrity positively called for entry into the life of faith or perserverance in it.

These are not only diverse judgments but diverse states of heart and mind. At the root of each lies a pattern of images and affects, sympathies and revulsions, tastes, evaluations, decisions, and commitments. How faith and integrity are related in the view of any particular person depends on his heritage of values and fund of experience, the reach of his powers and the goal of his conscious striving, for all these determine his horizons, i.e., the sum and limit of what is meaningful to him.

1. RELATIONSHIP TO 'THE THING' (*DIE SACHE*)

We begin by invoking 'the circle of things and words' (*Sache und Sprache*) formulated as follows: 'We understand words by understanding the things they refer to; we understand things by understanding the words that refer to them.'

The first limb states the more fundamental insight. It says why a blind man is bound to find a lecture on colour obscure and why talk of 'bondage' and 'liberation' is empty to anyone who has tasted the reality of neither.

The second limb supposes, first of all, the dependence of understanding on a sustaining flow of phantasms. This flow is not necessarily linguistic but in the life of literate man the linguistic component is important, for language is the peerless mediator of meaning. Moreover, we should distinguish with de Saussure between *langue* (the linguistic possibilities shared by a given speech community) and *paroles* (actual utterances).[1] 'We understand things by understanding the words that refer to them' is a true but pedestrian principle if 'words' is taken only in the sense of *langue*. It remains true but no longer pedestrian if 'words' is also taken in the sense of *paroles*. For now 'the understanding of things' becomes the mediation of reality to us not only through language in general but through worlds of determinate meaning; 'the understanding of words' becomes vital contact with whole literatures. In this sense 'the circle of things and words' points to a massive cultural fact. We successfully appropriate meaning and truth not by isolated, unaided efforts to decipher our experience but by a continuing participation in the experiments of contemporaries and the vast legacy of forebears.

It should be noticed that according to the circle of things and words the understanding of any communication supposes a pre-understanding (*Vorverständnis*) of the things communicated. If, for example, we are to grasp the sense of a literary work, we must already have some grasp of what it is concerned with. The principle of pre-understanding taken in this sense is obvious and age-old. Thus, without any claim to originality, Luther observes, *Qui non intelligit res non potest ex verbis sensum elicere* (He who does not understand the things cannot draw the sense from the words).[2] Here pre-understanding is nothing other than awareness of and attentiveness to 'the thing' (*der Blick auf die Sache*),[3] and this conditions all access to meaning. The movement of understanding is a recurrent spiral from the pre-understanding of things through the understanding of words to a firmer, sharper, more differentiated and penetrating understanding of things.

Language does not create, it solicits and evokes, drawing on resources already there. Its impact depends on what and how and how deeply the hearer knows and feels. Several related phenomena call for attention. First, the shabbifying of language points to a more than linguistic breakdown. An idiom or rhetoric deteriorates as the values that supported it wane. Standards and energies ebb together, formality replaces feeling, words wither and die. Yet speech can electrify, too, triggering insight or kindling generosity or unleashing resentment and aggression. What controls this? Pre-understanding, no doubt. But it is now clear that we must conceive pre-understanding in its integrity as the hearer's total relationship – intellectual, moral, emotional – to the thing (*die Sache*) expressed. This relationship may belie appearances, being either deceptively inflated and only simulating vitality, or potent but unformed, waiting in the twilight of consciousness for the call to take shape and rise. In any case the understanding of words cannot but vary in accord with one's total relationship to the things they intend. Even a dim and meagre understanding of words supposes some such pre-understanding; a clear, firm, and, above all, an appreciative understanding of words supposes a vital relationship (*Lebensverhältnis*) to the thing in question. The theme of vital relationship is thus a straightforward application of the principle of pre-understanding to affective and appreciative knowledge. Only such relationship allows one to catch tone and nuance, to savour value, to share in a sense of loss or in the élan of celebration.

We consequently find ourselves committed to rejecting, with Lonergan,[4] 'the principle of the empty head', according to which the less the interpreter has in his head, the more likely he is to avoid 'reading into the text' his own opinions and prejudices. To understand a lecture on colour in an objective way, it is no advantage to be blind. Therefore, experience (including sense data, images, and affects), intelligence, and judgment are not only an advantage but a *sine qua non* condition of coming to understand.[5]

This brings us to an observation of fundamental importance both for understanding the failures of the quest and for sustaining its successes. The quest got its start under the heady stimulus of the Enlightenment's *Sapere aude* (i.e., Have the courage to use your own intelligence instead of leaning on authority and tradition[6]). With the scientific revolution – the intoxicating experience of knowledge unmediated by the *auctores* – Europe reached a point where it had either to re-appropriate its traditions or disavow and debunk them. It fastened on the second option. The result was an era of wholesale 'prejudice against all prejudices',[7] which, through the mediation of a Romanticism superficially opposed to it, culminated in positivism and the 'objectivity' of the empty head.[8] Enlightenment critique, moreover, was aimed first and foremost against the double authority of the scriptures and of their Christian interpretation. The onslaught was so fierce and thorough and in time so successful that even when prejudice against presupposition was at last (in the wake of the first world war) denounced by theologians as profitless and self-deceiving, it turned out that positive affectivity for classical Christian dogma had meantime dried up and disappeared. Consider Chalcedon.

There is the much-quoted statement of William Temple who, back in 1912, in the symposium *Foundations*, said: 'The formula of Chalcedon is, in fact, a confession of the bankruptcy of Greek Patristic theology.' Of course, *Foundations* has been thought to mark a low point in Anglican theology, but Oscar Cullmann, who represents a high point in Protestant orthodoxy, says in *The Christology of the New Testament*: ' . . . all abstract speculation about the 'natures' of Christ is not only a useless undertaking, but actually an improper one.' Well, Cullmann is a biblical and positive scholar and perhaps we cannot expect him to have much time for Chalcedon, but then you get the highly speculative Paul Tillich telling us in the second volume of his *Systematic Theology* that Chalcedon defined two natures 'which lie beside each other like blocks and whose unity cannot be understood at all'. Such judgments seem positively benign when you read Chalcedon referred to [in a book review in *Theology*[9]] as 'sheer verbal rubbish'.[10]

David Friedrich Strauss instructively exemplifies the general law that understanding is conditioned by vital relationship to 'the thing' to be understood. Through hundreds of pages of analysis he showed himself stoutly impervious to the leading themes and motifs of gospel literature. At the same time the summary of Christian doctrine at the end of his *Leben Jesu* has the cold, deadly accuracy of a handbook of dogma. It is all there – Trinity, christology, soteriology – pinned to the page like a butterfly.

An even better hermeneutical paradigm is liberal theology. Markers in a half-forgotten graveyard, its scores of books on Jesus testify to the unauthenticity of a whole tradition. Yet liberal theology had begun ambitiously enough with an eclectic programme of mediation between traditional Christianity and the march of time. Its model was the mild humanist Melancthon; its ideal, freedom from dogma and commitment to presuppositionless history. A virtuoso of the movement was the historian Karl Hase, who, in Franz Schnabel's words,

mounted a last battle against an already staggering Rationalism and spent the rest of a long lifetime producing successive editions of his Church History, revised in accord with the latest developments in theological *Wissenschaft*. No creative soul but exceedingly receptive, he absorbed German cultural life on the broadest scale. An elegant writer and speaker, he introduced into theology the carefully honed artistic prose of classical tradition and in every historical phenomenon drew out the side that was beautiful. He was a representative of *Wissenschaft* in the most proper sense of the word. Raised to the nobility at a time when for professors this distinction was still rare, he oversaw a large household and each year spent several months in Italy. To students he provided what that liberal and bourgeois era was looking for. In a student's letter from Jena, where Hase taught from 1830 to 1883 we read: ' ... Eager to do justice to all sides and opinions, he makes a concession now to one side, now to the other ... developing in a really surprising way an understanding of all viewpoints. He has a remarkable capacity for accommodating himself to every alien mode of thought.' His stand on miracles was characteristic. Hase agreed with the Rationalist explanation but, unwilling to admit this, was evasive. Where it could be done without violence he offered a natural explanation, leaving open, however, the acknowledgment of a miracle. This had been Herder's method and that of the early Rationalists in general. Similarly, Schleiermacher in his lectures on the Resurrection of Jesus had proposed as equally possible a merely apparent death and a supernatural revivification. Just so, Hase wished to allow both possibilities, since a compelling proof of Jesus' death could not be adduced. (Decomposition, the one sure sign that the subject has expired, is nowhere established.) Exemplifying liberal theology's predilection for conceiving things rationalistically, Hase proposed a 'conjecture' on the real ground of Jesus' celibacy as follows: 'He out of whose religion there was later to come forth the ideal view of marriage so alien to antiquity found in his own age and youth no heart ripe for such a bond.'[11]

Theology like this is driven out only by prayer and fasting, neither of which seems to have figured prominently among the resources of liberalism. It would seem a safe proposition that liberal theology's conspicuous lack of relationship to 'the thing' that came to expression in the gospels related – not exclusively, to be sure, but significantly – to the theologians' involvement in the general cultural movement repudiating classical Christian dogma.

A third and last illustration might be Van A. Harvey's discussion of miracles in *The Historian and the Believer*. For present purposes we may take the discussion to have two foci: 'science and the miraculous' and 'miracles as prodigies'.

Certain apologists for orthodoxy in our time have been cheered by fluctuation and revision in the scientific community's understanding of the nature and scope of its own work. Harvey's comment on this belongs to a context where confident opinion has had free rein: that of scientists bravely stepping into the arena of cognitional theory, that of apologists taking quick comfort from the scientists' revisions, and that of the critics of the apologists who set out to explain exactly what had happened and what it all meant. Harvey, who belongs to the third group, assesses the apologists' thesis (viz., that it is no longer 'scientific' to reject miracles) as follows:

Nature, to be sure, may be far more refractory to mathematical description at the subatomic level than hitherto believed, but this does not warrant a return to the credulity once characteristic of a majority of the human race. The new physics, however much it may raise questions about a mechanical model for the universe, can hardly be utilized by a religious apologetic eager to find some small justification for believing in miracles . . .[12]

Does this assessment isolate the issue? The issue is not (a) whether it would be a good idea to return to the credulity once characteristic of a majority of the human race; nor (b) whether modern physics 'warrants' such a return; nor (c) whether apologetics ought to use physics as a justification for believing in miracles. The issue, rather, is one which Harvey has left unarticulated, namely, whether scientific knowledge has any bearing on the judgment that miracles are impossible and, if so, what this bearing is. When the principle of analogy was made to presuppose the impossibility of miracles, did it presuppose a grounded judgment or just an assumption? If it is grounded, what grounds it? Scientific knowledge? Philosophical reflection on scientific knowledge? Or what?

Whether scientific knowledge can and does ground it cannot in any case be resolved by the scientist as such. For science does not deal with questions like 'What is the nature of scientific knowledge?' In so far as the question under discussion inquires after the nature of scientific knowledge, it raises an issue for cognitional theory. But the account which cognitional theory gives of the nature of scientific knowledge does not ground the view that miracles are impossible. For the cognitional theorist observes that scientific knowledge is empirical. As science, it grasps the possible; as empirical, it grasps what possibilities are *de facto* verified. The key observation is that the formulations of empirical science stand in need of descriptive determinations to reach concreteness. For Galileo the formulations of science were not only intelligible but imaginable. Scientific laws attached to concrete particles; and since the laws were universal and necessary, they disclosed the nature of the universe as a mechanistic determinism. Galileo recognized

> that the relations of things to our senses must be transcended, that the relations of things to one another must be grasped, and that a geometrization of nature is the key tool in performing this task. Still . . . instead of speaking of the relations of things to our senses, he spoke of the merely apparent, secondary qualities of things. Instead of speaking of the relations of things to one another, he spoke of their real and objective primary qualities . . . [13]

The contemporary scientist may repudiate Galileo's mechanistic conclusions but keep his distinction between the real and the apparent. Only now 'the real is microscopic and random, while the merely apparent is the macroscopic in which classical laws seem to be verified'.[14] In this view verification can be only apparent, for whereas the laws are determinate, verifying measurements are only approximate. This is what cheered the apologists. If mechanistic determinism was in ruins, one might yet find in nature a place for miracles as Newton had found there a place for God.

But, in fact, the laws of science are not concrete and their verifiability need not be conceived in terms of absolute equivalence. The emergence from determinism was no doubt a forward step, but Heisenberg's principle no more opened up the concrete possibility of miracles than the law of the free fall had closed it down. The apologists missed the first point; their critics, the second.

Harvey asks how one is 'even to get into the position of asking' whether a miracle is a possible solution to a historical problem. There is, however, a counter-question at least equally valid: How is one to get *out* of the position of regarding miracles as an *a priori* impossibility? The issue is not whether 'miracle' is to be made a commonplace principle of explanation. The issue is whether persons testifying to miracles are by that very fact shown to be incompetent or dishonest or self-deceived, and this without reference to their credentials or to the particulars of the case but by ineluctable *a priori* law.[15]

In the gospels, at any rate, the supposition of the concrete possibility of miracles is fundamentally grounded in positive openness to a divine act of salvation as the intelligible context of the miraculous. If the salvific context is overlooked, the concrete possibility of miracle evaporates. In so far as 'miracle' evokes no more than images of the prodigious (Harvey's paradigm is 'a rain of blood'), it is fantasy, not seriously conceivable in relation to the real order of things and offering nothing at all by which a historian could 'even get into the position of asking' whether in a given instance 'miracle' might illuminate historical data. If, furthermore, the critic cannot seriously imagine anything which might give religious significance to a resurrection of Jesus (which, though not reducible to 'miracle', nevertheless involves a miraculous factor[16]), nothing of the sort can commend itself to him as a viable hypothesis in accounting for the transforming paschal experience of the disciples.

Three observations. First, we have reached a theoretical issue. Can a historian entertain the meaningfulness of 'saving acts in history' without abdicating his *métier*? This is the issue of whether history as a way of knowing and a kind of knowledge entails the historicist conception of events as a closed continuum (*ein geschlossener Wirkungs-Zusammenhang*). What in the operations of posing and answering historical questions grounds and clinches this entailment? The question, to be sure, is a variation on: 'Why do you wish to say that two and two make five?' The question will doubtless continue to be put until, in the matter of Troeltschean ideology, there comes to be more general agreement that two and two make no more nor less than four.

Second, the matter of differentiating history from historicism is, indeed, a theoretical issue; but inasmuch as theory in the modern sense is not merely contemplated but applied, it has a powerful impact on how history is done. If the historian of religions cannot entertain the meaningfulness of 'saving acts in history', then he cannot envisage miracle as a concrete possibility. There follows this dilemma. It is his business to give an account of data en route to answering questions about matters of fact. Now, in fact, he has no basis on which to exclude miracle *a priori* from either the data or the answer. On the other hand, he has pledged himself as historian not to envisage the possibility of miracles. He accordingly finds himself in a situation which does not allow him, as historian, to come to grips with history, for he cannot know whether or not the possibility he dutifully omits to consider offers the best account of a given constellation of data. I have no objection to the historian of Jesus who is satisfied to install himself in this conundrum, provided only that he acknowledge it for what it is. I need hardly add that I am not plumping for miracles as the heart of the matter in the story of Jesus. I am simply registering the anti-docetist observation that there is a loss regularly incurred by *a priori* rejection of miracles. It lies in a certain truncating of the full sense, scope, and force of the eschatological conceptions, purposes, words, acts, and total thrust of Jesus.

This introduces the third point. How it is that Harvey can deal with the question of miracle accounts without adverting to their all-commanding context in the gospels (i.e., without reference to the conception of miracles as signs of salvation)? The critic has allowed himself to be distracted from 'the thing' coming to expression in the texts on miracles. What is this 'thing'? It is salvation and nothing but salvation.

> Blind men see,
> cripples walk,
> lepers are cleansed,
> deaf men hear,
> dead men are raised,
> good news (= news of salvation) is broken to the poor! (Matt. 11.5 par.).

The gospels set such themes in the context of the question about who Jesus is; Harvey, confining the discussion to a context of science and credibility, cannot so much as 'get into the position of asking' whether such texts throw light on anything at all. 'The thing', the very principle of intelligibility in every miracle text, has vanished from sight, for the weather-beaten thesis of the closed universe has worked as an overpowering distraction.

Enlightenment luggage litters the contemporary Western psyche. Old scars and feeling-laden images are the 'absences which make us act',[17] half-conjured memories of the dark where the authority of 'holy writ' appears as ideology and dogma as just a tool of tyranny.

We have tried to locate hermeneutical and historical factors accounting for the failures that marked the prodigious effort of the quest, arguing that they derived proximately from lack of relationship to the thing (*die Sache*) that came to expression (*zur Sprache*) in the New Testament sources and, further, that at critical points this relationship was a casualty of Enlightenment critique. The critique, charged with resentment and levelled against Christian tradition in the name of Humanity, was strategically objectified in cognitional theory. That commitment to the critique was an awkward presupposition of inquiry into the figure of Jesus and that inquiry so conditioned could generate only misconceptions of him and his purposes should have been at least suspected from the start; for the dogmas of historical Christianity had simply objectified[18] the New Testament 'thing' and, in particular, Jesus as the New Testament church understood him, viz., as redeemer and Son of God.[19] Simultaneously to repudiate the dogmas and appropriate the meaning of the historical Jesus proved to be an ambitious but self-defeating project.

This is not, however, to define Christianity's dogmatic tradition as the unique point of access to the gospels. It is simply to assert a connaturality between classical 'doctrine and devotion' and a vital relationship to the New Testament 'thing'.

Some of those whose views would thus seem liable to hermeneutical critique (Bultmann, for example) not only acknowledged but pioneered the acknowledgment of the reciprocal mediation of things and words as well as the indispensability of a pre-understanding of and, indeed, vital relationship to, 'the thing'. The concrete way in which Bultmann exploited these gains was to call for a pre-understanding of the gospels in terms of the heuristic categories Heidegger articulated in *Being and Time*. These, argued Bultmann, represented the level of concern and questioning appropriate to the reading of New Testament texts.

There can be no argument with the light this has thrown on the task of interpretation and on orientation to the task, nor indeed with its actual productiveness. Such felt need is in any case enough to start with; actual transactions with the text on this basis are calculated to make known more ultimate needs which, as the theological career of Paul attests, is a matter of coming to terms with a new revelation. Bultmann's involvement in the Enlightenment legacy set severe limits on what would otherwise be the natural and spontaneous outcome of vital contact with the text. In the face of the text felt need, if remaining only that, is a limiting disposition. The whole New Testament attests a gift that not only meets man's felt and unfelt needs but incalculably outruns them. So kerygma theology talks earnestly of authentic existence whereas the New Testament celebrates life in 'abundance' (John 10.10), the inexhaustible (Eph. 3.8) treasures (Col. 2.3) that are the gift God makes of himself (cf. John 1.1–18; Heb. 1.3) in Son (Rom. 3.24 f.; II Cor. 5.19; John 6.32–58) and Spirit (Acts 2.38; John 4.10; 14.25; 15.26; Eph. 3.6).

Christianity's dogmatic tradition, though connatural with the New Testament 'thing', is not itself the grace of access to the gospels. We must
suppose, however, that vital relationship to the 'thing' that comes to
expression there is something like a divine grace of access. For, what
comes to expression in the gospels but *ta tou theou*, 'the things of God'? And
'no one comprehends the things of God (*ta tou theou*) except the Spirit of
God' (I Cor. 2.11). To natural man (the *psychikos anthrōpos* of Paul, which
roughly equals 'average carnal man') the things of God are 'folly' and 'he
is not able to understand them' (I Cor. 2.14); if Paul understands them, it
is because on his own testimony 'the Spirit of God' (I Cor. 7.40) and 'the
mind of Christ' (I Cor. 2.16) are his.[20]

2. THREE QUESTIONS

Our overarching concern is the relationship between faith and integrity
and the role played by historical knowledge in this relationship. Thus far
we have offered some few general considerations on access to the historic
figure, Jesus, and on how such access is conditioned. The principal condition is vital relationship to what the sources on Jesus and Jesus himself
represent and express.[21] This has occasioned the observation that the
repudiation of classical dogma has tended to limit and undermine this
relationship. But the observation touches only one facet of a many-faceted
question. We ought to say, then, how we delimit the question and what
facets of it we intend to discuss. We are discussing the views of
theologians. We are not discussing the views of those who leave faith out of
consideration, nor the views of those who affirm faith at the price of
renouncing reason or who affirm reason at the price of renouncing faith.
We shall only discuss efforts to secure simultaneously the integrity of both
faith and reason. Three questions arise. First, what is 'the integrity of
faith'? Second, how is the integrity of faith secured in the face of history?
Third, what are the purposes of history with reference to faith? In so far as
diverse answers to these questions turn out to be related among themselves, a final question is posed about the root of these relationships.

If the New Testament be taken to define normatively 'the integrity of
faith', the question remains how to interpret the New Testament. To
begin, we might differentiate in 'knowledge' between a final 'phase of
truth' (intended by questions calling for 'yes' or 'no') and an anterior
'phase of meaning' (intended by all other questions, e.g., 'What?' or
'Why?'[22]). But 'meaning', together with interpretation as the effort to
grasp and mediate meaning, becomes an acute question precisely when
what seems to be meant seems not to be so. Thus, Bultmann understood

what the writer meant by 'the Word was made flesh'; namely, 'a pre-existent heavenly being became man'.[23] Over and above such meaning, however, there remains the question, 'But did a pre-existent heavenly being actually become man?' If the answer is, 'no, that is unthinkable', alternative options present themselves: to abandon Johannine faith or to reinterpret it. Supposing the latter choice, a difficulty at the level of truth occasions return to an earlier moment in quest of a resolution at the level of meaning.

But a resolution of this kind (unless it were to mean repudiation of the initial interpretative insight into the intended sense of 'the Word was made flesh') must entail a systematically selective abandonment of the consciously and deliberately intended sense of texts in favour of another, deeper, more hidden dimension of meaning. It is thus no longer by recognitive interpretation (the quest of the intended sense) but by a new hermeneutic that 'the integrity of faith' is defined. Or as Strauss put it, 'the matters narrated in [the scriptures] must be viewed in a light altogether different from that in which they were regarded by the authors themselves'.[24] We might sum up the issue as 'recognitive' versus 'non-recognitive' exegesis.[25]

The second question: How is the integrity of faith secured in the face of history?

Practitioners of non-recognitive exegesis settle the matter with a single stroke cleanly severing faith from past particulars. History cannot threaten faith, for faith does not bear on past events. Historical inquiry, observes Bultmann, leaves open the possibility that Jesus suffered a collapse, was dragged unwilling to the cross, and died in despair.[26] But though this may have been the case, faith remains intact and unaffected, for it does not intend nor, consequently, hinge on past particulars.

Those committed to recognitive exegesis, on the other hand, are apparently confronted at this point with grave problems. It is evident that on the level of conscious, deliberate intention the faith of the New Testament churches did indeed bear on past particulars such as the expiatory self-sacrifice of Jesus 'for the many' (Mark 10.45 par.; 14.24 par.; cf. I Cor. 11.23–25; Gal. 2.20c; I Tim. 2.6 etc.). It is equally evident that the possibilities of successful historical inquiry are not coterminous with the scope of faith-affirmations. What can be ascertained historically often falls far short of what is affirmed by faith. Does faith, then, affirm without warrants? And is it put in perpetual jeopardy to the advance of historical knowledge? The answer to these questions must be yes, unless faith itself somehow guarantees the past particulars it intends.

The operative presupposition of this last possibility is that faith-affirmations are warranted but not by the intrinsic evidence of their objects. The warrant of faith is the fidelity of God. In this view God, not historical data, provides the ground and secures the truth of faith. It is a view elaborated from within the faith-perspective itself where truth is not a distant goal but a starting point and all the rest is only explanation. It may be an enlightening explanation. It will certainly invoke the categories of the supernatural (not in the current sense but in the classical sense of the disproportion between nature and grace). Still, the theology of faith will not dissolve in the slightest the scandal of unprovability. The sure sign of a mistake about faith is the announcement that the scandal of indemonstrable affirmation has been disposed of. Faith is not only a mystery and a scandal to the will by contradicting man's instinct 'to save his life' (Mark 8.35); it is a mystery and a scandal to reason by contradicting man's instinct for autonomous knowledge (II Cor. 10.5; cf. 'the obedience of faith' in Rom. 1.5 etc.).

Faith, then, is the risk of counting on the dark presence of the unknown that cannot be tested or controlled. Still, faith is not pure risk. It is not a guess or a bet, much less a *sacrificium intellectus*. It is a stepping out of the mastered, familiar world into the darkness where one is a child. The risk of faith is finally the risk of finding an identity in Christ by which 'we share abundantly in Christ's sufferings' (II Cor. 1.5). It is only unfaith – i.e., recoil from some substantial element of the faith-heritage – that runs the risk that 'our preaching is in vain' (I Cor. 15.14) or the risk that we might turn out to be 'of all men the most to be pitied' (I Cor. 15.19). Nowhere in the testimony of the New Testament is the risk of faith seen as the risk of illusion. Just the opposite: faith is refuge from illusion as from unfreedom and untruth.

In this view historical debates and discoveries cannot invalidate faith; they do, however, instruct it. They might, for example show a believer that he is not, in fact, committed by faith to his grandfather's understanding of the historicity of gospel narratives – a discovery which neither overlooks nor repudiates the New Testament confessions of faith but simply corrects a mistaken assumption.

The assertion that historical debates and discoveries cannot invalidate faith should not be mistaken for an obscurantism that refuses to be confused by facts. It supposes that faith intends the concrete particular past, and that the realm of the concrete, be it past, present, or future, cannot be internally contradictory. The faith-component in the assertion is that faith intends the concrete truly and that the pledge of its truth is the fidelity of God. But history, like personal experience, is instructive. For my part, I tend to think it excluded by faith that Jesus was dragged unwilling to the cross, but I acknowledge not knowing whether such a judgment is absolutely guaranteed. Is, then, anything at all absolutely guaranteed by faith? It seems to me that whereas a hypothetical brokenness and despair of the dying Jesus might not, perhaps, be finally incompatible with the faith-heritage of Christianity, faith does absolutely exclude *some* views of Jesus, e.g., that of Reimarus. That purely historical considerations regularly (though less apodictically) exclude views such as that of Reimarus adds a certain remote confirmation to the principle that faith, intending concrete events, carries its own warrant and guarantee of truth.

The third question: What are the purposes of history with reference to faith? For those who take faith to exclude the intending of past particulars, history renders a negative and purgative service. A half-century ago Barth and Bultmann hailed the collapse of the quest of the historical Jesus. The one positive gain of the quest, in their view, had been to demonstrate its own sterility for the life of faith.[27]

For those who understand faith to intend past particulars, the rise of history has had and continues to have a many-sided positive value with reference to faith. It has a corrective value, guiding an ongoing differentiation of Christian consciousness of what faith actually intends.[28] It has an apologetic value, allowing the believer consciously to appropriate the responsible character of entry into and perseverance in the life of faith. It has an instructive value, illuminating, for example, the originality of faith by the originality of Jesus, traced against the background of the world of piety in which he lived and died. At the coming of the eschaton, said Judaism, it is too late for ransom. No, said Jesus, the eschaton comes by ransom: my life for the world.[29]

So we have found quite divergent answers to three questions about faith and history. Though the diverging parties have a common aim (to affirm faith and reason without forfeiting anything of either), the divergences seem irresolvable by further appeal to the New Testament. They do, however, raise a further question about the root of the diversity.

There are both intrinsic and historic connections between the recourse to non-recognitive exegesis, the dissociation of faith from past particulars, and theological opposition to the critical history of Jesus. The combination is meant to solve a problem posed to faith by modern conceptions of the true and the good. Here 'the true' is defined in opposition to credulity and 'the good' in opposition to inhumanity. Both attest the indignation that powered the Enlightenment: passionate outrage at 'superstition' (i.e., at the manipulation of credulity) and at persecution for dissident belief or opinion. Historically, the presupposition of this movement was the crack-up of the medieval synthesis and the Cartesian quest of new foundations.

The Cartesian strategy – choice of the path of doubt to the goal of certainty – left its stamp on Enlightenment styles of thought and made the quest of apodictic epistemological foundations a central and permanent philosophical concern. At the root of those theologies which accuse every quest of the historical Jesus of being an unbelieving flight to security stands, ironically, a Cartesian hunger for definitively secured foundations of reason. This, indeed, belongs constitutively to the modern morality of knowledge with its critically rigorous scepticism. The result is a dichotomy between the lived experience of the believer and the account he gives of faith. The lived experience is a symbiosis of faith and reason, whereas the account posits their strict separation. The believer's effort to achieve coherence between himself and his account of faith may mean revision of the account; or it may mean the breakdown of faith.

The distinctive feature of 'the modern morality of knowledge' is this Cartesian contour. Critical and rigorous, the ideal functions both as a test of truth and a style of intellectual life. It represents an insistence on rational inference and a determination to withhold assent until it is compelled by evidence. Regard for evidence is its proudest claim, yet it greets all evidence with a sceptical eye. The whole issue is whether this scepticism is a virtue or a vice. In the present context, at any rate, it should be observed that a life of intelligence conducted according to this ideal stands in tension, if not antipathy, to the surrender that is faith. The Cartesian critic always runs the risk of strangling in his own suspicions.

This morality of knowledge is not of itself the adequate explanation of any particular contemporary theology. But a large part of contemporary theology, including that which refashions the New Testament world of meaning, dissevers it from the actualities of history, and repudiates knowledge of the historical Jesus as alien and irrelevant to faith, is unthinkable apart from a prior critical orientation which finds the classical form of Christianity repugnant.

The contrary theological position (commitment to recognitive exegesis and to the relevance of history to faith) is not, to be sure, disrespectful of evidence. Moreover, it is receptive to the obvious; namely, that communion in faith with the church of apostolic times is hardly more than an illusion if it fails to include credal commitments to the same revelation. This is the ultimate – the theological – rationale of opting for recognitive exegesis.

Central to this view is the primacy over all theology it accords to faith – a faith that lives in communion with its 'objects', that accepts prophecy as marking the limits of autonomous knowledge, and that rejoins the root allegiances of historical Christianity, pre-eminently including those of the New Testament churches.

There is a morality of knowledge at work here, too. In its pre-critical state it is the confident supposition that human intelligence intends the real and attains it. What specifies this pre-critical state as pre-critical is a new factor: the grounding of this confidence by the strategy of reflexively mediating the immediacy of knowledge.[30] Concretely, this consists in thematizing what is given in the performance of posing questions.[31] By this route it brings to light the realized conditions of the possibility of attaining the real by intelligence, thereby disclosing the further possibility that men should be 'hearers of the word'[32] and of the word in its integral fulness.

Thus, the issues on which we have distinguished antipathetic tendencies finally resolve back into two orientations and two schools: the orientation to doubt and the orientation to assent, the school of suspicion and the school of affirmation. As we understand them, both are coherent; but they are hardly on a par, for cognitional theory confirms the one and cripples the other. But *a priori* suspicion is not only crippled, it is crippling; and nowhere is its crippling effect more evident than in the meagre religious option it permits – the mere salvaging of remnants from the heritage of faith.

With this resolution of conflicting views into two orientations of the human spirit, we do not imagine we have vindicated the one and discredited the other. Our effort has been to locate ultimate roots of diversity. We consider that we have done this, and now wish merely to conclude with a last observation on whether the view favoured here is liable to the charge of 'immobilism'.

Some of those who posit the antinomy 'historically informed intellectual integrity versus traditional belief' facilitate their stand by describing traditional belief in static terms. But 'tradition' of itself connotes the living and adaptive. Dead traditions do not survive and lasting traditions do not stand still. Development, in fact, characterized Christian tradition from the start. Never more clearly than in our time has this been recognized as a hallmark of the apostolic era. The earliest Christian community had to *discover* that God's saving act temporally differentiated the enthronement of the Son of man from his judgment of the world[33]; it had to *discover* that the Gentiles' share in this same saving act demanded the launching of a world mission.[34] Indeed, the second of these developments was an aspect of vital accommodation to the first.[35] And it should be emphasized that this was not by straightforward and predictable deduction but was appropriated precisely as a discovery. Though such discoveries unfold in series, the participants in the history of the unfolding know neither the series nor even the next stage in its unfolding. Finally, as we are concerned here with matters of faith, the incorporation of such discoveries into the heritage of the church is nothing other than an ongoing 'discovery of (the) faith'.

Since the mid-nineteenth century and for the first time in history, discovery and development have become, in reflexly conscious fashion, salient features of 'traditional belief'. These, indeed, are seen now to belong indispensably to the conditions of the possibility of the perduring identity of faith and faith-community alike. To the discomfort of its critics, 'traditional belief' refuses to stand still and now[36] repudiates the claim to be doing so. Most significantly, in the framework of the present discussion, faith learns from history, i.e., from the march of time, from discovery of the historicity of knowledge, and from historical knowledge as such.

Let a single but striking instance – the radically altered course taken in this century by the most resolutely classical theologians on the topic 'the knowledge of Christ'[37] – serve to make the point. As Aquinas and Luther felt compelled by theological and psychological considerations (the full humanity of Christ and the indispensability to man as such of human intentional activity) to predicate of Jesus 'experimental knowledge' and thus real growth in knowledge, so all theologians of our century have been compelled, and perhaps by nothing as much as by considerations bearing on the historical intelligibility of the story of Jesus, to predicate of him ignorance, growth in 'wisdom', a 'listening' for God, a learning and teaching that saw divine signs in contingent events, and finally, a conscious recognition of the limits of his own prophetic insight.[38] Such perspectives have in a quite short time become almost commonplace aspects of 'traditional belief'. This one instance of the ongoing accommodation of traditional belief to never-ending differentiations of human consciousness is enough to explode in principle the antinomy of historian and believer or of intellectual integrity and traditional belief.

With this mini-salvo we conclude our discussion of hermeneutical issues. We hope only to have arrived at a beginning. But 'the beginning', as Paul Ricoeur once put it, 'is not what one finds first; the point of departure must be reached, it must be won'.[39]

PART TWO

THE AIMS OF JESUS

INTRODUCTION

For the man with 'aims', the non-drifter, aims are the man. They throw a flood of light on his history and they are the key to his historic selfhood.

But the self-fashioning connoted by 'aims' is ambiguous, for the radically antonomous man and the radically obedient man are both self-fashioners. The first – Adamic, Promethean, Faustian – wills to be rooted in himself. The selfhood of the second is rootage in the ground of being, where 'aims' equals 'vocation' or, as Ortega put it, 'destiny', which is not spontaneously devised or chosen but simply accepted or rejected.

The final historical question about the aims of Jesus may be cast in these terms. It asks whether he can be known historically to be a completely authentic man or whether, on the contrary, the figure of Jesus must remain permanently ambiguous. This is the question of aims as indices to the historic selfhood they both fashion and express (ch. IX). It is a modern question, posed on a different plane from the faith-affirmations of the New Testament and so not adequately met by them alone.

But an answer to the question about human authenticity depends, first of all, on how historical critique settles matters of fact bearing on the subject's purposes and performance. Jesus has, of course, found critics unconcerned with such laborious preliminary investigations.[1] But the effort to settle matters of fact touching purposes and performance is clearly indispensable to inquiry into a man's historic selfhood. In the present study concern for matters of fact finds expression in a sustained effort to locate the pattern or form or determining principle of Jesus' career. To this end we inquire into three sets of data: traditions relating to John the Baptist (ch. VI), public traditions on Jesus (ch. VII), and esoteric traditions on Jesus (ch. VIII). In each of these three inquiries the effort is to discern the shape of the historical reality attested by critically appraised and related traditions. Finally, we wish to know whether the results of these three efforts converge. Perfect convergence is not to be expected. But if the inquiries are productive, they should converge in some significant way on the principal unknown: the aims of Jesus and the historic form of his career.

Such is the strategy we intend to follow. Though its rationale can hardly be fully laid out and appreciated in advance, it may be well to offer two comments relevant thereto.

First, we systematically distinguish between public traditions (acts and words Jesus addressed to the public) and esoteric traditions (acts and words reserved for disciples). There is nothing artificial about this distinction. It is not only significant to the gospel redactions, it is inherent in the tradition prior to all redactions. The latter point imposes itself on condition that there are words of Jesus which clearly strike the esoteric note and which are found to be historical. This twofold condition, as we shall see, is fulfilled. To understand the data on Jesus it is accordingly indispensable to distinguish between public and esoteric traditions.

Second, where pre-redactional traditions can be discerned – and this is commonplace at least in the synoptic gospels – they are systematically detached from the redactions, i.e., from their peculiar functions in the service of any redactor's distinctive vision of things and distinctive purposes. Are traditions detachable in this way without being somehow damaged or destroyed? In some measure they obviously are. The gospel redactions in many instances have pressed materially the same traditions into the service of divergent purposes. To detach traditional data from their special uses in one or other or all of the redactions is simply to undo something only the redactors have done. The same holds in principle for the various restricted unities in pre-redactional and pre-literary tradition. The form critics may have underestimated the historical as well as the literary and theological worth of the redactions as such and they may sometimes have dismembered gospel traditions in a way that blocked rather than promoted insight into the material and its origin. But it would be a worse mistake, and one ruling out in advance all historical reconstruction, to treat the traditions as inseparable from the redactions and the redactions accordingly as inviolable monoliths.

In terms of the particular strategy sketched here, redaction criticism remains in the background, its role remote and oblique rather than immediate and direct. On occasion it will be necessary to treat explicitly (at least in a footnote) the special factors involved in detaching a given tradition from the redaction(s) (e.g. John 3.22ff. on Jesus' activity as baptizer). But wherever we judge the matter to present no special problem, we detach traditions from their special uses in the redactions with little or no comment. This certainly does not mean that we intend to pick now this, now that, tradition from the redactions to paste together a piece of wishful thinking in the manner of liberal life-of-Jesus research. We intend to deal with the whole mass of public traditions we judge to be historical and to try and discern the shape of the reality they attest. As for the esoteric traditions and many Johannine traditions, the writer does not feel equipped to assess them all. But the strategy of ch. VIII on esoteric traditions will be to deal with the most central issues.

There have been various studies of Jesus' intention, etc., in the past, but if the project as outlined here has been attempted before, the writer is unaware of it. A fairly extensive secondary literature – above all, the literature owing its achievements to excellence in philological and environmental research and Palestinian *Religionsgeschichte* (Dalman, Jeremias, Schürmann, Hengel, and others) – will repeatedly prove helpful in grasping the sense and assessing the historicity of discrete data. But the present work is intent on much more than that. It is most ambitious (and the writer most on his own) in orchestrating scores of inquiries into three inquiries and the three into a single inquiry. Still, there is nothing revolutionary about the systematically hierarchized procedures sketched here nor are they specially designed to produce revolutionary results. The inquiry is designed to proceed soberly toward the conversion of a significant unknown into a known – nothing more, nothing less.

VI

THE JUDGMENT AND SALVATION OF ISRAEL

1. UNDERSTANDING THE BAPTIST

The beginning of Jesus' public career is inextricably bound up with the
public career of John the Baptist. Both careers were prophetic appeals to
the nation. Both were short, abruptly ended by execution. But we have to
do here with more than 'parallel lives', for the two were significantly
related.

Initial sketch

John 'appeared' in the wilderness north of the Dead Sea 'in the fifteenth
year of the reign of Tiberius Caesar' (Luke 3.1); i.e., not earlier than the
autumn of AD 27 nor later than midsummer of 29.[1] Travellers found
themselves startled and stopped by a warning voice, a proclamation of
judgment and a summons to repentance which soon brought visitors, then
crowds, out to the wilderness to see and hear. Here was no theologian, no
enthusiast, but a prophet. And this alone was taken as a persuasive sign of
the truth of his message, a sign of the imminence of the end; for by now
Israel had lived so long without prophecy that common expectation postponed its appearance to the day of definitive salvation.[2] The very
phenomenon of the return of prophecy made John an eschatological symbol freighted with powerful, if ambiguous, meaning. Indeed, his career is
unintelligible apart from the interwoven symbols in which it was realized:
the pelt clothing that recalled Elijah;[3] the striking asceticism that made
Jesus say, 'John came neither eating nor drinking' (Matt. 11.18a par.) and
made the Christian community remember that 'his food was locusts and
wild honey' (Mark 1.6 par.); the imagery of judgment that filled his
preaching (Spirit and fire, wheat and chaff, winnowing fork and threshing
floor, axe and root). Two symbols especially defined his career: the
encircling wilderness and, at its centre, the water rite of baptism.

The wilderness (the word says simply 'uninhabited land') that was John's primary locale was the lower Jordan valley, east of Jerusalem.[4] But 'wilderness' was filled with connotation and symbolic meaning. It connoted, first of all, the impure, the demonic, the lethal. In the scriptures, however, wilderness (*midbar*) had become a multivalent symbol. In the wilderness Yahweh tested Israel and Israel rebelled and was punished. Above all, the wilderness signified the return to God by return to where God's transactions with his people began.[5]

It can be no accident that the wilderness chosen by John was within easy distance of Jerusalem.[6] Bent on confronting the whole of Israel with his proclamation, he was no doubt acutely conscious that the way Jerusalem went the nation would go. But John would not himself go to Jerusalem, e.g., to preach in the temple. No; he called Jerusalem out to him, to the wilderness, away from the whole network of current structures and commitments. He called the nation to a new beginning.[7]

The rite which won John the surname 'Baptizer' coheres with this interpretation. It was designed to symbolize and seal the conversion of Israel in the face of the approaching judgment – 'the wrath about to come' (Matt. 3.7 par.). In John's view, evidently, the supremely critical moment had come for Israel, a *kairos* charged with imperatives of purification. It is equally evident that in John's view the standing religious resources of Israel, e.g., cultic means of expiation, could not meet these imperatives. God called for the conversion and washing of the whole nation. It would only be by repentance and baptism that a renewed Israel could meet judge and judgment and survive.

This radical eschatology, grounded like classical prophecy in the conviction that the judgment to be turned against Israel would be unsparing, is implicit in the whole circle of symbols within which John operated. It is confirmed by a stinging word:

> Do not start saying to yourselves
> 'We have Abraham for our father.'
> I tell you:
> God can raise up sons to Abraham out of these stones!
> (Luke 3.8; Matt. 3.9)

God was now summoning the children of Abraham[8] to enter the scenario of the end-time. By repentance and baptism he would reconstitute his people for the messianic visitation.

> I baptize you with water for repentance;[9]
> but one comes after me mightier than me
> whose sandals I am unworthy to carry;[10]
> he will baptize you[11] with the holy Spirit and fire.[12]
>
> His winnowing fork is in his hand

and he will clear his threshing floor
and gather his wheat into the granary
but the chaff he will burn with unquenchable fire
(Matt. 3.11 par.).

These words supposed a scheme of salvation in two phases: the water
baptism of John and the 'mightier one's' baptism in 'the holy Spirit and
fire'. The two phases were related as prologue to judgment and judgment
itself. The second baptism would sort out, gather up, and purify the
righteous. But the unrepentant ('the chaff') would be doomed to hell-fire.

John's career had a public dimension (the call to the nation) and an
esoteric dimension (the guidance of disciples). Three traits typify the
latter: fasting, prayer, and teaching. On the basis of specific fasting practices John's discipleship was at least externally comparable to the
Pharisaic brotherhood (Mark 2.18; Matt. 9.14; Luke 5.33). More
significant, no doubt, for his followers' self-understanding were the
prayers John composed for them (Luke 11.1; cf. 5.33) but of which we
have no vestige. Finally, the heart of John's esoteric instruction was surely
his prophetic expectations of the messianic judge to come. We have too
little of his descriptive indications to match them with any eschatological
figure of biblical or Judaic tradition. The clear points are two: (1) John's
own mission was wholly relative to that of the coming judge (2) whose
messianic epiphany was imminent.

Analysis

How are we to understand the aims of John? It is clear that the world of
meaning within which he lived and operated was essentially shaped by
expectation of the eschatological judgment (Mark 1.2f. parrs.; Matt. 3.7
par.; 3.10 par.; 3.11f. par.).[13] But his own role with reference to the
judgment is revealed by 'the wilderness' where he took his stand and by
the baptizing which in contemporary estimation quintessentially defined
him. Hence, the question 'What were the aims of John?' is reducible to
'What was the meaning of his baptizing in the wilderness?' Generically,
the answer must be: 'to make Israel ready for the judgment.' But the
challenge is so to sharpen the focus of both question and answer as to
arrive at a differentiated understanding of John's presuppositions and
purposes.

It is historically out of the question that John conceived judgment along
the individualistic lines characteristic of later Western thought. Rather, he
conceived judgment in collective, or better, 'ecclesial', terms, i.e., in terms
of 'God's people, Israel'. To miss this is to miss the context – a massive
tradition – in which John consciously and publicly situated himself and
out of which came his every word and act. In Torah and prophets alike the

drama of history is the covenantal dialogue of God and people. Judgment is turned against *Israel* and *Israel* is the object of salvation. John's summons to baptism in the wilderness was accordingly directed not simply to all Israelites but to all Israel, i.e., to the nation as an ecclesial entity or to Israel as people of God. The response to his summons therefore could not be merely so many responses of individuals within Israel; it had to be the response of Israel as such. 'Prophet' is locked, as always, in engagement with 'people'. It would be a great mistake, then, to suppose that diversity of response could cancel the ecclesial character of the encounter. On the contrary, the diversity of response would concretely determine the destiny of Israel as such: its division (cf. the coming separation of wheat and chaff) and restoration (the wheat gathered into the granary). For the issue now was the judgment that would bring history to an end. Can John have supposed that, in the final act of the drama of God and people, some in Israel would be lost and some saved, but that Israel as such, neither lost nor saved, would simply cease to be a factor? Such a conception is totally alien to ancient Judaism as to the whole biblical tradition.

If it is Israel that is judged, it is Israel that is saved. But as judgment means the burning of the chaff, saved Israel is, in respect of its past collective selfhood, a remnant.

Prophetic tradition had converted 'the remnant of Israel' into a powerful symbol of restoration.[14] In and through the remnant of Israel God reconstituted his holy people. This both illuminates and is illuminated by 'wilderness' and 'baptism'.

In the language and imagery of John prophetic and apocalyptic schemes of thought went easily together and cohered. For all John's apocalyptic horizons (e.g. the definitive judgment and the mysterious figure of 'the mightier one' coming to judge), the wilderness thematic derived from prophetic sources. Apocalyptic threat invested John's prophetic themes with new urgency. In the face of judgment Israel was to be reconstituted as in the beginning:

> So I will allure her;
>   I will lead her into the wilderness
>   and speak to her heart ...
> She shall respond there as in the days of her youth
>   when she came up from the land of Egypt (Hos. 2.16f.; EVV 2.14f.).

By making his career 'in the wilderness' and so presenting Israel with a charged symbol (the *Urzeit/Endzeit* schema) by which to understand him, John purposefully evoked themes of eschatological restoration. This would seem to be the real thrust of the symbolic act of appearing and preaching 'in the wilderness'. As in the beginning Israel was made God's covenant people in the wilderness and so made ready for entry into the land of promise, so in the end-time Israel, renewed in the wilderness, would be made ready for the messianic judge. Moreover, this interior drama of reform was to be sealed by a rite of symbolic immersion in water:[15] Israel's 'baptism of repentance' (Mark 1.4; Luke 3.3) prophetically sponsored by John and designating in advance a people whose positive response to his call destined it for acquittal.

The analysis can be recapitulated in three points: (1) The question 'What were the aims of John?' is reducible to 'What was the meaning of his baptizing in the wilderness?' (2) It was in view of eschatological judgment that John summoned Israel as such to baptism in the wilderness. But: if John's mission (*a*) was undertaken precisely with reference to the coming judgment, (*b*) was directed to Israel as such (though envisaging a diversity of response to it among Israelites) and (*c*) consisted in proclaiming and realizing the condition on which Israel's survival of judgment hinged, it follows that John's goal was to gather the remnant of Israel destined for salvation.[16] (3) The symbols 'wilderness' and 'baptism' illuminate and support this conclusion.

Objections and precisions

Biblical criticism has failed to reach unanimity on the issue of John and the remnant of Israel because of numerous misunderstandings. We will mention five. It has been repeatedly but mistakenly supposed, first, that 'remnant' must signify a separate and organized community and, second, that the community so constituted must be a closed corporation. Third, it has been thought that remnant theology must suppose previous rupture of covenant. It has been unconsciously assumed, fourth, that John need not have conceived Israel as such to be the object of salvation, and fifth, that before specifying the aims of John as exactly as we have, we must first be able to settle all history-of-religions (*religionsgeschichtlich*) questions relating to him, his eschatology, and his baptismal rite. But none of these suppositions (which we will now take up in order) is well grounded; rather, all of them are misleading or false.

It is striking that the prophets who converted the age-old conception of the remnant into a vehicle of parenetic warning (*Drohpredigt*) and, eventually, into a potent symbol of survival and restoration, did not themselves undertake to gather the remnant of Israel prior to the outbreak of catastrophe. Perhaps they thought that this would be to presume to anticipate God's sovereign judgment. Nevertheless, two developments followed the prophetic use of the remnant theme, each exhibiting a distinctive 'realized eschatology'.[17] First, the exiles returning to the Holy Land from Babylon saw 'the remnant of Israel' realized in themselves in so far as they were indeed survivors of judgment. 'Remnant theology' became thereby a vehicle of national hope. Second, the Hellenistic crisis of the second century BC prompted the public appearance of more or less markedly apocalyptic communities of the pious which characteristically sought to realize in themselves the scriptural attributes of the holy remnant. Here the realized eschatology was of a distinct kind. Like the returning *gola*, they came to see 'true Israel' realized in themselves, but unlike the *gola*, they did not understand themselves as survivors of an already realized judgment of God in history. Rather, they made themselves ready by a right observance of the Torah for the judgment which would bring history to an end. The realized element in their eschatology lay in the very existence of the community as the realization of scriptures now read as law for the last days.

The summons of the Baptist, though tolerating a certain structural comparison with the eschatological self-understanding and purposes of these latter groups, was distinctive in virtue of its simplicity and incisiveness. The Baptist 'assembled' the remnant of Israel only in the sense that he sponsored a public and external rite to seal the decision of repentance and reform. Though the Johannite remnant, like contemporary remnant groups such as the Essenes or the Therapeutae,[18] was thereby 'assembled' in advance of the judgment, unlike them it did not exist as a separate, organized community. In this respect as in others the key to the distinctiveness of John's movement lay in its genuine openness to all Israel.

This introduces the second point differentiating John from contemporary movements. The one condition of acquittal at the impending judgment was repentance. The last hour had come, the blade of the axe was already sunk in the root of the tree. There was no time, no need, no place for long study of the Torah, for priestly robes, for isolation in *élite* groups, for a massively detailed *halaka* to guide the conduct of life. Indeed, there was no point in any of this. God's demand was radical and urgent. He called the whole people to a decisive break with sin. If this was to require less than did the mass of elitist prescriptions cultivated by the Pharisees, the Essenes, and like groups, it was also to require much more. Simple, urgent, incisive, the summons of the Baptist was keyed to evoke a response at a different and deeper level. The result is tangible. Other remnant groups were closed. The Johannite remnant was open.

In the sectarian groups contemporary with John the desire to embody 'true Israel' inspired (probably on the basis of Ex. 19.5f.) the self-imposition of a priestly standard of ritual purity. This separatist stance generated the Pharisees' condemnation of the unobservant and the Essenes' exclusion (from the final battle with the Gentiles) of the lame, the halt, the blind, and the dumb. John's mission was strikingly independent of such exclusivism. His call was addressed to all as a possibility for all. He proposed no special ritual code, no set of separatist rubrics, no distinguishing creed. He had disciples but organized no community. Whereas the self-understanding of the contemporary groups implied great claims, John

insisted on the renunciation of claims. His work was consciously preparatory and provisional.

'Remnant', therefore, was not defined by the limitation of John's mission to a given group. It was defined by the diversity of response (i.e.,
acceptance and rejection) *vis-à-vis* a summons addressed to all Israel. In so
far as John realistically foresaw that his appeal would divide the nation,
his goal was to bring into being 'the remnant of Israel'. In so far as this
remnant was the destined object of salvation, his goal was to make Israel
ready for its messianic restoration. Though John's controlling vision of
things was finally apocalyptic, both these facets of his purpose prolonged
the classic tradition of prophecy in Israel.

The third point: Our conclusion on the aims of John does not mean that
his summons necessarily presupposed previous rupture and collapse of the
covenantal relationship of God and Israel. In the face of judgment all
claims to salvation on the basis of racial solidarity with Abraham were
unavailing. This is the force of what we have called John's 'stinging word'
(Luke 3.8; Matt. 3.9). 'We have Abraham for our father' implied that
descent from Abraham was a guarantee of salvation. If the retort 'God can
raise up sons to Abraham out of these stones' meant that for John sonship
to Abraham was a matter of no consequence, then we are no doubt confronted with the motif of covenant-rupture. But more probably the sense
of the retort was: 'Sonship to Abraham is not physical descent!' On this
hypothesis the Baptist did not void 'sonship to Abraham' of its positive
thrust; rather, he affirmed the positive thrust[19] but, taking a stance in
radical continuity with themes of classical prophecy, he repudiated the
superficial reduction of sonship to mere racial solidarity. Those destined
for salvation were indeed sons to Abraham, and the baptism of John
related positively to the covenant, bringing it eschatological affirmation
and fulfilment.

The fourth point is the total implausibility of the assumption that John
might have conceived salvation in other than collective and ecclesial
terms. There is, of course, room in biblical and Judaic soteriology for the
important question of the individual, but the form of the question is
distinctive. It asks whether or not the individual belongs to the people to
be saved. In the traditional biblical conception, 'the saved' (survivors of
judgment whether past or future) are the reconstituted ecclesial entity,
Israel (cf. e.g. Isa. 4.2; Micah. 4.6f.). On this the biblical testimonies are
impressively at one.[20]

Lastly, the validity of our position on John's aims is not conditioned by
the antecedent need to answer all questions relative to his eschatological
vision and specifically to his baptismal rite. To suppose the contrary is to
forget that the conditions of the truth of any proposition are limited and
that the first step whether in the elaboration or testing of a hypothesis is

the selective determination of these conditions. The task, that is, is to find out what questions must be put and what answers verified to settle some prospective matter of fact. Related questions and answers may well have independent value; but, while potentially testing the hypothesis, they may also receive illumination from it.

2. JESUS AND THE BAPTIST

Among those from whom John's summons to baptism elicited a positive response was Jesus of Nazareth. But the baptism of Jesus,[21] unlike that of the many others who answered John's call, marked the beginning of a public religious career.

Jesus as baptizer

The synoptic gospels date the start of Jesus' public career from the arrest of John (Mark 1.14; Matt. 4.12; less clearly, Luke 3.19), leaving unexplained why Jesus had remained in Judaea until John's arrest (Mark 1.14; Matt. 4.12) and why the arrest should have had particular and decisive significance for him.[22] The lacuna is filled by data given in the Fourth Gospel: Jesus' public career had two phases, of which that opened by John's arrest and Jesus' return to Galilee (and recounted by the synoptists) was the second. Before the arrest he had already gathered followers about himself and with them worked as baptizer in alliance with (though apparently not alongside [John 3.26b]) John.[23]

In the context of our inquiry into the aims of Jesus these data immediately invite two questions. How, concretely, did Jesus' career as baptizer correlate with the career of John? And what in Jesus' career as baptizer correlated with his own later career?

The fact that Jesus could actively associate himself as he did with the Baptist's movement suggests that 'the baptism of John' (Mark 11.30 parr.; Luke 7.29; Acts 1.22; 18.25; 19.3f.; cf. 10.37; 13.24) be understood as 'the rite which John sponsored and whose sense and purpose he defined' but not as 'the rite which John had personally and physically to administer'.[24] Like John, Jesus preached repentance and baptism in the face of imminent judgment and stood as witness to the conversion of the repentant and its ritual sealing in water. We know of nothing distinctively his own in Jesus' participation in the call to baptism; only that it was effective. Some of John's disciples complained to their master that 'here he is, baptizing, and all are going to him' (John 3.26c.).

That Jesus not only responded positively to the Baptist's call to the nation but actively shared in it as an ally already stamps his horizons as eschatological and 'preparationist'. Moreover, intimate association with the Baptist's movement argues participation in his aim: the reconstitution of Israel in view of the eschaton. It was an aim that involved Jesus in the dangerous business of calling the powerful and the righteous to repentance. From the start, then, a seed of conflict was sown between him and the religious *élite* of Israel as between the same *élite* and John (Matt. 11.18f par.; Mark 11.29–34 parr.). These would seem the most significant of the correlations between Jesus' ministry as baptizer and his post-Johannite ministry. To them we should add a final remark on the repentance attested as a demand both of John and Jesus.

Repentance was not an arbitrary requirement, not a ticket to be turned in for admission to salvation. Rather, it intrinsically conditioned salvation by generating a new recognition of one's sins and sinfulness (Matt. 3.7b–8 par.;[25] Mark 1.5; Matt. 3.6; Matt. 3.11d par.[26]) and a new recognition of one's neighbour (see especially Luke 3.11–14). Radical repentance – the renunciation of claims and the opening of the heart to others – remains among the most compelling facets of the Baptist's religious stance. Jesus refined and extended it. To the representatives of Torah piety, repentance was supremely difficult for professional sinners such as publicans.[27] John's ministry showed the opposite (Luke 3.12–14; 7.29; Matt. 21.32). Repentance in the Baptist's sense, with its renunciation of all claims on God, proved supremely difficult to the professionally holy (Mark 11.29–33 parr.; Matt. 11.18f. par.; 21.32).

Is there still more which the opening phase of Jesus' career can tell us of his 'aims'?

As the Baptist's career evidences a prophetic self-understanding (see John 1.23; Mark 1.2 parr.; cf. Luke 3.15), so do the beginnings of the career of Jesus. Both his embarking on a ministry within the cadre of the Baptist's call to Israel and, even more, his withdrawal to Galilee on the signal of the Baptist's arrest[28] only to inaugurate a new proclamation and ministry of his own, point to an eschatological and prophetic self-understanding. Texts such as the baptism (Mark 1.9–11 par.; Luke 3.21f.) and temptation (Mark 1.12f.; Matt. 4.1–11 par.) narratives are designed to meet the questions which naturally arise from the fact of such activities: 'Who is this Jesus and what is he about?' Both the baptism and the temptation narratives depict him as Spirit-filled Servant of God and obedient Messiah, leaving open the specific contours of his vocation and destiny.

But these texts, it would seem, could give us data *immediately* relevant to our question on the aims of Jesus only if, biographical in intention, they ultimately derived from his personal testimony. This condition is not *a priori* impossible; but since the main thrust of the texts is situated on another plane, it is not easy to vindicate a genuinely biographical dimension.[29] We will therefore deal with the texts later, in terms of the community's interpretation of Jesus.[30]

Words of Jesus on the Baptist[31]

The work of the Baptist in the Christian view (Mark 1.3 parr.) as, no doubt, in his own self-understanding (John 1.23),[32] was to cry out in the wilderness to Israel to prepare the Lord's 'way' (Isa. 40.3; Mal. 3.1). More, 'John brought[33] you the way of righteousness' (Matt. 21.32), i.e., the way of repentance and baptism in view of the eschaton. A logion originally isolated in the gospel tradition,[34] this succinctly stated Jesus' understanding of the Baptist's career as the divinely commissioned role of revealing God's will for his people in the last days.

For our purposes this theme is among the most significant in Jesus' teaching, for his testimony to the Baptist cannot but throw a powerful if indirect light on his own self-understanding and intentions. This testimony was not wholly public. One element of it was esoteric, i.e., reserved, as apocalyptic secret, for his disciples. We will begin with public testimony and, first of all, that addressed to critics as self-defence and counter-attack.

> To what shall I compare this generation?
> It is like children sitting in the market place
> and calling to their playmates
>   'We piped to you and you did not dance,
>   we wailed and you mourned not.'
> For John came[35] neither eating nor drinking
> and they say, 'He is mad.'
> Then along comes one[36] who eats and drinks
> and they say, 'Behold, a glutton and drunkard,
> a friend of tax-collectors and sinners'.
> (Matt. 11.16 –19b; cf. par. Luke 7.31–34)[37]

The image is one of pouting children who, unwilling to join in with their playmates, sit on the sidelines grumbling that the others do not follow their whims. So 'this generation' piped and John did not dance; it wailed and Jesus did not mourn. Both violated the sanctity of custom: to feast and to fast in accord with specified tradition. But John's whole life-style was a break with this world of customary practices, and so was that of Jesus (Mark 2.19 parr.).[38] John and Jesus alike were signs of the eschatological break in the times. Though the signs were different – it is interesting that Jesus should indicate how fully conscious he was of the sharp difference between John's life-style and his own – they were signs pointing to one and the same thing: the coming of the consummation of history. The two were allied in common repudiation by a generation of sour critics satisfied to be installed in the assurances of holy routine.

Jesus' royal entry into Jerusalem for the pasch at which he would die, his cleansing of the temple, and the question about his authority to do these things, originally formed a single literary unit.[39] Its third and last element consisted in speech and counter-speech: his critics' demand for credentials ('By what authority are you doing these things, or who gave you this authority to do them?') and Jesus' response, posing a dilemma which reduced them to silence:

> I will ask you a question. Answer me and I will tell you by what authority I do these things. Was the baptism of John from heaven or from men? (Mark 11.29f. parr.).

The answer finally given was 'We do not know' (Mark 11.33 parr.).

Jesus' question may have been designed simply to stymie his critics. If so, it is still significant as incidentally implying that, for his part, Jesus considered John's baptism to be 'from heaven'. But there may be more here, namely, a veiled answer to the question posed by his critics. They asked by what authority he did these things ('these things': the royal entry into city and temple and the cleansing of the temple). Jesus' counter-question also turned on the authority theme, viz., that which authorized John's baptism. The element of 'veiled answer' lies in the implication: If John's baptism was 'from heaven', so is my doing 'these things'. The middle term in this logic remains to be specified. Why should the divine authority of Jesus to do 'these things' follow logically from recognition of the divine authority of John's baptism? The answer must be: Because the symbolic acts of both men converged perfectly on one and the same goal: the eschatological restoration of Israel.

Another tantalizing testimony is that which Jesus addressed to a general audience with the intent of defining for them, albeit cryptically, the sense of the Baptist's mission:

> What did you go out to the wilderness to see?
> A reed being shaken by the wind?
> Then, what did you go out to see?
> A man clothed in soft raiment?
> Behold, men wearing soft raiment are in the houses of kings.
> Why, then, did you go out? To see a prophet?
> Yes, I tell you, and more than a prophet!
> This is he of whom it is written:
>   'Behold, I send my messenger before your face
>   who shall prepare your way before you'.
> (Matt. 11.7–10; cf. par. Luke 7.24–27).

The main thrust here is the interpretation of the Baptist's career as a fulfilment event. God's messenger before the outbreak of judgment, John begins the fulfilment of eschatological prophecy. But the tantalizing element in this testimony is the mysterious identification of John as Elijah. 'If you are willing to accept it', says Jesus, 'he is Elijah who is to come' (Matt. 11.14); but that this disclosure was itself filled with hidden meaning is indicated by the formula which immediately followed: 'He who has ears to hear, let him hear' (Matt. 11.15).

Eschatological speculation formed the background of this designation of the Baptist. The prophet called Malachi, seizing on the Deutero-Isaian motif of 'preparation for the Day' implicit in the text 'In the wilderness clear the way of Yahweh!' (Isa. 40.3), specified this preparation as the task of Elijah returned to earth:

> Behold, I will send you Elijah the prophet
> before the coming of the great and terrible day of Yahweh;
> and he shall turn the hearts of fathers to their sons
> and the hearts of sons to their fathers
> lest I come and smite the land with a curse (Mal. 3.23f.; EVV 4.5f.).

The preparation consisted in purifying the priesthood (Mal. 3.1–3) and in putting an end to familial wrangling and strife in the face of judgment (Mal. 3.24). Ben Sira (48.10) adds that Elijah stood in readiness for the chosen time when he would not only 'appease the wrath before it breaks out' but also 're-establish the tribes of Jacob' (so fulfilling the mission of the Servant of the Lord, Isa. 49.6). Here, returning Elijah is the key figure of the end-time. In the Pseudepigrapha, on the other hand, the importance of Elijah has receded, and by the time of Jesus his eschatological role was variously conceived. But Elijah was thought of mainly, perhaps, as the 'forerunner' of the Messiah.[40] In the gospels the hidden sense of the identification of John as Elijah is its messianic reference: If the Baptist was Elijah, how imminent must the epiphany of the Messiah be!

Another and deeper meaning of the identification is disengaged and highlighted in an esoteric teaching (Mark 9.11–13 par. Matt 17.10–13) which typically remained charged with enigma.

> 'Why [asked the inner circle of Jesus' disciples[41]] do the scribes say: "First, Elijah must come"?' and he said to them, 'Elijah does indeed come first to restore all things. And how is it written of the Son of Man that he should suffer much and be despised? But I tell you Elijah has come, and they did to him whatever they pleased, as it is written of him' (Mark 9.11–13).

The text seems to have taken shape as a variation on a basic theme in the polemic between orthodox Jews and Jewish Christians. The basic theme: Jesus could not have been the Messiah, for Elijah has not come. Answer: Elijah *has* come – in the person of John. The variation on this theme: Jesus could not have been the Messiah, for Elijah's mission excludes a suffering Messiah. The answer to this objection rests on two presuppositions; namely, that no prophecy is to be fulfilled in a way which would exclude fulfilment of another prophecy, and that we have to do here with two sets of prophecies: Elijah is to come before the Messiah to reconcile (Mal. 3) and restore (Ben Sira 48.10) Israel; and the Messiah is to suffer much and be 'despised'.[42] On these presuppositions, the answer to the objection consists in interpreting the Baptist's historic destiny as the fulfilment of Elijah's mission. This not only denies that Elijah's mission rules out a suffering Messiah; it also presents John's (= Elijah's) martyrdom as a prophetically attested paradigm for the Messiah.

In the Markan text the disciples do not so much pose their own question as cite a scribal view of messianic eschatology according to which Elijah's mission of restoration would preclude any intelligible context for a suffering Messiah. Jesus' answer first brings out the point of the objection: 'Elijah does indeed come first to restore all things; [but, if so] how is it written of the Son of man that he should suffer much and be despised?' He then gives the solution: John fulfilled the Elijah role and it included his death!

Elijah, then, is (so to speak) demythologized. His return is not a literal reincarnation but a role in the eschatological scenario, and his mission of restoration is concretely accomplished by John's preaching and baptizing – not a restoration necessarily precluding a suffering Messiah. The last aspect of Jesus' answer – the affirmation that John's death was itself comprehended in the Elijah role – underlines this, alluding to the tradition that Elijah was destined for martyrdom.[43] Indeed, it would hardly be possible to align Jesus more closely and rigorously with John that does this early Christian reflection, or to imagine a level of alignment more profound.

There can be no reasonable doubt about the decisive significance of the Baptist in the scheme of the eschaton as Jesus understood it. 'The baptism of John' (Mark 11.30 parr.) was heaven-sent; 'the days of John' (Matt. 11.12) epitomized the inauguration of eschatological fulfilment. But 'the days of John' were no more than an inauguration. The *consummation* would transform the world. This may well be the sense of Jesus' eschatological riddle:

> No one greater has arisen among men than John
> and the least in the reign of God is greater than he
> (cf. Matt. 11.11; Luke 7.28).

Conclusion

To recover the meaning of the Baptist's mission is to win an insight into the perspectives of Jesus, for Jesus' response to the Baptist was unequivocally positive. Epitomized as 'a voice crying in the wilderness' to prepare for God's final visitation, the Baptist was first of all the bearer of an urgent warning. But this warning, and the confession, conversion, and washing to which it summoned its hearers, evoked a scheme of eschatological hope. Accents of warning and images of judgment (the felling of the tree, the winnowing of the chaff) yielded ultimately to promise-motifs and images of hope: the apocalyptic purification in holy Spirit and fire, the gathering of the wheat into the barn. The mission of the Baptist belonged to a scenario of fulfilment. His role was to assemble by baptism the remnant of Israel destined for cleansing and acquittal and so, climactically, for restoration.

The first observable act of Jesus' own career was to enter unreservedly into this scheme of prophetic meaning, sharing not only in the response to the Baptist's call but in the call itself. The legacy of Jesus' words on the Baptist supports this inference. He clearly affirmed the divine authenticity of the Baptist's mission. More: In particulars of the Baptist's career he read divine signs bearing on himself. He significantly aligned himself in the closest possible way with the trajectory of the Baptist's mission. The fact that Jesus was explicitly conscious of how sharply he differed from the Baptist in style of career gives particularly incisive definition to his alliance with the Baptist's purposes. There remains more to be said both about the distinctiveness of Jesus *vis-à-vis* John and about his words on John's mission. But without going further than we have already gone we are ready to offer the first formulation of a hypothesis on Jesus' own aims, i.e., on how he conceived his life's role. Like the Baptist, he understood his own role in terms of the age-old scriptural promise of the restoration of Israel; and, like the Baptist, he understood this restoration not as a divine act exclusively reserved for post-historical realization (located, that is, on the far side of a still future judgment) but as called for now and already begun! Its beginning was effected by 'the baptism of John'. As an ally of John, Jesus had already plunged into the prophetic and eschatological task he took to be his destiny.

VII

PUBLIC PROCLAMATION AND CAREER

1. PUBLIC PROCLAMATION AND TEACHING

Of the most fundamental importance, whether from the standpoint of exegesis or from that of historical reconstruction, is the distinction between gospel texts presenting Jesus' proclamation, teaching, and actions before the public and those, on the other hand, that present acts and words reserved exclusively to his disciples. Our inquiry into the aims of Jesus will centre in this chapter on 'public' traditions.

The reign of God

Why did Jesus cease to baptize after the arrest of John? No detailed and fully adequate answer lies ready to hand. But from the high probability that he did in fact put an end to his baptismal ministry at this point, it must be inferred that he saw the arrest of John as closing an initial, limited, distinct phase in the scheme of divinely willed fulfilment events. From this inference another follows: Jesus understood his own new career of proclamation, teaching, and healing as constituting another distinct phase in the eschatological scenario.

The transition from 'the days of John the Baptist' (Matt. 11.12a) to Jesus' independent career was signalled by the priority of 'the reign of God' over 'the wrath about to come'. 'The reign of God', *malkûtā' dē'lāhā'*,[1] was the distinctive term, in Jesus' proclamation, for God's final and climactic saving act. It is clear that John and Jesus alike understood the end of history in terms of both judgment and salvation. Nevertheless, John's proclamation and Jesus' post-Johannite proclamation differed in accent.[2] The call to baptism bore immediately on the judgment of Israel; the proclamation of God's reign bore immediately on the restoration of Israel and the concomitant salvation of the nations. The key to the difference is the motif 'free gift', with which Jesus charged the expression 'the reign of God'. This is why his proclamation came eventually to be known as 'gospel' or 'news of salvation'.[3]

Nowhere is the gospel-character of the proclamation more evident than in his macarisms:

> Happy the poor,[4] for the reign of God is for them!
> Happy those in mourning, for there is One[5] about to[6]
> comfort them!
> Happy the hungry,[7] for there is One about to give them
> their fill!

The apocalyptic macarism, as Jesus himself pronounced it, exclaimed at the eschatological blessings God had promised and was about to shower on the afflicted. How was it that blessings were about to come on the poor, the mourners, and the hungry? Because they were good? No. For Jesus the reason was: because God was good.[8]

Those Jesus designated as beneficiaries of the eschatological blessings were the literally poor, the literally mourning, the literally hungry – unlikely candidates for macarism. The macarisms were therefore deliberately startling. Their rhetorical structure consisted, first, in the setting up of a paradox (Happy the *poor*? the *mourners*? the *hungry*?), then in the resolving of it by showing the afflicted as *those whom God had chosen* as beneficiaries of his saving intervention. Happy the poor, the mourners, the hungry, for their time has come! The hour of great reversals has broken out! The theological savants of Israel, who 'bore the key of knowledge' (Luke 11.52), had in Jesus' view blocked the way to the reign of God rather than opened it (Matt. 23.12).[9] He himself did just the opposite, opening the way wide first and foremost to the mass of the afflicted: 'Happy the poor, for the reign of God is (above all[10]) for them!'

The theme 'salvation as pure gift' runs through the whole of Jesus' public proclamation. Its primacy is established by nothing so much as by his style of action, particularly his initiative toward and table fellowship with the irreligious.[11] Jesus repeatedly defended this style of action (which jarred and galled the contemporary religious *élite*) as climactically expressive of God's own goodness. In this, a decisive break with the tradition of Torah piety,[12] he was unique and it was especially this aspect of his historic uniqueness which defined his career as 'good tidings' precisely 'for the poor' or 'afflicted' (Isa. 61.1).[13]

For Jesus 'the reign of God' was the triumphant consummation of God's lordship over man and events. What does this mean? First, in his usage the term was invariably eschatological; second, he conceived the eschatology (in accord with biblical tradition in general) as climactic, i.e., standing implicitly in a positive relation to God's lordship over history; third, he conceived it (in accord with Judaic apocalyptic) as definitive, i.e., as signifying the end of time and the inauguration of the age to come.

Dalman long ago established that the Aramaic substratum of '*ē basileia* on the lips of Jesus was *malkûtā*' ('the reign').[14] The verbs Jesus used in conjunction with '*ē basileia/malkûtā*' show that he understood God's reign as an approaching 'order of things' to which men could be admitted and from which they might be excluded.[15] More recently, Jeremias's comparative study of late Judaic usage[16] has shown, first, that there is a profusion of coinages among the reign-of-God sayings which derive from Jesus himself. What do they say? First, they say 'free gift'. The reign of God is not achieved or developed or controlled or disposed of by men. It 'is near', 'comes', 'appears'; it 'overtakes' or 'comes upon' one; one may be 'in' it or 'not far from' it; one 'expects' or 'looks for' it and lives to 'see' it; one is 'called' or 'invited' to it, 'attains' or 'enters into' it or is 'cast out of' it; one 'seeks after' it and is or is not 'fitted' for it. God 'gives' it, man 'accepts' or 'takes' or 'inherits' (i.e., enters into specifically gratuitous possession of) it. Second, the new language coined by Jesus for the eschaton reveals a distinctively profiled consciousness that God's final saving act was already operative in Israel: Now is the new creation, time of the new wine and the new cloak (Mark 2.21f. parr.)![17] The fields are 'white' (John 4.35), the harvest 'great' (Matt. 9.37 par.)! Now is the wedding, the espousals of Israel! 'Can the wedding guests mourn?' (Mark 2.20 parr.). The young man dead through sin 'is alive again' (Luke 15.24, 32), so it is right to be glad.

> Blind men see,
> cripples walk,
> lepers are cleansed,
> deaf men hear,
> dead men are raised,
> good news is broken to the poor! (Matt. 11.5f. par.).

'The reign of God', in a word, 'has [already] come upon you!' (Matt. 12.28 par.).

It is hardly possible to exaggerate the explosive power which this combination of 'gratuity' and 'present realization' gave to Jesus' proclamation. The power is attested by the diversity and vehemence of the responses it evoked. As Jesus' macarisms show, the heirs of the reign of God were not 'the good' but 'the miserable'. Now, the miserable as such are not irreligious, but this hardly alleviates the scandal of the macarisms.[18] The point is that the heirs of the reign of God were the poor without qualification – not the deserving poor. They deserved nothing, yet salvation was theirs. Their virtue was merely to reveal God's goodness. They thus showed how it was that in Jesus God could offer salvation not only to the non-observant 'people of the land' ('*ammê hā'āreṣ*) but to the biblical 'sinners' (*rᵉšā'îm*). The coming of the *eschaton* did not validate, rather it reversed, the exclusion of the sinners from Israel![19]

The biblical theme of gratuity is as old as the promise to Abraham; yet in the light of biblical and post-biblical history the human animal would appear to be somehow incapable of keeping this heritage intact. How truly baffling: that God should be no less Saviour than Judge, that allegiance to him should be no less his gift than one's own decision and effort, that the decision and the effort should be part and parcel of the gift . . . . In rabbinic debate on the necessity of repentance for messianic redemption, repentance was considered indispensable, but the question how it related to redemption remained undifferentiated and so unanswered.[20] In Jesus' proclamation gratuity defined repentance. The reign of God was a gift; the core of repentance was acceptance of it *as* a gift. To repent, then, was to become a child. Repentance did not prompt God's mercy but attested it. It was joy and thanks as well as tears, remorse, resolution. It did not bring the reign of God near. Rather, the drawing near of the reign of God was the presupposition of the repentance for which Jesus appealed. As there could be no accepting without God's giving, so there could be no giving without the positive act of accepting. Salvation would not be a spectacular miracle nor Israel its inert, automatic, passive beneficiary. But if salvation had to be accepted as a gift, its acceptance meant nothing less than *the renunciation of all claims*. Such was the radical poverty of spirit that at once defined repentance and crossed the grain of Torah piety. To the *élite* of Israel (as we have already recalled) repentance was hard for the sinner and the publican. But the religious career of Jesus was peculiarly marked by and memorable for his acceptance of publicans and sinners. Repentance was hard for the pious, the upright, the holy.

The gratuity theme did not, then, preclude the traditional prophetic appeal for repentance and conversion. But it did situate the appeal differently and give it a new tonality. Because salvation was entirely free, repentance, rather than being a requisite condition of the gift of God,[21] became at once the acceptance of it *as* a gift and an expression of thanksgiving *for* the gift (e.g. Luke 19.1–18; cf. 7.41–47). The result was a phenomenon new in the history of religions, which has left its distinctive echo in the gospel literature: 'the joy of repentance'.[22] The reign of God was a wholly gratuitous blessing, a blessing bestowed in some sense even now; repentance arose as a joyous response to its coming.

'Gratuity' and 'present realization' – the electrifying immediacy of 'free' and 'now' – are probably the most distinctive accents in Jesus' message. Often overlooked, however, is another, equally fundamental, facet of the proclamation, undistinctive in itself (for it stands in conspicuous continuity with biblical and Judaic eschatology) but charged with consequence for the understanding of Jesus' career; namely, the tie between the reign of God and the restoration of Israel.

Why, indeed, should the reign of God have been the object of a proclamation to Israel as such unless it bore on the destiny of Israel as such? At this point, moreover, history supports and illuminates logical inference. The tie between the proclamation of God's reign and the salvation of Israel belonged to the history of biblical eschatology. In Deutero-Isaiah the old cultic cry 'Yahweh reigns!' became a proclamation of Israel's imminent redemption. More, the act of proclaiming was conceived as performing what it proclaimed: the ushering in of the new age.

> Salvation comes with the word of proclamation. By the fact that he [the herald (*mᵉbaśśēr*) of Deutero-Isaiah] declares the restoration of Israel, the new creation of the world, the inauguration of the eschatological age, he brings them to pass .... The watchers on the walls hear the word and repeat it with rejoicing. It rings through the city and messengers carry it through the land: 'Yahweh is king'; 'Behold your God.' A new era begins also for the nations. For Yahweh is a God of the Gentiles as well as Israel.[23]

The Psalms of Solomon (11.2) likewise correlate the proclamation of the herald (*euaggelizomenos*) with the salvation of the nation (*eleēsen 'o theos Israēl*). The Midrash on Ps.147.1 reads:

> When the Holy One, blessed be He, will be King, they will all be messengers bearing good news, as it is said, He who declares good things causes peace to be heard ... The Holy One, blessed be He, is King; it is fitting to praise him. Why? Because they are for the dominion (*malkût* [*basileia*]) of the Holy One, blessed be He.[24]

Three motifs from Isa.52.7–9, namely, the herald of salvation (*mᵉbaśśēr; euaggelizomenos*), the reign of God (*mālak 'ĕlōhāyik; basileusei sou 'o theos*), and the restoration of Israel (*niham YHWH 'ammô, gā'al yᵉrûśālāyim; eleēsen kyrios [Sion] kai errysato Ierousalēm*) make up a thematic constellation variously in evidence from the time of the exile on. In one of Qumran's most intriguing texts, 11QMelch, the herald (*mᵉbaśśēr*) of Isa. 52.7 is described as a messianic figure: one anointed with the Spirit (*whmbśr hw['h m]śwḥ hrw[ḥ]*, line 18).[25] It is significant that long before the rabbinic attestation of this identification,[26] Qumran had attested the motif of messianic herald. The motif had accordingly been established in advance of Matthew's definition (4.23; 9.35; cf. 11.5) of Jesus' messianic programme as consisting in proclaiming (*kēryssein*), teaching (*didaskein*), and healing (*therapeuein*). These data collectively indicate a context in which dissociation of 'the reign of God' and its proclamation from 'the restoration of Israel' is *a priori* implausible.

Scholarship ought never to have lost sight of this basic correlation. In the biblical perspective salvation was always and everywhere understood as destined precisely for Israel. 'Salvation' and 'Israel' were utterly inseparable. There was never a Saviour apart from a saved Israel, nor would there be a Messiah apart from messianic Israel. From end to end the Hebrew scriptures (as well as the non-canonical literature of Judaism) understood salvation in terms of: 'all Israel' (*kol-yiśrā'ēl*) or 'the people of Israel' (*'am yiśrā'ēl*), the assembly (*qāhāl*), the congregation (*'ēdâ*), and the like; Israel, in short, understood salvation in ecclesial terms. Where the salvation of the nations was promised or announced, this was conceived as an assimilation to saved Israel.

Exactly this frame of reference was operative throughout the gospel tradition. 'The reign of God' signified the salvation that God intended in the first instance for Israel (cf. 'the sons of the reign', Matt. 8.12). It was accordingly understood that the reign of God signified the *kairos* of eschatological fulfilment, the moment at which God would fulfil his age-old and often iterated promises to his people. 'Eschaton', therefore, inevitably evoked images filled with 'Israel': the banquet with Abraham, Isaac, and Jacob (Matt. 8.11b; Luke 13.28b; cf. Apoc. Elij. 3.67), the twelve tribes gathered anew (Matt. 19.28; Luke 22.30),[27] the temple Jesus would build in three days (Mark. 14.58 par.; 15.29 par.; John 2.19).

Particulars of Jesus' proclamation variously thematize the linkage between reign and restoration. First of all, the liturgical and scriptural resonances of the very phrase 'the reign of God' say 'the restoration of Israel'. The parallelism between the opening petitions of the Our Father,

> 'Let your name be hallowed!
> Let your reign come!' (Matt. 6.9; 10a; Luke 11.2),

and the Synagogue's *Qaddiš* or 'Holy Prayer',

> 'Let his great name be glorified and hallowed. . . .
> And may he let his reign reign . . . in the lifetime of
> the whole house of Israel speedily and soon',

indicates that the 'your reign' (*'ē basileia sou: malkûtak*) of the Our Father has its roots, like the 'his reign' (*malkûteh*) of the *Qaddiš*, in traditions and texts which themselves reflect the coincidence of God's eschatological reign with Israel's eschatological restoration (Isa. 24.23; 33.22; 52.7–10; Zeph. 3.14–20 [cf. Nahum 2.1, EVV 1.15; and Isa. 61.1–4]; Dan. 7.14; cf. Ps. Sol. 17.3). Clearly, this reading of the Our Father's 'your reign' cannot but illuminate Jesus' public proclamation of 'the reign of God'. As the final saving act of God, his 'reign' did indeed signify the consummation of human history; but at the centre of this consummation stood, as in Torah and prophets, the prime beneficiary of God's saving act: his people, Israel.

The decisive reason why this dimension of Jesus' proclamation has so often been overlooked is probably to be found not among the literary and historical data but simply in the climate of research, a carry-over from the last century.[28] On the side of the data, to be sure, there remains an ambiguity calling for resolution. The social entity 'Israel' rests on mixed foundations, ethnic and religious. In the post-exilic period these factors were more than once locked in subsurface competition for primacy in defining Israel's identity. Some years ago K. G. Kuhn urged an individualistic interpretation of the 'religious' factor. The prophets and rabbis, he argued, acknowledged a point at which 'man stands before God as an individual who must make his own decision, i.e., simply as man and not as the member of a particular people'.[29] According to Kuhn there consequently arose two eschatological 'concepts': that of the Messiah, which developed from a nationalist, secular matrix and looked to the end of 'the present age', and that of 'the reign of heaven', a purely eschatological theme which looked to a consummation beyond history. Here 'the purely religious concept of the *eschaton* achieves its full stature (God as All in All), so that there is no more place for the special thought of a national link with Israel.'[30] To be sure, it ought to be noted that Kuhn's view bears in the first instance on the content of a concept ('the reign of heaven') rather than on concrete literary usages. But even within these limits his case is doubtful. Whether in prophetic or apocalyptic or liturgical or halakic texts, whether with reference to this age or the age to come, the reign of God was bound up (as in the gospels) with images and themes of Israel. Finally, it would be difficult to adduce a single text to exemplify a religious self-understanding which positively abstracted from 'membership' in God's people. On the contrary, where the religious factor was most potent (i.e., where it most strenuously bid for primacy over the ethnic factor) the tendency was not toward individualism but toward new forms of corporate religious life.[31]

In summary: The epitome and the key to Jesus' post-Johannite public career was his proclamation of the reign of God. Salvation was dawning; it was free, a blessing for Israel and the nations, a renewal of the world. The very act of proclaiming initiated what was being proclaimed. As the proclamation was addressed to Israel as such, it summoned a national response. As it was addressed to the afflicted as the type of Israel-to-be-saved, it invited every hearer to accept salvation in simplicity, with thanks, like a child.

No account of the aims of Jesus could claim plausibility if it failed to accord with the central theme of his proclamation and teaching, the reign of God. The data thus far reviewed ground certain exclusions and certain expectations with respect to Jesus and his aims. It is excluded that he conceived his work in other than religious terms. It is further excluded that he conceived his work as a morally free option, a career he might take up or not, as he wished. These exclusions can be reformulated as a positive expectation and further specified: In view of his proclamation of the reign of God – an act prepared by a baptismal ministry and like that ministry pervaded with eschatological claims – Jesus must have conceived goals bearing on the life of Israel as such; and he must have conceived them as belonging to a divine scheme of fulfilment events. In a word, he must have conceived his work as *an eschatological vocation.*

Jesus' proclamation of the reign of God positively leads us to expect that his understanding of God and God's will, of Israel and Israel's destiny, constituted the vital context of his personal aims. For him as for the whole of Judaic tradition, God's will and Israel's destiny were one and the same and 'the reign of God' had immediate reference to it: At Yahweh's reign, no doubt, the ends of the earth would see salvation (Isa. 52.10) and Gentiles would sing the Lord a new song of praise (Isa. 42.10); but where and for whom, above all, would Yahweh reign? On the holy mountain and for Jerusalem (Isa. 24.23)! His reign would be his return to Zion (Isa. 52.3)!

The reign of God is a personal act, a decision to be given effect at the time of God's choosing. This personal and immediate reference to God repeatedly vitalized Jesus' phrase 'the reign of God', so making every exegetical inroad into it fruitful for inquiries such as the present one. To advance our effort to recover Jesus' distinctive world of meaning, we will offer a final observation on the immediate reference to God himself concealed and revealed by Jesus' reign-of-God idiom.

The phrase, of itself quite intelligible though hardly commonplace in the religious language of first-century Palestine, was subtly and richly laden with mystery by Jesus' use of it. Here we take as our point of departure related observations by Dalman and Jeremias on the periphrastic function of the phrase. Dalman pointed out that in the targumic literature 'the reign of God' appears as a reverential circumlocution for 'God' (as ruler).[32] Jeremias rightly finds this phenomenon in Jesus' idiom, as well, so that the words 'the reign of God is near!' virtually mean 'God is near' – at the door, or already here![33] The observation is not meant to muffle the resonances accruing to 'the reign of God' from the scriptures (cf. e.g. Ex. 15.11–21, esp. v. 18; Num. 23.21; 24.7; Nahum 2.1, EVV 1.15; Pss. 47; 93; 96–99, etc.) or from the new linguistic uses to which Jesus put the phrase. It is meant rather to affirm that 'the reign of God' was both intended and understood to have immediate reference to God's own saving act. Now what does this mean? It means that this pithy phrase, which might easily be mistaken for a trite technical formula in Jesus' usage, was inevitably charged with his own religious intentionality: his existential understanding of God (i.e., of how he himself related to God) and his understanding of God's will for the world and activity in it at this moment. Thus, in his macarisms Jesus at once exemplifies the periphrastic function of the phrase ('the reign of God' reserved for the poor stands in perfect parallelism with 'the One' about to comfort the mourning and 'the One' about to give the hungry their fill) and expresses – not thematically but performatively, by the very act of speaking the macarisms – a sovereign prophetic claim to insight into God's good pleasure at the present moment, his will to lavish the blessings of the eschaton on the poor, the mourners, the hungry. 'The reign of God' signifies 'God' and signifies God precisely as Jesus knows him. This is what loads the phrase with meaning and calls for it to be unpacked.

The point of unpacking it is to arrive at the point of the proclamation. Why did Jesus proclaim the reign of God, if not to summon 'the sons of the reign' (Matt. 8.12) to their heritage? The point was salvation. The goal was the banquet with God, epilogue to the long drama of sin and grace recorded and illuminated by the scriptures. This, to be sure, would be the banquet of mankind (Matt. 8.11); hence the imagery of universal renewal which periodically glinted in Jesus' language (e.g. Mark 2.21f. parr.). But two conditions were always understood. The post-historical restoration of mankind would hinge on the historically rooted restoration of Israel. And Israel's restoration would not be realized without a willed act of acceptance.

To have come this far in ascertaining the point of the proclamation is already to have made a decisive inroad into the understanding of Jesus' aims. For, all his words and actions were relative to the reign of God. They were meant to lead men into the proclamation, to unriddle it, to nuance and reinforce it, to dramatize and realize it.

Eschatological Torah

Our purpose now is to consider briefly the teaching of Jesus in the hope that this will provide us with a distinct avenue to knowledge of his purposes, i.e., knowledge of how, concretely, he understood his mission. The inquiry requires that we answer several questions. What, in fact, was the burden of Jesus' teaching? Did it have any centre of gravity and controlling perspective, or was it a somewhat random collection of wise parables and sayings? What were its express and unexpressed presuppositions?

We may begin by emphasizing the observation with which we have just concluded our consideration of the reign of God, an observation of basic heuristic importance: The words and actions of Jesus – the whole of his career, therefore – were consciously and all-pervasively relative to the reign of God and its proclamation. The theme of the proclaimer is God's initiative; the theme of the teacher, man's response. In Jesus proclaimer and teacher were one. Proclamation determined teaching at every point and accounted for all its traits.

Jesus' proclamation of the reign of God meant both salvation (for accepters of it) and ruin (for rejecters of it). His teaching accordingly comprehended antithetical themes: the cost and joy of discipleship (e.g. Matt. 13.44f.) versus the warning and threat of judgment (e.g. Luke 13.6–9); the appeal for confidence in the coming fulfilment (e.g. Mark 4.26–29) versus counter-attack on the critics of indiscriminate goodness to sinners (e.g. Luke 15.11–32).

It nevertheless remains a question whether there was a unique and original perspective in which the particulars of Jesus' teaching were meaningful and coherent and, if so, whether we can recover it. In the Jesus-literature of the past two decades the sources have sometimes been drawn on almost as if they were a thesaurus of ambiguities like the Sibylline Oracles; hence, the jumbled variety of proposals on Jesus' perspective. Yet the way to some security of insight would seem open and clear: observance of the law of parsimony (Remain within the limits of the verifiable) and application of reciprocal controls (Check A against B, B against A) to proclamation and teaching and, within the teaching, to general perspective and particular detail. Taking this way, we shall examine a single teaching of Jesus and use it as the basis for a set of anticipations bearing on his teaching generally. We shall then take up several other particular teachings to see if the anticipations are in fact met. But first of all we shall seek to 'place' the teaching of Jesus, i.e., to set it in its own context.

In general, this context must be the reign of God and its proclamation. To judge from 'the Holy Prayer' (*Qaddiš*)[34] as well as from 'the Prayer' (*Tᵉphilla*),[35] the response evoked in Jewish antiquity by the phrase 'God's reign' was one of longing, for God's reign and his people's restoration could not but be one:

> And may he let his reign [*malkûteh*] reign in your lifetime and in the lifetime of the whole house of Israel speedily and soon. . . . .
>
> > (*Qaddiš*)
>
> Restore our judges as of old
>   and our counsellors as in the beginning,
> remove from us sorrow and sighing
>   and reign over us, O Lord, you alone. . . .
>
> > (*Tᵉphilla*, eleventh benediction).

Had 'his reign' been cheapened in the popular consciousness (as had happened in biblical antiquity to 'the day of Yahweh' and parallel expressions) so as to signify simply the miracle of a happy ending? This may be a more or less common tendency of popular piety (though the *Qaddiš* and the tenth and eleventh benedictions of the *Tᵉphilla* essentially reflect the heritage of exilic and post-exilic biblical eschatology). In Jesus' own usage, in any case, 'the reign of God' was coupled from the start with the call for conversion. We have already observed that the reign-of-God texts in the gospels show that Israel was not to be the 'inert, automatic, passive beneficiary' of eschatological salvation and that Israel's restoration 'would not be realized without a willed act of acceptance'.[36] A disposition conditioning the whole conduct of life – appetite for the will of God – belonged integrally to the act of accepting his reign. Repentance, the acceptance of salvation as a gift, involved an 'ethical' commitment.

But the teaching of Jesus, defining the right response to a divine initiative, was anything but a natural ethic. It did not look to man's nature but to God's will. Nor was it a scribal ethic, i.e., legitimized by exegetical appeal to the Torah. It was, above all, an eschatological ethic, for the divine initiative calling for response was the advent of the eschaton. Finally, there is a question about the eschatology of Jesus which historical analysis of the teaching may help to settle; namely, was this eschatology exclusively futurist, or did Jesus himself understand the proclaimed eschaton to be in some way already in process of realization?

We may start with a single and singularly instructive teaching of Jesus: his prohibition of the dismissal of one's wife. The basic text is Mark 10.2–9; Matt. 19.3–9.[37] Jesus is put to the test on an issue on which he was, perhaps, antecedently suspect: 'Is it permitted a man to dismiss his wife?' (Mark 10.2). He responds with a counter-question: 'What has Moses commanded you?' As expected, the answer is a reference to the relevant Deuteronomic provision (Deut. 24.1ff.). But Jesus at this point takes a stunning tack. Rather than comment on the Deuteronomic text, he flatly declares it irrelevant!

'In view of your hardness of heart he [Moses] wrote that commandment. But from the beginning of creation "he [God] made them male and female". "For this reason a man shall leave father and mother and shall be joined to his wife and the two shall become one". So they are no longer two but one. What therefore God has joined let man not separate!' (Mark 10.5–7; cf. Matt. 19.4–6, 8).

Given the historicity of this prohibition as indicated by a variety of considerations,[38] what was its rationale?

Doubtless, the datum most central to the understanding of the crucial final word ('What therefore God has joined let man not separate!') is the text's eschatological perspective. Drawing on the familiar scheme 'as in the beginning, so in the end', it defines *Paradise* as the beginning and leaves it to be gathered from the present renewal of the original will of God that *now* is the end! Second, Jesus is shown in the act of judging the Torah to be imperfect, defective. The statute on the dismissal of one's wife, promulgated 'in view of your hardness of heart', represents a falling off from the authoritative word of the Creator: 'the two shall become one'. Third, we have here not a teaching which observes or analyses but one which declares a command. Each of these three points invites reflection.

The prophets had long since exploited an imagery typically associated with Paradise to depict the bliss to come.[39] Ezekiel and Deutero-Isaiah had explicitly correlated the expected time of salvation with the Paradise of the first age.[40] The theme found further elaboration in pseudepigraphical texts and rabbinic tradition.[41] At several points the New Testament presents Jesus as the restorer of the paradisal communion with God shattered by the sin of Adam (e.g. Mark 1.13b; cf. Rom. 5.17–19). But the most significant parallel to the present text is Jesus' use of Isaian language – language depicting the time of salvation by means of Paradise images and motifs (Isa. 29.18f.; 35.5f.; 61.1f.) – to designate the present moment as the onset of the eschaton:

> Blind men see,
> cripples walk,
> lepers are cleansed,
> deaf men hear,
> dead men are raised,
> good news is broken to the poor! (Matt. 11.5f.; cf. Luke 7.22).

What is happening in the public career of Jesus? Restoration of the ideal order of things!

The theme of disparity between the present order and the ideal order is not necessarily limited to eschatological horizons. Greeks and Romans acknowledged that slavery, though everywhere legally established, was repugnant to natural law. An accommodation to a defective world, law sanctioned the second-best. David Daube, in a reflective account of the background to Jesus' prohibition of divorce, recalled Plato's expression of this view.[42] But Daube naturally accented the biblical and Judaic antecedents and parallels. In the Old Testament the most striking concession to human weakness and sinfulness was the monarchy, a regimen conceived as detracting from God's rule over his people. It had been sanctioned, so to speak, 'in view of your hardness of heart'. This is in a class with Hillel's *prozbul*[43] and with other applications of the Torah seen by the rabbis themselves as necessary concessions to human frailty. All such acceptance of 'things as they are' is obviously innocent of the eschatological note, for what eschatology affirms is precisely the closing of the gap, the restoration of the ideal. With the advent of the eschaton toleration and 'realism' and the mass of makeshift legal arrangements giving them effect are rendered obsolete. The provisional – and now even the Torah is seen in its provisional aspects – is finished. Such is the thrust of Jesus' word on divorce.

The command character of the word should not be overlooked. It is a prohibition. And it is a prohibition addressed, almost provocatively, to critics whose question had been meant as a trap. If Jesus were to condemn current practice, as he may well have been expected to do, he could be tagged as a rigorist. His stand on divorce was every bit as radical as his questioners had suspected, or else it was even more radical, more objectionable, than anything they had expected. The flat answer seems almost designed to disconcert.[44]

This is no isolated phenomenon in the gospel literature. As T. W. Manson pointed out long ago,[45] Jesus' vocabulary, themes, tone, and point differ in accordance with how his hearers are disposed and related to him. Often the narrative scheme 'public pronouncement/private explanation' emphasizes this: What Jesus says in public puzzles or startles his disciples, who question him in private on his meaning (Mark 4.10ff. par.; 7.17ff. par.; 10.23ff. parr.).[46] What was dark and harsh is now clarified and set in context or complemented by further considerations, but this explanatory follow-up is strictly reserved for disciples. In the present instance, however, the additional instruction (Mark 10.10–12) simply amplifies and emphasizes Jesus' stand on divorce. It does not deal with such issues as 'why?' or 'how?' The upshot is that Jesus' prohibition of divorce might at first sight seem to express no more than a naively utopian religious impulse. Is this the fact of the matter?

Not if the prohibition, far from being a bare, flat insistence on the full rigour of God's will, is conceived as *Torah for a graced and restored Israel*!

Now, this is precisely the case. Restoration of the norm of Paradise does not thematize, but it does suppose, a radical cure for 'your hardness of heart'. The Torah of Moses was defective in so far as it had been accommodated to a defective Israel. But now is the hour of the eschatological espousals (Mark 2.19), the time of the *agatha* or 'good things' (Matt. 7.11; cf. LXX Isa. 52.7) to be lavished on Israel. It is the disciple who discovers this, for his life reveals it. His very life, that is, reveals that discipleship is transforming. It produces good fruit. And *the fruit is good because the tree is good* (Matt. 7.17f. par.)! The disciple is a changed man.

'The reign of God' did indeed signify an order of things destined for man but beyond his reach. That a rich man should enter into it called for the 'impossible' (Mark 10.27 parr.). In full accord with this realism stand the repeated warnings of ultimate division at the judgment to come and the unmistakable tone of urgency in such words as 'Travel by the narrow pass!' (Matt. 7.13[47]). The question 'Who can be saved?' (Mark 10.26 parr.) or 'Are the saved to be few?' (Luke 13.23; cf. Matt. 7.14) is recurrent.

Yet all this represents but one side of the matter. The 'impossible' is evoked only to set in relief the affirmation

For men (it is) impossible
but not for God (Mark 10.27, cf. parr.).

That the saved are *a vast assembly* is assumed (e.g. Mark 4.8 parr.; 4.32 parr.). The disciple is not simply constrained by the uncompromising rigour of his code. Code implies gift and 'joy' attests the gift

(Matt. 13.44–46[48]). The way of celibacy, for example, is 'given' (Matt. 19.11, divine passive: God gives it) to some. The implicit renewal of the disciple himself is the buried treasure in Jesus' eschatological act of restoring marriage to its primaeval state. This act of restoration finds its only credible context in the restoration of God's people, Israel. Both John and Jesus, it is true, conceived the restoration of Israel as belonging to the final, post-historical act of God: The wheat would be gathered into the granary when the chaff would be consigned to the fire (Matt. 3.12 par.). But, as we have observed, both understood their baptismal activity to constitute the beginning of this consummation. There is no doubt at all that the now reaffirmed command of the Creator ('The two shall become one') refers not to the ultimate constitution of Israel on the far side of judgment (when, indeed, people would 'neither marry nor be given in marriage', Mark 12.25 parr.), but to the *kairos* defined by present proclamation. Still more specifically, it is the present public career of Jesus which stands as the fulfilled condition of his restoring marriage to its original permanence; and this restoration is ultimately addressed to the restored Israel coming into being in response to his call.

It is only in the light of these subsurface, implicit, and contextual facets of the text that Jesus' teaching on divorce is revealed in its full sweep. Here he taught *'ōs exousian echōn* (Mark 1.22 par.; cf. Matt. 7.29; Luke 4.32): as one having power, 'not like the scribes' (Matt. 7.29). The scribes' authority was Moses-bound. Jesus' authority transcended the Mosaic economy, correcting and perfecting it. This inevitably struck a harsh polemic note. In the 'now' of restoration the Torah was revised. More: The whole scribal system, its rationale and its prestige, was suddenly and totally *passé*. The authority of the teacher, Jesus, would at once shape and respond to the eschatological state of affairs brought about by his proclamation.

Consideration of Jesus' teaching on divorce generates certain anticipations about his teaching in general. We would expect to meet three characteristics of that teaching: first, that it be eschatological; second, that it be prescriptive; third, that it specifically transcend the Mosaic Torah.

We anticipate from this single prohibition that the teaching of Jesus will comprehend not only an eschatological ethics (great demands posed by the advent of the reign of God) but an ethics of realized eschatology. The demands were meant for – and in the last analysis could only be meant for – a community of the transformed. Like the warning of the Baptist and his rite of baptism, like the proclamation of Jesus and his appeal for conversion, they called for an eschatological Israel. They called on the nation to be stripped clean in the face of the approaching reign of God. The challenge of God's will and the transformation of the community were equally eschatological. Challenge made transformation necessary; transformation made the meeting of the challenge possible.

Second, we anticipate from this single prohibition that the teaching of Jesus will be prescriptive, made up of specific commands rather than educible from and reducible to a global insight or principle. In declaring the restoration of marriage to its primal state Jesus did not ground this in the general law of love; he derived it from and grounded it in the sacred order of creation and the express will of the Creator. His teaching was concentrated on the plenary fulfilment not simply of the nature of the sexes or of the family or of society but, above all, of God's good pleasure at the present moment in the understanding that God revealed this through the prophetic medium of verbally formulated commands.

Only a prescriptive ethic would cohere with the conception of the reign of God and with the specific force of its advance proclamation. Revelation of the full will of God had been reserved for the end. God's reign was the goal of history, now entering history to shape it from within before bringing it to its appointed end. It was shaping a unique *kairos* defined precisely by this full and final revelation. The provisional was yielding to the definitive. God was imposing his reign, putting an end to the jerry-built casuistry and compromises that had veiled his will, and revealing the full measure of his demand.

If the ethics of realized eschatology meant an end to the provisional, what of the many necessarily provisional aspects of custom and casuistry in the Torah itself? No longer relevant to the divinely wrought eschatological situation of Israel, they would be rendered null and void! The Torah would be thereby surpassed, indeed, but only in its own direction. The inner dynamism of Torah had always been the honour of God and of one's parents and the rights of one's neighbour. Now this inner dynamism would be not transcended but realized; only the Torah's external forms and limits would be transcended and rendered obsolete.

We may test these anticipations against several particular texts from the Matthean Sermon on the Mount, beginning with the 'antitheses'.[49]

You have heard that the men of old were told,
  'Thou shalt not murder; the murderer deserves condemnation (to death).'[50]
But I say to you:
  Whoever gets angry at his brother deserves condemnation (to death);
  whoever says to his brother 'You blockhead!' deserves the (death-) sentence
of the high court;
  whoever says 'You idiot!' deserves condemnation to the fiery pit.

You have heard that it was said,
  'Thou shalt not commit adultery.'
But I say to you:
  Whoever looks at a woman lustfully
  has already committed adultery with her in his heart.

Again you have heard that the men of old were told,
  'Thou shalt not swear falsely; thou shalt perform to the Lord what thou hast sworn.'
But I say to you:
  Do not swear at all!

You have heard that it was said:
  '(No more than) an eye for an eye and (no more than) a tooth for a tooth.'
But I say to you:
  Do not set yourself (at all) against the man who wrongs you.

You have heard that it was said
  'Thou shalt love thy neighbour, though thine adversary thou needst not love.'[51]
But I say to you:
  Love your adversaries and pray for those who persecute you ...
(Matt. 5.21f., 27f., 33f., 38f., 43f.).

These five antitheses stand apart from traditional religion for their boldness in both form and content. It is probable that the antithetical form, accenting as it does the scandalous view that the Torah as it stands does not suffice, derived from Jesus himself.[52] The content is an extreme radicalization of Torah prescriptions. In a given instance (e.g. either or both of the last two antitheses) such radicalization might be interpreted not as accentuating but as suppressing a Torah prescription. This, however, would be to miss the angle of vision of these antitheses. In both cases (as also in the earlier antitheses) the Torah is thought of as imposing a limit on man and the new prescription of Jesus as imposing a severer limit of the same sort. Thus, the Torah limits vengeance to an appropriate measure; Jesus, banishing vengeance altogether, has carried the Torah prescription to its ultimate. He did not thereby undermine the Torah; he endorsed it *à outrance*.

Why this radical condemnation of judicious measure? The answer, once again, lies in Jesus' central proclamation. The reign of God was God's supreme and climactic gift to Israel and the world, not just goodness but boundless goodness. How could the time-tested, customary, quotidian morality of the Torah be an appropriate response to boundless goodness? The bursting of limits in the antitheses correlates with the message of the herald of salvation (*m^ebaśśēr*) and strikingly satisfies the anticipation of a teaching at once eschatological, prescriptive, and (with reference to the limits of the Torah) transcendent.

This presupposition of Jesus' moral teachings – his prior proclamation of divine benevolence, boundless and on the brink – is also relevant to the question of the transforming impact of God's reign on the person who accepts it. 'The reign of God' signified a revelation of extravagant goodness, generosity appealing for generosity, depth calling depth into being.

But this transformation – the anthropological supposition of a code excluding the angry word and the lustful look, the blustering claim, the spirit of vengeance, the natural instinct to be a good hater – was left wholly unthematic. The immediate point was the revelation of the commands themselves rather than of the conditions of their fulfilment. But the rigour of the commands inevitably poses the question of resources for their fulfilment; for, humanly speaking, all of them are a 'mystery to the will',[53] contradicting and baffling, not intelligence, but appetite. They would yield their secret, however, precisely in so far as they were lived out as the code of a community of disciples. Discipleship was communion with *mārē*', the Lord whose 'authority' was also 'power' (*exousia, šoltān*).

The commands of Jesus were the heart of his teaching, reflecting the revolutionary significance of the reign of God and specifying the right response to it. Nothing was to be left as it was. The eschatological reversal of fortunes (now it was to be the turn of the poor, the hungry, and the mourners) was matched by an eschatological transvaluation of values.

Is wealth what everyone wants and can never have enough of? Then sell what you have and give it to the poor (Mark 10.21 parr.).

> Sell your possessions
> and give aims,
> provide yourselves with purses
> that do not get old,
> with a treasure in heaven
> that does not fail,
> where no thief approaches
> and no moth destroys;
> for where your treasure is
> there will your heart be, too[54]
>   (Luke 12.33f.).

The last motif is set in focus by the story of the rich man (Mark 10.17–22 parr.), which makes clear that to be without goods has a positive point. The sequence of Jesus' command (Mark 10.21 parr.) is 'Go, sell, give, and come follow';[55] detachment is for the sake of attachment, poverty is ordered to discipleship.

Does the whole world hanker to be first? Then be last. 'If anyone would be first, he must be the last of all and the servant of all' (Mark 9.35; 10.43f. parr.). This is simply to adapt to a law of the eschaton: 'And many that are first will be last, and the last first' (Mark 10.31 parr.); or, still more concisely, 'The last will be first and the first last' (Matt. 20.16; Luke 14.11; 18.14). Salvation would turn on the most secret quests of the heart; but now all the heart's quests are revalued and the hierarchies of history reversed.[56]

Piety that wins the approval of the righteous is redefined as hypocrisy.

> But when you give alms
> your own left hand should not know
> what your right hand is doing
> so that your giving may be secret
> and your Father who sees what is secret
> will reward you ...
>
> But when you pray,
> 'Enter your room
> and shut your door',
> and pray to your Father who is unseen,
> and your Father who sees the unseen
> will reward you ...
>
> But when you fast,
> anoint your head
> and wash your face,
> so that no one can see you are fasting,
> except your Father who is unseen;
> and your Father who sees the unseen
> will reward you ...
>
> (Matt. 6.3f.,6,17f.).

Inasmuch as Jesus excluded as impossible a simultaneous praise from men and God, the thrust of his teaching was toward 'a piety which is wholly secret'.[57] What this amounts to is the radical devaluation of religious prestige.[58]

Did this eschatological code of discipleship simply 'radicalize' the Torah? Or did it in reality dispense with the Torah and take its place? If the code proposed by Jesus was the response to a boundless benevolence, the inmost spirit of the Torah had always been epitomized in the prescription of a love boundless in principle: 'Thou shalt love the Lord thy God with all thy heart and with all thy soul and with all thy might' (Deut. 6.5). This 'great commandment' called on man, as Walther Eichrodt has rightly insisted, 'to leave all earthly security and cling to God's word alone'.[59] But the mass of determining prescriptions by which flesh and blood translated principle into practice reflected the unheroic morality of the small landowner. The teaching of Jesus, on the other hand, had no other point than to realize the Torah's inmost spirit of self-forgetfulness in its full purity, fierce and flawless. In all their concrete radicalness and definiteness his commands simply gave eschatological body to this inner dynamism and spirit. They could not have been predicted or deduced from the Torah, but they presented themselves as its supreme form.

Nor did this diminish the personal dimension in Jesus' teaching. His distinctive signature is evident in the incisiveness and vehemence with which he condemned sins of the tongue and unmasked peculiarly religious faults: those especially of the ungenerous heart (the refusal of faith, the perverse flair for the irrelevant truth or value, recoil from mercy to sinners) and of the righteous spirit (ostentatious piety, readiness to burden and condemn others and, as the real foundation of all the rest, confidence in the system). Positively expressed, Jesus' judgment on sins of the tongue and on the false consciousness of the professionally good was his quest of the heart set not on tradition but on God. Hence, sins of the tongue and, even more, the righteousness in which the pious installed themselves fixed Jesus' attention. 'Tongue' revealed 'heart': from the overflow of the heart the mouth speaks (Matt. 12.34; cf. Luke 6.45), i.e., mouth articulates what heart is full of. To condemn 'sins of the tongue' is to call for reform and renewal of the heart. The peril of self-conscious piety lay in its power to mask from the pious man himself the secret resources and conations and tangents of his heart. The latter phenomenon, as we shall presently see,[60] had a direct and dramatic bearing on Jesus' encounter with the religious *élite* of Israel.

Clearly, the teaching of Jesus was not a random collection of wisdom sayings. As defining in concrete detail the appropriate response to the reign of God and its proclamation, it did have a controlling centre of gravity. Thus far, however, we have not satisfactorily answered the question whether Jesus held together in a single thematic perspective all the prescriptive particulars of his eschatological ethics. In its full scope and reach, this question focuses not only on the terms in which he conceived the whole of his teaching but also on the correlative terms in which he understood himself as teacher.

We might begin by asking which of two alternative views found in the synoptic tradition better reflects the mentality of the historical Jesus. The first is that of Matt. 5.17:

> Do not think that I have come
> to annul the Law [or the prophets],
> I have come not to annul
> but to fulfil!

according to which Jesus' aim is to mediate the final, climactic revelation of God's will, thus bringing the teaching of Torah and prophets to its full, divinely predetermined, eschatological measure of completeness.[61] The second is that of Luke 16.16 (cf. Matt. 11.13):

> The Law and the prophets [held sway] until John [but] from that time [forward] is gospelled the reign of God!

according to which 'Torah plus prophets' and 'reign of God' are related antithetically. Quite apart from the high likelihood that the formulation of the Lukan text is secondary,[62] the issue remains which of the two views (the crowning completion of Torah and prophets or their final displace-ment) better represents the view of Jesus. The answer should take account not only of the prohibition of divorce, the formulation of 'antitheses' (it was said/but I say) and 'reversals' (be last; sell what you have, etc.), but also of Jesus' word on the 'first' (Mark 12.28) or 'great' (Matt. 22.36) commandment as well as of his subversion of the sanctity of ritual law (Mark 7.15 par.). But this much may be anticipated from the start: If Jesus affirmed the abiding validity of the Torah, he must have understood it as 'Torah transformed'. (This does in fact correspond with conclusions already reached above.) But did he in fact affirm the abiding validity of the Torah? If so, how was it transformed?

Among the traditions certainly reflecting the stance of the historical Jesus toward the Torah it is easier to find evidence of discontinuity and originality than to find professions of fidelity to tradition. There are, nevertheless, indications of Jesus' affirmation of the Torah. In the encounter with the rich man (Mark 10.17–31 parr.[63]), for example, the dialogue between the two does both: It affirms and it transcends the Torah. But the Torah is not affirmed merely to be transcended, so that the affirmation in the end is simply empty. The dialogue makes three points: that the Torah (in the sense of the decalogue) specifies the way 'to inherit eternal life'; that observance of the commandments (the possibility of which is assumed: 'Master, I have obeyed all these [commandments] from my youth.' And Jesus looked at him and loved him . . .' [Mark 10.20f.]) is the right response to God, and not merely right but requisite; and that, whereas the observance of the commandments is a limited response, the response solicited by Jesus is boundless: 'Go, sell what you have and give the money to the poor . . . and come follow me' (Mark 10.21). The climactic 'response without limits' goes beyond the decalogue but not by contradicting or nullifying it. It is evident that Jesus here understands allegiance to the decalogue as a seedbed of discipleship.

But how, if at all, did observance of the ritual law figure, according to Jesus, in Israel's appropriate response to God? This is a vexed question for several reasons. It is not immediately clear what data are relevant to it; obviously relevant data are not extensive; and the witness of the early church is divided. The issue ultimately poses questions never thematized in the sources, such as: How did Jesus understand the soteriological situa-tion of Israel? Did he perceive the cult as an availing resource in this situation? We reserve these questions for later. For the present we shall simply touch on a few matters obviously relevant to the question of Jesus and the ritual law.

Against the background of contemporary religious movements Jesus appeared as a 'secular' figure. He lived in the world and freely associated with all, unconstrained by that mass of purity prescriptions which expressed the power of sacral taboo in Judaism. This life-style was provocative and (as analysis of the parables reveals) a fertile source of criticism and debate. Jesus did not deny the validity of the ritual order as such. But when he did refer to the ritual order it was only to assert the moral order as the condition of its efficacy (Matt. 5.34) or to specify that 'the weightier matters of the law' belonged to the moral order (Matt. 23.23) or to attack ritual casuistry used to circumvent the moral law (Mark 7.10–13 par.; Matt. 23.16–22). Calling for special attention, however, is the saying of Mark 7.15 par.:

> Nothing that goes into a man from outside can defile him
> but [only] what comes out of a man [speech] defiles him.

The first limb of the *māšāl* functioned in one branch of early Christian tradition as declaring all foods to be clean (Mark 7.19b; Rom. 14.14). Does this render the historical sense of the saying?[64] Before answering, we should observe that the accent falls not on the first but on the second limb of the *māšāl*, so that in its main thrust it was a polemic against that self-deception which met moral demands with ritual observances (cf. Mark 7.10–13 par.; Matt. 5.34; 23.16–22, 23, 25f. par.). Granted this, we may still ask how the first limb functioned to support this meaning. There are two basic possibilities: 'Nothing that goes into a man from outside can defile him [in any sense at all]', and 'Nothing that goes into a man from outside can defile him [in the proper, the deep and significant, sense of "defile"].' That the second possibility yields the correct sense seems probable to me inasmuch as it can be supported with parallels.[65] This sense does not render the saying harmless or deprive it of its sting. It remains a very sharply formulated relativizing of the ritual law. If the first possibility yielded the correct sense one would have expected to find more echoes in the synoptic tradition of Jesus' repudiation of the practice of distinguishing between clean and unclean foods. To account for the lack of such echoes one might, to be sure, appeal to the hypothesis of a 're-tora-izing' (*Rethoraisierung*)[66] of the entire synoptic tradition from a very early date. Thus far this hypothesis does not seem to me to have been made plausible.[67]

Jesus is represented in the same passage of Mark as differentiating between 'the command of God' and 'the tradition of men' (Mark 7.8; cf. Matt. 15.2–6). Since we know that he did not hesitate to transcend Mosaic statutes in a way which abolished them *prout stabant* (Mark 10.5, 9 par.; cf. Matt. 5.38f.), numerous critics consider the distinction to be an artifice of the early church meant to tone down Jesus' more radical stance. But in all probability it was Jesus himself who distinguished the two, precisely to single out scribal *halaka* as a target.[68] In post-exilic Israel scribal tradition had made the distinction clean/unclean (*katharos/akathartos*; Heb.:

ṭāhôr/ṭāmēʾ), of which in many cases the primitive rationale had long since been forgotten, more important than ever as a distinguishing trait of Judaism and so a token – even a pure token[69] – of religious allegiance. But the *halaka* ran the risk (as in various ways do all systems of pious observance) of becoming a fatal distraction from the values it was designed to protect.

In the time of Jesus the *halaka* was en route to being absolutized. Brusquely he challenged its pretension to embody the will of God. In its place he put his own commands of eschatological discipleship. The key to his harsh critique of the *halaka* (Mark 2.17 parr., 18f. parr., 27; 3.4 parr.; 7.1–15 par.; Matt. 8.21 par.; 11.16–19 par.; etc.) was the advent of the reign of God: Torah piety might call for fasting but at Israel's wedding-feast fasting was out of place (Mark 2.19 parr.).

He not only appealed to the new eschatological context established by his proclamation, he commended that context itself by appealing to the stubborn fund of religious good sense which the *halaka* inhibited but failed to extinguish. This was a feature of the controversies over cures on the sabbath. For his critics the issue Jesus posed was 'cures as the breaking of sabbath laws'; but to Jesus his critics stood for 'appeal to sabbath laws as blindness to salvation'. You yourselves, he argued, must acknowledge that to do good, to save, to heal, on the sabbath is permitted (= God permits it). God permits what the scribes forbid! 'Who among you, if he has a sheep and it falls into a hole on the sabbath, will not take hold of it and lift it out?' (Matt. 12.11 par.).[70] It is ironic that by the third century of the Christian era the rabbis had expressly forbidden this. But the rhetorical question supposes that the contrary practice prevailed in the time of Jesus and is an instance of his exploiting the gap between theme and performance on the part of his critics. This was a recurrent feature of debate. It might be that the scribe prescribed the right thing but failed to follow it himself: 'They talk but do not act' (Matt. 23.3). On the other hand, he might do the reasonable thing (water his ox or rescue his sheep on the sabbath) but prescribe against the cure of a man (Mark 3.1–5 parr.). The earliest Christian communities, conscious that their own conflicts with the orthodox over the sabbath *halaka* were rooted in the prior conflict between Jesus and the scribes, extended the stock of sabbath conflict stories by outfitting miracle stories with a sabbath setting (Luke 13.14–17; 14.3–6; John 5.9–16; 9.16).[71]

The ritual order received neither accent nor development in the proclamation and teaching of Jesus. On the contrary, his central themes of eschatological consummation repeatedly crossed the grain of ritual tradition and so violated religious sensibilities (Mark 2.15 parr., 19–21 parr., 23–28 parr.; 3.4 parr.; 7.1–23 par.; 10.3–9 parr.; Matt. 8.21f. par.; 11.16–19 par.; 17.24–26; Luke 15.1f.; 19.5–7; John 2.19 [=Mark 14.58 par.; 15.29

par.]). Jesus' teachings could not fail to be in discord with the prevailing Torah piety, for they flowed from a new presupposition and source: the coming of the reign of God. Grace and Torah were correlative. The grace that was the reign of God was both climactic (i.e., related to Israel's history as its fulfilment) and new. The Torah correlative to this grace was likewise climactic and new: climactic, in endorsing ancient directions and, above all, the commandment of undivided and unlimited love (Deut. 6.4); new, in the bursting of the ancient limits.

Thus, the Markan dialogue on which was the first of all the commandments concludes on the pleasing note of mutual approval by Jesus and the scribe (Mark 12.32–34). But in the context of Jesus' proclamation and teaching the great commandment had a new orientation. The scribe affirmed the commandment of boundless love and everything remained in place. With Jesus everything was changed: divorce abolished, vengeance outlawed, wealth, power, and piety devalued, the *halaka* rejected. Whoever affirmed boundless love as the first of the commandments was 'not far from the reign of God' (Mark 12.34). But the commandment now turned toward a new compass point – precisely the reign of God, impending and already effective, with its own economy of demands and dynamisms. The abiding validity of the great commandment lay in the open-endedness of boundless love. But, though exodus and Sinai were not voided in the new context of Jesus' proclamation, the reign of God took over the covenantal role of the exodus and his own code of discipleship brought Sinai to completion.

The unique and original perspective of Jesus' teaching, the context in which all the particulars of that teaching fall into place, was 'Torah for a graced and restored Israel'. It was Torah transformed by reference to the new and public revelation set before Israel in Jesus' proclamation of the reign of God and his apodictic teaching of the new imperatives which flowed from it. This Torah teaching was not interpretation but revelation. As teacher, then, no less than as proclaimer, Jesus was not a rabbi but a prophet and, like John, 'more than a prophet'. He was the unique revealer of the full final measure of God's will.

Only on the hypothesis that such was the understanding and self-understanding of Jesus are the traits of his teaching fully intelligible. Among these traits we take three to be decisive: that his teaching strictly correlated with his proclamation of the reign of God; that it regularly transcended the Mosaic economy; and that its authority was personal rather than exegetical.

The hypothesis is that Jesus understood himself to be the unique revealer of the full, final measure of God's will. The data relate to the hypothesis in this way: The first two traits of Jesus' moral teaching (its tie with the proclamation of God's reign and its transcending of the Mosaic system) set up an expectation to which the hypothesis corresponds and which the third trait (personal, not exegetical authority) fulfils. First, proclamation of the reign of God, implicitly and of its very nature, presented itself as an act of divine revelation, the act not of a scribe but of a herald holding a unique commission from God. But similars should be interpreted similarly; that is, teachings and commands strictly aligned with (though undeducible from) proclamation of the reign of God similarly present themselves as divine revelation. Second, since the Mosaic code was conceived to have been divinely revealed, any code claiming to supersede it had somehow to include the claim to be equally revealed – indeed, to belong to a superior revelation. No doubt, there is a certain indeterminacy in the expectations set up by these two traits, but all vagueness vanishes in the light of Jesus' repeated claims, implicit and explicit, to the highest personal authority as teacher. It was precisely through him that God disclosed his saving will for the world. Hence the emphatic 'I' (*egō*) of 'But I say to you . . .' (Matt. 5.22–44)[72] and the distinctive 'amen' of 'Amen, I say to you . . .' (Mark 3.28; 8.12; 9.1, 41; etc.).[73] The secret and ground of this authority found expression in the (esoteric) word of Matt. 11.27 par.:

> All things have been delivered to me by my Father;
> just as only a father knows his son,
> so only a son knows his father,
> and anyone to whom the son chooses to reveal him.

The linguistic observations of Dalman and Jeremias have cleared the way for an understanding of this text and an assessment of its historicity. The first line compactly alludes to the teaching and training of sons by fathers.[74] Lines two and three 'constitute a detailed Oriental mode of expressing the reciprocity of intimate understanding'.[75] The last line likewise belongs to the sphere of everyday experience. But the four lines refer parabolically to Jesus and his heavenly Father. Hence Dalman's deft definition of their intention: 'He who stands in so uniquely close a relation to God' is God's 'only possible' and 'absolutely reliable' revealer.[76] Confirmation that Jesus understood his own words as divine revelation comes from his references to the special activity of God inclining hearers of those words to understand and accept them (Mark 4.10 parr.; cf. Matt. 11.25 par.; 16.17); this divine activity was itself called revelation (Matt. 11.25 par.; 16.17).

The question whether Judaism before the time of Jesus had already worked out the theme of the 'Messianic Torah' still remains without a certain answer,[77] but in the present context the question has limited significance. In any case Jesus presented his teaching as the definitive revelation of God's will for Israel. This revelation discredited the tradition of the scribes but it 'fulfilled' the Torah. It is solidly probable that Jesus conceived this fulfilment in accord with the well-attested scheme of 'appointed measure'.[78] His crowning revelation 'fulfilled' the Torah by bringing it to its appointed eschatological completion.

The teaching of Jesus and his self-understanding as teacher show, once again, that his purposes fit into an interlocking scheme of divine and human acts. The point of proclamation and teaching was to bring eschatological Israel into being. The teaching prophetically defined the shape of the 'yes' God sought from his people. For us it confirms that Jesus' world of meaning was eschatological, that the eschatology had an ecclesial character and a realized element and, finally, that in his own view Jesus himself belonged to the centre of the eschaton as its revealer.

2. PUBLIC ACTIONS

The public actions of Jesus include the call of disciples and the sending of disciples to Israel; miraculous signs of salvation; table fellowship with sinners; public debate and public formulations of mission; and, finally, the entry into Jerusalem to 'cleanse' the temple. We shall interrogate these actions in quest of the meanings with which Jesus charged them. The final question will be: On what do these meanings converge?

The call and sending of disciples

Jesus was not a teacher to whose circle prospective members applied for admission and were accepted or not. The discipleship surrounding him arose typically, and in all probability exclusively, through his call. The call was peremptory (Mark 1.17 par., 20 par.; 2.14 parr.; 10.21 parr.; Matt. 8.22 par.; Luke 9.61f.; cf. John 1.39, 43), tolerating no delay in response (Mark 1.17 par., 20 par.; 2.14 parr.; Matt. 8.22 par.; Luke 9.61f.) and no competing claim, whether of Torah, piety, and custom (Matt. 8.22 par.)[79] or of family love (Luke 9.61f.; cf. Matt. 10.37 par.). A full-time commitment, discipleship excluded the rootedness of a fixed abode (Matt. 8.19f. par.; cf. Mark 3.14 ['*ina ōsin met' autou* = 'to be with him (wherever he was)']; Acts 1.21 [*synelthontōn 'emin* =' who travelled with us'[80]]). The context for this remarkable rigour was the abrupt, proleptic entry into history of the reign of God and its demands. Though no close parallel to the discipleship of Jesus presents itself,[81] there is at least a point of comparison with the discipleship of the Baptist. The 'disciple' was meant not to study but to serve the master in his mission. As the missions differed, so did the discipleships: Jesus and his disciples did not take their stand in the wilderness but confronted Israel in town and village.

The historicity of the deliberate act of choosing twelve disciples to participate most intimately in his mission (Mark 3.13f. par.; 6.7–13 parr.; cf. Matt. 19.28 par.) is beyond reasonable doubt.[82] The number twelve was symbolic; hence 'the twelve' (Mark 3.16; 4.10; 6.7 parr.; 9.35 parr.; 11.11; 14.17 par., 10 parr., 20, 43 parr.; Matt. 10.2,5; 11.1; 19.28 par.; Luke 8.1; 9.12; John 6.67,70f.) were themselves a 'sign'. Generically, the reference was to, the people of God, in its fulness twelve tribes (Gen. 35.22b; 49; Num. 1; 26). But inasmuch as the loss of the Northern Kingdom (722 BC) had left only two and a half tribes,[83] 'twelve' in the eschatological herald (*mᵉbaśśer*). This had been presaged and its whole Israel could only signify *Israel restored*.[84] By his appointment, then, Jesus made the twelve a sign of the future, i.e., of the imminent restoration of Israel. Against the backdrop of Judaic piety, they were a startling sign, made up of radically disparate elements, Galilean (Mark 14.70 par.; John 12.21) and Judaean,[85] religious (John 1.35–39) and irreligious (Matt. 10.3; cf. Mark 2.14 parr.), Johannite (John 1.35–39) and Zealot (Luke 6.15 par.; Mark 6.18 par.).[86] As this could hardly have been accidental, there follows the real, if as yet indeterminate, expectation that the restoration of which the twelve were the sign would itself have a startling character.

Jesus, moreover, made the twelve more than a sign of the future. He gave them a share in its coming-to-be, by sending them (Mark 6.7 parr.) in groups of two (Mark 6.7) to enlist Israel's welcome of the reign of God (Mark 3.14; Matt. 10.7; Luke 9.2). Thus they entered into his role of eschatological herald (*mᵉbaśśer*). This had been presaged and its whole point and purpose defined in advance by the *maśal*: 'Come, follow me, and I will make you fishers of men' (Mark 1.17 par.), an image alluding (through Jer. 16.16) to the eschatological task of gathering Israel.[87] The fate of the nation would hinge on its response to their message. Acceptance would bring eschatological blessing; refusal, eschatological condemnation (Mark 6.11; Matt. 10.12–15; cf. Luke 10.10–12). In the light of these data on the twelve, their historicity and symbolic thrust, it is impossible to define the aims of Jesus plausibly without reference to a mission or task, central and urgent, set by the imminence of God's eschatological reign, bearing on the whole nation of Israel, and pressing Israel to a decision of faith or unfaith.

Miraculous signs of salvation

> Behold, I drive out demons
> and perform cures
> today and tomorrow,
> and on the third day I complete my course (Luke 13.32).

Jesus thus epitomized his public career not as words but as exorcisms and cures. Our interest centres on recovery of the original context in which such actions could incarnate the intentions of Jesus. Since 'context' and 'intentions' are interactive, we cannot discover either without reference to the other. We shall simply take up a series of texts and question them on both topics.

What texts? The long history of exegetical and historical analysis of the miracle narratives has made it clear that the most promising avenue for our inquiry is not the narratives themselves but the separately transmitted sayings which make reference to Jesus' exorcisms and cures.[88] There are numerous narrative details which point to reminiscence, but by and large the history of the narrative material is a laborious and rarely certain route either to secure judgments of historicity or to grasp of the significance Jesus himself attached to his exorcisms and cures. Indeed, their most striking and original dimension is indicated only rarely in the narratives.

We shall briefly consider six sayings in turn: the double *māšāl* on Beelzebul and the advent of the reign of God (Matt. 12.27f. par.); the *māšāl* on the dynasty and the household divided against themselves (Mark 3.24–26 parr.); the *māšāl* on the binding of the strong man (Mark 3.27 parr.); Jesus' sending out of the disciples with power over demons (Mark 3.14f.; 6.7; Matt. 10.7f; Luke 9.1f.); his answer to the question of the Baptist (Matt. 11.5 par.); and, finally, his refusal of the demand for a sign from heaven (Mark 8.11f. par.; Matt. 12.38f. par.; Luke 11.16; cf. John 4.48; 6.30ff.).

> If I drive out demons by the power of Beelzebul,
> by whose power do your sons drive them out? . . .
> But if by the spirit [finger, Luke] of God I drive out demons,
> then the reign of God has overtaken you (Matt. 12.27f.; Luke 11.19f.).

The historicity of these words is guaranteed by a convergence of indices: the sheer offensiveness of the charge of sorcery; the risk of relativizing the exorcisms of Jesus by reference to those of others; the precise, though implicit, allusion to a scriptural text;[89] the distinctiveness of the combination of exorcisms with apocalyptic eschatology. Formal indices support not only historicity but the authenticity of the conjunction of the two sayings: The antithetical parallelism of question and statement is a trait typical of the speech of Jesus (cf. Mark 3.33f. par.; 8.12; 10.18 par.; 11.17; Matt. 7.3–5 par.; Luke 12.51; 22.25).

The issue was the sense or thrust of his exorcisms. As he epitomized it in response to a malicious charge, the question was whether his exorcisms were effected by the power of Beelzebul or of God and, if by the power of God, what they meant. It took Jesus himself to thematize the second step: The exorcisms pointed beyond themselves to the dawning of God's reign! In terms of the history of religions this gives an entirely distinctive profile to the exorcisms of Jesus. They become, like proclamation and prophecy,

– and precisely in function of the particular prophetic proclamation of Jesus – *signs of the eschaton*. They signified God's imminent triumph over all evil. The emergence of this new meaning was doubly conditioned. First, it supposed a view of evil radicalized by the firm correlation of 'demons' and 'Satan', i.e., by the unity of evil and its bondage-character.[90] Second, it supposed the peculiar circumstance that by an eschatological proclamation the exorcist had generated an all-commanding context or frame of reference for his encounter with the demons.

The charge of sorcery also guarantees the historicity of the mini-parable on dynasties that assure their own downfall:

> If a regime be divided against itself
> that regime cannot last,
> and if a house be divided against itself
> that house cannot last;
> so, if Satan has risen up against himself and is divided,
> he cannot last, but is coming to an end (Mark 3.24–26).

Supposed once again is the continuum of evil and its solidarity with Satan who stood at the source of sickness and madness, self-destruction and moral corruption. Jesus does not say that Satan is finished. He says that if the charge of his critics were well founded, it would follow that Satan is finished. Now, the charge is ill-founded and illogical. But the only alternative to the supposition that Satan is divided against himself is that Jesus is locked in combat with him; and on the basis of this changed premise, the conclusion remains the same: Satan is coming to an end. We have here an index to the absolute terms in which Jesus set his own interpretation of the exorcisms. The whole argument, its explicit line and its implicit line, its imagery and idiom, is absolutist; i.e., the exorcisms of Jesus – that they are successful is uncontested – are absolutely decisive for the life of man. The combat evoked is not the endless seesaw of history's long haul but the apocalyptic turning-point. Hence, sayings like the present one legitimate the maximizing of symbolic hints and pointers in the otherwise simplistic-seeming folklore of the exorcism narratives, with their shouts and counter-shouts (Mark 1.24–26 par.; 5.7f. parr.; etc.),[91] the wind and sea tamed like wild animals (Mark 4.39f. parr.), the swine plunging down the precipice to drown (Mark 5.13 parr.), and so forth.

The point is made still more graphically by another image:

> No one can enter a strong man's house and plunder his goods
> unless he first binds the strong man;
> after that he can plunder his house (Mark 3.27 par.; cf. Luke 11.21f.).

The image defines an antecedent condition of Jesus' successful and absolutely decisive exorcisms: He has defeated Satan *already*. A stunning claim! When and how had this happened? There is no answer among the words of Jesus; but the Christian community early answered the question by its accounts of Jesus' victory over Satan (Mark 1.13) or 'the devil' (Matt. 4.1ff. par.) on the threshold of his public career, with the consequent restoration of communion between God and man (Mark 1.13) or God and Israel (Matt. 4.11).[92]

As Jesus combined his proclamation with exorcisms and cures, he commissioned the twelve to do likewise (Matt. 10.7f.; cf. Mark 3.14f.; 6.7; Luke 9.1f.). In fact, the commissioning of the twelve throws a shaft of light on the significance of the exorcisms and cures. The disciples' mission, like that of Jesus, was a distinct eschatological task: the winning over of God's people. Hence, proclamation, cures, and exorcisms were strictly reserved for 'the lost sheep' that were 'the house of Israel' (Matt. 15.24; 10.6).[93] Cures and exorcisms imaged and actualized the reign of God (cf. Matt. 12.28 par.) and, like the reign of God itself, were an entirely gratuitous gift (Matt. 10.8b–10[94]). The restoration of Israel evoked its paradisal beginning in the wilderness where, prior to the sin with the golden calf, there were 'none with fluxes, no lepers, no dumb, blind, or deaf, no imbeciles, and even death was ruled out'.[95] The theme correlates with Jesus' compassion for 'this woman, a daughter of Abraham, whom Satan has kept bound for eighteen years' (Luke 13.16). Exorcisms and cures signified the perfection of Israel restored and began to actualize it already.

This note of realized eschatology is struck again in a text which both Matthew and Luke transmit as Jesus' response to the question of the Baptist:[96]

> Blind men see,
> cripples walk,
> lepers are cleansed,
> deaf men hear,
> dead men are raised,
> good news is broken to the poor! (Matt. 11.5 par.).

The words evoke three Isaian passages on the coming dawn of salvation (Isa. 35.5–7; 29.18f.; 61.1f.), but they add 'lepers' and 'dead men' to the Isaian lists of the beneficiaries of salvation.[97] According to Matthew and Luke Jesus' words specifically referred to his miracles and, in the last line, to his proclamation. If this was Jesus' own intended sense (as seems likely[98]), the words support the historicity of a great variety of miraculous signs of salvation and are relevant to the historicity of numerous gospel narratives (e.g., those narrating the raising of the dead, Mark 5.21–24, 35–43 parrs.; Luke 7.11–17; John 11.1–46). It is noteworthy that in contrast to other texts alluding to his miracles, there is here no explicit reference to exorcisms, an omission probably due to the immediate function of these words, namely, to signal just that aspect of his wonder-working which corresponds to scriptural promises of restoration. If, on the other hand, the words of Jesus were originally intended simply to evoke in traditional symbols the dawn of salvation as realized in the act and content of his proclamation and in positive responses to it, they still attest a point relevant to the larger context of our inquiry, for they still define the terms in which Jeşus understood his work, namely (in harmony with the overarching theme of the Isaian passages) as the salvation or restoration of Israel.

It would be a mistake in historical interpretation to adopt a minimizing attitude toward the miracles of Jesus. Though the narratives themselves are extremely various – some purely folkloric and unhistorical (e.g. Matt. 17.27), some bearing the hall-marks of reminiscence (e.g. Mark 1.21–33 par.[99]), and the mass of them insusceptible of firm historical judgments *in individuo* – we have good evidence (Luke 13.32; Matt. 11.21–24 par.)[100] that Jesus himself judged his *dynameis* (Aram. *g^{e}bûrtêh*; 'his powerful deeds', see esp. Matt. 11.21 par., 23) to be decisive signs of the dawning eschaton. They ought to have spurred all Galilee to repentance; in the face of them unbelieving Chorazin and Bethsaida and Capernaum were doomed (Matt. 11.21–24 par.).

A minimizing attitude toward the miracles would be especially mistaken if it presupposed their reducibility to the popular prodigies of the surrounding world, whether Jewish or Greek.[101] The miracles of Jesus were not magic. They were evoked by his word in a context of religious faith. They signified the reign of God in a way that illuminated its relation to world and history and bodily life precisely as fulfilment; as harvest, wedding, and banquet, as *Weltvollendung*, not the mere end but the consummation and re-creation of the world.

The 'sign from heaven' (Mark 8.11 par.; Luke 11.16) which unbelieving critics called for in vain (Mark 8.11f., par.; Matt. 12.38f. par.; Luke 11.16; cf. John 4.48; 6.30ff.) was in all probability understood as a miracle of accreditation, a circus prodigy such as a parting of the waters in imitation of the Moses tradition[102] or the feat of floating down from 'the pinnacle of the temple' sustained by angels (Matt. 4.5f. par.). Such marvels were conceived as sacred, unambiguous proofs of divine approval. Jesus' flat rejection of the demand for 'a sign from heaven' differentiates the intentions incarnated in his cures and exorcisms from the flamboyant conceits of prophetic or messianic pretenders.[103]

Table fellowship with sinners

To his contemporaries it was a staggering phenomenon that he did not shrink from dining with the irreligious; indeed, he did so at his own initiative, whether the meal was at home (Mark 2.15[104] parr.; Luke 15.1f.) or abroad (Luke 19.5). Numerous gospel texts reflect directly

(Mark 2.16f. parr.; Matt. 11.19 par.; Luke 15.1f.; 19.8) or indirectly (Matt. 20.1–16; 21.28–32; Luke 7.41–43; 15. 4–7, 8–10, 11–32) the powerful impression this made on contemporary Israel and the intense reactions to it: the shock and resentment of the religious (Mark 2.16 parr.;[105] Matt. 11.19 par.; Luke 19.7; cf. Luke 15.25–32), the sheer delight of the irreligious (Luke 19.9; cf. Mark 2.19 parr.).

The intensity of the reactions becomes fully intelligible only in the light of the socio-religious situation of the time. Here we shall touch on the two main points: the significance of table fellowship and the division between 'the righteous' and 'sinners'.

Dining in common established among its participants a special bond, table fellowship, violation of which was rank betrayal (Ps. 41.10). Likewise, exclusion from dining together signified repudiation of social ties generally. Social lines and associations were accordingly sharper and firmer than in our world. Moreover, from age-old tradition table fellowship had had a role in sacral ceremony (Ex. 18.12; 24.11; I Kings 3.15) and even in everyday life maintained a sacral character, first of all through the blessing at the meal's outset and its responding 'amen'.[106]

It was through table fellowship that the ritual distinction of clean and unclean (*katharos/akathartos*, Heb.: *ṭāhôr/ṭāmē'*) and the moral distinction of the righteous and sinners (*dikaioi/'amartōloi*, Heb.: *ṣaddîqîm/rᵉšā'îm*) found concrete social expression. Since Gentiles were unclean (Deut. 14.21) and uncleanness was contagious, Jews were not to eat with them (Jub. 22.16). But the rule applied by Jews to Gentiles was also applied by the religious to the irreligious within Judaism. The possibilities of table fellowship contracted in accord with how one concretely defined the irreligious. Inasmuch as false teachers were irreligious, seduced and possessed by demons, and unclean,[107] they and their followers were excluded. For at least some associations of the religious *élite* this practically meant that only their own membership were possible table fellows.

What held on a ritual basis held also on a moral basis. In fact, the ritual and moral orders tended to interpenetrate. But it was specifically on a moral basis that table fellowship with publicans (*telōnai*, Aram.: *môkᵉsîn*) was excluded. Publicans were not levitically unclean; they were simply despised as immoral.[108] 'Sinners', in the phrase 'publicans and sinners' (probably coined by Jesus' critics, cf. Mark 2.15f. par.; Matt. 11.19 par.; cf. Luke 15.1) included public and/or professional sinners (like prostitutes, cf. Matt. 21.31f., 'publicans and prostitutes'). But the tendency of Torah piety was to regard the ordinary run of men (*'oi loipoi tōn anthrōpōn*), Luke 18.11) as greedy or dishonest or adulterers.[109]

The distinctions of clean and unclean and of righteous and sinners shaped and permeated the self-understanding of Judaism. To subvert these distinctions was not a breach of religious etiquette but a challenge to the social order. Jesus, as we have seen, sharply relativized a central aspect of the first distinction ('Nothing that goes into a man from outside can defile him'); and by admitting the unconverted, public, professional sinner to his table fellowship (Luke 19.5) he shattered the social form of the second.

The exclusion of the morally evil from the social life of the morally good was not at all akin to Victorian respectability. It was a principle deeply rooted in the imposing religious and moral tradition of the nation. The legacy of Torah and prophets had burned into the consciousness of post-exilic Israel the absolute incompatibility of good and evil. The God of Israel had never been tolerant: 'For I, Yahweh, thy God, am a jealous God ...' (Ex. 20.5). This motif of exclusive claim went hand in hand with Yahweh's moral will: 'I will not acquit (*'aṣdîq*: justify, pronounce innocent) the wicked' (Ex. 23.7c). 'Yahweh', declared Nahum, 'is a jealous God and avenging' (Nahum 1.2): 'Yahweh is slow to anger and of great might and Yahweh will by no means clear the guilty' (*wᵉnaqqê lo' yᵉnaqqeh YHWH*, Nahum 1.3). For Judaism the bottom of the barrel morally was that warped judgment which contrary to the word of God (e.g. Ex. 23.7c; Nahum 1.3) acquitted the wicked and cleared the guilty, a nadir of perversity figuring in the accusation the Code of Damascus levelled against Israel:

> They pronounce the guilty innocent (*wayyaṣdîqû rāšā'* = justify, acquit the wicked man)
> and pronounce the innocent guilty (*wayyaršî'û ṣaddîq* = condemn the righteous man, CD 1.19).

This simply echoed a theme of traditional wisdom:

> He who justifies the wicked (*maṣdîq rāšā'*) and he who condemns the righteous (*ûmaršia' ṣaddîq*)
> are both alike an abomination to Yahweh (Prov. 17.15).

Now, if this religious and moral economy is radically upset in the Pauline account of God as one 'who justifies (*dikaiounta* = acquits, makes righteous) the ungodly' (Rom. 4.5),[110] this has its concrete presupposition in Jesus' revolutionary contact and communion with sinners.

We should recall the historical (*religionsgeschichtlich*) setting. Repentance and conversion were important traditional themes in Judaism, regularly brought to mind by the synagogue and finding regular cultic expression in the temple. The new element in the preaching of the Baptist was his presupposition that at the threshold of judgment the ordinary economy of Mosaic religion did not suffice. God called all Israel to repent, to confess its sins, to seal its confession by a rite of washing. But the Baptist maintained the classic biblical structure of repentance: conversion first, communion second (Matt. 3.7–10 par.; Luke 3.10–14; cf. *Antiquitates* 18.117).

The *novum* in the act of Jesus was to reverse this structure: communion first, conversion second. His table fellowship with sinners implied no acquiescence in their sins, for the gratuity of the reign of God cancelled none of its demands. But in a world in which sinners stood ineluctably condemned, Jesus' openness to them was irresistible. Contact triggered repentance; conversion flowered from communion. In the tense little world of ancient Palestine, where religious meanings were the warp and woof of the social order, this was a potent phenomenon, comparable in our world, perhaps, to the first public responses to a charismatic political leader.

Is it possible at this point to feel our way into the horizons and intentions of the historical Jesus?

First, the act of initiating table fellowship with sinners was not an erratic development calling for a special effort to relate it in some intelligible way to Jesus' proclamation. On the contrary, it was the perfect translation of the proclamation into action, the perfect counterpart in action to Jesus' eschatological macarisms (Matt. 5.3ff. par.). Word and act illuminate one another; and Jesus' table fellowship with sinners confirms the characteristic motifs we have associated with the reign of God. It was free and now and related to the restoration of Israel. Nothing, in fact, could have dramatized the gratuity and the present realization of God's saving act more effectively than this unheard of initiative toward sinners. Nor could anything have been more fundamental to the eschatological restoration of Israel.

For, what exactly was at stake in this initiative toward sinners and fellowship with them? The answer is twofold. First, the forgiveness and conversion of sinners was at stake. That this is how Jesus conceived the issue emerges with force and clarity from historical analysis of the parables by which he defended his actions (e.g. Matt. 20.1–16; 21.28–32; Luke 7.41–43: 15.4–7, 8–10, 11–32).[111] But there was a second factor. The sinner won back to God was also restored to his rightful family, Israel. Salvation belonged to Zacchaeus, said Jesus, 'for he, too, is a son of Abraham!' (Luke 19.9). It would seem that in entering into table fellowship with sinners Jesus was intent on a mission of reconciliation, not only between God and man but between man and man, the good (*dikaioi/ ṣaddîqîm*) and the wicked (*'amartōloi/rᵉšāʿîm*) in Israel. Nothing could have been more fundamental to the eschatological restoration of Israel than the seemingly impossible feat of healing the division between the good and the wicked without forfeiting the claims of the moral order.

But following Jesus' extraordinary impact on sinners (Mark 2.14f. parrs.; Luke 7.37f.; 19.6,8) the great problem in this work of reconciliation became the winning over of the good, the innocent, the pious (*dikaioi/ ṣaddîqîm*), so named not ironically or sarcastically but in frank acknow-

ledgment of their moral performance. The parables defending Jesus'
initiative to sinners call for interpretation not only as theme (mercy) but
as performance (defence). It should be emphasized that this was not the
defence of an embattled man concerned with his own honour nor was it a
polemical put-down of his critics. It was above all an appeal, one
repeatedly renewed and recast, designed not to humiliate the opposition
but to win it over. Such was the intended thrust of the parables of the Two
Sons, of the Two Debtors, of the Lost Sheep, of the Lost Drachma, and,
above all, of the Prodigal Son, where the appeal to the *dikaioi* is particularly evident and poignant. The story ends on this note of appeal, with the
words of the father to the elder son: 'But we had to celebrate and be glad,
because your brother was dead and has come back to life; he was lost and
is found' (Luke 15.32). How the elder son would respond to this is left
open and undecided; it was up to the hearer, the *dikaios/ṣaddîq*, to decide
this matter for himself. Successful or not, Jesus' appeal to the righteous
was a persistent effort; and it was part and parcel of an eschatological task
of reconciliation (Mal. 3.24) aimed at re-establishing the tribes of Jacob
(Sir. 48.10; Isa. 49.6).

Public debate and public formulations of mission

We have already made reference to the public conflict between Jesus and
his critics from among the religious *élite* over Jesus' breaking the sabbath
by a miraculous cure (Mark 3.1–5 parr.; for another sabbath cure, cf.
Mark 1.21–28 par.; on debates over sabbath cures, cf. Luke 13.14–17;
14.3–6; John 5.9–16; 9.16). Our question at this point is: What was at
stake in the collision between Jesus and Torah piety? We may answer
from the outset in general terms: a certain claim on the part of Jesus and a
certain claim on the part of Israel's religious *élite*.

A cleanly formulated system designed to fill the whole of life down to its
nooks and crannies, Torah piety had impressive and attractive traits.
What in it and in Jesus could account for their collision? The answer must
somehow include the theme of 'system', Jesus' distance from it and the
contemporary *élite's* immersion in it. Evidenced by his table fellowship
with sinners and in his attitude toward dietary and sabbath prescriptions,
Jesus' freedom from system had its immediate source in his sense of God
and view of God's will. He based his table fellowship with sinners on the
need of the sinners ('It is not the healthy but the sick who need a physician', Mark 2.17 parr.), yet even more extensively and emphatically on
the boundless goodness of God (Luke 15.11–32); hence, on God's 'joy'
over a converted sinner (Luke 15.7,10). With respect to Torah prescriptions, it is in the nature of the case that Jesus' view of 'how things are'
('Nothing that goes into a man from outside can defile him', Mark 7.15
par.; 'God did not make man for the sabbath but the sabbath for man',

Mark 2.27[112]) derives from a prior, more fundamental view of 'how *God* is', i.e., what he wills (Matt. 12.7; cf. 20.14f.) or what pleases him (Matt. 18.14; Luke 15.7,10). On the other hand, Torah piety was systematic and, like all such piety, was liable to the risk of fatal entanglement in system, the risk of losing that craning toward and listening for God which would keep the system open. Thus, Jesus' cures called for interpretation. Some saw in them signs that climactic and definitive salvation was imminent; the cures were launching it. 'The reign of God has overtaken you!' (Matt. 12.28 par.), said Jesus himself. It took a confident scribal *élite* to interpret a miracle as the infraction of a law. Impeccable logic: It could not be God who was acting in these cures for in that case they would not contravene the sabbath laws. Jesus confronted this closed world as its crisis: Not man for the sabbath but the sabbath for man! (Mark 2.27). Utterly unassimilable to casuistry of any kind,[113] the saying receives its sense from Jesus' polemic engagement with casuistry. 'Is it permitted (*exestin*, cf. rab. *muttār*) on the sabbath to do good or to do evil, to save life or to kill?' (Mark 3.4 par.; cf. Matt. 12.12). The question, its force dramatized by the immediately following cure, contradicted the confident claim that God could be counted on to operate within the confines of Torah and *halaka*. At the same time it presented Jesus' counterclaim to a divinely endorsed eschatological mission. The conflict, therefore, was not exclusively tied to an isolated event but was recurrent and substantial.[114]

Jesus' claim to a divine, eschatological mission inevitably became a theme of public debate, as the brilliant historical work on Jesus' parables over the past fifty years has shown. Nothing, in fact, has better illuminated Jesus' debates than parables-analysis, for as C. H. Dodd insisted, the genre 'parable' belonged very much to the arsenal of debate. Here we shall exemplify the technique of such analysis, drawing on a parable especially relevant to the definition of Jesus' mission: the Mustard Seed (Mark 4.30–32 parr.).

To the speaker of a parable the occasion and starting point was an objection or problem together with his own view of the matter. Then came the parable itself, giving figurative expression to his view. Reversing this process, we begin with the figurative expression, the parable. In the original situation this made its point by a comparison (as X is to Y, so A is to B). But the parable gives us only one limb of this equation ('as X is to Y'). The task is to recover the other limb ('so A is to B'); i.e., to recover the answer together with the problem or issue it answers. The unknowns are the audience, the issue, and the stand of Jesus.

Besides the expectation of a debate context, we have a starting point in the parable's imagery. In the parable of the Mustard Seed (Mark 4.30–32; Matt. 13.31f.; Luke 13.18f.; Thomas, 20) we are presented with a marvel: the great plant from the tiny seed. It has a twofold grounding, the continuity of seed and plant (the plant comes from the seed) and the discontinuity between the two (the seed is tiny, the plant great). Accordingly, the parable is both 'a parable of growth' and a 'contrast parable'. 'As the smallest of all seeds becomes the largest of all plants, so. . . .' How fill out the 'so . . .'? Apart from the fact that the answer has to do with the reign of God, we know only that it involves two related terms: A is to B as the tiny seed is to the great plant. That is, B comes from A; but B so contrasts with A that to have come from it is a marvel. That 'marvel' and 'reign of God' should be associated is only to be expected. But out of what metaphorical 'tiny seed' does the great plant, somehow imaging the reign of God, grow? The generically correct answer must be: Out of apparently meagre and unimpressive beginnings comes – the reign of God! But, though generically correct, this still leaves the original issue abstract and unfocused.

Clues to its concrete definition lie in the image of the birds and in the word *kataskēnoun* ('to nest'). The birds nesting in the great shrub evoke Gentiles taking refuge with Israel; and *kataskēnoun* is a technical term for the eschatological assimilation of the Gentiles to the people of God.[115] The original issue must accordingly have been the unimpressiveness of Jesus' following. If he really had a divine mission, ran the objection, he would not be surrounded by this rag-tag band, but by the best and the brightest. The parable answers:

> With the same compelling certainty that causes a tall shrub to grow out of a minute grain of mustard-seed . . . will God's miraculous power cause my small band to swell into the mighty host of the people of God in the Messianic Age, embracing the Gentiles.[116]

Appealing for faith and confidence, the parable invites the hearer to see in Jesus' followers the seed of the vast communion of the saved. Like many of the parables, this one warns: Do not be misled by appearances! Out of this unprepossessing band of disciples is destined to come the restored people, not only the lost sheep of Israel's house but the nations, as well. Here we glimpse a unique self-understanding. Jesus not only understood himself as the revealer of God's final saving act but as the author of its nascent realization in time.

The distance between question and answer is significant. The question was a question about Jesus (Was he not in some way discredited?). The answer was an answer about God's reign. The horizon of the question was narrow, that of the answer, vast; for what in Jesus' following fell under the critique of men came to expression in the parable, indirectly but incisively, as a revelation of the will of God. He did more, then, than defend his following and himself against objection. He invited the critic or doubter to find in them, and in himself, an omega-point, an aspect of God's climactic and definitive self-revelation.

Jesus' parabolic teaching, in no small part a follow-up on his proclamation of the reign of God, is filled with warnings and appeals addressed to the unresponsive: the learned, the pious, and the crowds (cf. the Children in the Marketplace, Matt. 11.16f. par.; the Deluge, Matt. 24.37–39 par.; the Snare and the Bird, Luke 21.34f.; the Useless Salt, Mark 9.50 parr.). These warnings pointed to an urgent issue bound up with Jesus' career. Thus, the supposition of the parable of the Sterile Fig Tree (Luke 13.6–9) was that Jesus' mission regarded the whole nation of Israel, whose salvation or ruin would turn on how it responded to him. Depicting this mission as the holding off of judgment – for a while, the parable warned that time was borrowed and running out.

Such warnings were not controversies. Jesus' controversies were not with the *massa indolens* but only with the learned (scribes) and the pious (Pharisees). The learned were theologians, public figures with social prestige on a par with the nation's hereditary *élite* (the temple clergy and the leading families of the capital). This aspect of the social context, reflecting the primacy of religion in Judaism's history and self-understanding, is a presupposition of the intense conflicts generated by Jesus' public career. Let us conclude our discussion of them by examining the claim to an eschatological mission in the context of debate over Jesus' initiative toward sinners and over his non-conformism to sabbath traditions. That this eschatological factor was decisive is not immediately evident; without reference to it, however, the conflicts remain opaque.

In his defence of the initiative toward sinners the eschatological note is struck in the motif of imminent judgment. The 'joy in heaven' (Luke 15.7,10), for example, refers by circumlocution to God's delight at finding sinners to acquit at the judgment.[117] In the parable of the Good Employer (Matt. 20.1–16) the last labourers engaged image the 'sinners' and the payment at the end of the day images the judgment. Here both the righteous and the sinners are saved. Elsewhere in Jesus' dialogue with the righteous, sinners are saved because at the last moment (= now) they repent (cf. the Two Sons, Matt. 21.28–31), whereas the righteous refuse to. 'Amen, I say to you: Publicans and prostitutes are about to enter the reign of God – and not you!' (Matt. 21.31).[118] Judgment is imminent; but, if so, its imminence and Jesus' mission are reciprocally defining.

Eschatology is likewise the key factor in the sabbath conflicts. Sayings such as 'God made the sabbath for man, not man for the sabbath' (Mark 2.27) might easily be given a gnomic sense, but there is no sign in the gospel tradition that Jesus wished to offer sapiential principles applicable to all time. His whole attention was concentrated on the present moment as conditioned by the imminence and the already operative presence of the reign of God. The charged present moment rather than a better and wiser grasp of the Torah therefore fuelled the debate and focused

Jesus' perspective on the debate. It was *halaka*-as-usual versus Israel's destined wedding feast and the new wine and new cloak of the time of salvation (Mark 2.19–21 parr.); *halaka*-as-usual versus miracles pledging and inaugurating the age to come (Mark 3.1–5 parr.; cf. the same thematic in Luke 13.14–17; 14.3–6; John 5.9–16; 9.16); *halaka*-as-usual versus God's messengers at the last hour (Matt. 11.16–19 par.); *halaka*-as-usual versus Torah brought to perfection (Mark 10.3–9 parr.; Matt. 5.21–48); *halaka*-as-usual versus the rigour (Matt. 8.20–22 par.) of discipleship for the reign of God.

Because it was the claim to a divinely sponsored eschatological mission that was ultimately at stake in Jesus' public debates, they elicited from him explicit statements about his mission. The *ēlthon*/*'ătêt* ('I have come') series includes public statements bearing on two themes: the salvation of sinners and the revelation of God's will: 'I have not come to call the righteous but sinners' (Mark 2.17 parr.). The formulation *ēlthon* ('I have come' = Aram, *'ătêt*) may signify: It is my intent, will, task.[119] The following infinitive concretely names the intention or will or task. In this case *kalein* (to call, summon) names the task of the messenger (cf. Luke 14.16f.) commissioned by his master to tell the invited guests that the banquet is ready. The summoning of the sinners showed that all Israel had been invited! The pointed antithesis, 'not the righteous but sinners', is polemic. It reflects the debate over Jesus' table fellowship (just the context in which the evangelists transmit it) and in this context is especially revealing. 'Why do I invite sinners to my table? This is my mission: to summon them to the banquet of salvation.' The theses of Lohmeyer,[120] Jeremias,[121] and others are accordingly well grounded: Jesus himself conceived his dining with sinners as an anticipation of the banquet of salvation with the patriarchs in the reign of God.

In thematic parallel to this text stands that of Luke 19.10: 'The Son of Man has come to search for what was lost and to save it.'[122] The sense is the same but the image is different. Here Jesus is not the messenger but the shepherd. Whereas Matthean texts (9.36; 10.6; 15.24) reflect an emergency situation in which the shepherd's task is to regroup the whole scattered flock, the present text evokes a different situation, that of the shepherd who, having just counted his flock and found a sheep missing, sets out in search of the straggler. This, says Jesus, is my mission.

The second theme of the public sayings in the *ēlthon*/*'ătêt* series is the revelation of God's will:

> Do not think that I have come
>   to annul the law [or the prophets[123]],
> I have not come to annul
>   but to fulfil (Matt. 5.17).

The historicity of the saying is probable.[124] Its key image is conveyed by the word *plērōsai*, which here means 'to fill to the full'. Presupposed is a view of world process as divinely determined and governed. God sets the measures of all things: space and time, life and death, good and evil. Thus, 'the time is fulfilled' (Mark 1.15; cf. John 7.8; Luke 21.24; *plērōma* in Gal. 4.4; Eph. 1.10) means that the appointed measure of time has been reached, as if a certain vase ordained for the measure of time were now filled to the brim (cf. 1QpHab 7.12–14). In the present text there is question of 'the law' ('*o nomos*; Aram: '*ôrāyᵉtā*'), i.e., the revelation of what God willed from Israel. The speaker declares that it is not his task to detract from this revelation but, on the contrary, to bring it to its appointed fullness. The motif of detracting indicates a debate context: Jesus is under attack as an antinomian.[125] The positive motif of filling to the full correlates with the claim that his Father had taught him (handed over or handed down to him) 'all things', 'everything' (Matt. 11.27 par.).[126]

Moreover, it fits into a larger and fuller scheme of meaning. Jesus presented his mission as the fulfilment of ancient promises and prophecies (Matt. 11.5 par.) and this, as biblical tradition eloquently attested (e.g. Josh. 21.43–45), signified a change of measure all along the line, an end to the fractional in favour of the full. Just as Elijah had come to restore 'all things' (Mark 9.12), so the call of Jesus was to all Israel (cf. 'the twelve', the inviting of sinners, Mark 2.17 parr., etc.); all the children of Abraham had a claim on him (Luke 19.9; cf. 13.16; Matt. 10.6; 15.24), especially 'all who toil and are burdened' (Matt. 11.28). He pledged that there was One who would meet 'all' the needs of those who put the reign of God first (Matt. 6.33) and arrival at his destined goal (*teleioumai*, Luke 13.32) would be bound up with the filling of all the appointed measures, including those of iniquity (Matt. 23.32), of suffering (Luke 23.28–31), and of historical time (Mark 14.25; Luke 22.16; cf. Luke 21.24).[127]

Among the sayings of the *apestalēn*/'*ištaddarît* ('I am sent') series,[128] we should mention the public word of Matt. 15.24: 'I am sent only to the lost sheep of Israel's house'. High probability attaches to the historicity of this saying.[129] In the distinctive context of Jesus' ministry, however, it may well have been enigmatic, for Jesus took a positive attitude toward Samaritans (Luke 10.25–37; 17.11–19) and the Gentiles. He consistently criticized (by the polemic technique of deliberate omission) the traditional theme of eschatological vengeance on the Gentiles (Luke 4.22; Matt. 11.5f. par.[130]) and he positively included the Gentiles among the saved in the reign of God (Mark 4.32 parr.; Matt. 8.11 par.; 12.41f. par.; 25.31–46). Why, then, this explicitly formulated limiting of his mission to Israel? The solution is given in Jesus' view of the scheme of salvation. His own task and so that of his disciples exclusively regarded the winning over of Israel, for the Gentiles would find salvation by assimilation to saved

Israel at the judgment bringing history to an end (cf. the eschatological pilgrimage of the nations of Zion, Matt. 8.11 par.[131]).

Entry into Jerusalem and cleansing of the temple

Originally, the entry into Jerusalem (Mark 11.1–10 parr.), the cleansing of the temple (Mark 11.15–19 parr.) and the question about authority (Mark 11.27–33 parr.) constituted a single narrative unit and reflected a single continuous event.[132] In no other event set before Israel had the themes of Jesus' public career and those of his esoteric instruction of disciples so dramatically converged. The public background to the event includes the riddles and symbolic acts by which he focused the significance of the reign of God. We shall review these briefly and offer as much of an interpretation of the temple-cleansing complex as is possible at this point (that is, without reference to the esoteric traditions which we reserve for later consideration and in the light of which we shall also reconsider the entry and cleansing).

Riddles and symbolic acts have in common a deliberately provocative aspect. They say, in effect, that to understand one must construe, and must do so deftly and with insight. Jesus was acutely aware of being a riddle to 'the wise and intelligent' (Matt. 11.25 par.), to 'those outside' (Mark 4.11), and even to his disciples (Mark 7.17–23 par.). He used riddles to solicit the effort to understand him. Though most of his riddles belonged to the esoteric teaching, there were also those spoken in public. It was doubtless enigmatic to the crowds, for example, that no one greater had arisen among men than the Baptist but that the least in the reign of God was (or would be) greater than he (cf. Matt. 11.11; Luke 7.28). There were also sayings which, to be sure, were intended to be understood at face value but whose originality of content and trenchant formulation made them surprising and puzzling; e.g., that the poor and the mourners and the hungry were 'blessed' (Matt. 5.3f. par., 6 par.) or that to dine with sinners and invite them to salvation was precisely Jesus' task (Mark 2.17 parr.).

Under the heading 'symbolic acts' we do not include all acts which have a symbolic value nor all acts the narratives of which have a symbolic intention. We include only those acts whose symbolic thrust we judge to have been conscious and intentional on Jesus' part. Thus, though the narrative notices on Jesus' practice of prayer doubtless have a symbolic and exemplary function, it is improbable that the practice of the historical Jesus should be described as intentionally symbolic. He prayed 'in private' (Luke 9.18), whether through the night (Luke 6.12), before sunrise (Mark 1.35), or in the afternoon (Mark 6.45 par.); usually in the 'wilderness' (Mark 1.35; Luke 5.16) or the 'hill country' (Mark 6.46 par.; Luke 6.12; cf. 9.28); and his praying was not meant to be seen (cf.

Matt. 6.5). Again, the Lukan notice on Jesus' weeping over Jerusalem (Luke 19.41) has prophetic and symbolic force; but if, in fact, Jesus wept over Jerusalem, it is doubtful whether his weeping was a deliberately intended symbolic act.

On the other hand, his understanding of his public career as a divine mission to Israel bringing the work of Moses and of all the prophets to climactic and definitive completion – nothing less is implied by the convergent phenomena of his public proclamation and teaching – converted public actions into symbolic actions. He willed his public actions to be open and transparent, to epitomize his views and values and to signify his purposes. His use of the number 'twelve' was symbolic; choice of the disparate personnel that were to be 'the twelve' was a symbolic act as was his sending of the twelve to Israel. His own exorcisms and cures as well as theirs were symbolic acts. His non-fasting was symbolic; and his dining with publicans and sinners was symbolic through and through.

Now, symbol calls for interpretation and Jesus was himself the guide to the interpretation of his symbolic acts. He contested and corrected mistaken or malicious interpretations, as we know from his debates with critics. His parables were designed to help Israel decipher all these actions and to read in them the message they were meant to carry. This message was definite and intelligible and it was a message of salvation. At the same time, Jesus was fully conscious of the distance between the demand for insight built into his actions and the capacity for insight on the part of the public. He once said to his disciples:

> To you One has given the secret of the reign of God
> but to those outside he imparts everything in riddles (Mark 4.11).[133]

The unriddling called for by his words and actions was beyond flesh and blood (Matt. 16.17). Learning was no help (Matt. 11.25 par.). His symbolic acts met with failed insight or malicious misconstruction. This he understood to be the normal situation, that of average man ('flesh and blood') confronted by One whose ways were not man's ways (Isa. 55.8), and who, moreover, was 'doing a new thing' (Isa. 43.19). When understanding occurred, Jesus attributed this to God (Mark 4.11; Matt. 11.25 par.; 16.17; cf. Luke 12.32), interpreting the total situation of misunderstanding and understanding as a gracious economy of divine predilection for the poor, the mourning, and the hungry, the deaf, dumb, and blind, the publicans and prostitutes, and his own pick-up team of disciples.

> I thank you, Father,
> Lord of heaven and earth,
> that, hiding these things from the wise and intelligent,
> you have revealed them to the simple!
> Yes, Father,
> for it is your gracious will that it be so (Matt. 11.25 par.).

The cleansing of the temple triggered a sequence of events which brought Jesus to his death on a cross outside the city wall. Was he aware that such actions as driving 'sellers and buyers' (Mark 11.15 parr.) out of the temple forecourt, overturning 'the money-changers' tables and the stalls of the pigeon-sellers' (Mark 11.15 par.) would lead the temple clergy and the scribes to 'seek a way to destroy him' (Mark 11.18)? This much was surely evident: To disrupt temple operations and to do so at the head of a crowd of messianic-minded pilgrims come to Jerusalem for Passover, was to perform an explosive act. The inherent danger of being interpreted in terms of sedition was doubtless one reason for the deliberately contrived contrast between Jesus' violent action on arrival at the temple and the symbolism of non-violence in his riding in procession from the Mount of Olives on the colt of an ass. In the consciously assumed trappings of non-violence, he headed for the temple and for public violence. Everything about the entry into city and temple and the immediately following expulsion of the temple concessioners was calculated. It is most unlikely that the provocative act of cleansing the temple was born of a sudden impulse. The temple was the goal of the procession and the procession was planned. Putting a strain on his policy of avoiding any explicit messianic claim, he now did nothing to inhibit the acclamation of the pilgrim crowd, probably Galileans like those who, according to a plausible Johannine tradition, had already tried 'to make him king' (John 6.15).[134]

The historicity of the solemn entry is plausible and that of the cleansing of the temple is solidly probable. The sense of this integral act, however, has been no less a challenge to critical interpretation than to the interpretation of Jesus' contemporaries. A first sure step is to recognize that the sense of this astonishing initiative cannot be contained within its immediate context. Jesus doubtless intended a real critique and reform of temple practice. The notice, 'he would not allow anyone to carry anything through the temple' (Mark 11.16) has the ring of serious intent to keep the temple hallowed here and now. But current custom was not the only, nor even the central, issue. Jesus' act was symbol-charged and signified the imminent eschaton. It brought the capital city and the temple into relation to the reign of God. Like the hosannas of the crowd, which Mark says proclaimed 'the coming reign of our father, David' (Mark 11.10), the temple cleansing signalled the dawn of a new era and a restoration of cult appropriate to it. We are far from having plumbed the sense of the temple cleansing; but further than this we cannot go for the present.

3. CONVERGENCE

Judging from Jesus' public words and actions, what was the point of his career? Was he a social reformer? How was his task limited? Did it consist simply in issuing warnings 'like one of the prophets of old' (Mark 6.15; cf. Luke 9.19)? (The Baptist's mission, as we have seen, went far beyond that.) What should be added in order to do justice to Jesus' mission? Perhaps we should begin from the beginning, with his proclamation of the reign of God.

The reign of God signified the age to come (*'o aiōn 'o mellōn*) under the modality of God's sovereignty. In this understanding the defining note of the eschaton was not Paradise regained (*gan 'ēden*) but the fulfilment of God's will. God's reign meant the realization of his intention, pleasure, will (*eudokia, rāṣôn*); and Jesus proclaimed that this intention, pleasure, will was on the point of realization. As the public traditions amply demonstrate, however, he did not proclaim (on the supposition that what God willed was a known quantity) merely that its time had come. The indirect object of the message 'The reign of God is at hand!' was the revelation of what God willed, what he had prepared for Israel and the nations, what he was doing for, and what he demanded of, Israel now.

What had he prepared for Israel and the nations? For Israel, climactic and definitive restoration; for the nations, participation in the salvation of Israel (Matt. 8.11 par.). The present moment did not fit neatly into the scheme of 'this age' versus 'the age to come', for the reign of God (the age to come) was operatively present (Matt. 12.28 par.) already in 'this age'.[135] Present by operation but future in its fulness, the reign of God was being mediated by its proclaimer. It was being mediated as a pure gift, attesting God's goodness, not Israel's, demanding the renunciation of claims, and offering the joy of repentance (the becoming like a child before God). Jesus' message, summons, promise was specially directed to an unexpected combination of groups and classes within Israel: the simple, the afflicted, and the outcasts.

Here evidently we have arrived at a densely packed datum. What does it mean that Jesus should have specially directed his proclamation and mission to the simple, the afflicted, and the outcasts?

It means, first of all, that his career had a powerful symbolic dimension. The crippled, the lepers, the blind, the poor, the hungry, the mourners, the sinners, the ostracized, the unimportant, unpowerful, and unpromising, were all types imaging the real – not the stubbornly illusory – situation of Israel *vis-à-vis* God. They were types of Israel-to-be-saved. The eschatological reversal of their situation – the poor made rich, the mourners comforted, the lepers cleansed – imaged the eschatological restoration of Israel.

Second, the distinctive directing of his mission to the unlikely had a powerful reconciliatory dimension. All the children of Abraham were to share in their heritage. If the ignorant had been depreciated by the learned (John 7.49; cf. Abot 2.5), the sinners by the righteous (Mark 2.16 parr.), the crippled by the pure and priestly (1QSa 2.4–7), Jesus by his every word and act – concretely, by his proclamation and teaching, his miracles and table fellowship – represented a completely new valorization of depressed elements in Israel: the simple (*nēpioi*, the inarticulate, and *mikroi*, *elachistoi*, the socially insignificant, to whom we should assimilate women and children), the afflicted (*ptōchoi*, *penthountes*, *peinōntes*, *kopiōntes*, *pephortismenoi*, *daimonizomenoi*, *kakōs echontes*, i.e., the poor, the mourners, the hungry, the fatigued, the burdened, the possessed, and the sick, including the blind, deaf, dumb, cripples, lepers, etc.), and the outcasts (*'amartōloi*, i.e., professional sinners like publicans and prostitutes and public sinners from among the mass of the unobservant; with these we should associate another group, the *akathartoi* or those 'unclean', like the practitioners of the despised trades, tanners, herdsmen, and so on).

In view of this reconciliatory and integrationist aspect of his public career, Jesus might indeed be mistaken for a social reformer. But, for one thing, social reform anticipates ongoing time, whereas Jesus anticipated the judgment about to inaugurate God's eschatological reign. Jesus' work should rather be interpreted in accord with the eschatological horizons of such texts as Mal. 3.24 and Sir. 48.10 on the task of Elijah. He was totally taken up with Israel's long-sought, final restoration. Though scriptural themes threw light on it, the restoration he was engaged in preparing and in already realizing was startling and new. It set in relief the presumptions and oversights and limits of eschatological expectation in Israel. Nothing, it would seem, had been so overlooked and unexpected as God's boundless goodness toward the simple, the afflicted, and the outcasts; accordingly, nothing in Jesus' career was so thoroughly misconstrued and resented as his resolute, unabashed, symbol-charged dealings with them. What appears in Christian retrospect as a compelling epiphany of love appeared in the swift unrepeatable drama of history as a contemptuous trampling on tradition. It was nothing less than a dismantling of the Torah and a seduction of Israel.

Earlier we said that in the light of their disparate make-up the twelve were 'a startling sign' and that, since their make-up was hardly accidental, there followed the real if as yet indeterminate expectation that the restoration of which they were the sign would itself have a startling character. At this point we can affirm that the relevant data on Jesus and the simple, afflicted, and outcast give definite shape and substance to the expectation. The restoration Jesus was intent on effecting startled everyone who came into contact with him – the crowds, the learned and pious, the simple, afflicted, and outcast, the disciples, the priestly and aristocratic *élite* – firing fierce allegiances and inciting deadly hostilities. This divisive impact (as we shall see in the next chapter) was perfectly conscious on

Jesus' part. It externalized the incongruence of Israel's dispositions and his own distinctive aims.

These aims had an element of the extravagant. If contemporary wisdom would call on a reasonable casuistry to bridge the chasm between human frailty and the divine will, Jesus would reveal a divine will that shattered the limits of Torah and *halaka* and he would bridge the greater chasm that resulted by calling into being a graced discipleship in which 'your hardness of heart' (Mark 10.5 par.) would be cured.

From the public traditions it would appear, then, that nothing short of a stunningly unexpected restoration of Israel defined the historic form of Jesus' career. Symbolic words and actions imaged this restoration as eschatological reversal. 'The twelve' as such evoked restoration motifs that had stamped the hope of Israel since the days of Ezekiel (see Ezek. 47.13–48.29). But Jesus did more than call on Israel to accept its rightful destiny of restoration. His exorcisms and his fellowship with sinners effected the restoration they signified. A leading purpose of his parabolic teaching was to heal religious divisions in Israel. The bold stroke of cleansing the temple laid a claim on the whole nation, pressing it to acknowledge the dawning reign of God.

These conclusions have a greater specificity than those drawn from our study of the Baptist and Jesus' stance toward him. Otherwise the two sets of conclusions remarkably converge.

VIII

THE SECRET OF THE REIGN OF GOD

The present chapter deals mainly with esoteric traditions (gospel texts depicting Jesus alone or Jesus and the disciples alone) and especially with Jesus' esoteric teaching (teaching reserved for his disciples). My purpose will be to show that this related to his public career as theme to performance, in the sense that the esoteric teaching promoted Jesus' public performance to the level of explicit thematization, and as solution to riddle, in the sense that it also presented the full scheme of meaning, the interpretative and explanatory perspective, in which he invited his disciples to grasp the whole of his words and acts and, in particular, the significance for Israel and the nations which he attached to his personal destiny.

1. FROM PERFORMANCE TO THEME: THE QUESTION 'WHO IS JESUS?'

In the course of its evolution toward critical history scholarship on the historical Jesus took two opposing detours. The 'critics' adopted that 'whole world-view' which Ernst Troeltsch maintained was necessarily entailed by 'the historical method'.[1] The 'apologists' in the meantime took their heuristic categories from systematic or biblical theology or both. Thus, with reference to the question of messiahship the critics made it clear that nothing more was at stake than whether or not Jesus happened to have drawn on a certain set of current concepts and titles to shape his self-understanding and to make himself intelligible to others. ('Messiahship' accordingly had no reality other than that of an idea.) Like the critics, the apologists dealt not with messiahship as such (which, however, they understood to have the reality of a divinely appointed role in a salvation history governed by God) but with Jesus' messianic consciousness, for whereas messiaship lay beyond the reach of the historians as such, messianic consciousness did not. The apologetic task was to keep the way open for a religious affirmation of Jesus' messiahship by offering historical evidence for his messianic consciousness.

If the historicism of Troeltsch now turns out to have been mere ideology and, indeed, ideology that thwarted access to the historical Jesus, the delicately balanced and nuanced apologetics of yesterday neglected historical interpretation and explanation in favour of dogmatic concerns such as the correspondence between the Testaments, the fulfilment of expectations associated with messianic titles, and the like. The apologists' choice of questions and categories was a more fundamental shortcoming than their uncritical exposition of Old Testament texts. The status they reserved for titles I reserve for aims, in the conviction that the key to historical understanding is the grasp of intentionality, i.e., perspective and purpose. But I preface consideration of the esoteric traditions with these remarks because, as it happens, there figures in the traditions a title which in my opinion Jesus understood to specify thematically the comprehensive aim of his mission.

The first question and the quest of a base from which to project an answer

The synoptic gospels represent Jesus as offering his disciples[2] private explanation of public teaching from the beginning of his public career (e.g. Mark 4.10–20 parr., 34; 7.17–23 par.). They nevertheless reserve the core of his esoteric teaching for a particular moment in the story, namely, that following Simon's confession of Jesus as 'the Christ [(the son) of (the living) God]' (Mark 8.29; Matt. 16.16; Luke 9.20). Successive pericopes inseperable in the synoptic tradition (Mark 8.27–30, 31–33; Matt. 16.13–20, 21–23; cf. the merger of the two pericopes in Luke 9.18–22) effect a thematic progression from the confession of Jesus as Messiah to the revelation of his coming repudiation, suffering, death, and resurrection. It is generally recognized that these conjoined Caesarea Philippi texts have considerable significance at least for the ordering of traditions within the synoptic gospels. Though each of these gospels has its distinctive structure, all three present Jesus' word on his coming destiny as the inauguration of a distinct, final phase both in his teaching and in his career; and all of them set this final phase under the sign of Simon's recognition and confession of Jesus as 'the Messiah'.

This commonplace observation imposes a strategy of inquiry; for, first of all, it seems unreasonable to hope to understand the data of the esoteric teaching attributed to Jesus without examining what the synoptic tradition explicitly presents as the central presupposition of these data, namely, the acknowledgement of Jesus as Messiah. Moreover, we take it that such questions as: 'Did Jesus identify himself as Messiah? Did the disciples of the pre-paschal period identify him as Messiah?' define an issue apt to generate light on Jesus' aims. These two related reasons positively invite us to make the first object of our inquiry into the esoteric traditions, and especially into the esoteric teaching, the messianic thematization of Jesus and his mission.

It would be extremely advantageous if, prior to any detailed consideration of texts whose sense and historicity remain under debate, we could articulate a well grounded expectation with regard to the thematization of Jesus and his vocation or mission as messianic. A heuristic base of this kind would be especially welcome in view of the possibility urged by Wrede, his followers, and many others, that the messianic texts of the synoptic gospels are the precipitate of a fundamental and far-reaching early Christian reconstruction. Though we have no advance guarantee that we can establish such a base, an exploratory effort at least is in order.

What, then, might offer indisputably solid ground on which to shape and base a guiding anticipation of the answer to our question about the messianic thematization of Jesus? There appear to be two candidates: the explicit christology of the Easter church and the almost certainly historical *titulus* on the cross, 'The King of the Jews' (Mark 15.26; cf. Matt. 27.37; Luke 23.38; John 19.19). We shall consider them in turn. But first the question itself ought to be stated as clearly and carefully as possible.

It is a historical, not a theological, question. It is exclusively concerned with gauging historical probabilities, not with specifying requisites for the truth of christological confession. The theologian may urge: 'What is decisive with regard to the object under consideration is not that the confession [of Jesus' messiahship] found expression [in his lifetime] but that Jesus really was what the confession affirmed of him.'[3] But we are not here concerned with what is decisive from a religious or theological standpoint. Without the least regard to whether or not Jesus was what the church's christological confession affirmed him to be, there remains the question: What must be supposed in order to account for the very emergence of the church's christological confession?

To answer this particular question it would not suffice to debate the proposition: 'The career of Jesus was performatively messianic.'[4] Whether finally made plausible or implausible, this proposition of itself would not cast so much as one ray of light on our question. Nor would matters be much improved by centring inquiry on the proposition: 'Jesus was himself consciously persuaded that he was the Messiah.' For on what grounds are the pre-paschal consciousness of Jesus and the paschal consciousness of the church to be treated as interchangeable? We may leave aside the question whether either or both the above propositions represent conditions, *de facto* fulfilled, of the coming to be of the church's messianic proclamation. For what is at stake is not *de facto* history but a heuristic anticipation thereof, and from this standpoint the above propositions neither singly nor together represent sufficient conditions of the Easter proclamation. Since we are not concerned with the truth, but simply with the emergence, of the Easter proclamation, the issue turns not on the object of the proclamation but on its subject, the proclaimers – who have been left out of both of the above formulations. Our precise question, then, is this: What must be supposed of the (pre-paschal and paschal) consciousness of the proclaimers, if we are to account for the coming into being of their specifically messianic proclamation?

Without necessarily having formulated the question in just this way, scholars have arrived by different routes at contradictory answers to it. 'Form criticism', wrote Hans Conzelmann in the late 1950s, could discover 'no connecting link' between Jesus and christology 'except the Easter experience of the disciples'.[5] Bultmann and his followers in particular followed Wrede in considering the Easter proclamation to have derived whole and entire from the Easter experience of the proclaimers. A frequently expressed objection to this view is based on the lack of any relation of entailment between 'resurrection' and 'messiahship'. Albert Schweitzer took note of this in his critique of Wrede, asking: 'How can the appearances of the risen Jesus have suggested to the disciples the idea that Jesus ... was the Messiah?'[6] Or, as N. A. Dahl put it in declarative form: ' ... from the appearances of the Resurrected One it could be inferred that Jesus lives and is exalted to heaven. But from this it could not be inferred that he is the Messiah.'[7]

There is a still more fundamental problem, however, which neither the critique offered by Schweitzer and Dahl nor the position under critique has satisfactorily addressed: How are we to gauge what was or was not possible under the impact of 'the Easter experience of the disciples' without a firm hold on the character and content of this experience? Wrede and the form critics did not arrive at their position out of a positive effort to show that the Easter experience of the disciples was of a nature to generate the proclamation of Jesus as Messiah. They had simply backed into their position from the premise that the history of Jesus had been unmessianic; and they felt confirmed in their position by confessions of faith (e.g. Rom. 1.4; Acts 2.36) which appeared to date Jesus' messiahship from the resurrection. But since they made 'the Easter experience of the disciples' a fertile source of epoch-making religious affirmations while offering little more than perfunctory conjectures about the nature of the Easter experience, the whole procedure has seemed to its critics cavalier and unconvincing. In their view 'the Easter experience of the disciples' had been turned into a magic top-hat from which, like so many rabbits, there unexpectedly emerged the church itself, its messianic proclamation, and its basic soteriology.

On the other hand, how is one to pronounce securely on what 'the Easter experience of the disciples' could *not* do? If, for example, one supposed that the Easter experience was such as to arouse the conviction that with Jesus eschatological resurrection had begun, i.e., that he was 'the first to rise from the dead' (Acts 26.23) in the sense of entering into 'the age to come', why might not the disciples have simply correlated this supreme eschatological event with what they clearly took to be the supreme role in the eschatological scenario, namely, that of the Messiah?[8] Even if other resources and data relevant to the messiahship of Jesus were lacking, how could such an Easter experience have failed to compel the conclusion that Jesus filled the supreme eschatological role? The lack of antecedent conceptual congruence between 'resurrection' and 'Messiah' would doubtless be a factor if we could be sure that the Easter experience guaranteed the strict logic of a careful graduate seminar.

But owing to the lack of studies cogently illuminating the character of the Easter experience as such,[9] it remains unclear whether or not this experience might of itself account for the church's proclamation. This makes Wrede's view problematic; but it makes that of his critics no less problematic, for, it would seem, we do not have a firm enough hold on the nature or content of the Easter experience to validate their verdict, namely, that this experience could not of itself generate the beginnings of christology. Consequently, the explicit christology of the Easter church does not meet the hope for an indisputably solid base from which to project an anticipation of these beginnings. Until we are better instructed on the Easter experience, the appeal to it as to a certainly adequate or certainly inadequate 'connecting link' between Jesus and christology is bound to look like a classic pursuit of *ignotum per ignotius*.

The death of Jesus by crucifixion outside Jerusalem establishes that the Roman administration executed him on a charge of political sedition and the *titulus* on the cross establishes the charge more exactly: He was executed as a claimant to kingship (= a messianic pretender).[10] It is therefore attested beyond any reasonable doubt that there had been some pre-paschal thematization of Jesus as Messiah. The question is whether this of itself allows us to block out a guiding expectation with reference to the pre-paschal consciousness of Jesus and his disciples. And the answer must be 'no'; for, the crucifixion of Jesus as 'the King of the Jews' entails only that he was charged with claiming a status incompatible with Roman policy and punishable by death. It entails nothing either of Jesus' self-understanding or of his disciples' understanding of him.

Prior to consideration of debatable texts, then, we are unable to articulate a well grounded expectation calculated to forward our inquiry. But the state of the question for heuristic moves of this kind has been improved, I hope, by insisting that the inquiry, in so far as it is made to begin from the church's explicit christology, be precisely focused on the evolving consciousness of the proclaimers; and that to ground judgments of possibility and probability concerning the endlessly invoked 'Easter experience of the disciples' we must have arrived at a more exact knowledge of its nature than has so far been achieved. It is widely recognized, on the other hand, that the crucifixion itself and the titulus 'The King of the Jews' are not of themselves an adequate base for projecting an effective anticipation of the mentality of Jesus and the disciples.

But this state of affairs need not fundamentally inhibit our inquiry. The church's christology is a fact and it does lead us directly back to the *titulus* on the cross; the *titulus* is a fact and it leads us back to Jesus' trial, which, though debatable, has come into sharper historical focus than ever before thanks to the debates of the past three decades. For our purposes it is not necessary to establish the historicity of the trial before the Sanhedrin. It is in the Markan account of the trial, however, that we shall find the historically solid point of departure for our inquiry. And though the historicity of the trial as such is not crucial to our argument, we do in fact take the Markan account to have a historical grounding.

First, the literary and historical arguments proposed by Hans Lietzmann in 1931 against the historicity of the trial before the Sanhedrin (Mark 14.55–65 parr.) have been largely eroded under intense examination. The Sanhedrin's limited juridical competence (John 18.31b) in particular has been shown by a convergence of lines of evidence to have high probability.[11] The studies of Paul Winter, beginning with his 1961 work *On the Trial of Jesus*, have similarly served to sharpen critical focus on the relevant literary and historical issues and (contrary to Winter's own views and intentions) to fill out, nuance, and tighten the case for historicity.[12]

Second, a Qumran text (4QFlor 1–13) applying Nathan's oracle (II Sam. 7) to the Essene brotherhood has also thrown light on the trial of Jesus.[13] Otto Betz, in particular, has explored the relevance of the oracle of Nathan to the thematization of Jesus as Messiah and specifically to the Markan scene of Jesus before the Sanhedrin.[14] Interpreted eschatologically, the ancient text of II Sam 7 was made to reveal the underground connections linking the testimony of the 'false witnesses' on Jesus' word about the temple (Mark 14.58), the question of the high priest (Mark 14.61), and the response of Jesus (Mark 14.62). Nathan's oracle, i.e., Yahweh's word to David, reads in part:

> When your days are fulfilled
> and you lie down with your fathers,
> I will raise up your offspring after you,
> who shall come forth from your body,
> and I will establish his reign.
> He shall build a house for my name,

and I will establish the throne of his reign forever.
I will be his father and he shall be my son ... (II Sam. 7.12–14a).

Just as this oracle had stood at the source of biblical tradition identifying the Davidic king as God's son (Pss. 2.7; 89.27; 110.3), defining the building of the temple as his task (Hag. 1.1f.; 2.20–23; Zech. 6.12f.), and promising the perpetuity of the Davidic dynasty (II Sam. 23.5; Isa. 9.5f., EVV 9.6f.; Ps. 89.3–5, 20–38), so an eschatological valorization (cf. 4QFlor 1–13) of the words:

> He shall build a house for my name,
> and I will establish the throne of his reign forever.
> I will be his father and he shall be my son,

provides the clue to the structure of meaning that holds the Markan trial scene together. In the Markan sequence the relevant motifs occur as follows: (Destruction and) construction of the temple (Mark 14.58; II Sam. 7.13); 'the Messiah, the Son of the Blessed One' (Mark 14.61; II Sam. 7.14); definitive enthronement (Mark 14.62; cf. Luke 22.69; II Sam. 7.13). These motifs, moreover, provide the intelligible ground of the following charge of blasphemy and sentence of death. For in all probability the 'blasphemy' (Mark 14.64a par.) lay in dishonouring 'the Blessed One' by the claim – ostensibly false inasmuch as Jesus stood utterly powerless before his judges[15] – to be his 'Son'. And blasphemy was punishable by death (Lev. 24.16; cf. Num. 15.30f.; Mark 14.64b par.). As the root of the thematic complex 'temple, Messiah, Son of God, enthronement', the oracle of Nathan has thus contributed directly to the Markan scene's intelligibility and indirectly (by resolving objections based on the scene's supposed incredibility) to the issue of its historicity.

Our interest, in any case, focuses on what now appears as the hinge word of the entire scene: 'We heard him say: 'I will destroy this temple that is made with hands, and in three days I will build another, not made with hands' (Mark 14.58 par.). Though garbled in the version of the witnesses and modified by a Christian, perhaps Markan, addition,[16] the temple saying (cf. Mark 15.29 par.; John 2.19; Acts 6.14) is certainly a word of the historical Jesus.[17] In the light of the substantially attested biblical and post-biblical traditions deriving from the oracle of Nathan it is clear that 'the building of the temple' could easily be made to carry messianic connotations[18] and that in the strictly eschatological and symbolic form which this motif has assumed in Jesus' saying, a messianic sense is implicit (Mark 14.58 par.; 15.29–32 = Matt. 27.40–42; cf. Matt. 16.16–18). We conclude that in the word on building the temple in three days we have found a solid point of departure for dealing with messiahship as a determining factor in Jesus' understanding of himself and his mission.

The temple riddle

In the synoptic gospels the temple saying is cited by Jesus' enemies (Mark 14.58; 15.29; Matt. 26.61; 27.40; cf. Acts 6.14). In the gospel of John it is spoken by Jesus himself (John 2.19) and interpreted by the evangelist as a reference to 'the temple of his body' (John 2.21). That the Christian community found the saying thoroughly problematic is attested by three factors: the diversity of form (as cited by his enemies Jesus says he himself will destroy the temple, whereas when represented as speaking the word himself [John 2.19] he says: 'Destroy this temple . . .'); the lack of direct attestation in the synoptic tradition for the original word; and the need sensed by John for an explanatory comment as well as the artificiality, from the standpoint of critical history, of the comment itself.[19] Problematic for special reasons to the Christian community,[20] the saying was baffling also for its first audience. It had been deliberately formulated as a riddle. In this it is very like two other public words, likewise spoken to critics and cryptically relating Jesus to the coming eschatological crisis and its resolution, namely, the saying on the sign of Jonah (Matt. 12.39 par.; cf. Mark 8.12; Matt. 16.4) and the 'three days' saying on Jesus' divinely destined course (Luke 13.32). To unriddle the word on the temple calls for recovery both of its original form and of the full field of meaning in which it has its intelligibility.

It is quite probable that the form given the first limb of the saying by the witnesses at Jesus' trial and the taunting bystanders on Golgotha did not derive from Jesus. True, he maintained to a chosen inner circle of disciples that the temple would be destroyed (see Mark 13.2ff. parr.). But in his view the fall of the temple belonged to the tide of evil which he called the 'ordeal' or 'test' (['o] *peirasmos*; Aram.: *nisyôn[ā']*, e.g. Matt. 6.13 par.). Such was the eschatology of trial and tribulation. Fierce but brief, it would be followed by the eschatology of grace: the divine intervention that would put an end to the ordeal and repair its ravages. Moreover, the very fact of 'the cleansing of the temple' excludes, in the last analysis, the negative mentality of the destroyer (*katalyōn*). The original or historical form of the first limb of the temple saying may very well be given in John 2.19, 'Destroy this temple . . . ,' an imperative with the force of a condition.[21]

In the second limb Mark and Matthew give the time notice as *dia triōn 'emerōn*, whereas John gives it as *en trisin 'emerais*, formulas which presumably are translation variants of Aram. *lit'lātā' yômîn*.[22] *Dia triōn 'emerōn* can mean 'throughout three days' or 'within three days' or 'after three days'. Antithetical parallelism which neatly juxtaposes 'destroying' and 'building' excludes the first, durative, sense. The punctiliar sense, corresponding to the apocalyptic conception of the new temple miraculously raised and revealed, would still leave open the second possibility (favoured by the Johannine *en trisin 'emerais*, cf. Mark 15.29 par.) and the third (cf. Vulg. Matt. 26.61, *post triduum*). In either case we have an eschatological scheme which (as we shall see) is entirely characteristic of Jesus' esoteric words on the imminent future: The eschatology of tribulation (in this case the destruction of the temple) is followed swiftly (here within or after three days) by the eschatology of triumph (here, the new temple).

To specify fully the field of meaning in which the saying has its intelligibility we should take other gospel texts into consideration. But we can begin with a few words on the 'three days' motif and on the meaning of 'temple'. We shall then be able to propose a view on the probable historical context in which Jesus spoke the temple word.

The 'three days' motif derives from Semitic idiom, which variously compensates for the want of a word like 'time', an abstract noun with a durative sense. Joachim Jeremias has pointed out that to signify 'some (little) time' the Bible draws on such concrete expressions as *yāmîm* (lit. 'days', Gen. 40.4), *yôm 'ô yômaim* (lit. 'a day or two', Ex. 21.21), *yāmîm 'ăḥādîm* (lit. 'some days', Gen. 27.44), etc., and, above all, *šelôšet yāmîm* or *šelôšâ yāmîm* (lit. 'three days').[23] Accordingly, such expressions as 'for three days' or 'in three days' or 'after three days' and 'on the third day' do not necessarily refer to three calendar days. They sometimes have a vague sense: 'in a while, shortly, soon' (cf. e.g. Josh. 2.16; II Kings 20.5, 8). Context must indicate the duration of the while, i.e., say what the shortness of time would concretely amount to in any given case. It must also indicate whether the accent in a particular instance falls on shortness as such. So much for ordinary usage. In the symbolic language of the Bible, as the rabbis noted, 'the third day' brought salvation because God did not leave the righteous in need for more than three days (Gen. 42.17f.; Ex. 19.16f.; Josh. 2.16; Hos. 6.2; Jonah 2.1, EVV 1.17, etc.).[24] The 'three days' sayings of Jesus (besides Mark 14.58 parr., cf. Luke 13.32f.; John 16.16f., 19) carry a symbolic sense. The time is determined by God, and the third day signifies the *kairos* of salvation. The time prior to it need not be conceived as crisis nor need the shortness of time be accented (cf. Luke 13.32f.). But in the saying under consideration, in which the eschatological scheme of crisis/crisis-resolution is evident, the sense does call for an accent on the limitation and shortness of time. The imminent crisis epitomized in the destruction of the temple would swiftly yield to the salvation epitomized in the new temple to be built by Jesus.

'This temple' in the first limb of the saying evidently refers to the temple of Jerusalem: imposing in dimension, dazzling in beauty, charged with meaning for Israel. The temple was central not only to the cultic but to the political, commercial, financial, and social organization of national life. But neither its physical nor its functional reality exhausted its meaning for Israel. Long before the time of Jesus the temple had been invested with extraordinary symbolic significance. At the turn of the sixth century BC the cry *hêkal Yahweh* ('The temple of Yahweh!') had summed up the Israelite sense of election as God's people and epitomized its covenant claims on God's favour and protection (Jer. 7.4). When the armies of Nabuchadnezzar stormed Jerusalem and destroyed the temple, they also shattered a world of religious assumptions and provoked a national crisis of faith. The major effort of the post-exilic years had been concentrated on rebuilding the temple. The splendour of the Herodian renovations begun in 20/19 BC and not completed in final ornamentation until the early 60s, more than thirty years after Jesus' death, made the temple one of the world's wonders. To evoke, even conditionally, the destruction of 'this temple' was to touch not just stone and gold and not only the general well being but history and hope, national identity, self-understanding, and pride.

The already potent symbolism clinging to the temple, all its parts and appurtenances, the mountain on which it was built, the city in which it stood, was magnified by classical eschatology and even more by transposition from relative to absolute (or apocalyptic) eschatology.[25] We know from the public proclamation and teaching of Jesus that for all the sobriety of his language he stood in the tradition of absolute eschatology. There is, of course, a relevant biblical background, a rich one especially in the prophets, to Jesus' word on the temple he would build in three days. But we must remember that the laborious, historical-critical appropriation of the relative eschatology of the prophets is only remotely relevant to the effort to reconstruct the operative field of meaning of Jesus' words. It was in the mode of absolute eschatology that he appropriated the entire biblical heritage. Here we shall simply fasten on a few texts on the temple taken from the book of Isaiah and read them in a way corresponding to this mentality.

The temple, then, would have a role not only in Israel and for history but for the whole world at time's end in the reign of God (Isa. 2.2–4; 56.1–8). This would be the last and eternal – the eschatological – temple, located on a Zion (Isa. 2.2–4; 28.16) rebuilt in carnelians and sapphires (Isa. 54.11) after a final devastation:

> Yes, the LORD will comfort Zion
> and have pity on all her ruins;
> he will make her wilderness like Eden,
> her waste land like the garden of the LORD (Isa. 51.3).

The final ransoming of Israel would turn on an act of faith. 'Behold,' says the Lord, 'I set on Zion a stone', a stone of crystal crowning the temple portal and inscribed 'He who believes shall not be shaken' (Isa. 28.16). Copestone signified Messiah; temple, the messianic remnant of believers.[26] And once the Lord had taken it in hand to reclaim and restore his people for the last time, then Messiah and messianic people, the temple on Zion, would draw the dispersed of Israel from the corners of the earth (Isa. 11.12; 56.8) – together with the Gentiles! For on that day the Davidic king would himself be 'a signal for the nations'; they would seek him out, 'for his dwelling shall be glorious' (Isa. 11.10).

> I will bring them to my holy mountain
>   and make them joyful in my house of prayer.
> Their holocausts and sacrifices
>   will be acceptable on my altar.
> For my house shall be called a house of prayer
>   for all peoples (Isa. 56.7).

A world in darkness would raise its eyes to the radiance of restored Israel (Isa. 60.3) and the nations would stream to the holy mountain at the centre of the world.

To read the Bible in this way – that is, understanding its mass of promise and prophecy to refer to today and to a tomorrow on the point of dawning, and understanding this tomorrow as the climactic and definitive consummation of time and history – is to grasp something of what the new temple meant to Jesus. *This* temple no one could build but God himself – or the Messiah transcendently enthroned at his right hand.

Is it plausible that Jesus should have spoken openly of such themes as these? No. But his word on the temple was not open language. It was a riddle. The only context which early Christian literature supplies for the temple riddle as originally spoken is the demand for a sign (John 2.18) establishing Jesus' authority to cleanse the temple (John 2.14–17). Was this, in fact, the historical context of his word? To break the question down into parts: Was its original context the demand for a sign? In favour of a 'yes' stands a historical parallel, the Jonah riddle. On another occasion the certainly historical and doubtless repeated demand for a sign elicited from Jesus his words on 'the sign of Jonah' (Matt. 12.39; Luke 11.29), an equally disconcerting and similarly eschatological and christological riddle.[27] Was the original context of the temple riddle the quest of a sign apropos of the cleansing of the temple? A sure answer can hardly be expected; but it is striking, first, that among the relatively few parallels between John and the synoptic gospels for the period prior to the passion is the sequence: temple cleansing/question about authority (John: demand for a sign) and, second, that according to the synoptic tradition, historically preferable here, the cleansing of the temple is what triggered the determination to do away with Jesus (Mark 11.18; Luke 19.47), i.e., as it concretely turned out, to bring him to the trial at which the temple saying would be cited as evidence against him.

The saying was a riddle. But, though both its limbs were cryptic, neither was unintelligible. Ultimately, their riddle character lay less in their sense than in their significance, i.e., less in the indecipherability of the words (the high priest at the trial deciphered them) than in the chasm between the horizon of the speaker and that of his audience. To this audience the words were outlandish, pretentious, insulting, with the motif of the temple's destruction smacking of impotent threat. Over and above having a riddle form, the temple saying was a riddle in the deeper sense: 'To those outside [God] imparts everything in riddles.'

To get a firmer hold on the sense of the temple saying and especially to discover how this sense was anchored in the perspectives and purposes of the historical Jesus, we shall examine two other texts which draw on temple motifs to signify the eschatological restoration of Israel: the rock (*kêpā'*) saying of Matt. 16.17–19 and, once again, the cleansing of the temple. In conclusion we shall reconsider Jesus' riddle and its significance.

In the region of Caesarea Philippi

The text of Jesus' response (Matt. 16.17–19) to Simon's declaration of messianic faith (Matt. 16.16) reads as follows:

> 17 Blessed are you, Simon Bar-Jona,
> for flesh and blood has not revealed [this] to you
> but my heavenly Father.
> 18 And I say to you: You are Peter ('*o Petros*; Aram.: *Kêpā'*)
> and on this rock I will build my church
> and the gates of Hades shall not prevail against it.
> 19 I will give you the keys of the reign of heaven
> and whatever you bind on earth heaven shall bind
> and whatever you loose on earth heaven shall loose.

The three verses constitute a single unit.[28] Verse 18 draws on the master image of the cosmic rock, the divinely appointed site (in the ancient Near Eastern alphabet of symbols) for the central sanctuary or temple and the lid over the netherworld (cf. the allusion to 'the gates of Hades').

This age-old imagery had been adopted in biblical tradition (cf. Bethel ['house of El'] as the sacred point of contact between heaven and earth in Jacob's dream, Gen. 28.11–19) and turned to eschatological account by the prophets (the holy mountain, navel of the world, to be the sanctuary of the nations: Isa. 2.2–4; 60; Zeph. 3; Zech. 8; cf. Jer. 3.17 etc.). The cosmic rock's wealth of attributes, numerous and various to the point of apparent incoherence, find their intelligibility in a basic mythological image: the emergence of the hollow mountain from the primaeval flood.[29] Its peak was the world's topmost and centremost point, offering access equally to Hades and to heaven. To the rabbis the cosmic rock was the site of creation, of Paradise and the tree of life, source of the rivers of the world, proof against the Deluge. Here was the altar on which Abraham was ready to sacrifice Isaac; here, too, was the altar of Melchizedek; here, the house and throne of God and the destined locale of the judgment of the world.[30]

Concretely, the cosmic rock was identified first of all with Zion and the altar of holocausts; later, with the *'eben šᵉtiyyā'* in the holy of holies.[31] In later Jewish literature Abraham, 'the rock from which you were hewn' (Isa. 51.1), would be interpreted as the cosmic rock that braved the subterranean flood and bore the house of God.[32] Or the twelve patriarchs would be so identified.[33]

If the image of the cosmic rock is the key to the content of Jesus' word, the oracle of Nathan is the key to its context. For, once again, the thematic complex originally established for biblical tradition in this oracle provides the unarticulated link between confession and commission. The text's operative presupposition is that the task of 'the Messiah, Son of the living God' (Matt. 16.16) is precisely to build the eschatological temple. Here temple is translated by 'church', the community of restored Israel, or rather by 'my church', for the restored community of Israel is messianic.[34]

Though few gospel texts have been branded unhistorical more emphatically than Matt. 16.17–19 has been, the evidence favours both its historicity and the originality of its placement in the Caesarea Philippi scene.

Quite apart from Matthew, the gospels are at one in relating that Simon received the name Peter from Jesus (Mark 3.16; Luke 6.14; John 1.42). In Mark and Luke this datum is left altogether unexploited. It receives neither special accent nor thematic development. The only way in which this lack of emphasis, whether on the name itself or on its bestowal, can affect the judgment of the critic is to support a verdict of historicity. Even in the Fourth Gospel, where the original Aramaic form of the name is indicated, the force of *Kēphas* (Greek transliteration of *Kêpā'*) and of *Petros* (Greek translation of *Kêpā'*) is supposed rather than highlighted or developed. The conclusion, with a rating of good probability, is that Jesus did in fact give Simon the totally new name *Kêpā'*.

But no rationale for this new name other than that offered by Matt. 16.17–19 has ever been made even minimally plausible. That '[the] Rock' was a sobriquet alluding to Simon's appearance or character traits is trivial and groundless. On the other hand, the character and importance of the role of 'Cephas' in pre-Pauline (I Cor. 15.5), Pauline (Gal. 1.18; 2.9,11,14; I Cor. 1.12; 3.22; 9.5; 15.5), and post-Pauline (Acts 1–15;[35] all four gospels) estimation accords exceedingly well with the distinctive force of the Matthean text. That the giving of the name should be located in the pre-paschal period follows from the unity of Matt. 16.17–19[36] and is affirmed by all the gospels (Mark 3.16; Luke 6.14; John 1.42).

It is probable on structural grounds alone that the original context of

Matt. 16.17–19 was the Caesarea Philippi confession.[37] But this probability is independently fortified by the thematic complex Messiah/Son of
God/building of temple (cf. II Sam. 7) by which vv. 17–19 interlock with
v. 16 and so with the substance of the Caesarea Philippi pericope.

The structure of this pericope as it appears in any of the synoptic
gospels tells against the conjecture that the tradition at any stage intended
to represent Jesus as rejecting Simon's confession of messiahship. True,
one aspect of the thematic progression from this to the following pericope
lies in the firm bond between messiahship and enthronement. Dalman
long ago made the point that 'Messiah' meant ruler and so supposed
enthronement; and he applied this observation to the Caesarea Philippi
pericopes: 'When Jesus attached to the messianic confession of Peter the
first intimation of His violent death, He did so in order to make it clear
that the entrance upon His sovereignty was still far distant. . . .'[38] The
relation of enthronement and messiahship was a feature of the riddle of
David's 'son' and 'Lord' (Mark 12.35–37 parr.), the point of which was
the mystery of the enthronement. It would be stunningly transcendent
and supernatural (Ps. 110)! This is why the inspired David called his son
'Lord': he had heard God bid him sit at his right hand, a cosmic victor.
Again, Jesus' insistent conjunction of messiahship and enthronement was
the climactic moment of the trial scene before the Sanhedrin (Mark 14.62
parr.) and was the heart of the Son-of-man thematic in its original form.[39]
Granted these qualifications on enthronement (and, by implication, on
the destiny to be realized prior to enthronement), it would still be a
mistake to suppose that the tradition ever knew of Jesus' rejection of
Simon's messianic confession. The pericope's indispensable opening move
is the question by which he himself initiated the issue: 'Who do men say
that I am?'

Obviously, the force of this 'Who?' was to relate Jesus in a specific way
to Israel's eschatological scenario. Thus, the Fourth Gospel represents the
priests and levites commissioned to inspect the claims and purposes of the
Baptist as asking: 'Who are you?' (John 1.19) and the range of possible
answers included 'the Messiah', 'Elijah', and 'the prophet' (Deut. 18.15–
18), all scripturally attested figures. If the Baptist added to this list, it was
still by reference to biblical prophecy (Isa. 40.3). The same pattern was
present in Jesus' identification of John as Elijah (Mark 9.13; Matt. 11.10
par.), in the conjecture of Herod and others to the effect that Jesus was the
Baptist come back to life (Mark 6.14 parr., 16 par.), or some other
prophet *redivivus* (Mark 6.15 par.; 8.28 parr.). Again, it was the 'Who?'
question and a prospective answer ('the Messiah') which 'everybody'
according to Luke (3.15) entertained about the Baptist and the Baptist
about Jesus (Matt. 11.3 par.). The disciples were often led by striking
phenomena in Jesus' career to ask themselves who he was. Miracles trig-

gered the question 'What is this?' (Mark 1.27. cf. Luke 4.36) which then
led to 'Who can this be?' (Mark 4.41 parr.). But it should be noted that
the point of finding an answer to the 'Who?' question was thereby to find
an answer to the question of what exactly the sense and significance of the
work, whether of the Baptist or of Jesus, was. Identification by reference to
Israel's eschatology was meant to illuminate the final meaning of words
and actions already interpreted as signs of the eschaton.

Hence, the scene we have been considering was in effect the hidden
turning point of Jesus' career. The eschatological character of this career
had clearly registered on the public which instinctively located Jesus
within the framework of the biblical and post-biblical theme of the
prophet come back to life to carry out eschatological tasks (e.g.
Mal. 3.1ff.). How to understand the eschatological task of Jesus was
accordingly the thrust of the question he himself put to the disciples: 'Who
do you say that I am?' Christology, in short, was 'functional', and Jesus'
question led directly into the issue which is our main inquiry. Indeed, the
sequel to his question puts us in possession of the symbol-charged terms in
which he thematized his work of national restoration: it was the messianic
task of building on rock, secure against death, the living temple of the last
days.

Now, this historical construing of the data of Matt. 16.17–19 represents
a minority, out-of-season, opinion. An effort is accordingly called for to
show in detail why it is preferable to the majority view and how it is
defensible against objections which derive either from the data or from
suppositions connected with the majority view. To this end I should like,
first, to offer an exposition and critique of average current opinion on the
exegesis and historical analysis of Matt. 16.17–19 and, second, to state
and respond to the most serious objections against the minority position
defended here.

Happily, average opinion has recently been made available, as if to
order, in an exposition of Matt. 16.16b–19 prepared by a committee of
American scholars.[40] In their view the text of Matt. 16.17–19 had its
origin in a tradition on the resurrection.[41] The hypothesis of Markan
priority places the burden of proof on whoever would affirm the Matthean
form of the Caesarea Philippi scene to be earlier than the Markan form.[42]
Moreover, the material present in Matthew and absent from Mark is also
absent from the parallel scenes of Luke 9.18–22 and John 6.66–71.
John, to be sure, offers parallel material scattered through his gospel
(John 1.41f.; 6.67–71; 20.23); but this only shows that Matthew may well
have assembled materials from another setting or from several other set-
tings and inserted them into the Caesarea Philippi scene.[43] Again, the
Matthean form of Simon's confession ('You are the Christ, the Son of the
living God') expresses a faith in Jesus as divine, and this especially ties in

with a resurrectional setting.[44] In line with this reasoning the words 'reveal' and 'flesh and blood' (Matt. 16.17; cf. Gal. 1.16), the macarism form (cf. John 20.29), the reference to a 'church', to 'the gates of Hades', and to binding and loosing (cf. John 20.23), all have special ties and parallels with resurrectional texts.[45] In average opinion it was Matthew who converted Simon's words into a fully accepted profession of faith. Mark had taken Simon's confession of messianic faith either as wrong or as incomplete. The Matthean transformation was inspired, then, not by the Markan text but by a tradition originally centred on Simon and the risen Christ.

The force of this analysis depends on the cogency of its individual elements as well as on their convergence. Though some elements might claim more cogency than others, no single one stands out as virtually clinching the conclusion by itself and so reducing other considerations to a merely confirmatory role. We shall accordingly weigh each individual element, treating in turn Markan priority, parallels in Luke and John, the Matthean form of the confession, and the link in motif and vocabulary between Matt. 16.16b–19 and the resurrection.

First, apropos of Markan priority we should recall the two basic distinctions discussed earlier, in Part One: that between relative antiquity among redactions and relative antiquity among traditions and that between the antiquity of traditions and the claim to historicity.[46] To apply these principles to the present instance is only to repeat our rejection of the principle that with regard to the relative antiquity of traditions 'Markan priority holds until proved otherwise'; it is also to be disabused of the supposition that the claim of Matt. 16.17–19 to historicity is settled in the negative on condition that the Markan form of the pericope is older than the Matthean.

But that the Markan form is older is in any case entirely unlikely, as we have observed, on form-critical grounds. Possibly, the Caesarea Philippi tradition came to Mark in truncated form. More likely, he himself omitted the response of Jesus to Simon in favour of making Simon's confession (which, like all the parallels, e.g. Matt. 16.16; John 1.41; 6.69; cf. Mark 1.1, 34; Mark presents in an entirely positive sense) strictly functional to the central theme of his gospel, namely, entry into the messianic mystery of the Son of man's death and resurrection. The acknowledgment of Jesus as the Messiah was the condition of this thematic development (already, in all probability, in pre-Markan tradition); Mark has seen to it that the confession is severely limited to the role of bringing this condition to fulfilment. Mark's own placement of the notice on the naming of Simon (Mark 3.16) had a merely topical basis; and he doubtless supposed that its sense – Simon is the foundation rock (*Petros*, Mark 3.16) of the eschatological temple (cf. Mark 14.58) – was clear (cf. John 1.42).[47] To think that

Mark presents the confession of Simon as 'wrong' is to overlook its identity with post-paschal Christian confession generally (cf. Mark 1.1); to conjecture that the Markan Jesus sees it as inadequate not only psychologizes the scene in a way congenial to modern but alien to Markan writing; it also overlooks the difference between a thematic progression (from Mark 8.27–30 to 8.31–33) which is believably pre-Markan and Markan, and a thematic merger of the two pericopes, which has no parallel elsewhere in Mark. Finally, this view affirms, despite the formal conclusion bringing the first pericope to an end (v. 30) and the formal introduction opening the second (v. 31, *kai ērxato didaskein autous*, 'and he began to teach them'), that the sense of the first pericope anticipates and derives from the second. This specifically means that Mark has suspended the intelligibility of the prohibition in v. 31 until the conclusion of the following pericope (whereas in fact Mark has already presented the rationale for the so-called messianic secret, cf. Mark 4.11f., and thereafter offers no further explanation.) In a word, average current opinion overloads Markan priority with a significance for literary criticism which it does not have, especially by blurring the distinction between priority among redactions and priority among traditions; it overlooks the form-critical grounds for denying the priority of the Markan text *vis-à-vis* Matt. 16.17–19; it slights the formal indices distinguishing and relating the confession and the prediction pericopes in Mark; it misconstrues the prohibition of Mark 8.30 and, consequently, the sense of Simon's confession and the relation between it and the following pericope.

Second, the parallels in Luke and John are significant in a way which, if anything, tells against rather than for average current opinion. In the text of Luke 9.18–20 the confession names Jesus *ton Christon tou theou*, 'the Christ of God' (v. 20). This differs from the Markan form ('the Christ') and correlates, through the phrase *tou theou*, with both Matt. 16.16 ('o 'uios tou theou* ... 'the Son of God') and John 6.69 ('o 'agios tou theou*, 'the holy one of God').

In assessing the evidential force of the parallel between the Matthean and Johannine texts, we should first of all correlate *Simōn Bariōna* in Matt. 16.17 with *Simōn 'o 'uios Iōannou* in John 1.42, and *Petros* (as well as the play *Petros/petra*) in Matt. 16.18 with *Kephas/Petros* in John 1.42. Given the solidly probable independence of the Matthean and Johannine texts with reference to one another, the correlations attest the conjunction in common Christian tradition of the motifs of Matt. 16.17, 18. This further subverts the plausibility of average opinion to the effect that these verses were first correlated in the Matthean redaction.

A last comment on the relevant Johannine material. Three texts parallel Matt. 16.17–19, namely, John 1.41f.; 6.67–69; and 20.23. Average opinion inclines to the supposition that this Johannine diffusion is more original than the Matthean unity. But this disregards at least one feature of the Johannine redaction: the programmatic character of the testimony of John 1.19–51, in which the identification of Jesus and his saving role (e.g. 'We have found the Messiah!' v. 41) is placed at the head of the ministry (cf. the early placement of the cleansing of the temple, John 2.13–22). In accord with his programmatic design John has equivalently pre-placed the Caesarea Philippi scene (John 1.41). It should be particularly noted that in the Johannine tradition the word of Jesus to Simon (John 1.42) is conjoined with the designation of Jesus as Messiah (*'Eurēkamen ton Messian*, 'We have found the Messiah!' John 1.41), so paralleling the conjunction of messianic confession and Simon's new name (as in Matt. 16.16–18).

Third, the sense of the Matthean form of the confession ('the Messiah, the Son of the living God', 16.16) should be considered not only redactionally but tradition-historically. Indeed, this holds for the whole pericope.[48] In the redaction 'the Son of the living God' probably does express faith in Jesus as divine. But is this also true of the phrase from its earliest use? There are good reasons for doubting it. 'Son of God' occurs too often, too variously, with too determinate a reference to the role of Messiah for the probability of an original purely messianic sense to be overlooked. The gospels might seem to retroject quite spontaneously the maximum post-paschal sense to all traditions on Jesus. If so, 'Jesus, the divine Son of God' would be an issue thematized by the voice from heaven (Mark 1.11 parr.; 9.7 parr.), confronted by the demons (Mark 3.11; 5.7 parr.; cf. Matt. 4.3 par., 6 par.; 8.29; Luke 4.41), acknowledged by the disciples (Matt. 14.33; 16.16; cf. John 1.49; 11.27), evoked by Jesus' enemies (Mark 14.61 par.; John 19.7; cf. Matt. 27.40, 43; John 10.36) and executioners (Mark 15.39 par.). But one need not agree that this seemingly wholesale retrojection was intended in all cases by all the redactors. Neither Mark nor Luke unambiguously attributes to the disciples, prior to the resurrection, faith in Jesus as divine. But I do not wish to burden the present discussion of 'the Son of the living God' (Matt. 16.16) with a fully articulated statement on 'Son of God' in the Markan and Lukan redactions. It is enough to make the point that the purely messianic sense presents itself as the link between pre-Christian tradition (II Sam. 7.14 grounding I Chron. 17.13; Pss. 2.7; 89.27; 110.3; and appropriated in a messianic sense in 4QFlor) and the full-blown christology of the post-paschal church. The sense intended by the Matthean redactor in 16.16 hardly forecloses the possibility that in the earliest tradition the sense of 'Son of God' was simply messianic. Indeed, wherever in synoptic texts 'Son of God' evokes a determinate role understood as attested in advance by the scriptures (e.g. Matt. 4.3 par., 6 par.; in the light of Luke 4.14 cf. Mark 3.11; 5.7 parr.; also: Mark 1.11 parr.; 9.7 parr.; 14.61 par., etc.), there is reason to think that originally the phrase carried a purely messianic sense, open to but not of itself demanding the new sense – that is, the sense transcending merely messianic sonship – which it in fact came to have. In a word, the probability lost sight of in average opinion is that in pre-Matthean tradition the confession was simply messianic; and that the redactor changed its form by adding *tou zōntos* ('the Son of *the living* God', cf. Matt. 26.63) and its sense by investing it with a plenary post-paschal faith.

Fourth, parallels between the vocabulary of Matt. 16.17–19 and resurrectional texts supply average opinion with support far short of compelling; in some cases the alleged links are tenuous or even fanciful. *Apokalyptein* ('to reveal') in Matt. 16.17 has its closest parallel not in any resurrectional text but in the logion of Matt. 11.25 par. where, as in Matt. 16.17, the Father's revealing is correlative to the insight of faith, and the correlation 'revelation/faith' is placed in the present of the ministry. Did this word of Jesus (Matt. 11.25 par.) originate in post-paschal tradition? That this is unlikely is indicated positively by the well attested pre-paschal theme of divine predilection for the ordinary run of men (who, unobservant in terms of Torah piety, responded favourably to Jesus) and by the distinctive use of *nēpioi* ('the simple') to designate them; it is indicated negatively by the lack of any distinctively post-paschal trait or title. The next closest parallel, Matt. 11.27 par., similarly locates the revelation in the present of the ministry; and once the original idiom of this logion is recognized, the ground for positing a post-paschal origin dissolves, as we have already remarked.[49] The specific tie seen by average opinion to connect the phrase 'flesh and blood' with the resurrection is largely fanciful (contrast John 1.13; Eph. 6.12; Heb. 2.14). It rests on the parallel between Matt. 16.17 and Gal. 1.16. One might suppose that both texts reflect a specifically resurrectional context, but so far as Matt. 16.17 is concerned this is *mere* supposition. The macarism form of Matt. 16.17 is more fully paralleled by pre-paschal (e.g. Matt. 5.3ff.; 11.6; 13.16) than by resurrectional (John 20.29) texts. The reference to 'the gates of Hades' would, of course, be perfectly appropriate in a resurrectional text. It belongs, however, to the theme of the ordeal which (as we shall see) is a demonstrably pre-paschal element of Jesus' esoteric teaching on the future (e.g. Matt. 6.13 par.). Verbally, *ekklēsia* ('church') is otherwise unexampled in the gospels (apart from Matt. 18.17). But 'church' as it is used in Matt. 16.18 bears a meaning by no means alien to the words of Jesus. It appears where 'temple' would be expected and expresses in the literal mode (the 'assembly' of God's people) what the temple symbol symbolizes (cf. Mark 14.58 par., etc.). Moreover, though *ekklēsia* does not otherwise occur among the words of Jesus, images of the eschatological community (flock, plant, city of God, family of God) are well attested and the idea of Israel's restoration, at once ecclesial and eschatological, pervades the whole gospel story. 'Binding and loosing' does have a parallel in a resurrectional text (John 20.23) but exactly what or how much should be made of this remains an open question. Thus, of the mass of literary detail invoked to establish as probable the hypothesis that Matt. 16.16b–19 originally belonged to a resurrectional context, there is next to nothing that of itself evokes such a context. This does not necessarily mean that the hypothesis is groundless, but it does suggest that its real ground has been misconstrued. That real ground is the character of Jesus' messiahship as conceived in gospel texts. Messiahship was a destiny; the consummation of that destiny would be death and resurrection; and this set up an exigence with respect to messianic confession in the period of the public ministry to which the thematic progression from Mark 8.27–30 par. to Mark 8.31–33 responded.

But is our view of the Matthean text any less vulnerable to objection than average current opinion on Matt. 16.17–19? We shall not take up the long list of commonly repeated but finally insubstantial objections against the historicity of Matt. 16.17–19. We shall deal only with two objections, both of them significant.

First, does not the text show signs of the Matthean redaction? And is not a verdict in favour of historicity excluded by the numerous motifs (rock, church, gates of Hades, keys of the reign of heaven, binding and loosing) otherwise foreign to the synoptic tradition? In response: The text is Matthean not in the sense of exhibiting traits of the redactor's own composition but in the sense of reflecting pre-redactional Matthean tradition. Thus, *'o pater mou 'o en tois ouranois* ('my heavenly Father') in v. 17 is irreducible to Matthean redactional composition[50] but typical of the Matthean tradition (though not limited to it, cf. Mark 11.25; Luke 11.13). Again, *'e basileia tōn ouranōn* ('the reign of heaven') in v. 19 is pre-redactional terminology limited among the synoptics to the Matthean tradition. Matt. 16.17–19 exhibits no distinctively redactional linguistic trait.[51] The question of the historicity of the tradition is hardly affected by these observations, but they do raise a question about the most original form of the text.[52]

As for the seeming isolation of the motifs church, gates of Hades, keys of the reign of heaven, binding and loosing, the basic observation is that they appertain more or less closely to the controlling image of the cosmic rock; so the question comes down finally to whether this particular symbol is alien to the synoptic tradition of Jesus. Symbolic language as such is not alien to it (Mark 2.21f. parrs.; 3.27 parrs.; 14.58 par.; Matt. 12.39f. par., etc., relate to the master builder [*oikodomēsō*, Mark 14.58 par.; Matt. 16.18]; the symbols of the shepherd, Matt. 15.24; Luke 12.32; Mark 14.27f. par.; the physician, Mark 2.17 parrs.; the messenger, Mark 2.17 parrs., etc.); the theme of the Messiah, builder of the temple is not alien to it (again, Mark 14.58 par.; 15.29–32 par.); the election of men to participate in

Jesus' eschatological functions is not alien to it (Mark 6.7 parr.; Matt. 10.7 par.). But the most satisfactory response to the objection would no doubt be a positive analysis setting the motifs in both literary and historical context. This we shall offer in three swift steps: the sense of the name Peter independent of the Matthean text; the *petra* image with reference to church, gates of Hades, etc.; and the articulation of themes in the text as a whole.

Petros translates Aramaic *Kêpā'*. The evidence for this is the Pauline (Gal. 1.18; 2.9, 11, 14; I Cor. 1.12; 3.22; 9.5) and pre-Pauline (I Cor. 15.5) use of *Kēphas*, a grecized (added final *s*) transliteration of *Kêpā'* to refer to the man Peter (= Simon, Simeon, Simon Peter). The correlation, moreover, is formal and explicit in John 1.42. But *kêpa'* means 'massive rock, bedrock'.[53] As the appellation of a man, *kêpā'* evokes – in preference to all other rock and stone motifs in Judaic and biblical tradition – rock on which to build.[54] Thus far, we have not touched Matt. 16.18, but the Matthean text simply makes this sense explicit.

Prior to recognition that *petra/kêpā'* draws on a specific symbolic scheme (the cosmic rock), the text with its concentrated assembling of words rare in the gospel tradition (church, gates of Hades, etc.) was bound to seem historically problematic, but the situation is changed when these motifs are grasped as elements of a whole. There is no effort in the Matthean text to image the rock precisely as the lid of the netherworld or the site of the gate of heaven (cf. Gen. 28.17). But the total schematic image (netherworld – rock and temple – gate of heaven) provides a background which has clearly conditioned the text. Thus, the text offers a non-figurative equivalent of temple (namely, *ekklēsia;* Aram.: *'edtā'* [cf. Heb. *'edâ* in 4QpPs37 3.16] or *q'hillâ* or *q'hālâ* or *ṣibbûrā'* or *k'ništā'*), a reference to the netherworld (in 'the gates of Hades') and an eschatological analogue or counterpart of the cosmological conception of the gate of heaven (in 'the keys of [= to] the reign of heaven'). There is no artificiality at all in the way the text moves from the name *Petros* to the symbolic scheme which explains it. The name of itself was open to and oriented to this scheme; the scheme supplies the context, the only known context in ancient Palestinian Judaism, in which 'rock' is intelligible as the appellation of a man.

We have said that the text moves from the name[55] to the symbolic scheme which explains it. More exactly, it moves from the bestowal of the name to the promises the name was meant to epitomize. Now, the pivotal promise – *epi tautē tē petra oikodomēsō mou tēn ekklēsian* ('on this rock I will build my church') – brings two thematic schemes to expression, that of the cosmic rock and that epitomized in *Christos/oikodomein* (Matt. 16.16, 18; Mark 14.58–61 par.; 15.29–32 par.) which belonged to classic biblical messianism (II Sam. 7.13f.; I Chron. 17.12f.; Hag. 1.1f.; 2.20–23; Zech. 6.12f.; cf. Isa. 28.16; 4QFlor 1–13). The two schemes are not juxtaposed but fused and the fusion takes place by reference to Simon. It has often been noticed that Simon's confession and Jesus' response are linked rhetorically by the parallel *su ei 'o Christos* ... *su ei Petros* ('You are the Messiah ...' 'You are Peter ...'). But the deeper bond between confession and response is thematic rather than rhetorical, and it is effected by *oikodomēsō* ('I will build'). Acknowledged as Messiah, Jesus responds with *oikodomēsō mou tēn ekklēsian* (classical messianism). But acknowledged precisely *by Simon*, Jesus responds with a macarism ('Blessed are you, Simon Bar-Jona ...') explained by the following distich (God, not man, had made Simon the recipient and bearer of revelation) climaxing in the definition of a personal role for Simon in the eschatological scenario. Through *oikodomēsō* the scheme of the cosmic rock (and the new name, 'Rock', deriving from and alluding to it) has been inserted into the scheme of the Messiah, builder of the house of God. The result, thematically, is a new creation. *Christos/oikodomein* (cf. II Sam. 7) has become *Christos/ Petros-petra/oikodomein*. But if this is a new creation it is also a flawless unity, and in grasping the unity of the text a long forward step has been taken toward locating it in its historical context: that of Jesus' words and acts bearing on the new temple, the premier symbol of God's eschatological people.

The second objection against the historicity of Matt. 16.17–19 was given classic form a generation ago by Bultmann in an article specifically devoted to this question.[56] Bultmann urged (among other things) that we cannot plausibly attribute to Jesus the sense intended in Matt. 16.18 by *ekklēsia*, for here the word referred to a community which, though identified in the ideal order with eschatological Israel, concretely amounted to 'an empirical, organized community of which Peter is the head ...'[57]

Bultmann observed that the ideal aspect of the *ekklēsia* theme is well attested in the hope of ancient Israel. Present Israel was scattered among the nations; the eschatological *ekklēsia* would be gathered again into one. Present Israel was made up of the godless and the pious side by side; in the eschatological *ekklēsia* Israel and the pious would be identical. Furthermore, this eschatological *ekklēsia* was an ideal unity which would comprise all individual communities within Israel; it would not be just one community among others. But in the Matthean text the ideal *ekklēsia* assumed the empirical form of a *Sondersynagoge* (separate or sectarian community) presided over by Peter – thus corresponding not to the goal of Israel's hope but simply to that ecclesial reality which emerged in the course of history as believers in Christ, identifying themselves with the ideal *ekklēsia*, increasingly found themselves separated from Israel at large and reduced perforce to just one among many groups competing for Israel's allegiance. Thus, the *ekklēsia* of Matt. 16.18, which corresponded to the situation and mentality of the primitive post-paschal community organized under Peter, could be nothing other than a community product. It was the community's historical selfhood retrojected in the guise of prophecy into the ministry of Jesus.

To this Bultmann added a reflection of Jesus' aims. Jesus certainly never intended the founding of a mere sectarian community, for such an intention would not have been compatible with his appeal to all Israel, and we can specify no point in time after which Jesus' appeal to all Israel is abandoned. Bultmann observed that what in fact emerged out of Jesus' career was a sectarian community within Israel; he hastened to add, however, that this was a result, not an intention.

So far as historicity is concerned, Bultmann's reasoning followed the standard pattern of hard-line methodical scepticism. From the positive correspondence between the text and the post-paschal 'organized community of which Peter is the head', Bultmann automatically inferred non-historicity. But, as we have seen, hard-line methodical scepticism's pattern of inference is invalid.[58] More interesting are Bultmann's reflections on the aims of Jesus. It is doubtless correct that in so far as Jesus addressed his appeal to all Israel, he could not have intended *per se* the limitation connoted by 'separate or sectarian community'. Bultmann's argument, however, rests on two unexamined assumptions. First, Matt. 16.18f. does indeed evoke a community under the authority of the bearer of the keys to the reign of heaven. But the community envisaged is eschatological Israel and this is an open concept; that is, it calls for concrete realization or embodiment but of itself determines only in a general way what that realization or embodiment is to be. Nothing in the text (even though 'binding and loosing' include the notion of 'admitting and excluding') specifically posits a separate or sectarian community within Israel. Bultmann, having correlated the text with the post-paschal church, has gratuitously transferred to the former a trait which belongs to the latter, namely, the status of separate or sectarian community within Israel. Second, in differentiating between the intention of Jesus and the result of his work, he has too flatly correlated 'all Israel' with the intention and 'sectarian community' with the result. The intention is conceived as a call, but without reference to the response called for. The result is conceived as unintended, i.e., as a response, but without reference to the call responded to.

Certainly, Jesus addressed his call to all Israel, but it was a call for faith. Was the intention of Jesus simply defeated if all were called but not all responded? There is extensive and decisive evidence to the contrary which we shall review in due time. For the present let it suffice to distinguish two fundamental facets of Jesus' intention: the address to all Israel and the demand for a deliberate, positive response. It was clearly not the aim of

Jesus to bring all Israel to eschatological restoration regardless of how Israel responded to his call. And it would be entirely gratuitous to suppose that in the perspective and intention of Jesus, it was 'all Israel' or nothing. He called all Israel, the simple, the afflicted, and the outcast along with the wise, the flourishing, and the just. But the call he addressed to all Israel demanded a certain insight and generosity and (especially among the secure) a certain loss of poise, a collapse of defences. . . . Hence, the call of Jesus was consciously and inevitably divisive of Israel, but he did not retract it on that account. In so far as his call was a call for faith, all responses of faith were an intended result, a result positively corresponding to his aims, regardless of whether those responding with faith were all or some, many or few. The result, to be sure, would have corresponded not only positively but *perfectly* to Jesus' intention, only if all Israel had in fact responded with faith. In any case, the Matthean tradition on the exchange between Jesus and Simon in the region of Caesarea Philippi says nothing about whether the eschatological *ekklēsia* embraces all Israel or a remnant of Israel. It says only that Israel was destined to find eschatological restoration in those who, like Simon, would come to confess Jesus as 'the Messiah, the Son of [the living] God'.[59] They would be the temple built on rock. The Messiah chose the rock and would build the temple.

The cleansing of the temple

Earlier we alluded to the Deutero-Isaian motif of 'preparation for the Day' (Isa. 40.3) presupposed and developed by traditions like the return of Elijah (Mal. 3.1–5; 3.23f. [EVV 4.5f.]; Sir. 48.10) and given historic actuality by John's programme of baptizing and Jesus' proclamation, teaching, and symbolic acts. The first point to make about the cleansing of the temple is that it belonged to this selfsame context. It epitomized in action the message 'The reign of God is at hand!' and the demand 'Repent!' For all its immediacy as dramatic act and present demand, it pointed ahead – like Elijah's task of purifying the priesthood (Mal. 3.1–4), reconciling families (Mal. 3.24 [EVV 4.6]), and restoring the tribes of Jacob (Sir. 48.10) – to imminent judgment and restoration. And like John's baptism and Jesus' proclamation, it urgently addressed all Israel, not just the temple clergy or the Sanhedrin. Planned for prime time and maximum exposure, it was a 'demonstration'[60] calculated to interrupt business as usual and bring the imminence of God's reign abruptly, forcefully, to the attention of all. As proclamation, demand, and warning, it said what Jesus had always said. If it was an especially startling and provocative act, this simply gave added edge to one of the basic traits of Jesus' whole career.

But to categorize his act as a 'demonstration' is of itself hardly adequate. It was at once a demonstration, a prophetic critique, a fulfilment event, and a sign of the future.

The critique pointed straight at temple practice and so presented the unmistakable contour which has rightly given the event its name: the cleansing of the temple. It was an act of prophetic indignation attesting an uncompromising conception of God's honour and Israel's vocation as cult community (Ex. 19.6). There was, moreover, another element in the critique. Entry and cleansing evoked the heritage of temple/Zion/Jerusalem themes. Now, the popular appropriation of these themes constituted a response to divine election. It could take the form of a self-effacing obedience of faith; it could also take the form of a self-congratulatory sense of security, lightly varnished or heavily solemnized by religious convictions and practices and in either case a besetting distortion which the prophets never ceased to denounce. By his action in the court of the temple Jesus equivalently set an ancient word before Israel: 'Reform your ways and your deeds, that I may remain with you in this place' (Jer. 7.3) and, as the text of the oracle continued: 'Do not put your trust in the deceitful words, "This is the temple of the LORD, the temple of the LORD, the temple of the LORD!" ' (Jer. 7.4). The cleansing of the temple was an attack on 'this generation's' obstinate confidence in its status. This aspect of the cleansing had as its horizon the imminence of judgment.

But the cleansing of the temple said 'restoration', too, and was already itself a fulfilment event. 'On that day', declared the last words of the book of Zechariah, 'there shall no longer be any merchant in the house of the LORD of hosts' (Zech. 14.21).[61] The fulfilment, to be sure, was partial and proleptic and in this respect comparable in structure and function to the classic biblical 'sign'. Linked with some prophecy, the biblical 'sign' (*'ôt*) served as a present guarantee of the prophecy's future fulfilment (cf. II Kings 20.9; Isa. 7.11; 38.7; Jer. 44.29; Ezek. 4.3). As the evangelists suggest by their citations of Isaiah, Jeremiah, Zechariah, and the Psalms, and especially by their citation of Isa. 56.7 on the eschatological temple, the 'prophecy' linked with the cleansing was the entire treasury of oracles celebrating the restoration of temple, Zion, and Jerusalem. No matter how pointed in its historic immediacy, the restoration realized in Jesus' cleansing of the temple was essentially parabolic. The gospels present it as a single, discrete happening. The tables and stalls of the buyers and sellers and money-changers were doubtless soon back in place and Jesus, who did not shrink from collision with authority, did nothing to make the reform permanent. Rather, his action presented itself to the public as a parable demanding to be construed and deciphered and veiling the potent claim to be a hinge moment in the eschatological scenario. It was at once a fulfilment event and a sign of the future, pledging the restoration of temple, Zion, and Jerusalem. Since these were symbol and synecdoche for the whole people of God, the cleansing of the temple pledged the perfect restoration of Israel.

This brings us to the last and most distinctive aspect of Jesus' act. His mode of arrival at the temple gave the whole event a unique specificity. Form-critically the entry *récit* is a legend garnished with motifs from religious folklore. Mark's account (11.1–10) all but spells out the Zecharian oracle which Matthew in fact explicitly cites (Matt. 21.5). In the prophet it reads:

> Rejoice greatly, O daughter Zion,
>   shout for joy, O daughter Jerusalem!
> See, your king comes to you,
>   a righteous saviour is he,
> lowly and riding on an ass,
>   on a colt, the foal of an ass (Zech. 9.9).

Jesus, the disciples, and the pilgrim crowds combined to make the entry a messianic event, so investing the cleansing of the temple with a messianic dimension.

This, to be sure, is not a datum but a conclusion and a necessarily tentative one. The tradition of the entry with its heavy overlay of folkloric (Mark 11.1–6) and midrashic (Mark 11.9 parr.; John 12.13)[62] motifs, especially in view of the all but intolerable strain it imposes on the ordinary framework of Jesus' public career (eschatological but otherwise deliberately unspecific and in this neutral sense 'unmessianic' or, if messianic, then only performatively, not thematically), might seem to rule historicity out altogether. Alone, however, form-critical and stylistic considerations rarely settle substantial historical questions. According to the synoptic tradition a strain on the secret was characteristic of the last part of Jesus' ministry, when the fiercely urgent will to press Israel to decision and the hopeful will to win it over for the reign of God ignited flashes of self-revelation in riddles and parables (Mark 12.10 parr., 35–37 parr.). To this corresponds an entry into Jerusalem designed to raise just such questions (cf. Matt. 21.10) as had once agitated the disciples: 'What is this?' and 'Who can this be?' and, finally, 'Who do you say that I am?' Moreover, the cleansing itself has good claims to historicity; and according to a fixed, age-old symbolic structure, this act – generically, a restoration of cult – supposes and interlocks with just such royal motifs as the entry supplies.[63] The conclusion, though not compelling, derives positive probability from these contextual considerations. The Galilean pilgrims (Matt. 21.8,10f.) and the company that regularly travelled with Jesus and the twelve (Luke 19.37) responded to a consciously symbolic act. The entry into Jerusalem and the cleansing of the temple constituted a messianic demonstration, a messianic critique, a messianic fulfilment event, and a sign of the messianic restoration of Israel.

In so far as the cleansing of the temple was a harsh and dramatic

critique, its messianic aspect was an implicit presentation of credentials.
But in the deeper sense, i.e., in so far as the total event was both a partial
fulfilment of Old Testament prophecy and a pledge of perfect completion,
the messianic aspect was the ultimate rationale of the event. It said
why the reign of God had overtaken Jerusalem. If 'on that day' there
was no longer to be 'any merchant in the house of the LORD of hosts'
(Zech. 14.21), 'that day' had come because the Messiah was there. The
restoration of temple, Zion, and Jerusalem – nothing less than the salvation of Israel and the nations – was already under way.

This reading of the event implies that Jesus understood his messiahship
as do synoptic texts which present his pre-paschal career as actually but
proleptically messianic. For on the one hand he is understood in these
texts (e.g. Mark 12.35–37 parr.; Matt. 11.2–6 par.) not as Messiah-
designate but as Messiah; on the other, pre-paschal messiahship stands in
advance dependence on an enthronement conceived in transcendent
terms. It is interesting that the rabbis of the third century sensed a problem in Zech. 9.9, for it presented a Messiah 'lowly and riding on an ass'.
How harmonize this with 'one like a son of man coming with clouds'
(Dan 7.13)?

> R. Alexandrai has said: R. Jehoshua b. Levi has contrasted 'Lo, with the clouds
> of heaven came one like a son of man' with 'Lowly and riding on an ass'. If they
> [Israel] have merits, he comes with clouds of heaven; if they have no merits,
> lowly and riding on an ass (Sanh. 98a).

What the rabbis differentiated on the basis of 'Israel with merits' and
'Israel without merits', Jesus appears to have differentiated as present
status and future status (cf. David's 'son' and David's 'Lord',
Mark 12.35–37 parr.), the line of division between present and future
being drawn by the prospect of transcendent enthronement (cf.
Mark 12.36 parr.). If this is so, the status of the lowly but royal figure of
the entry and cleansing was consciously proleptic, and the functions of the
Messiah were apportioned to successive phases of his messiahship. How
did the aims of Jesus correlate with a messiahship conceived in this way?

With this question we return to the riddle: 'Destroy this temple and in
three days I will build another.' We have already ascertained that in this
saying the building of the temple is conceived as an instantaneous act
signalling the post-historical resolution of the coming 'ordeal' or 'trial'
(*peirasmos*). Here 'temple' was symbolic of messianic Israel in the glory of
its restoration. We are now in a position to relate this cryptic and
extravagant saying to the very substance of Jesus' career; for the sense of
the post-historical temple Jesus would build within three days has been
mediated now by a word (the *kêpā'* word which responded to Simon's
messianic confession) and an act (the entry into Jerusalem and cleansing

of the temple) which bring the riddle into relation with the mass of words and acts that constituted his life.

Jesus had publicly represented himself in the evocative figures of shepherd (Matt. 15.24; Luke 19.10), physician (Mark 2.17 parr.), and messenger (Mark 2.17 parr.), images that bore on his appeal to sinners and belonged to the apologia by which he sought to reconcile righteous and sinners under God's reign. But the image in which he caught the whole of his work and disclosed its hidden, final sense belonged to the esoteric traditions: He was the builder of the house of God. Jesus spoke this word only in response to a faith that had intuited the secret of his supreme role in the plan of eschatological salvation. If we take Simon's confession and Jesus' response together (as, historically, we should), we find that the role of Messiah specifies thematically the comprehensive aim of his mission. The Messiah was the master-builder who would raise on rock the living temple, his *ekklēsia*. The riddle of the miraculously built temple had its roots here, in Jesus' thematization of his life's work as the bringing of messianic Israel into being.

The royal entry into Jerusalem and the cleansing of the temple likewise relate the temple riddle to Jesus' historic career. First, the theme of messiahship binds the riddle to the cleansing. If the central term of the riddle, the building of the temple, designated an implicitly messianic task, Jesus came to the cleansing of the temple as messianic judge and restorer. The event was a veiled irruption of esoteric themes onto the public stage. Critique and warning had often figured in Jesus' address to the crass and indifferent and to the critics who with the fullest self-assurance rejected him. But when the messianic dimension was added and the target of the critique was Jerusalem – settled, together with the *élite* of the national leadership, in a stupor of unknowing throughout the whole 'time of your visitation' (Luke 19.44) – critique and warning took on new gravity. 'The Lord whom you seek will suddenly come to his temple' (Mal. 3.1), warned the prophet. Powering the prophetic indignation with which Jesus cleansed the temple was precisely the consciousness of coming to it as Lord and judge.

It is plausible, furthermore, and even probable that the temple riddle belonged to the cleansing of the temple as a postscript (John 2.18).[64] The cleansing was not a matter of courts and buildings but of people, of all Israel but particularly of its leaders, who were ever ready with the tactical demand for a sign. As in the days of Jeremiah unbelief could find assurance in the massive fact of the temple. But the cleansing was a parable of judgment (cf. Luke 19.39–44) and to unbelief Jesus would offer no sign but that of the 'other' temple he would build within or after three days of the destruction of 'this' one. Like the sign of Jonah, this sign would come too late to serve as a motive for belief, for it would be nothing other than that climactic vindication at which, for good or ill, belief and unbelief would yield to vision.[65]

As for how Jesus conceived his aims to correlate with a messiahship in two phases, the answer lies in his classically scriptural affirmation of the messianic task. In both phases this was one and the same. The temple – dazzling, miraculous, everlasting, centre of the new heaven and new earth, goal of the pilgrimage of the nations – was the image thematizing in symbol the scope of his work. If we further ask what, if anything, the theme of messiahship added to the eschatological restoration of Israel and the attendant salvation of the nations, the answer must be: the affirmation that in this mission with its earthly and heavenly phases the scriptures of Israel were coming to complete and superabundant fulfilment.

2. THE ESOTERIC TEACHING: HOW JESUS WOULD ACHIEVE HIS GOAL

Epitomized in the radiant image of the temple, the goal of Jesus' career was the messianic restoration of Israel. But this does not say how he envisaged this restoration in the concrete and how he intended to realize it. The interpretative and explanatory perspectives in which he invited his disciples to grasp his words, acts, and destiny are only partly given in the promise to build his *ekklēsia* on the rock of Simon, in the hinge event of the cleansing of the temple, and in the riddle of the destruction of the temple and the building of another within or after three days. The course of his destiny as he envisaged it remained a puzzle even to his disciples.

The line of scholarship which, so far as I can judge, has made most headway toward reconstructing the eschatology of Jesus is that which runs from Weiffenbach to Jeremias. First, we shall sketch this development and briefly take up its leading motifs; then we shall consider what it implies from the standpoint of Jesus' aims; finally, we shall ask how he concretely envisaged the process by which restored Israel would come into being.

Jesus' vision of the future

In 1873 Wilhelm Weiffenbach published *Der Wiederkunftsgedanke Jesu*.[66] It was an effort to recover the original form of Jesus' vision of the future. As Albert Schweitzer describes it, the principle of Weiffenbach's criticism was to distinguish the bare promise of a second coming from all the concomitant trappings of Judaic eschatology. 'In the end', comments Schweitzer, 'Weiffenbach's critical principle proves to be merely a bludgeon with which he goes seal-hunting and clubs the defenceless Synoptic sayings right and left.'[67] Still, he credits Weiffenbach with being the first to pose clearly and unequivocally the question of how resurrection and second coming were related in Jesus' esoteric teaching: 'For the first time it had dawned upon historical criticism that the great question is that concerning the identity or difference of the Parousia and the Resurrection.'[68] According to Weiffenbach it was only after the death of Jesus that his disciples differentiated between the two. The original prophecy of Jesus was of his parousia, a theme standing in organic connection with the announcement of his approaching death. The resurrection component in the predictions of death and resurrection was a *vaticinium ex eventu*, supposing the post-factum differentiation of resurrection and parousia.

In chapters two and three of his 1935 work, *The Parables of the Kingdom*,[69] C. H. Dodd reviewed the evidence of the synoptic gospels on the future as Jesus conceived it. He began by discussing references to 'forthcoming historical events'[70] (chapter two) represented in the prophetic manner and portraying an 'eschatology of woe' (*Unheilseschatologie*):[71] suffering and death for Jesus himself and some of his followers, disaster for the Jewish people, capital, and temple. Some of Jesus' predictions, such as that in three days he would 'build another temple', could not be plausibly fitted into any strictly historical future envisaged by Jesus. Dodd accordingly turned to a new framework, that of apocalyptic events (chapter three), in which to set them.[72] This framework was established by choosing (from the standpoint of historicity) sayings that spoke equivalently, if not literally (e.g. Luke 17.24), of 'the Day of the Son of Man' (esp. Matt. 24.37–39 par.)[73] over two other sets of sayings: those that supposed the 'traditional conception of Doomsday'[74] as 'a Great Assize'[75] (Matt. 10.15 par.; 11.21f. par.; 12.41–47 par.) and those that set 'a long series of signs'[76] before the Son of man's appearance (Mark 13.14–25 parr.). This vision of the future was unified by reference to Jesus' own career (cf. esp. Luke 12.49–53).[77] Jesus himself saw his career 'moving rapidly to a crisis' which would bring about 'a general upheaval'[78] in which the power of Rome, mediating an 'effective judgment'[79] on the sin of this generation, would make an end of the Jewish nation, its city and temple (cf. Matt. 23.34–36 par.). Second, the apocalyptic eschatology of bliss (*Heilseschatologie*),[80] 'the Day of the Son of Man',[81] would be the vindication of Jesus. Like Weiffenbach, Dodd took this 'Day' to have originally signified a single event. 'It is noteworthy', he observed, 'that there is no saying which predicts both resurrection and second coming.'[82] 'Where [Jesus] had referred to one single event, [the early Christians] made a distinction between two events, one past, His resurrection from the dead, and one future, His coming on the clouds ... Thus the eschatological scheme of early Christianity was constructed.'[83] Once this was grasped, it was possible to work out the probably original sense of parables (the Faithful and Unfaithful Servants, Matt. 24.45–51 par., the Waiting Servants, Luke 12.35–38 par., the Thief at Night, Matt. 24.43f. par., and the Ten Virgins, Matt. 25.1–13) which appeared to suppose an interim between Jesus' death/resurrection and his parousia.[84]

Dodd's handling of the future sayings in the synoptic gospels must rank as a brilliant *tour de force* in the service of a systematic view ('[totally] realized eschatology') little congenial of itself to the profusion of graphic images with which the synoptic sayings depict the future. Cool, deft, never protesting, Dodd at least touched on every one of these images and in so plausible a way that the reader finds himself insensibly nudged to a vantage point from which, it suddenly appears, the future as such has vanished. Or rather it is here and now. For the first disciples Jesus had converted classical images of judgment into a set of present challenges; and what to him and them had still been future (resurrection/exaltation/parousia) was here and now to the church. The future had not come and gone but come (in the sequence of events recounted in the gospels) and stayed.

Joachim Jeremias presented Dodd's view revised and refocused in an appreciative review article in 1941.[85] He criticized the terminological distinction between historical events presented in the prophetic manner and supernatural events presented in the apocalyptic manner. All the events, historical or post-historical, were conceived as elements in a divinely initiated, supernatural sequence; at the same time the whole belonged qualitatively to the tradition of the prophets. Abandoning almost without comment the distortions which systematic commitment to 'realized eschatology' had introduced into Dodd's final assessments, Jeremias was nevertheless able to retain and exploit key elements of the analysis and, above all, its central insight: the original non-differentiation of resurrection and parousia. Only now the resurrection did not exhaust, rather it guaranteed, the eschatology of future triumph. 'Now' was originally defined by Jesus' career. Beyond this 'now' stood a future dominated first by the eschatological crisis to be opened by the repudiation, suffering, and death of Jesus himself (Luke 23.28–31) and destined to engulf his disciples and all Israel. Dreadful but short, it would be brought to an end by the Son of man whose appearance would open the last act of the eschatological drama: resurrection, judgment, the banquet of the saved.

The positive achievement represented by this line of investigation is manifold. First, in virtue of the holistic approach, i.e., beginning by bringing all the relevant data together and searching for an intelligible pattern therein, one found the whole in terms of which otherwise baffling parts (e.g. Matt. 10.23; Mark 9.1 parr., etc.) became intelligible. The approach had the virtue not only of thus arriving at a wholly intelligible whole vision of things but of leaving no masses of data out of account in the process. Jesus' scheme of the future was single and simple: crisis events (his own death, the persecution of his followers and martyrdom for some of them, the suffering of Israel, the attack on Jerusalem, the ruin of the temple) followed by resolution events (the day of the Son of man, the resurrection of the dead, the pilgrimage of the nations, the enthronement of the disciples, etc.).

Second, by confronting all the data at once the interpreter stayed free of the temptation to tinker with the motif of 'imminence' in particular texts (e.g., the fall of the temple); though he might attempt (like Dodd) to render the whole futurist dimension ultimately harmless, this approach to the data encouraged him to do full justice to the original unity of conception. Thus, part and parcel of Jesus' vision of the future was the brief time-span within which it was to be contained. Time was short between now and the opening of the eschatological ordeal (Matt. 26.18; Luke 12.49; 13.33; cf. John 14.19; 16.16a; Mark 14.42) and especially between the now of Jesus' suffering and the outbreak of suffering for Israel (Mark 14.25 par.; Luke 22.18; 23.28–31); between the opening of the ordeal and its closing (Mark 9.1 parr.; 13.29 parr.; 14.58f. par.; 15.29 par.; Matt. 10.23; cf. John 2.19; 16.16b); and so between the now of the ministry and the globally conceived, publicly proclaimed final consummation (Mark 1.15 par.; 8.38 par.; Matt. 10.7; 12.39 par.; Luke 11.5 par.; etc.). The theme of 'shortness of time' conditioned public proclamation (Mark 1.15), the call of disciples (Matt. 8.22 par.), missionary instructions (Luke 10.4), the demand for conversion (Luke 13.6–9), the consolation of followers (Mark 9.1 parr.; Matt. 10.23), and the condemnation of 'this generation' (Matt. 12.39 par.; 24.34; cf. Mark 14.62 parr.). Jesus signified the shortness by such words as 'soon' (Matt. 26.64 par.; cf. Luke 12.52), 'tomorrow' (Matt. 6.11 par.),[86] 'within' or 'after' three days (Mark 14.58 par.; 9.31 parr.), 'on the third day' (Luke 13.32), etc. Imminence, swiftness, certainty typified the whole.

Third, access to an intelligible whole grounded an effective approach to historicity judgments amid just that mass of data which had so often and so thoroughly defeated the merely atomistic approach (as the chaotic critical literature on Jesus' view of the future attests). The lack of reference to a whole view posited on the basis of all relevant data has occasioned the most arbitrary denials of historicity even of acutely problematic sayings which for that very reason have an especially strong claim to historicity (e.g. Matt. 10.23; Mark 9.1 parr.). The pervasive supposition of imminence, inasmuch as it proved to be 'unfulfilled', favoured the historicity of the whole. Connections within the whole confirmed the historicity of particular parts. For example, fulfilled prophecies (such as the sudden ending of Jesus' career) were secured as historical by their intimate linkage with 'unfulfilled' prophecies (such as the destined baptism of James and John, obviously conceived to be imminent, like that of Jesus: Mark 10.39 par.).

Fourth, in Dodd's and, still more, in Jeremias's analysis the Weiffenbach hypothesis was made to operate in historically fruitful ways. It decisively helped to locate the original centre of gravity not only of the so-called parousia parables but of many more texts requiring to be somehow located in Jesus' conception of the future. Though the early church doubtless understood everything in accord with its own eschatological schemes, the hypothesis provided a touchstone for differentiating between materials that were verbally revised in accord with those schemes and those that were left verbally unrevised, e.g., the 'three days' sayings.

Fifth, this line of investigation has had hermeneutical significance. On the one hand, it refused to short-circuit the emergence of problems by flattening out and equivalently dismissing from the outset 'time' as a meaningful factor in eschatological prophecy. On the other, it represented a clean break with the naive practice of retrojecting the interpreter's own view of 'fulfilment events' (e.g. the fall of the temple in AD 70) into the historical Jesus' vision of the future. Finally, it makes clear, in my opinion, that the hermeneutic appropriate to prophecy is an appreciation of symbolic knowledge, a topic to be taken up in the next chapter.

The leading motifs in Jesus' vision of the future were, then, the coming ordeal and its resolution by the triumph (enthronement[87]) of the Son of man.

The theme of the ordeal had a remote background in the whole of biblical tradition, where salvation derived its meaning from Israel's misery and helplessness as well as from the benevolent initiative of God (cf. the theological overture to the book of Judges, Judg. 2.8–19). The prophets and psalms gave a new intensity to the correlatives of distress and salvation:

> Thus says Yahweh:
>   We have heard a cry of panic,
>   of terror and not of peace . . .
>
> Oh, how mighty is that day,
>   there is none like it!
> It is a time of distress for Jacob
>   though there is One who shall yet save him out of it (Jer. 30.5, 7).

Apocalyptic eschatology heightened this theme. 'This distress' became *the* distress, climactic and final. It could not be otherwise for whoever supposed that the imminent reversal of present distress meant the end and consummation of historical existence:

> There shall be a time of distress such as there never has been
>   from when nations began until that time;
> at that time there shall be One to deliver your people,
>   everyone whose name is found written in the book (Dan. 12.1).

In public preaching Jesus warned the indifferent of the coming crisis. It was much more than a warning of the 'great assize' (which, however, he repeatedly affirmed). The warning drew a circle around this particular set of contemporaries. The last generation stood in a unique danger, one leading up to but irreducible to the post-historical judgment of the world. Danger threatened 'this generation' which did not threaten the dead (who would also be called up for judgment) nor the Gentiles (who stood outside the drama of Jesus' personal prophetic confrontation of the world):

> This is why the Wisdom of God said, 'I will send them prophets and apostles and some of them they will kill and some they will persecute': [namely,] that there may be One [i.e., God] to exact from this generation the penalty for the blood of all the prophets shed since the foundation of the world. . . . Yes, I tell you! There is One who shall exact the penalty from this generation! (Luke 11.49–51; cf. Matt. 23.33–36).

If 'this generation' pays the blood-debt it is not only because it is the last generation and the debt is to be paid in history but because 'this generation' is engaged in repudiating God's climactic and definitive revealer. We have here a public saying which evokes the image of a frightful suffering to take place in history, to be undergone by those whom Jesus addressed and who sealed their historic fate (it still belonged to 'this age') by their settled, persistent refusal. A comparable text is the word of Jesus to the pious association of women who were singing the death lament for him as he went to his execution: 'Daughters of Jerusalem, do not sing the dirge for me, sing it for yourselves and for your children . . . If this is what they do when the wood is green, what will happen when it is dry?' (Luke 23.28, 31).

The last words of this text, like the whole of the previous text, insinuate the judgment character of the coming distress. Jesus' public career had been a holding off of judgment on Israel (Luke 13.6–9); now this respite was all but gone. The time of the sword was about to break out with that special suffering imposed by the rupture of family ties over the word and person of Jesus (Matt. 10.35f. par.); thus, the judgment word of Micah (7.6) and Zechariah (13.3) would be brought to fulfilment. Jesus' lament over Jerusalem expressed the judgment character of the ordeal for Israel: God would abandon the temple (cf. Ezek. 11.23).

> O Jerusalem, Jerusalem, killer of prophets, stoner of those sent to you,
> how often I have wanted to gather your children together
> as a mother bird gathers her brood under her wings but you refused!
> Behold, there is One who shall abandon your house! (Matt. 23.37f. par.)

For the refusers of Jesus the coming distress (so he instructed his disciples) would not be reversed but confirmed by the day of the Son of man. Judgment would come like the flood that swamped and drowned the

world (Luke 17.26f.), like the fire that fell on Sodom and Gomorrha
(Luke 17.28f.).

For the disciples themselves the ordeal (*'o peirasmos*; Aram.: *nisyônā'*)
would test and purify, like refining fire. This, too, was the reprise of a well
attested biblical theme.

> Search me, O Yahweh, and try (*nissâ*) me,
> refine my soul and my heart (Ps. 26.2).

God tried the just man so that in his temptations (*b^enisyônotaw*) he would
acquit himself well.[88] The righteous, not the ungodly, were tried. Here the
Abba prayer which Jesus taught his disciples is revealing. It supposed the
understanding of the ordeal as test and it supposed the ordeal as the
setting and context of the prayer.

> Father!
> Let your name be hallowed! Let your reign come!
> The bread of tomorrow give us today,
> and forgive us our debts as we now forgive our debtors,
> and do not let us fall victim to the ordeal![89]
> (Luke 11.2–4; cf. Matt. 6.9–13).

In and through the address *Abba* ('Father'), which bore the stamp of
Jesus' personal idiom,[90] the disciples entered the shelter of his unique
relationship to God. 'Let your name be hallowed!' meant: Let the acclamation ring out! The reference was to the hallowing of God's name by the
new song (Isa. 42.10) that would greet and acknowledge God's final saving act. Like 'Let your reign come!' (with which it stands in synonymous
parallelism) it was a cry for God's triumph over evil. That is, 'God can
shorten the time of distress for the sake of the elect who cry to him day and
night (Luke 18.7f.); he can hear the cry 'Thy kingdom come'.[91] The
context of the ordeal was equally supposed in the contrast between 'today'
and 'tomorrow' and the urgent need today of the bread of tomorrow, i.e.,
the bread of life, the power and goodness of God mediated to the present
not only by bread but by everything that sustained men, their courage and
hope. Again, forgiveness had as its context distress, tribulation, trial. The
petitioners begged divine forgiveness and, on the occasion of the prayer
itself, placed their own act of forgiveness. If the rupture of the closest ties
was explicitly a theme of the ordeal, so was forgiveness, which would
frustrate evil, break its rhythm, heal its ravages, and convert into redemp-
tive power the energy evil would otherwise claim for itself. Finally, the last
petition expressed a crystal clarity on where the danger of the ordeal lay:
not in slander, suffering, death, but in infidelity. It was the cry: Save us
from ourselves! and supposed that God willed to do so (cf. Mark 13.20;
Matt. 10.22).

It is solidly probable that the role played in public proclamation and teaching by the coming of the reign of God was played in esoteric teaching after the confession in the region of Caesarea Philippi[92] by the day of the Son of man.[93] This probability has its solidity from a triple cord: first and foremost, from the fact that the data called on to support it – i.e., the whole of the material bearing on Jesus' 'vision of the future' – are relatively massive and interlock easily, coherently, in reciprocally reinforcing fashion. Whether beginning from Jesus' words on the ordeal or from his words on its resolution, some kind of transcendent vindication and exaltation of Jesus is positively demanded. A vision of the future which would include his sharing the fate of the prophets (Matt. 23.29–32 par., 34–36 par., 37–39 par.; Luke 13.33), his 'baptism' (Luke 12.50; Mark 10.38f.) and drinking of the 'cup' (Mark 10.38f. par.; cf. 14.36 parr.) etc., but in which reversal and vindication were lacking is altogether improbable. Again, if within three days of the temple's destruction Jesus would build the new temple belonging to the eschaton, it is inescapable that he supposed for himself a mysterious, unfathomably transcendent condition. The theme of the exaltation/enthronement of the Son of man meets the demand in both cases. Second, the probability that the day of the Son of man was the counterpart in esoteric teaching after Caesarea Philippi to 'the reign of God' in public proclamation derives from oblique inferences of the historicity of texts in which, contrary to secondary descriptions (e.g. Mark 13.24f. parr.), the epiphany of the Son of man comes unannounced, like a sudden interruption (e.g. Matt. 10.23; 24.27,37; Luke 17.22–24, 26–30). Third, this probability is confirmed by the fact that no substantial or serious alternative to the Son of man thematic is present among the available data.

The force and scope of the first point in particular must not be loftily dismissed. Whereas the historicity of Jesus' words on the main elements of the ordeal is beyond reasonable doubt, the ordeal itself – to be launched by Jesus' own suffering and death, to include the persecution of his disciples and death for some of them, to divide families over him, to bring the last Gentile attack on Jerusalem and a new and final destruction of the temple – could not possibly be the final state of the future he envisioned. That the final state should rather be the total reversal of all this is a necessity intrinsic to the pattern of all synoptic data on eschatology. The disciples would be enthroned, the tribes of Israel restored (Matt. 19.28 par.), the temple rebuilt (Mark 14.48 par.; 15.29 par.; cf. John 2.19); and, just as the rejection of Jesus would launch the ordeal, so his vindication would signal its reversal. Antecedent expectation that Jesus should envisage this vindication is met by the evidence of synoptic texts on the exaltation/epiphany of the Son of man and, it would seem, by nothing else.

The messianic remnant

This vision of the future tells us what Jesus thought was at stake in his encounter with his nation. That nation's destiny was at stake. His mission was to elicit Israel's acceptance of salvation, but not all would accept it. He would call his countrymen together to a life beyond Torah and *halaka*, he would gather them together in a common renunciation of claims and mutual forgiveness and reconciliation – 'but you refused!' (Matt. 23.37 par.). Everything turned on acceptance or refusal. Blessed were they who heard God's word and accepted it (Luke 11.28) for only they would enter the reign of God. Descent from Abraham would count for nothing, neither would the claim to the scriptures, covenants, and prophets. Those who rejected him would be rejected. 'Unless you repent, you will all perish!' (Luke 13.3). His task was to herald news of salvation but its rejection would raise the frightening question, 'Are only a few to be saved?' (Luke 13.23).

These sentences epitomize an awesome event: the division of Israel and the coming into being of the messianic 'remnant'.

To deal securely with this debated thesis, we might begin by recalling the specious objections against our earlier conclusion that John the Baptist by his baptism sought to assemble the remnant of repentant Israel: (1) 'Remnant', an assembling or gathering of Israel, signifies a separate and organized community. Response: Not necessarily. The originality of John lay in the simplicity of his mission and its openness to all Israel. He 'assembled' the people of God in advance of judgment but only by baptizing, not by segregating and organizing the baptized. (2) The remnant must be closed. Response: This, too, is a gratuitous requisite. Only the repentant and baptized would be saved but this did not require that they be called into being as a closed community. (3) Remnant theology supposes lapse of covenant (cf. Ezra 9.10–15). Response: Not necessarily. John did suppose, however, that in the face of imminent judgment the standing resources of Israel were inadequate, for God required all Israel to repent and be baptized. (4) John addressed all Israelites but not necessarily Israel as an ecclesial entity. Response: Any such notion is anachronistic.[94] In biblical and post-biblical antiquity Israel is always conceived as an ecclesial entity, not as a mere aggregation of individuals. (5) The data on John are inadequate to specify as his intention the gathering of the remnant of Israel. Response: The conditions of the truth of the proposition are limited to three, all of them fulfilled. First, John's mission was undertaken with reference to the coming judgment; second, it both aimed at all Israel and envisaged a diversity of response to it among Israelites; third, it consisted in setting a choice before Israel, not an optional choice but one indispensable to survival of judgment, understanding this to be the final, irreversible judgment. This requisite, too, John met by proclaiming and realizing the condition (baptism sealing conversion) on which Israel's survival of judgment depended.

It is immediately evident that the considerations which apply to John apply to Jesus. Jesus' mission was eschatological through and through. He understood judgment either as an element in the effective imposition of God's reign[95] or as the essential prelude to it. In either case his mission was relative to judgment, a theme which became explicit and prominent in the face of indifference to or refusal of his proclamation of God's reign. Again, he called all Israel but he was fully conscious that not all Israel accepted or would accept the call. Finally, he made it clear that both the offer and the demand implicit in 'reign of God' were divinely authoritative; the gift was free (not earned or earnable) but acceptance was requisite (not discretionary, optional). What Matthew would call a 'better righteousness' (Matt. 5.20) conditioned entry into God's reign. In a word, Jesus pressed a decision on Israel, so engendering the crisis that created the remnant of the last days.

This is the basic context within which the call and sending of the twelve, the cures and exorcisms, the dining with publicans and sinners, the temple cleansing, all take on their full intelligibility, for all these restoration-intending acts were appeals for faith and acceptance. They could all be discounted, misconstrued, rejected. All of them could thereby become and did in fact become acts divisive of Israel.

Rabbinic Judaism would declare that all Israel had a share in the age to come. Jesus declared that the natural heirs or 'sons' of the reign of God would be cast into the dark and their place taken by the nations (Matt. 8.11f. par.). The ordeal would continue to divide Israel (Matt. 10.34) because restoration would not be a spectacular miracle nor Israel its passive beneficiary. It would have to be accepted in faith as a gift.

The debate on Jesus and the remnant of Israel has gone on over a fifty-year period in desultory fashion and without satisfactory result. In the years between the two wars Ferdinand Kattenbusch,[96] Karl Ludwig Schmidt,[97] Gerhard Gloege,[98] and T. W. Manson[99] urged that it had been the intention of Jesus to gather the remnant of Israel. They have been opposed by Rudolf Bultmann,[100] Albrecht Oepke,[101] Werner Georg Kümmel,[102] Joachim Jeremias,[103] and others. Though the debate has often been tangled in semantic confusions, several points have emerged firmly from the critique of the remnant thesis. Contrary to Kattenbusch and Schmidt, Jesus never abandoned the will to win all Israel over; he did not simply limit his mission to the little nucleus of his disciples. Gloege, in turn, failed to establish his point that 'remnant' was no quantitative concept, that those who responded to Jesus with faith would still be the remnant, 'however great their number might be, even if it had included all Israel'.[104] T. W. Manson defended a thesis we may summarize in three points. First, following the remnant theology of Isaiah, the exilic period brought a bifurcation in tradition. Deutero-Isaiah envisaged 'the saving remnant', which would be a light to the nations; Ezekiel, 'the saved remnant', according to which 'restored Israel ... turns to enjoy salvation, whatever may be the fate of the rest of the world'.[105] Second, the remnant idea was the essential feature of 'the Servant' in Deutero-Isaiah, the 'I' of the pious in the later Psalms, and the 'one like a (son of) man' in Daniel; Jesus carried this through into his own Servant and Son of man themes. Third, from the pre-exilic prophets to the Pharisees and Jesus, remnant theology represented a 'decisive step' toward the emergence of individualism in religion.[106] All three points touched significant issues but none of the three could be accepted without qualification: and since the almost universal rejection of Manson's views new proposals on Jesus and the remnant of Israel have rarely been put forward. The debate proper as well as more recent developments and contributions have nevertheless made it possible to outline the critical points for a renewal of the conversation.

First, the individualism anachronistically affirmed of Jesus and earliest Christianity by many scholars, including such diametrical opposites as Manson and Bultmann, should be sharply reformulated. The currently widespread disillusionment with existentialism as an adequate guiding light for New Testament studies and especially the protest against isolating Jesus and early Christianity from cosmos, history, and society[107] should commend a reconsideration of how the mission of Jesus stood *vis-à-vis* Israel precisely as people of God. 'In the apocalyptic view', according to Bultmann, 'the individual is responsible for himself only ...'[108] The transition in the history of Israel's religion was accordingly from the salvation of the nation to the salvation of the individual. Is this accurate? Was it not rather a transition from the salvation of Israel as ethnic community to the salvation of Israel as religious community?[109] This is a historical question, but of the kind which depends not only on data but very particularly on the horizon of the historian. In no small part the power of existentialism lay in its appreciation of decision as the peak of human intentionality; its deficiency lay in attending to decision almost exclusively in its solitary moment. Though decision and, above all, conversion is intensely personal and utterly intimate, it is not so private as to be solitary (as Lonergan has insisted).[110] And in fact, despite a long tradition to the contrary in German scholarship,[111] early Christianity was not an essentially fortuitous collection of individuals, nor was the very earliest Palestinian community a phenomenon with 'no real history'.[112] To Bultmann the new covenant was not grounded on an event of the history of Israel.[113] But to reaffirm as Jesus' intention the gathering of the messianic remnant is simultaneously to locate the event – the historical prologue – on which the new covenant was grounded. This event was recounted in the gospel literature and, indeed, is coterminous with the whole gospel story. It is the story of a trenchant eschatological demand which effected a division within Israel between those who accepted and those who rejected it.

Second, this aspect of Jesus' mission – division – calls for renewed and concentrated attention. Two sayings from the *ēlthon/'ātêt* series make the significant point. The first reads:

> I have come to kindle a fire on earth
>   and how I wish it were already burning!
> I have a baptism to be baptized with
>   and how I am torn until it be accomplished! (Luke 12.49f.).

The 'fire' was the ordeal; the 'baptism', Jesus' own immersion in it (cf. Mark 10.38f.). *Synechomai* ('I am torn', cf. Phil. 1.23) points to a tension between opposites: a passionate commitment to his mission versus an instinctive recoil from pain and repudiation and death. The saying has a special fascination from this rare glimpse of Jesus' response to the drama of his destiny; but the much more significant point – in fact, the central thrust of the saying – is the explicit comprehending of the ordeal in the aims of Jesus. He wept over Jerusalem and he recoiled from suffering, but he willed the ordeal and here he instructed his disciples that to launch it was precisely his mission. The second saying reinforces and sharpens this sense:

> Do not think I have come to bring peace on earth;
> I have not come to bring peace but a sword (Matt. 10.34).

The sense of the antithesis 'peace/sword' is clarified both by the Matthean context and in the Lukan parallel (Luke 12.51). It does not refer to military conflict but to the division among persons forced to decide for or against the reign of God and its proclamation. Since the decision determined one's lot at the judgment (Matt. 10.32f. par.), the mission of Jesus was like the oracle in Ezekiel: 'Let a sword go through the land' (Ezek. 14.17). The sense of Jesus' saying was that he fully intended and willed to press a radically divisive decision on Israel. But inasmuch as he took no satisfaction at all in the ruin of refusers, the secret of his willing the division had to lie in its positive aspect: the assembling of the heirs of restoration. What was this but the remnant of Israel?

If there is any doubt about the meaning of the division Jesus effected in Israel, it is removed by a word which occurs in his missionary instructions to the twelve:

On entering a household
  offer it the salutation [of peace].
If the household is worthy of it,
  let your peace be upon it;
if it is not worthy,
  let your peace return to you.
And if someone is unwilling to welcome you
  or hear your words,
leave that house or that town
  and shake off the foot-dust [from your clothes].
Amen, I say to you:
The land of Sodom and Gomorrah will fare better
on the day of judgment than shall that town (Matt. 10.12–15).

The disciples' shaking off of the dust was to signify a broken communion heavy with consequence, for the town that rejected the envoys of God's definitive revealer would exclude itself from true Israel,[114] the Israel destined for restoration. In their proclamation of the reign of God and summons to conversion, the disciples would participate in Jesus' own fateful function of division. Faith would be the way to life, unfaith the way to death; and Jesus envisaged whole towns opting for death. Compare the word, 'And you, Capernaum: shall you be raised up to heaven? You shall go down to Hades!' (Matt. 11.23 par.). Like a sword, the news of salvation would divide Israel and render the divided segments ripe respectively for restoration and ruin.

Third, the sense of the motif of 'gathering' should be clarified and traced through Jesus' ministry. The state of the question on the aims of Jesus was advanced in 1971 by Rudolf Pesch, the heart of whose argument was that the cleansing of the temple, a key to the intention of Jesus, signified the eschatological gathering of Israel as the presupposition of salvation for the nations.[115] Heinz Schürmann has objected to the 'gathering' motif,[116] thus raising both a semantic and a substantial question. So far as the semantic question is concerned, the language of 'gathering' need not imply full-fledged segregation and in fact did not in the gospels (cf. Matt. 12.30 par.; 23.37 par.). Like Jesus, the disciples were gatherers (messengers, Mark 6.12 par.; cf. Matt. 22.1–10 par.; fishermen, Mark 1.17 par.; harvesters, Matt. 9.37 par.). But their task was simply to win the response of faith. Jesus' 'following' accordingly came into being not by settling in the wilderness but simply by internal acts of conversion and hope and transient external acts like table fellowship with him and his disciples. As for the substantial question, it is twofold. First, neither in the disciples alone nor in the far wider circle of those who accepted the proclamation of the reign of God was the restoration of Israel an already fully accomplished reality. The full accomplishment was reserved for the coming of God's reign (Matt. 13.24–30, 44–46;[117] cf. Mark 13.27 par.). But those who accepted the proclamation were the seed of the final assembly (Mark 4.30–32 parr.). Moreover, the disciples were in a special sense heirs of restoration: 'Do not be afraid, little flock, for it has pleased your Father to give the reign to you' (Luke 12.32; cf. Dan. 7.27).[118] Second, there is the question whether Jesus provided for the emergence of his following into visible community. The *kêpā'* word (Matt. 16.17–19) and the Last Supper orient us, as we shall presently see, in the direction of a nuanced 'yes'.

These critical points specify the sense in which the aims of Jesus comprehended the remnant of Israel. A salient trait (and indirect confirmation) of Jesus' gathering of the remnant was his predilection for those who figured in prophetic tradition as 'the remnant of Israel', namely, the poor and lowly, the simple or childlike, and the afflicted. These were exactly those Jesus viewed as favoured beneficiaries of God's reign (Matt. 5.3ff. par.; 11.5 par.); he could appeal to them because he was one of them (Matt. 11.29). But in the messianic remnant which Jesus brought into being the traditional themes of the *'ănāwîm* (poor, lowly) would be immeasurably deepened. We can learn how by considering the relationship between the messianic secret (the answer to the public 'Who?' question posed about Jesus[119]) and the messianic mystery (the sense of Jesus' personal destiny, exclusively a theme of esoteric teaching) stylized in the synoptic tradition by the transition from the messianic confession of Jesus to the following pericope.

The confession (Mark 8.27–30 parr.) and the first prediction of the passion (Mark 8.31–33 parr.) are distinct but related pericopes in Mark and Matthew. The distinction is marked stylistically (Mark 8.30 = Matt. 16.20 functions as a conclusion formula; Mark 8.31 = Matt. 16.21 is a narrative reprise) and thematically (the new themes of the second pericope are repudiation, suffering, death, resurrection) but the nexus between them, if implicit, is unmistakable. The reprise which opens the second pericope implicitly presents the confession of messiahship as the condition and signal for the prophecy of suffering; and the figure of Peter is presented as a didactic paradigm, a positive example in the first pericope and a cautionary example in the second. The readership, then, is invited both to affirm Jesus' messiahship and to learn to 'savour the things [= intention, will] of God': repudiation, suffering, death. But there is more here than a simple juxtaposition of themes. The prediction pericope is an esoteric instruction on messiahship. It does not cancel out this theme as it came to expression in the previous pericope but it completes and transforms it by integrating the destiny of Jesus into it. In virtue of the thematic progression from the one pericope to the other,[120] Jesus is represented as seeing to it that he is Messiah specifically in this context. The way to enthronement would be through repudiation, suffering, and death. What follows is almost the equivalent of a new call to discipleship: 'If any man would follow me, let him deny himself and take up his cross and *so* follow me' (Mark 8.34 parr.).[121]

Such is the classic picture of the synoptic gospels. The critique that would test it – dealing with a long- and much-disputed question 'competently, respectfully, and honestly'[122] – only verifies it in its main lines. This, it seems to me, has emerged from several studies of the past few years concerned with how, if at all, the historical Jesus regarded his still future death. Of these studies I would signal two, the more complementary for being distinct from one another in hermeneutical stance and methodical procedure, that of Jeremias[123] and that of Schürmann.[124] It would not be appropriate or possible to review these detailed efforts here; let it suffice to allude to these examples of work challenging the plausibility of the view that Jesus had no awareness of heading toward mortal conflict and death or that, if he did, we cannot know what he might have made of this. Such studies likewise diminish the plausibility of the conjecture that he was executed by mistake, a view which often turns out to be systematically motivated, i.e., meant to make a point about 'faith', as if the purity of faith were enhanced by subverting the congruence of word, deed, and fate which a sane hermeneutics anticipates of Jesus and which research tends to verify and in large measure does verify. The synoptic picture (messiahship and the immediate transition from messiahship to suffering messiahship) is not required by but it does fit in with Jesus' vision of the future as a whole, emergent from a larger reservoir of data and distinct from the eschatological scheme of the primitive church.

Jesus repeatedly associated his own death with the coming ordeal (Mark 10.39 par.; 14.27 par.; Matt. 23.29–32 par.; Luke 12.49–59, cf. par.; 22.35–38); but the ordeal was not only an evil to be reversed, it was a good somehow intrinsically designed to generate the reversal. This 'dialectical' nature of the ordeal came to expression particularly in a set of Lukan texts: the *synechomai* ('I am torn') of Luke 12.50; the contrast between Jesus' tears over Jerusalem (Luke 19.41) and his fierce appetite for his own entry into the ordeal (Luke 12.50; 22.15; cf. Mark 8.33 par.; John 12.27). The secret of his willing 'fire' and 'baptism' certainly lay in their positive role of somehow mediating the dawn of the new age, the consummation and restoration, the reign of God. How fire and baptism were to do this is not, however, spelled out and so remains a question calling for an answer.

Synoptic data individually and in the mass thus bring us to two ascertainments: Jesus understood his immediate messianic task to be the division of Israel between faith and unfaith; and he understood his messianic destiny (formally, enthronement and rule) to be scheduled for fulfilment only as the outcome and reversal of repudiation, suffering, and death.

Why did he set out to elicit a messianic confession from his disciples (Mark 8.27 parr., 29 parr.)? If the confession pericope is taken by itself, the answer is: so that they could grasp his mission as the messianic restoration of Israel (cf. esp. Matt. 16.17–19). But if we consider the same question in the light of the following word on his death, the answer must be: so that they could grasp the terms in which he himself grasped his imminent death, namely, as a constituent element of the messianic event.

We have observed, first, that Jesus could not have envisaged his death as the ruin of his mission; second, that as 'baptism', i.e., eschatological vocation (Luke 12.50; Mark 10.38f.), it could not but have a positive significance; third, it remained a question as to wherein this significance lay. The two pericopes we have been considering (Mark 8.27–30 par., 31–33 par.) do not define it any more than do the esoteric sayings on Jesus' baptism (Luke 12.50; Mark 10.38f.), his drinking of the cup (Mark 10.39 par.), his being anointed beforehand for his burial (Mark 14.8 par.) and so forth. But that the question had implicitly been posed pertains to the logic of the conjoined pericopes (Mark 8.27–30 par., 31–33 par.) and is confirmed by the texts that follow. For now (Mark 8.34ff. parr.) Jesus' esoteric teaching became a mystagogy centred on suffering and death, the meaning of which somehow depended on the still undefined meaning of his own destiny. Riddles (Mark 8.35 parr.; cf. Matt. 10.39; Luke 17.33) and questions (Mark 8.36f.) underlined the baffling issue. What can a man use to pay for life? (Mark 8.37). The classic and expected answer was 'nothing' (Ps. 49.8). But Jesus' ultimate answer was not the expected answer. Man could not buy life. But he, the Messiah, could ransom the mortal and the dead. He could *give* life to the world. As the climax and conclusion of the mystagogy pervading the central section of his gospel, Mark set a word which anticipated a motif of Jesus' eucharistic words: 'The Son of man has not come to be served but to serve: to give his life as a ransom for many' (Mark 10.45 par.).[125]

In common with his contemporaries, Jesus understood the prophetic vocation to entail violent death (Luke 13.33).[126] The 'ransom for many' gave the sense of this death. It alluded to the Isaian ransom theme (Isa. 43.3f.) assimilated to the expiatory suffering of the Servant for 'many' (Isa. 52.13-53.12). It thereby also supplied the missing link between the salvation of Israel and the salvation of the nations. The expiatory value of the death of Jesus would not be limited to Israel. It would be boundless (Isa. 52.15; 53.4–6, 10–12). With a single stroke this defined Jesus' view of the situation of the nations – their immersion in sin and liability to eschatological death – and supplied its resolution. The paradox that saving one's life was losing it and losing it, saving it (Mark 8.35 parr.) took its sense finally from the destiny of Jesus, which would convert death

– in biblical orthodoxy, the punishment for sin – into purification from sin and entry into life.

Expiation as the positive sense of Jesus' death was not an issue he could or did set before Israel; but it confirms his understanding of the situation not only of the nations but of Israel as well. Outside the ambit of his own saving mission there was only death and the dead (Matt. 8.22 par.). The standing resources of Israel could not effect eschatological life. It was not that the Mosaic dispensation had been a failure from the start; it was simply that the concluding revelation had been reserved for the eschaton. This was not the revelation of some ineluctable necessity structurally intrinsic to salvation. It was rather the revelation of God's pleasure, wisdom, will. The motif of the Servant's universal expiation revealed that it pleased God to restore Israel and save mankind – by Jesus' death.

If his willing of the ordeal was an index to its reversible or ambivalent character, we have a clue to the sense in which his death was comprehended in his aims. Jesus did not aim to be repudiated and killed; he aimed to charge with meaning his being repudiated and killed. That he could and ultimately did combine the promise of God's reign with the prospect of his own violent death is inferred from his refusal, on the eve of death, to 'drink of the fruit of the vine until the coming of the reign of God' (Luke 22.18) when he would 'drink it new' (Mark 14.25).[127] It was an implicit promise of table fellowship beyond death. This, indeed, was just the kind of expectation that conditioned the possibility of the temple riddle. In both words Jesus conceived of life beyond death as on a continuum with his earthly career.

The ordeal was to be the revelation of evil; the day of the Son of man would have its greatness from victory over evil; and the victory would have its inner form from the messianic mystery. Evil would not be simply crushed by power. On the contrary, by subjection to evil Jesus would render it impotent. Betrayal, desertion, repudiation would only promote and realize his aims. By submitting to evil he would take its measure, establish its futility, shape it to his own purposes. The faith reflected in the esoteric teachings on repudiation (Mark 8.34 parr.),[128] losing one's life (Mark 8.35 parr.), poverty (Mark 10.17–31 parr.), and the like followed no pattern of piety attested in contemporary Israel. A deft, assured, original foray into iniquity and redemption, it gave a new and matchless depth to the *'ănāwîm* thematic.

Schürmann has shown that the *'yper* ('for, on behalf of', as in 'for many', Mark 10.45 par.; 14.24, or 'for you', Luke 22.20; cf. I Cor. 11.24) of Jesus' death was already integral to his life, to a convergent mass of acts and words, public and esoteric.[129] The same should be said of the covenantal sense (cf. 'covenant' in Mark 14.24 par.; Luke 22.20; I Cor. 11.25) of Jesus' death, for not only the symbolic gestures of the Last Supper[130] but the mass of Jesus' acts and words, public and esoteric, were bent on the restoration of Israel (ultimately to the benefit of the whole world, cf. Matt. 8.11f. par.). Still, it is of real significance for the understanding of Jesus that these charged motifs should have come to explicit articulation; and, in fact, the historicity of both motifs, expiation and covenant, is probable.[131] On the brink of death, Jesus interpreted his death as expiatory for the world (*'yper pollōn*, 'for many', Mark 14.24; *eis aphesin 'amartiōn*, 'for the forgiveness of sins', Matt. 26.28; *'yper 'ymōn*, 'for you', Luke 22.20; I Cor. 11.24; cf. *'yper tēs tou kosmou zōēs*, 'for the life of the world', John 6.51) and as a sacrifice sealing a new covenant (*to 'aima mou tēs diathēkēs*, 'my blood, the blood of the covenant', Mark 14.24 par.; *'ē kainē diathēkē en tō 'aimati mou*, 'the new covenant in my blood', Luke 22.20; cf. I Cor. 11.25).[132] This combination of interpretative motifs defined the messianic community to be born of the new covenant as a people whose sins were forgiven.

The word 'community' brings us back to the substantial issue raised by Schürmann's objection against describing the aim of Jesus as a 'gathering' of eschatological Israel. We remarked above that 'to gather' need not be understood in the sense of segregation. On the other hand, Jesus' maintenance to the end of the will to win all Israel for the reign of God does not rule out the possibility that he considered the disciples, whom he *had* gathered to himself in the full sense, as the core of the messianic people to be. This, indeed, is just what he made them to be by the eucharistic words and their share in the eucharistic bread and wine. They thereby became covenant partners bound to one another and to him in ineffable communion. This represented no new direction; it was rather a solemn fulfilment of intentions prefigured in the countless common meals that bound them in table fellowship. By the command 'Do this' (Luke 22.19; cf. I Cor. 11.25) he enjoined the continuation of this fellowship in his absence and endowed it with a distinctive social and cultic act.[133] This was to be the visible unifying factor of a community otherwise remaining scattered throughout Israel. In the eucharist his followers would have the bread of tomorrow for as long as the ordeal would be their today. So equipped, they were the house built on rock. The power of Hades would try to swamp it and fail, for it belonged to the ordeal as a unique realization of the eschatology of grace. At the judgment heaven would endorse the binding and loosing word (Matt. 16.19) by which it would dispense condemnation and forgiveness. Until the definitive gathering of the saved at the end of time the aims of Jesus would be incarnated in this community, at once the remnant and first fruits of messianic Israel.

3. CONCLUSION

We have now studied the traditions relating to the Baptist, the public traditions on Jesus, and the esoteric traditions on Jesus in an effort to discern the form of his career and the purposes that powered it. In the transition from our first set of conclusions (on Jesus and the Baptist) to our second set (on the reign of God for the simple, the afflicted, and the outcast) and again in the transition from the second to the third set (on Jesus and the remnant of Israel destined for that final restoration symbolized by the new temple) there is a clear progression from lesser to greater differentiation and specificity. The three sets of conclusions converge, but in their convergence the second set sublates and interprets the first, the third sublates and interprets the second. Let us briefly review how this works out in the concrete.

The prophetic and apocalyptic elements that went into the Baptist's career made up a unique symbolic structure. They had been selectively drawn from biblical tradition to define both the looming future (judgment) and the ever diminishing present (the last call to conversion). The Baptist's career was an *Entscheidungsruf* (call to decision) which implied not a christology but an ecclesiology, not the closed ecclesiology of a reformist sect but the assembling by baptism of an open remnant: the Israel of the converted, soon to be purified by Spirit and fire. Jesus affirmed this scheme of meaning by entering into it as an ally and by qualifying John as 'more than a prophet' and his baptism as 'from heaven'.

When John was arrested, Jesus left Judaea for Galilee and embarked on a career as herald of the reign of God. Again, the extremely diverse elements that entered into this career made up a unique symbolic structure. They included exorcisms and cures as well as proclamation and teaching, and these elements were (so to speak) doubled by a circle of disciples instituted to share in the same eschatological tasks. From the standpoint of historical criteriology and its application to the major blocks of data we have distinguished (e.g. Jesus' teaching, the choice and sending of the twelve, cures and exorcisms, table fellowship with sinners, etc.), it would be a mistake to pronounce any of them (say, 'miracles' or 'the twelve') to be non-historical. But even apart from historicity as a narrowly conceived issue, excisions of this kind would represent no gain at all for the understanding of Jesus' career as an intelligible unity, pattern, form. The reduction of authentic materials to the barest minimum might seem proportionately to reduce this problem of unity or form, but its main effect would rather be to lessen the chance of solving it, for it would rule out the data on which any promising hypothesis of unity might be based. The unity in question must not be conceived in merely moral terms – 'he went about doing good' – for these would not account concretely either for his going about or for the particularity of the good he did. But the unknown to be known is precisely the *raison d'être* that would account for the particularity of the particulars of his career.

The reign of God was the focal point. Proclamation and teaching centred on it; cures and exorcisms were signs of it. But what has neither been clearly seen nor probed for its consequences is that the reign of God as imminent meant the imminent restoration of Israel, and the reign of God as already overtaking Israel in Jesus' words and acts meant that Israel was already in process of being restored. His teaching was Torah appropriate to restored Israel and requisite to perfect restoration. His wonder-working signified the restoration of Israel and effected it by restoring the afflicted to their heritage as children of Abraham. The appeal to 'the sinners' likewise belonged to this context. Offering forgiveness and eliciting conversion, it was designed to restore the outcasts to Israel. This is confirmed by Jesus' repeated efforts to reconcile the righteous to this move toward socio-religious integration.

In sum, once the theme of national restoration in its full eschatological sweep is grasped as the concrete meaning of the reign of God, Jesus' career begins to become intelligible as a unity. For this is the point at which all the particulars converge, the theme supplying the original why and wherefore of Jesus' public performance. Its distinctive notes are, first, the gratuity and present actuality of Israel's restoration and, second, the choice of its privileged beneficiaries: the simple, the afflicted, and the outcast.

Moreover, 'eschatological restoration' correlates the whole of Jesus' post-Johannite public ministry with his earliest activity as an ally of John and with his career-long affirmation of John's eschatological role. But if the public traditions thus provide a context in which to grasp more fully and securely the sense of Jesus' earliest acts (his being baptized, his alliance with John in the call of others to baptism), the esoteric traditions provide the fully differentiated context in which to set the whole of his career.

The thrust of Jesus' esoteric teaching was to structure the present and the future in a way which we may represent to ourselves as thesis, antithesis, synthesis. Thesis was Jesus' self-understanding as messianic builder of the house of God. Antithesis was the ordeal that would supervene upon his mission and appear to frustrate it: The shepherd would be stricken, the flock scattered (Mark 14.27 par.). Synthesis was the day of the Son of man, the coming of the reign of God, the shepherd's return to the head of the reassembled flock (Mark 14.28 par.), the building of the new temple. Now, elements of this scheme coincided with numerous public actions and teachings of Jesus. Nevertheless, his esoteric teaching transvalued the whole of his public performance, revealing it as integral to the drama of the end of time. The great theme of apocalyptic – the victory over evil and especially over the adversaries and oppressors of Israel – was now made to incorporate a historical moment: God's final controversy with Israel in the face-to-face encounter between prophet and people. This moment included the proclamation that divided believers and unbelievers, the persecution of Jesus and his followers, the national disaster epitomized in the fall of the temple. Restoration was reserved for the messianic remnant self-assembled by faith.

Some may suppose that to define the aims of Jesus in terms of so grandiose a vision of things is to do theology, not history. But the history of Israel in general, and above all in the centuries preceding and following Jesus, was not the prosaic affair evoked by a facile division between theology and history. All the issues and actors were immersed in religious schemes and visions. As we shall presently see, they were the hinges on which Israel's history turned.

IX

CONFIRMATION AND REFLECTION

By relating Jesus, first, to the history of Israel and especially to the religious movements dating at least from the time of the Maccabees and, second, to early Christianity, its self-understanding and understanding of Jesus, we may hope to find confirmation of the view that the aims of Jesus bore on the restoration of Israel and that in accord with these aims 'restoration' came to proleptic fulfilment in those who by responding to his mission constituted the messianic remnant of Israel. This we set under the heading of 'confirmation'.

We shall conclude the inquiry with an effort of reflection on the disparity between 'imminent end' and ongoing time, on the problem this raises with respect to Jesus and his mission, and on some misconceptions and problems relating to Jesus' human and religious 'authenticity'.

1. CONFIRMATION

Jesus' absorption in Israel's destiny related him to the central movement of the past: the immediate past of the Baptist and of the competing religious parties in Judaism and to the remote past (which they brought to life in their own way) of Moses and the prophets. All these figures contributed to the dialectic of 'ethnic' and 'religious' community. The sea-change in the history of ancient Israel was, in fact, the evolution from ethnic to religious community.[1] Hence the emergence of a major condition of the possibility of Jesus' mission, namely, that the religious factor should become absolutely decisive for the self-definition of Israel. Compared to this sea-change, political events like the advent of the monarchy, its division and collapse, its re-establishment, its relapse into vassalage, its final disappearance, were merely episodic.

The point of departure: solidarity in early Israel

The selfhood constituted and revealed by Israel's self-understanding as people of Yahweh brought into being by the exodus and the covenant was a compound of race and religion, the major components of Israel's historic idiosyncrasy. Not only was it through covenant (*bᵉrît*) that the tribes came to constitute a people, but the blood relationship of the tribes themselves was in part simply posited, as indicated by the contrived character of the various genealogies meant to relate all to a common ancestor.

Israel's earliest social organization reflected the quasi-organic solidarity of house (*bayit*), clan (*mišpāḥâ*), and tribe (*šebeṭ*) typical of nomad life. Solidarity forestalled individuation. That the individual should sustain an autonomous existence or line of action lay outside the horizon of possibilities. He belonged to the collectivity as limb to body. His material and conscious life was participation in family, clan, and tribe. Reciprocal obligations bound him to the living whole of this triple circle which in turn pledged him protection in every phase of life. This was the presupposition of social institutions such as the blood-feud, the law of the levirate, group suppression of the guilty, and so forth.

Cult sacralized all social bonds, those of blood and those of covenant. From family to tribal league every social unit was cultic and every cultic unit was maintained by sacrifice and feast, binding participants in the cult to one another and all of them to the deity. Hence, rebellion against Yahweh had two possible outcomes. Either the rebels would be annihilated before infecting the whole people (Dathan and Abiram, Num. 16; Achan and his house, Josh. 7) or the whole people would be infected and punished as when, in the wake of rebellion by the 'scouts' (Num. 13–14), Israel was condemned to forty years' wandering in the wilderness. It was simply his solidarity with a sinful people (according to Deuteronomy) that excluded Moses from entry into the land (Deut. 1.37; 3.26).

In the myths that opened his epic and the sagas that followed, the Yahwist retained the savour of Israel's nomadic past: the sacrifice of the keeper of flocks was accepted, that of the tiller of the soil rejected; the murderer and his line were founders of cities and inventors of the arts; the tower that aspired to the heavens was disastrous arrogance. Abraham, chief of a nomad clan, recalled the strong and pure past. But, as the Yahwist knew, the instinctive antipathies of the nomad would give way with time to alien satisfactions. Deuteronomy epitomized them as 'great and goodly cities which you did not build and houses full of all good things which you did not fill and cisterns hewn out which you did not hew and vineyards and olive trees which you did not plant . . .' (Deut. 6.10f.). The challenge to Israel's identity of the way of Canaan would not be met by the rally of tribe and clan to the holy war but by the rise of prophets who would effect a change in the nation's self-understanding.

The Yahwist had prepared the way. Though his work as a whole steadily reflected the presupposition of corporate solidarity, there were probes which modified it, such as the dialogue between Abraham and Yahweh about the fate of Sodom (Gen. 18). It opened with Abraham's question: 'Wilt thou indeed destroy the righteous with the wicked?' The question supposed the traditional moral economy of crime and punishment but re-conceived its concrete operation, for it implicitly differentiated a purely moral from a purely social solidarity. The following dialogue developed the question. Righteous and wicked remained in solidarity. But because punishment of the righteous was repugnant, the solidarity functioned in a new way. The righteous would not be punished; rather, the wicked would be spared. Inasmuch as social and moral solidarity were differentiated, their relation could be conceived in a new way.

The prophets and the remnant of Israel

It was owing to their repudiation of the popular notion of the covenant as a guaranteed source of blessings that the prophets effected a change in the self-understanding of the nation. God's word to Israel was not salvation on 'the day of Yahweh' but judgment!

> Hear this word ... against the whole family which I brought up out of the land of Egypt:
> 'You have I favoured more than any family on earth; the more reason to punish you for all your iniquities!' (Amos 3.1f.).

What of the definitiveness of the covenant? Amos acknowledged no such thing. If Israel were to change, to hate evil and love good, then 'perhaps' God would 'graciously spare a remnant of Joseph'[2] (Amos 5.15). Survival was not assured on the basis of the covenant. Hope could turn on nothing but conversion and then, since it was a matter of God's sovereign decision, it was qualified by a 'perhaps'.

The notion and literary motif of 'remnant' was age-old and the common property of the Near East.[3] But through its adoption by the prophets, apparently beginning at an early date, with Elijah (I Kings 19.15–18), 'remnant' was made to function in two new ways. First, it became a vehicle of parenesis. Second, it emerged as a charged symbol of restoration after judgment. The first development began with Amos. The beginnings of the second are attested in Zephaniah and still earlier in the powerful currents of Isaiah's theology.

Isaiah represented his call to prophecy in a scene (Isa. 6.1–13) of special significance for the history of the remnant theme. The scene unfolded in three phases: vision, purification, and mission. *Vision*: The Lord was enthroned in the temple, the seraphim hovering over him and crying, 'Holy, holy, holy is Yahweh of hosts! The whole earth is filled with his glory!' Suddenly filled with a cloud, the temple shook. *Purification*: 'I am doomed!' cried Isaiah. 'For I, a man of unclean lips, living among a people of unclean lips, have seen the king, Yahweh of hosts!' At this, one of the seraphim flew to him and touched his lips with an ember from the altar: 'Your evil is gone, your sin purged!' *Mission*: Then Isaiah heard the Lord's voice, 'Whom shall I send? Who will go for us?' and he cried out 'Here I am, send me!' The Lord's reply:

> Go and say to this people:
>   'Listen carefully – but you shall not understand!
>   Look intently – but you shall not perceive!'
> You are to make the heart of this people obtuse,
>   to dull their ears and close their eyes;
>   otherwise their eyes will see, their ears hear,
>   their heart comprehend, and they will turn and be healed.
> Then I said, 'How long, O Lord?'
> And he said
>   'Until cities lie waste without inhabitant
>   and houses without men, and the land is left in ruin,
>   and Yahweh removes men far away
>   and desolation is great in the midst of the land.
>   And though a tenth remain in it
>   this in turn will be laid waste like a terebinth or an oak
>   of which, when it is felled, only a root stock remains.'
> A holy seed is the root stock.

This majestic scene expresses the aspects of Isaiah's proclamation most relevant to our sketch of development. Yahweh met his people in the person of Isaiah – a numinous encounter. His holiness ('Holy, holy, holy . . .') laid bare the nation's sinfulness and the vision woke a cry of dread. But the cry was followed by Yahweh's lifting the single figure of Isaiah out of Israel's impurity. This cleansing was the condition of the sending. The sending again evoked the underlying and controlling theme of vision, dread, and purification, namely, the disparity between the holiness of Yahweh and the iniquity of Israel. From this disparity followed the prophet's mission – and the nation's disaster. For it grounded the harsh paradox of a mission designed from the start to confirm Israel in its blindness. The dominant tone of the conclusion was therefore doom, an awesome judgment. When Amos said that God would save a remnant of Israel he made the force of these words clear by adding 'as a shepherd snatches from the lion's mouth two legs or the tip of an ear' (Amos 3.12). The conclusion of the Isaian scene was similar. The announced catastrophe was not absolute (absolute catastrophe would be expressed by *negating* the survival of a remnant), but the prospect of slightly mitigated disaster was not cheering.

And though a tenth remain in [the land]
this in turn will be laid waste like a terebinth or an oak
of which, when it is felled, only a root stock remains.

The 'tenth' left in the land was the remnant of Israel. Even this fraction
would again be racked with disaster. The remnant of the remnant was the
root stock. Though the image connoted potency for life, it was so little
calculated by itself to set flags of hope flying that a comment (Isaiah's or
his disciples' or an editor's) had to be added to Yahweh's speech for the
image to be recognized as one of hope: 'A holy seed is the root stock.' The
remnant of the remnant lived. There was hope for the future, for the
disaster-stricken handful was what God required his people to be: 'holy'.

The structure of Isaiah's remnant theology was condemnation of present Israel and projection of a future Israel, the survivor of an all but
annihilating catastrophe. The determining principle of this structure was
faith: 'If you do not believe, surely you shall not endure' (Isa. 7.9).[4] The
remnant which 'shall again take root downward and bear fruit upward'
(Isa. 37.31) was idealized in terms of faith. It would be holy (Isa. 4.3) for
it would lean upon Yahweh (Isa. 10.20). Though Isaiah saw in himself
and his children a 'sign' of Israel to be (Isa. 8.18), he did not retroject this
future into the present. Purified Israel lay on the far side of a still future
judgment.

The main motifs of this theology resonate in other prophetic passages.
Without pretending to date the texts, we may recall some of them. The
theme of restoration after judgment appears in Micah:

On that day, says Yahweh,
   I will gather the lame
and assemble the outcasts
   and those whom I have afflicted;
I will make of the lame a remnant
   and of the outcast a strong nation
and Yahweh shall reign over them on Mount Zion
   from this time forth and forever (Micah 4.6f.).

The most striking aspect of the text is the parallelism of 'remnant' and
'strong nation'. The destiny of the remnant was restoration (Isa. 37.31) in
accord with God's promise to the patriarchs (Micah 7.20). The survivors
would 'increase and multiply' (Jer. 23.3). The dispersed would be
gathered again (Jer. 23.3; 30.8f.; 31.10; Ezek. 34.15f.). Moreover, the
saved remnant would be made up of forgiven sinners:

What God is like thee, removing guilt
   and pardoning sin for the remnant of his inheritance?
He is not one to stay angry forever
   for he delights in covenant-love;
he will again have compassion on us

trampling our guilt underfoot.
Thou wilt cast all our sins
  into the depths of the sea ... (Micah 7.18f.).

In the latter seventh century, with Zephaniah, we meet a key development in remnant theology. The remnant in which earlier prophets had seen the restoration of a shattered nation is now identified as 'a people humble and poor':

On that day you shall not be put to shame
  because of your rebellious acts against me,
for then I will remove from your midst
  your proud boasters
and you shall no longer exalt yourself
  on my holy mountain.
But I will leave in your midst
  a people humble and poor (*'anî wādāl, praün kai tapeinon*)
and they shall seek refuge in the name of Yahweh,
  the remnant of Israel ... (Zech. 3.11–13).

There had been a preparation for this theme in Amos, Micah, and Isaiah. Amos had exploited the traditional idea that the poor and lowly (*'ebyônîm, dallîm, 'ănāwîm; penētes, ptōchoi, tapeinoi*), unable to protect themselves, were placed under the special protection of Yahweh; therefore their oppression especially cried for justice. The right of the poor to help was the bridge between poverty as social fact and as religious theme. Micah had seen the coming restoration as a gathering up of the survivors of judgment: the lame, sick, and afflicted (Micah 4.6f.; cf. Zeph. 3.19). For Isaiah the remnant would be 'holy' because it would be cleansed by judgment (Isa. 1.24–26; 4.2–6). But, as Zephaniah was the first to see the remnant precisely as a gathering of the 'lowly', so it was he who saw that the one hope under the menace of judgment was to seek humility.

Seek Yahweh, all you humble (*'ănāwîm, tapeinoi*)
  of the earth who do his will,
seek righteousness, seek humility!
Perhaps you may be hidden on the day of Yahweh's anger (Zeph. 2.3).

Previously the vocabulary associated with the remnant had been drawn from the promises and the covenant. Heir to the whole legacy of Israel, the remnant would have the covenantal blessings epitomized in 'the fruit of the land' (Isa. 4.2). As in a new exodus (cf. Isa. 11.15f.), Yahweh would create over Zion a cloud of smoke by day and a fire by night (Isa. 4.5). The prophets identified the remnant in the traditional image for God's people, the flock (*ṣ'ôn, 'ēder; probata, poimnē, poimnion*; cf. Micah 2.12; Jer. 31.10). Now, with Zephaniah, 'poor' and 'poverty' (*'ănāw/'ănāwâ*; cf. *'ebyôn, 'ānî, dal, šāpāl*) acquired a lasting prominence in the remnant tradition. Albert Gelin[5] pointed out the thematic constellation of covenant, righteousness, poverty, and flock in Trito-Isaiah, prophet among the returned exiles: *covenant* ('people', 57.14; 58.1; 60.21; 62.12; 63.8; 65.10, 19, 22; 'eternal covenant', 61.8; 'blessed race of Yahweh', 65.9, 23; 'holy people', 62.12; 'elect of Yahweh', 65.9, 15, 22; 'redeemed of Yahweh', 62.12); *righteousness* (the 'just' or 'righteous' as opposed to the wicked, the sceptical, the idolaters, thieves, and the hard-hearted); *poverty* (the 'humble' and the 'broken-hearted', 61.1f.; the 'contrite and lowly', 57.15) and *flock* (65.10).

Efforts towards restoration

The exile and post-exilic period brought about several transpositions of the remnant theme. For the first time an identifiable social entity applied the theme to itself. The returning exiles understood themselves to be the remnant of Israel. The background of this development was the idea that the survivors of national catastrophe were the seed of restoration. The *gola* returned to Palestine in the consciousness of a vocation: to build the temple (Ezra 1.2–4; 3.1–6.22) and to realize 'Israel' as a religious ideal (Ezra 10.2–5). The prophets had designated a pure and perfect future beyond catastrophe and this future had now come. Its salient trait was separation from 'the peoples of the land' (Ezra/Nehemiah). Positively stated, it was a drive to purity. The goal of the community so constituted in rigorous observance of the law was to realize in itself the scriptural attributes of Israel, an ambition destined for repeated renewal in the period from Ezra to the Maccabees.

What grounds the exiles had for identifying themselves alone as Israel is shrouded in darkness. The literature which remains has suppressed, or in any case taken no account of, the right of other groups to the name of Israel. As in classical prophecy the remnant was conceived to be all there was of Israel. The case is different with the anonymous groups of the pious which arose in the Persian period and whose hand is discernible in some of the Psalm literature. Now we find groups, their hallmark a spirituality of 'lowliness', which sought to realize the equation between themselves, the *'ănāwîm* of the present, a small fraction of the nation, and, on the other hand, ideal Israel:

> For Yahweh takes pleasure in his people, he glorifies the lowly (*'ănāwîm*) by saving them (Ps. 149.4).

The parallelism of 'people' and 'lowly' recurs in Ps. 37, where those who 'inherit the land' are variously described as 'those who wait for Yahweh', (v. 9), 'the blessed of Yahweh' (v. 22), 'the righteous' (v. 29) and 'the poor' or 'lowly' (v. 11). Again, the miracle of the exodus, the epiphany of Sinai, and the entry into the land of promise were all for the sake of the '*anî/ptōchos* (Ps. 68.8–11). As the poor man had been the beneficiary of the exodus, the very type of salvation, so the '*ănāwîm* were the beneficiaries of restoration (Ps. 69.33–36). The traditional terminology of the righteous (*ṣaddîqîm/dikaioi*), the upright (*yᵉšārîm/eutheis*), the chosen (*bᵉḥîrîm/ eklektoi*), the holy (*qᵉdôšîm/'agioi*), the pious (*ḥasîdîm/'osioi*), the simple (*pᵉtā'îm/nēpioi*), and so forth was now more and more applied to an *élite*.[6] This heritage from classical prophecy, transmuted by the experience of the exile, imbued with priestly ideals, reserved for a pious *élite*, would be met again in certain groups brought to light by the Hellenistic crisis of the second century or brought into being in the wake of it.

The priesthood and priestly ideals as expressed by Ezekiel as well as in the priestly traditions of the Pentateuch early established an atmosphere conditioning religious developments in post-exilic Israel and directing the transition in self-understanding from nation ('*am*) to cultic community (*'ēdâ*). The rebuilding of the temple was indispensable to the rebuilding of Israel in Judah. The high priest became the central figure in the post-exilic community. A new understanding arose both of what Israel represented in the world and of its relationship to the nations. Where interest in the destiny of the nations waned (e.g. in the books of Chronicles, under pressure of opposition to the Samaritans), eschatological interest in general receded. The Judaean restoration could thus take on the aspect of a *societas perfecta* and set up a potential opposition between eschatology and the 'theocracy' of Jerusalem.

The book of Maccabees indicates that at the time of the Maccabean revolt the 'Assideans' (*synagōgē Assidaiōn*, I Macc. 2.42) already existed, since what period, it is impossible to say. Though the origins of groups such as the Essenes,[7] the Pharisees,[8] the Sadducees,[9] the Therapeutae in Egypt,[10] and the baptist movement in the Jordan Valley[11] are exceedingly obscure, the Hasidim probably stood in some kind of genetic relationship to most if not all of them. Again, to define the relations between the intertestamental literature we possess and the religious groups we know of is difficult and uncertain. The Essenes are currently better known to us, especially through the strictly sectarian portion of the Qumran texts, than any other group, but whether we are justified in interpreting other groups on the Essene model is a question. Granted all such grounds for caution, it still seems possible to learn enough from the religious parties and movements to define the broad current which they collectively represented and within which they were competitors.

The issue underlying the competition was the settling of what Israel was to become. As people of God, Israel had a vocation; it could not be itself without becoming other and better than itself. It lived under the imperative of its heritage: the Torah and the prophets. The agonizing reappraisals of national life begun by the traumatic experience of the exile created a lasting consciousness among the most able and responsible of the gap between vocation and performance. Against this background the rise and diversity of religious parties was inevitable. Not all were agreed on wherein the gap lay nor in any case were all concerned about it and resolved to close it. But for those who were, their life's aim was to realize the attributes specified for Israel in the covenant. Ultimately, after the disastrous revolts against Rome, this ideal would find concrete realization in the triumph of the Pharisaic *halaka*[12] and the subsequent normative definition established for Judaism by the rabbis and crystallized in the Mishna (turn of the third century AD). We are concerned with an earlier period, 'that colorful and tension-laden world'[13] in which Pharisees, Sadducees, Essenes, and Zealots all laid claim to Israel's allegiance and competed for it. These were religious initiatives aimed at the restoration of Israel and setting before Israel a claim to this effect. Of immediate interest is the nature of the claim and the manner of laying claim which such movements represented. This is almost the equivalent of asking what they understood themselves to be. We shall be satisfied to deal briefly with the question, without discussing all the movements and without aspiring to trace their origins and development.

The common note of these movements in any case was the drive to define and realize the biblical ideal which was Israel itself. Theologians did the defining; the pious translated it into practice by their lives. Since the definitions varied, so did the appeals for Israel's allegiance. But we may distinguish two fundamental forms of appeal: the *transformist*, represented pre-eminently by the Pharisees, and the *separatist*, represented pre-eminently by the Essenes. The Essenes supposed empirical Israel to be a *massa damnata* and appealed to the pious to separate themselves from it. Pharisaic suppositions and perspectives are more difficult to determine and may have been less unified than in Essenism. But in principle at least Pharisaism regarded empirical Israel as a *massa salvanda* and appealed to it to be transformed.

Let us return for a moment to the Hasidim. This term is vague and the groups indeterminately covered by it were no doubt various. According to I Macc. 7.12–14 the Assideans (in I Macc. 2.42, a group of soldiers) correlated at least in part with 'a group of scribes'. The readiest explanation is that the Hasidim/Assideans were pious groups of several sorts and various orientations (e.g. in policy toward the Hellenizers and Maccabees, respectively) and that 'scribes'[14] provided them with religious guidance. As for the Pharisees, there are no solidly probable references to them in the book of Maccabees. The oldest text referring to them is in the New Testament, where Paul describes himself as having been 'as to the law a Pharisee' (Phil. 3.5). Here 'Pharisee' is defined by a certain way of understanding and observing the Torah. The earliest point in time for which their existence is attested is the era of Hyrcanus (135–105 BC). Here (*Antiquitates* 13.288–300, cf. 297) they are described as transmitters of ancient laws not written in the Torah. Such references as well as many rabbinic texts might lead one to suppose that the Pharisees were a class of theological scholars.[15] On the other hand, certain New Testament texts indicate that (like the Hasidim) the Pharisees were guided by scholars but were made up of the theologically untrained pious.[16] Were they members of 'closed societies', i.e., the *ḥăbûrôt* of the rabbinic texts?[17] Specialists in rabbinic literature are divided on this significant issue,[18] with the result that the work of historical triangulation (New Testament, Josephus, the rabbis) and reconstruction of the phenomenon of Pharisaism remains in many respects uncertain.

I believe that the term 'transformist', however, can stand. Pharisaic scholars approved of traditional popular customs even when they lacked scriptural sanction and they alleviated the burden of Torah observances by interpretation and casuistry. A certain 'popular' thrust, then, is evident in Pharisaism. The Pharisees wished somehow to extend to all Israel the possibility of meeting God's demand for 'a holy people' (Ex. 19.6; cf. Lev. 11.44f.; 19.2; 20.7).

To this extent they were a people's party and, as Josephus frequently affirmed,[19] enjoyed popular support. But the ordinary people, who welcomed Pharisaic approval of popular custom and Pharisaic alleviation of obsolete and burdensome obligations, did not for all that commit themselves lock, stock, and barrel to the whole programme of Pharisaic observances. In the view of the Pharisees, then, the mass of the people were non-observant and it is entirely unlikely – uncharacteristic in general of the period and specifically uncharacteristic of Torah piety – that the Pharisees simply took this in their stride in a spirit of enlightened toleration. Hence an ambivalent relation of Pharisaism to the mass of Jews. The Pharisees laid a claim on all Israel and the response fell short; the result was tension on the Pharisaic side between condemnation and the sustaining of the appeal.

The gospel literature offers an important clue to the distinction between Pharisees and common people. Pharisaic observances notably included ritual handwashing before meals (Mark 7.3,5; Matt. 15.2; Luke 11.38) and special tithing prescriptions (Luke 18.12; Matt. 23.23 par.). These practices went beyond the letter of the law for Israel, according to which ritual purity played a very limited role in the everyday life of the layman.[20] What, then, was the significance of such practices? In all probability the Pharisees, mostly laymen, were applying to themselves prescriptions proper to the priesthood.[21] Why? Presumably, because the scriptures defined Israel as 'a kingdom of priests' (Ex. 19.6). In so far as the Pharisees thus sought to realize in themselves the attributes of scriptural Israel, they constituted an *ecclesiola in ecclesia* – not a sect, for they remained *in ecclesia*, but the restoration in which all Israel would live as it ought, in full fidelity to the Torah, consisted precisely in following Pharisaic *halaka*. To this extent the Pharisees were not only a leaven within Israel. Israel was being told that in Pharisaism lay its true vocation.

Despite the differences between 'transformist' and 'separatist' policy, therefore, there was a structural resemblance between the Pharisees and the Essenes. The difference lay in the Essene conviction that empirical Israel at a certain point in time, namely, in the mid-second century (perhaps in the wake of the popular vote by which Simon Maccabee and his sons were made high priests forever in 141 BC) had become 'a community of apostates' (CD 1.12). This was the era of 'the Scoffer' who 'let pour over Israel the water of lies' (CD 1.14f.). Only a remnant, led by the Teacher of Righteousness who was to give Essenism its distinctive direction, remained faithful to the Torah. This division followed the pattern of sacred history from time immemorial as epitomized in the paradigm set at the head of the Damascus Document: 'When they were unfaithful and abandoned him, he hid his face from Israel and its sanctuary and gave them over to the sword; but remembering the covenant of the ancients, he left Israel a remnant . . .' (CD 1.3–5; cf. 2.3–13). From the outset the first members of the covenant of old had been divided between the rebellious and the faithful (CD 3.7–11); it was only with 'the remnant which clung to the commandments' (CD 3.12) that God made his covenant forever. Likewise, in fulfilment of his promise (Ezek. 44.15; cf. CD 3.21–4.1f.) he made a 'new covenant' (CD 6.19; 8.21; 19.33f.; 20.12; 1QpHab. 2.3) with the remnant of the last days (cf. 1QM 13.8f.; 14.8f.) which he himself would raise up and purify (1QH 6.7f.).[22]

The sect therefore frankly appealed to pious Jews to join 'Israel'! Pursuing its idea with unblinking attention to symbolic detail, it modelled itself on the Israel of the scriptures; hence its divisions into clergy (the house of Aaron) and laity (the house of Israel), into twelve tribes (cf. Gen. 49: Num. 1; 26), into thousands, hundreds, fifties, and tens (cf. Ex. 18.21; Deut. 1.15) and, in military operations to take place at the end of time, into four camps of three tribes each (cf. Enoch 82.9–15). All these divisions (1QS 2.19–22; 6.8f.; CD 14.3–6; cf. 1QM 3.13–16; 4.1–5) collectively constituted 'the people of God' (*'am 'ēl*, 1QM 3.13).[23]

This remnant was, axiomatically, the seed of Israel's restoration, its intention being to be constituted as Israel in perfect purity according to the right understanding of the Torah. The right understanding radicalized the Torah by applying to the whole sect the most rigorous moral and ritual standards, including the norms of purity originally designed for priests when officiating in the temple. This was in all probability the perspective in which the sectarians of Qumran adopted celibacy.[24] This is supported by what we know of the Therapeutae of Egypt, a group similar to and perhaps historically related to the Essenes. According to Philo these contemplatives practiced an asceticism even sterner than that of the Essenes, the key to which, once again, was the priestly ideal. Thus, Philo writes: 'Abstinence from wine is enjoined by right reason as for the priest when sacrificing, so to these [Therapeutae] for their lifetime.'[25] The same perspective emerges from other details. On feast days the Therapeutae celebrated a sacred meal of bread and water. The bread was leavened and the salt mixed with hyssop 'out of reverence for the holy table enshrined in the sacred vestibule of the temple on which lie loaves and salt without condiments, the loaves unleavened and the salt unmixed. For it was appropriate that the simplest and purest food should be assigned to the highest caste, namely the priests ... and that others while aspiring to similar privileges should abstain from seeking the same as they.'[26] Celibacy, which Philo's description suggests without explicitly mentioning, again belonged, no doubt, to the thematic of priestly ritual purity.

If we are to set John the Baptist and Jesus in the context of this pre-70 competition for Israel's allegiance, how ought we characterize their claim and appeal? The post-paschal Christian community was both separatist (like the Essenes it regarded itself as the community of the new covenant and the unique heir of the promises) and transformist (it launched a major missionary effort to win over all Israel). But neither term hits off the perspective in which the Baptist and Jesus regarded Israel at large. Neither John nor Jesus worked out a distinctive *halaka* designed to transform Israel nor did either consider Israel a lost cause from which only an *élite* of the pious might escape. Both conceived restoration itself in immediately and strictly eschatological terms. The claim and appeal of the Baptist and Jesus was *preparationist*. The whole point of both appeals was to prepare Israel for the imminent consummation of history. Neither considered the very constitution of the remnant of Israel to hinge (as in Essenism and, if the Pharisees ever applied the remnant idea to themselves,[27] in Pharisaism) on a right understanding and observance of the Torah. The Pharisees as well as the Essenes had an eschatology,[28] but in neither case was eschatology the immediate and decisive principle of the movement's very existence. For the Baptist and for Jesus, on the contrary, the remnant of Israel was constituted precisely by response to a trenchant eschatological demand.

Essenism went beyond Pharisaism in subordinating the ethnic to the religious factor in the effort to realize 'true Israel'. But this line of radicalization took the form simply of exclusion, the exclusion of children of Abraham from salvation. Jesus' radical eschatology envisaged Gentiles in the place of Jews at the banquet of salvation with the patriarchs (Matt. 8.11f. par.). Alluding to the great passage on the Isaian Servant of

God (Isa. 53), he named the Gentiles beneficiaries of his expiatory death. It was the Christian community that took the ultimate step, admitting Gentiles as Gentiles (Acts 10; 11.20; 13.1–3) into Israel (Gal. 6.16) and celebrating the supreme 'secret': 'that in Christ Jesus through the news of salvation the Gentiles are fellow-heirs with the Jews, made one body with them, and co-sharers of the promise' (Eph. 3.6).

The contrast with Essenism is dramatized by the midrash on Nathan's oracle (4QFlor 1–13). Christian agreed with Essene that God would build Israel a house in the last days (2); that in the sanctuary he himself had built (Ex. 15.17f.) the Lord would reign forever (3); that the community itself was that house (3); that Satan would fail against it (7–9); that the words of the oracle designated the Messiah, the Branch of David (10f.) who would arise in Zion at the end of time (11f.). But at a certain point there was a parting of the ways in opposite directions. The Essene heard God say: 'This is the house into which [there shall] never [enter] the Ammonite nor the Moabite nor the half-breed nor the foreigner nor the stranger' (3f.; cf. Deut. 23.2–7, EVV 23.1–6); the Christian heard him say: 'my house shall be called a house of prayer for all peoples' (Isa. 56.7; Mark 11.17). . . .

Zealots, Pharisees, Sadducees, and Jesus

So far we have referred to religious parties in Judaism simply with a view to locating the context in which to set the aims of Jesus and to clarify by contrast with other groups the character of his appeal to Israel. Now, however, we shall consider the parties with a view to locating concretely the conflicts which marked his career and brought it to an end.

The Essenes did not figure in the gospel story. The so-called 'Herodians' (Mark 3.6; 12.13 par.) figured in it, but our lack of information on them makes it impossible to reconstruct with any assurance the terms and motives of their conflict with Jesus. That leaves the Zealots, the Pharisees, and the Sadducees.

The Zealot movement, once it is set in the context of Palestinian Judaism's unremitting recalcitrance toward its alien political masters from the Macedonians of Syria (Maccabean Revolt, 167–141 BC) through the half-Jew and Roman protégé Herod (war of 40–37 BC) and his son Archelaus (abortive revolt of 4 BC) to Rome itself (resistance to Gabinius and Pompey, 63 BC; revolt under Cassius, c. 52 BC; Zealot movement inaugurated, AD 6–7, and operative in a ceaseless succession of incidents until the war of AD 66–73, appearing again in the Diaspora revolt of AD 116–117 and the revolt of Bar Kochba, AD 132–136), appears not as an erratic phenomenon running against the Judaic grain but as a native and durable feature of the Judaism of the time. The Zealots promoted a liberation movement under the aegis of the reign of God. Submission to foreign masters, e.g. by payment of tribute, was idolatry. They were apocalyptists but, unlike the book of Daniel, did not expect salvation by divine miracle alone. God's reign would come by force of arms, including terrorism as preparatory for revolt. From Judas the Galilean through Theudas to Menahem, son of Judas, and beyond to Bar Kochba, the movement produced a succession of messianic prophets or pretenders.

The proclamation and teaching of Jesus stood in flat contradiction to the Zealots, their distinctive tenets, their whole religious perspective. Both were passionately bound to Israel and both saw its restoration in the reign of God; but the radicalizations of the Torah specified by the Zealots and by Jesus respectively pointed in opposite directions: here to vengeance and violence, there to forgiveness and acceptance.

Apparently, the Zealots did not single Jesus out for special enmity; he was no collaborationist. But the movement was fundamental to the history of Jesus, often surfacing anonymously as a determinant of the tense social scene (Mark 12.14–17 parr.; 15.6–15 par.; cf. 10.38f. par.; Matt. 5.38–48 par.) and without reference to it the story of Jesus' death would obviously be unintelligible.

The two religious parties that came into direct conflict with Jesus were the Pharisees and the Sadducees. Pharisaism's most indisputable trait was its absorption in the *halaka* by observance of which Israel was to be made a holy people. For the time of Jesus it is not clear whether any or all Pharisees excluded a new Torah for the messianic age; but with reference to the present the economy of the Torah was complete and fully adequate and its observance according to Pharisaic *halaka* had a role in the scheme of things comparable to that which Christians were to attribute to messianic redemption. It was the *movens* of history (as observance of the great commandment had been in the Deuteronomistic view), radicalized as such by the emergence of apocalyptic and its absolute eschatology.

The cardinal importance of observance of the Torah – structurally, the task corresponding to the grace of election and the stipulation on which the Mosaic covenant turned; historically, the permanent religious reaction to the national trauma of the exile, interpreted in Torah and prophets as condemnation for non-observance – generated the horizon of Torah piety shared by all the religious parties and established the context within which they disparaged one another.

Given Jesus' sharp differentiation between the word of God and the tradition of the scribes and his depreciatory view of the latter, or – to put it more fundamentally and more positively – given his sense of plenipotentiary sovereignty as the final revealer of God's will, friction with Pharisaism was inevitable. Its central issue was Jesus' radical and repeated offence to Torah piety by word and act. If in post-exilic Judaism the sabbath commandment was the most important part of the divine law, he managed to violate it – by curing the sick. If, on the other hand, the Pharisees practised the most rigorous ritual observances, he managed to find fault with this by contrasting outer with inner purity. He did not differ from the erudition of Pharisaic scribes and the piety of their followers as the Sadducees did, essentially conceding the rules of the game and haggling over the score. He overturned the game, rejecting Pharisaism root and branch. The response, according to the unanimous testimony of the gospels – which, to be sure, calls for a sober historical critique in particular texts and with reference to the over-view of each redaction – was bitter enmity.

It is a well grounded observation that in the passion predictions and the passion story the prime movers of events are not the Pharisees but the Sanhedrists (Mark 8.31 parr.; 10.33 par.; 11.18 par., 27 parr.; 14.1 parr., 10 parr., 43 par., 47 parr., 53–55 parr.; 15.1 parr., 31 par.): the chief priests (the current high priest, the retired high priests, the captain, overseers, and treasurers of the temple), the elders (the family heads of Jerusalem's lay aristocracy) and the scribes (Sadducees and Pharisees). In the time of Jesus the balance of power in the Sanhedrin was held by the Sadducees.

Known to us through the New Testament (e.g. Mark 12.18–27 parr.; Acts 4.1; 5.17; 23.6–9), Josephus (*Bellum Judaicum* 2.119, 164 166; *Antiquitates* 13.71, 173, 293–298; 18.16f.; 20.199; *Vita* 10), and the Talmud (cf. Billerbeck IV, 343–352), the Sadducees have left no writings of their own. While they are not to be simply identified with the priesthood, their strength lay in the hereditary lay and priestly aristocracy and the temple was their special preserve. Their characteristic doctrinal stance was conservative. They cultivated an exegetical *halaka* without understanding it as oral tradition from the time of Moses (as the Pharisees did). Doctrines unattested by the Torah such as angelology and the resurrection of the dead, they rejected. But Sadduceeism cannot be defined simply by its rejections. What were its affirmations? These relate to the situation and mentality of the post-exilic hierocracy.

The common matrix of the three major religious parties had been a priestly world of cultic piety and the evolution of the parties accorded with patterns they forged from this heritage. In Pharisaism and Essenism development was far bolder than in Sadduceeism, which affirmed land, temple, and Torah in line with the pre-Hasmonean ideology of the temple state. The hereditary sons of Zadok appear to have held the high-priestly office and to have headed the Judaean hierocracy since the return of the *gola* (cf. Hag. 1.1 with MT I Chron. 5.29f., 34, 40f.) and evidence from Ben Sira attests this state of affairs for the period c. 190 BC (Sir. 45.25; 50.1–21; 51.12 ix). Among the incidents pertaining to the crisis of the high priesthood – part of the larger crisis instigated by Antiochus Epiphanes –

were the flight of the Zadokite Onias IV to Egypt (*Antiquitates* 12.237, 387) where c. 154 BC he established a temple in Leontopolis, and the withdrawal of the so-called Teacher of Righteousness to Qumran with a group of like-minded followers among whom the priestly element named itself 'sons of Zadok'. It may well be that the term Sadducees (*saddoukaioi*, Heb.: *ṣaddûqîm*) meant Zadokites as well, so implicitly claiming priestly legitimacy (cf. Ezek. 40.46; 43.19; 44.10–15). However this may be, genuine Zadokites did not figure in the long list of Sadducean high priests of the period between 37 BC and AD 67. If 'Sadducee' meant 'Zadokite', perhaps the Sadducees had their name from before the Hellenistic crisis; in any case, the religious persuasions of the Sadducees did hark back, as we have said, to an older priestly ideology:

> To have the mind of the Zadokite or Sadducee is to be sustained by the concept of a particularist temple state which along the lines of traditional [= this-worldly] eschatological hopes is the seed for the purification of the Holy Land, its liberation from all Gentiles and semi-Gentiles, and the restoration of the idealized kingdom of Israel as David once reigned over it ... [29]

In this reconstruction even the Sadducees looked to the restoration of Israel.

Under the Hasmoneans they had at first flourished. From the time of Salome Alexandra's accession to the throne (76 BC), however, they took second place to the Pharisees, and when Herod ended the Hasmonean dynasty the power of the Sadducees (who had taken sides against him) went into temporary eclipse. Herod nevertheless appointed a Sadducee, Simon, son of Boethus, to the high priesthood (22–5 BC), and this office remained in Sadducean hands practically until its end in the revolt against Rome. In this period Pharisaic scribes figured in the Sanhedrin as a force to be reckoned with, but priestly and lay Sadducees were the main mediators between the native population and Roman authority.

If Jesus provoked the hostility of the Pharisees by his critique of the *halaka* and radicalization of the law, he aroused the mortal hatred of the Sadducean higher clergy by his cleansing of the temple, an event without known parallel in the tense history of Palestinian Judaism under the Romans. Over and above this brusque and jarring critique of temple administration – directly offensive to Sadducean temple officials and Sadducean entrepreneurs controlling the concessions – the cleansing of the temple was rightly interpreted as an act of prophetic symbolism (cf. the charge implied by Luke 22.63f., cf. Mark 14.65 par.) subverting Sadducean dogma and identity. In the Sadducean perspective Jesus had practically broken with the covenant; he had laid violent hands on the untouchable and would pay for it with his life.

The conflicts between Jesus and the contemporary religious parties could not have been more fundamental. He demolished the legitimacy of the Zealot programme with a single word (Mark 12.17 parr.). He condemned the Pharisaic *halaka* as a perversion of the will of God (Mark 7.8 par.): its rigour frustrated the command of love (Mark 3.4 par.) and its leniency was connivance with the will to disobey (Mark 7.10–12). To the Sadducees, whose very selfhood was peculiarly bound up with the temple, he evoked the temple's destruction and promised to build a new one 'in three days'.

Confirmation from early Christianity

Both by its self-understanding and its understanding of Jesus, early Christianity offers significant confirmation of the view that the goal of Jesus' career was the eschatological restoration of Israel. We may begin with confirmation from early Christian self-understanding.

From the start this was an essentially ecclesial self-understanding. Its first categories – the community of the outpoured Spirit, the Zion of the last days, the remnant of Israel, the restored *qāhāl* of the desert – corresponded in substance and sometimes in striking detail to what we take to have been Jesus' goal.[30]

In the part of the epistle to the Romans which dealt with how God integrated the unbelief of Israel into his plan of salvation for the world (chs. 9–11), Paul asked (Rom. 9.22–24) whether the scriptures had been contradicted and defeated by the non-entry of the bulk of Israel into messianic salvation. His answer (Rom. 9.27–29) was that the scriptures had been fulfilled! The Isaian threat/promise that a remnant would be saved (Isa. 10.20–23) had found historic realization. Paul's intention was to make a statement not on the aims of the historical Jesus but on the providential aims of God. The statement found its full expression in ch. 11. Had God rejected his people, Israel? The answer – no! (Rom. 11.1) – was developed in terms of remnant theology, beginning with the classic text of I Kings 19. As in the Israel of Elijah's day, 'so, too, at the present time there is a remnant, chosen by grace' (Rom. 11.5). The following sequence (Rom. 11.7–12) culminated in the theme of unbelief made to serve God's saving purpose: 'If their failure only means riches for the nations, how much more will their full inclusion mean!' (Rom. 11.12). This, in turn, set up the *mystērion*: God would save all Israel (Rom. 11.27) for his gifts and his call were irrevocable (Rom. 11.28). Paul's subsumption of the historical encounter of Christ and Israel (cf. Rom. 15.8f.) under the category of the salvation of the remnant correlates well with how we have defined the perspectives and purposes of Jesus. So does his naming the church 'the Israel of God' (Gal. 6.16).

The confirmation offered by the earliest categories of ecclesial self-understanding and by Paul's account of how believing and unbelieving

Israel stood *vis-à-vis* the destiny assigned Israel by the scriptures is rein-
forced by a development within the synoptic tradition. Jesus' vocabulary
for those who were favoured beneficiaries of God's reign had borne a
discernible relationship to the *'ănāwîm* vocabulary of the remnant thematic
after Zephaniah. But as Jesus used this vocabulary it implied no community organization. Now this vocabulary was transformed. In so far as the
transformation took place in the sayings material attributed to Jesus, it
suggests an interpretation of him as the founder of a remnant brotherhood. If the line of the argument is clear, its material elements may be
summarily presented. The literally poor, whose lot Jesus had promised
was about to be reversed, now became the *'ănāwîm* (*'oi ptōchoi tō pneumati*,
Matt. 5.3. cf. 5.5,7–11) in the sense of the prophets and Psalms and of
sundry post-biblical religious groups (Pss. Sol. 10.7; 15.2; 4QPs37 2.8f.;
3.10.; 1QpHab. 12.3, 6, 10; 1QM 11.13; CD 19.9, applying Zech. 11.11 to
the Essene brotherhood). The socially insignificant (*mikroi, elachistoi*) now
became those in the community most easily hurt by bad example
(Mark 9.42; Matt. 18.6 par., 10, 14). With this one might compare the
distance between Jesus' use (Matt. 11.25 par.) of *nēpioi* (Aram.: *šabrîn*; cf.
Heb. *pᵉtā'îm*) for the naive and unlettered (and so open-hearted) with
Paul's use of *nēpioi* to signify the spiritually immature in the community
(I Cor. 3.1). In line with other transformations within the synoptic tradition, Matthew attributed to Jesus a vocabulary typical of remnant groups:
'brothers' (*adelphoi*) used in a community sense (Matt. 18.15,21,35), the
'elect' (*eklektoi*, Matt. 24.22,24,31; cf. 1QS 8.6; 9.14; CD 4.3f. etc.), the
'perfect' (*teleioi*), a term in the community for the advanced and mature
(Matt. 5.48; 19.21; cf. I Cor. 2.6).

We turn now to early Christian interpretations of Jesus and his mission.
In the baptism narrative (Mark 1.9–11; Matt. 3.13–17; Luke 3.21f.) the
voice from heaven signifies the sense of the scene: Jesus, Son of God, was
anointed by the Spirit of God (Isa. 42.1) for the role of the Servant: to be a
covenant to Israel and a light to the nations (Isa. 42.6). In the following
account of Jesus in the wilderness, he has broken the power of Satan. The
essential point of the three 'ordeals' depicted by Matthew and Luke was to
present Jesus as at once 'the obedient Messiah' and 'the new Israel' – a
combination evidencing the consciousness of early Christians that 'Messiah' was inseparably bound up with 'messianic community'. Jesus typified it and they themselves constituted it. Three times Jesus was urged to
initiate his messianic career without waiting on God. The rejection of this
option was by the same token the acceptance of his divine vocation. The
content and character of the vocation was obliquely indicated by the
eschatological scheme 'as in the beginning, so in the end' (cf. Barn. 6.13:
ta eschata 'ōs ta prōta). Whereas ancient Israel had collapsed under the test
in the wilderness (Deut. 8.2f.; cf. Matt. 4.4; Luke 4.4), the Israel of the

last days, Jesus himself, emerged victorious from it. The result was the restoration of communion between God and man evoked by symbols of Paradise (Mark 1.13, 'he was with the wild beasts' and 'the angels ministered to him', [cf. Matt. 4.11]). The baptism and temptation narratives are thus replete with allusions to Israel and its restoration. As bearer of the Servant's role, Jesus was to bring it about; as representing Israel, he incarnated it.

In the transfiguration account (Mark 9.2–8; Matt. 17.1–8; Luke 9.28–36) pre-redactional tradition presented a narrative filled with covenantal images and allusions (the figures of Moses and Elijah, the tabernacles motif, the cloud, the Old Testament citations) and the redactions variously exploited this line. In Matthew the covenant theme is mediated by 'the new Moses'; in Mark and Luke, by Jesus' death (cf. Mark 14.24; Luke 22.20). Mark by his special accent on Elijah (named before Moses! Mark 9.4) has managed practically to transpose the scene's centre of gravity to the following dialogue (Mark 9.28–36): Elijah's mission of restoration, a type of the mission of Jesus, comprehends a martyr's death. In the Matthean conception the centre of gravity is the role of Jesus as revealer of the new Torah for Israel (cf. the new Moses motif in Matt. 17.2: 'and his face shone like the sun', cf. Ex. 34.29–35), the major accent falling on 'Listen to him!' (Matt. 17.5; cf. Deut. 18.15, 18). In Luke the centre of gravity is the theme of 'departure' (*exodos*, denoting death and probably connoting 'assumption'; see Luke 24.51; Acts 1.9; cf. the assumptions of both Moses and Elijah in intertestamental tradition). In all the texts the nexus between 'new Israel' and the personal mission and destiny of Jesus is unmistakable.

Let these brief observations serve as a pointer to what is a major and pervasive theme of the earliest Christian theology.[31]

2. REFLECTION

We conclude our inquiry not with an effort to specify what might be its positive yield but simply with an effort to withdraw from some misunderstandings it may have generated. They relate to the human and religious authenticity of Jesus.

We have said that his proclamation bore on the imminent advent of God's reign; and in this context, while setting words like 'unfulfilment' and 'unfulfilled' in inverted commas, we have referred to aspects of the disparity between Jesus' word and the actuality of events as to so many indices of the historicity of his word. The time has now come to pose the question: 'Was the proclamation of Jesus mistaken?'

Second, we referred at the outset to the result of Jesus' career (in its positive moment, the coming to be of his *ekklēsia*, in its negative moment, the break between Judaism and Jesus) and asked how 'aims' and 'outcome' correlated here. The aim immediately commanding his historic career was to win all Israel over to eschatological restoration; on this was to hinge the salvation of the nations. But the eschatological restoration of all Israel turned, itself, on a hinge, a *sine qua non* condition: the response of faith to proclamation of the reign of God and so to its messianic proclaimer. In 'all Israel' and 'faith' we have accordingly seen distinct facets of Jesus' aim. History dissociated them. 'All Israel' did not take the path of faith in Jesus and his proclamation. But 'faith' took primacy in his aims over the 'all' in 'all Israel'; and those who did take the path of faith uniquely constituted, in their own view as in his, the remnant in which Israel would find messianic restoration. The only perfect correlation between aims and outcome would have been all Israel's entry into messianic salvation. In its positive moment, therefore, the actual outcome of his career (concretely, his *ekklēsia*) was in fundamental and substantial, but not in absolutely perfect, accord with his aims; and in its negative moment (the division between Judaism and Jesus) the outcome was in fundamental and substantial, but not in absolute, discord with his aims. Such is the background of our concluding reflections on the human and religious authenticity of Jesus. Nourished in part by themes of contemporary New Testament scholarship, in part by the observations of certain Jewish thinkers on Jesus and Judaism, in part by recognition of the futility of pretending to evaluate Jesus, these reflections attempt to correct or forestall misunderstandings relative to eschatological promise and fulfilment, 'apocalyptic and Jesus', the 'messianic secret', Jesus' invitation to Judaism, and, finally, on what made Jesus go as he did to his death.

Was Jesus mistaken?

'If what the prophet says does not happen, you need not fear that prophet' (Deut. 18.22).

There is a tradition running from the radical deists to the present which, applying this principle to Jesus and his vision of things, has found him and it wanting. Another tradition, running *pari passu* with the first, has consisted in a laborious effort to meet the problem of the disparity between vision and history and to highlight aspects of Jesus' perspectives and purposes which in some sense were independent of his prophecy of the imminent coming of God's reign.

The view of the deists has about it a kind of clean simplicity. Jesus foretold and expected the imminent end of history, but he was wrong; it did not come. And there is an air of evasion about the views of the many theologians who, in substantial if often unarticulated accord with this ascertainment of the deists, nevertheless insisted on going further in the hope of freeing the core of Jesus' message from its now evidently obsolete husk. These were the theological salvagers who, much more than the Reimaruses and the Bruno Bauers, produced 'the quest of the historical Jesus' and bequeathed to posterity this imposing but ambiguous monument.

In the hard-line deist view Jesus' error was no trifle. It meant the collapse of his claim to the status of infallible revealer. Among many of the theologians, on the other hand, the 'error' was so doubtful and so minor as finally to have been forgotten. Johannes Weiss's recalling it forcefully to mind in 1892 broke over the heads of these scholars like a thunderclap and Jesus' eschatology has not been forgotten again.

Since the days of the deists, to be sure, this eschatology has posed a problem different from the problem it posed for the ancient church. Ancient believers lived within it. Modern believers are largely unaware of it and modern theologians merely objectify it and examine it from the outside. In early Christianity the non-advent of the parousia was a lived puzzlement arising from a lived faith and it found a lived solution in the same faith. The major element of the solution was a persevering watchfulness and persevering hope; the minor element consisted in some *ad hoc* explanations of delay, often made to correlate with missionary concerns (cf. e.g. Rom. 11.25 32; Acts 3.19–21). But since the Enlightenment the non-advent of the parousia has become a theoretical problem calling for an equally theoretical solution. First formulated for discussion by controversialists absorbed in the issue of natural versus revealed religion, it has since been relegated to academic experts expected to be able to work out an informed opinion on it. This should not be understood as if meant to reduce the problem to insignificance. It is a significant theoretical problem related vitally, but still in the realm of theory, to the authenticity of prophecy and prophet. In this light it seems unlikely that we should be able to arrive at a true appreciation of the aims of Jesus without taking account of this now long-standing problematic.

Since 1892 some theologians, most recently Eta Linnemann,[32] have been persuaded that the problem of 'delay' had little to do with Jesus. True, he had spoken of a future coming of the reign of God, but he had not said that it was imminent. Others, finding evidence that Jesus had in fact proclaimed an imminent coming of the reign of God, frankly acknowledged that the prophecy was mistaken. Of these Albert Schweitzer stood almost alone in not feeling the least need to save Jesus from himself by explaining, reinterpreting, and redeeming the error.

C. H. Dodd, as we have seen,[33] had no hesitation about detailing Jesus' original view of the imminent reign of God, for the whole could be transposed into the spiritual categories of a lasting present which was as much a fulfilment of Jesus' prophecy as there would ever be. Dodd distanced himself in various particulars from the nineteenth-century liberals, but his theological strategy, namely, the transposition of eschatology into other categories, differed from theirs only, or mainly, in being more conscious and more sober. The strategy was conceived still more consciously and executed still more systematically by the existentialists who, with Bultmann, named this process 'demythologizing'. The terms into which Jesus' eschatology was transposed were new but the strategy itself was at least as old as Gnosticism.

Romano Guardini proposed that if all Israel had answered the summons of the reign of God, the consummation of history would have taken place just as Jesus had predicted; God's allowing history to continue responded to Israel's refusal.[34] Joachim Jeremias has offered a comparable solution.[35] In contradistinction to apocalyptic conceptions (a calendar of future events with fixed and unchangeable dates, cf. II (4) Ezra 4.33, 37), Jesus in the parable of Luke 13.6–9 revealed that God could lengthen an appointed time; according to the petition 'Thy Kingdom come!' he could shorten an appointed time; and according to Mark 13.20 he had already decided that for the sake of the elect he would shorten the last time of distress. Unlike Guardini, who absolved Jesus of error by invoking God's power to revise the schedule of eschatological consummation, Jeremias conceded that Jesus erred in affirming an imminent end. Since to err is human, the error accorded with the christological tenet of the *vere homo*. The important point was Jesus' revelation of a gracious God who for men's sake could change the appointed measures of time.

According to most conservative scholars, Catholic and Protestant, Jesus envisaged an interim between resurrection and parousia. In Oscar Cullmann's view, he thus foresaw an era of the church having the lifetime of a single generation.[36] Though he was mistaken about the length of time involved, the significant point was his having willed in principle the same eschatological and salvation-historical scheme as the church of all times has affirmed.

Others, such as Rudolf Schnackenburg, adopted a judicious agnosticism about the originally intended sense of those sayings of Jesus which set a limit on the time between 'now' and the end (e.g. Mark 9.1 parr.; 13.30 parr.; Matt. 10.23).[37] Béda Rigaux and Anton Vögtle, on the other hand, offered positive explanations of these texts. Differentiating between affirmation and expectation, Rigaux located in Jesus' sayings a genuine and basic affirmation: he did not know 'the day and the hour' of the consummation (Mark 13.32 par.). Words that seemed to say otherwise belonged to the thematic of expectation, exhortation, hope, watchfulness, as 'conjectural affirmations' on which apocalyptic literary convention imposed an absolute form.[38] Vögtle argued that in just those details which went beyond Jesus' basic affirmation of not knowing the day and the hour (Mark 13.32.), the sayings were secondary, reflecting a church anticipating by hope the end of the ordeal.[39]

This swift, unsystematic, but fairly representative sampling of opinion indicates the problem which the eschatology of Jesus has posed and still poses. But the various solutions proposed all appear to be more or less unsatisfactory.

On the level of historical-critical interpretation it is hardly possible to excise 'imminence' from Jesus' proclamation.[40] At the opposite extreme, Schweitzer's reconstruction of Jesus' eschatology is exegetically and historically indefensible.[41] As for the systematic translation of apocalyptic eschatology whether into timeless truths or existentialist self-understanding, the suspicion arises, even where the end-result exhibits some positive accord with the kerygma or some religious gain (as when liberal theology and, later, kerygma theology make Christianity a live option for many heirs of the Enlightenment) that the integrity of the faith has fallen victim to the translation. Concretely, the exclusions effected on the basis of the modern world-view and, in the case of kerygma theology, the austere limits of the new categories into which eschatology had been translated combine to deepen that suspicion. The past could be only fractionally appropriated, and the real, as distinct from the figurative, future simply evaporated. Guardini's notion that God subsequently changed the scheme of things which Jesus had proclaimed can hardly be anything other than a *deus ex machina*. Jeremias's observation on New Testament texts supposing divine transcendence *vis-à-vis* even divine plans for history is valuable, but does it meet the problem at hand? The issue is not *vere homo* (error in any case does not pertain any more than sin [Heb. 4.15] to the genuineness of humanity); the issue is *vere propheta*. How can he be an authentic prophet whose prophecy is mistaken? Obviously, the question is addressed to many theologians of this century, not only Jeremias but Bultmann, Cullmann, and countless others. The question to Schnackenburg, Vögtle, and many others is how, in the light of the striking unity of Jesus' conception of the future, one can suppose that the problem of his eschatology might be resolved if only those few texts which set an express time limit for the end could be satisfactorily explained. Even if those texts did not exist we would have essentially the same problem with Jesus' eschatology, for what is problematic is the implicit time limit which pervades the whole. Thus, Vögtle's proposal (namely, that the crucial parts of the most troublesome texts are secondary) does not go far enough to be of any real help. Many other sayings – e.g. the Jonah riddle, the temple riddle, the answer to the high priest – are implicitly *termingebunden*, i.e., they express time limits which in fact were not met. Indeed, this is the case for the entirety of the relevant material. Rigaux's recourse to literary genres is pertinent to the question but not entirely equal to it. The problem bears finally on genres of knowledge, not merely of expression.

It is a twofold problem, involving the intention of Jesus' prophecy and the relation between this prophecy and the actual course of events.

How are we to grasp the intention of Jesus' prophecy? Our preceding chapter offered a positive assessment of the reconstruction of Jesus' prophecy presented by Dodd and revised by Jeremias. This reconstruction was characterized by a holistic approach to the data, by a follow-up dealing with particular aspects of the whole scheme and particular sayings, and by adoption of the Weiffenbach hypothesis of an original conception globally identifying resurrection/exaltation/parousia. But have we grasped the intention of Jesus' prophecy simply by reconstructing his vision of the future? The answer, as two observations suggest, is no.

First, there is a special complexity about the intention of prophecy. It belongs essentially to the prophetic phenomenon that the prophet present himself as speaking for God. He does not speak his own word nor on his own behalf: ' . . . the word which you hear is not mine but the Father's, who sent me' (John 14.24). What the prophet wills to speak is precisely God's message. All else is functional to this and apart from it is just a contingent residue. Second, to judge once again from the whole biblical tradition, it belongs essentially to the phenomenon of prophecy that the message be expressed in symbols. Jesus' word on the future intended a symbol-charged two-act drama of crisis and resolution. But if symbol is intended, symbol also intends. It stands for something further. It points beyond itself to something related to but different from itself.

Taking a point of departure from these unobjectionable premises, I would propose this thesis: In prophecy what the symbol intends is identical with what God, for whom the prophet speaks, intends. This may enter the prophet's own horizon only partially and imperfectly. If the question 'Was Jesus mistaken about the future?' is accordingly recast, it may be put this way: 'Did Jesus have determinate knowledge of what God intended by the symbolic scheme of things which Jesus himself was commissioned to announce?' The answer, again, would seem to be no.

Prophetic knowledge thus appears as limited knowledge. It also appears as distinct in kind from empirical knowledge. It is a mistake to conceive of prophetic knowledge on the model of the common experience of knowing. We should not underestimate the importance or misconstrue the nature of prophecy's characteristic symbolic idiom, as if prophetic knowledge were a kind of empirical-knowledge-by-anticipation but with symbolic frills and trimmings. We should not imagine that any prophet ever had before his inner eye the kind of scenario that history, on cue and according to schedule, might literally follow.

Consequently, a correlation between prophetic word and actual event may appear before the eye of faith; but of itself the correlation is ambiguous. The ambiguity is denied equally by the fundamentalist's simplistic affirmations of fulfilment and the rationalist's simplistic discernment of mistakes. If God speaks in prophecy, he speaks in the history that follows on prophecy, and it is history, history grasped within the perspective of faith, that does what the prophet cannot do – namely, decipher prophetic symbol, translating image into event, schematic sequence into actual sequence, and symbolic time into real time.

In this light let us consider a prophecy of Jesus: 'I tell you, Many will come from east and west and recline [to banquet] with Abraham, Isaac, and Jacob in the reign of God ...' (Matt. 8.11 par.). The sense of this saying is illuminated by a long tradition. Watching crowds of Israelites pour into Jerusalem for a pilgrimage feast, Isaiah saw in them a figure of all the nations of the world, for like the Yahwist (Gen. 12.1–3) he understood Yahweh to be the Lord not only of Israel but of all nations. If, then, history had its meaning from the lordship of Yahweh, it would necessarily entail not only the realized destiny of Israel but the realization of the nations' destiny, as well. Zion would be raised to the peak of the world and all peoples would stream to it as to the world sanctuary (Isa. 2.2–4). This pilgrimage of the nations became a *topos* of eschatological prophecy in both biblical and post-biblical literature. It evidently defined the way in which Jesus conceived of the Gentiles' entry into salvation. What actually happened? The most historically charged event of late antiquity was the entry of Mediterranean Gentiles into the Christian movement. It was not, then, through a pilgrimage to Zion that Gentiles would come into the eschatological heritage of Israel; it was rather through an energetic missionary movement that this was already beginning to come about! To the eye of faith the visionary imagery of Jesus was being translated into time, place, and action by the world mission. The centripetal movement of the vision became the centrifugal movement of history from Jerusalem 'to the end of the earth' (Acts 1.8).

A more instructive example of the relation of prophetic utterance to actual history could hardly be asked for. The prophet envisioned the future in a manner unique to prophecy. To the cold eye of the unbeliever Jesus' vision of things may seem like an exotic hallucination; to the believer it stands in profound and creative continuity with an ongoing history of salvation yet to find its final culmination.

In his 1961 study of the role played by one biblical text (Hab. 2.3) in post-biblical Judaism's encounter with the problem of a seeming 'delay' in the fulfilment of biblical prophecy, August Strobel provided a solid index to the non-isolation of 'the delay of the parousia'.[42] Indeed, the problem which so many theologians supposed was peculiar to the prophecy of Jesus was in fact recurrent through the whole history of biblical prophecy. Israel did not repudiate prophetic predictions on the ground of disparity between the regularly recurrent motif of imminence and the regularly recurrent lack of immediate fulfilment but rather, while hoping and praying for early fulfilment, learned to expect it in the *kairos* of God's own choosing. Similarly, it did not occur to the first Christians to repudiate the predictions of Jesus on the ground that they were not immediately fulfilled. On the contrary, for all their puzzlement over 'non-fulfilment', they repeated, restated, reaffirmed the prophecy.

Where, then, does 'illusion' belong? It hardly describes the consciously limited (Mark 13.32 par.) symbolic knowing of the prophet. It hardly describes the commonsensical accommodation of the believing community to the actuality of eschatological realization. It may describe that phantom community – not the one that actually existed in history but an imaginary projection, perhaps a distorted image of the imaginer himself – which was not a believing community but one forever trying to decide whether to believe or not and half-inclined, in the light of the delay of the parousia, to disbelieve. But 'illusion' may best of all describe the confident supposition of Enlightenment men that unprejudiced reason provided the exactly right vantage point from which to view and weigh and pronounce on prophecy. As it now turns out, it would seem that the ancient church and, indeed, the church of the long pre-critical period from primitive Christianity to the deists managed, by muddling through in faith and hope, to construe the prophecy of Jesus more profoundly, more appropriately, and more accurately than the deists or even many of the critical theologians with their industrious, well-intentioned salvage operations.

The man of faith, however, need not entrench himself in pre-critical positions. Prophecy retains its claim on faith for as long as history goes on, for fulfilment within history never involves faith's yielding to vision. But there is point in the modern and contemporary effort to appropriate religious tradition in fully adult fashion. Under the lordship of the same God as spoke through the prophet, the actuality of events discloses to the believing community the divine intention charging the prophet's symbols. The prophet knows mainly the symbols; history – and the end of history – reveal what they symbolize. A disappointing conclusion, no doubt, to whoever insists in the name of human autonomy that faith cease to be merely faith, but to the man of faith an enriching conclusion; for, in striving toward some basic understanding of prophecy and prophet, he is thus led to locate himself once again in a history that is meaningful from beginning to end because, as prophecy has revealed that the end is consummation (*Vollendung*), it has revealed that history itself is redeemed, that despite rack and stake, holocaust and Gulag archipelago, its redemption at times 'will flame out like shining from shook foil' and is always gathering to a greatness: a divinely destined goal.

The view of eschatological fulfilment commended by this understanding of prophecy is exactly expressed by the term 'eschatology in process of realization' (*sich realisierende Eschatologie*). The term describes the view of the primitive church from its earliest moment, when resurrection was differentiated *ex eventu* from parousia. It also describes the view of the contemporary believer who, though unable to 'decipher' it in advance, affirms the still future day of the Son of man. Eschatology, then, designates the present situation of mankind as Augustine depicted it in the didactic narrative of *De catechizandis rudibus*. Recounted to first-stage catechumens (*rudes*), the narrative ran from creation to the resurrection of the dead at the end of time. 'Eschatology in process of realization' describes the last part of the story: from Jesus of Nazareth to the resurrection of the dead. Such is Christianity's absolute eschatology. It is ultimately rooted in the eschatology announced and already coming to realization in Jesus' proclamation of the reign of God.

An ambiguous figure?

Can Jesus be known historically to be a completely authentic man? Or must the figure of Jesus remain permanently ambiguous?

We have said that 'he willed his public actions to be open and transparent, to epitomize his views and values and to signify his purposes'.[43] At the same time 'the unriddling called for by his words and actions were beyond flesh and blood (Matt. 16.17)' and failed insight was 'the normal situation' of 'average man' encountering him.[44] Apropos of the conundrum of 'open and transparent actions' versus 'enigma' and the need of 'unriddling', we should recall the sense of the so-called messianic secret in Jesus' career and the fact that his world of meaning drew upon apocalyptic.

Modern scholarship has given apocalyptic a bad press. It is said to connote stilted symbolism, a presumptuous calendar of the future, impotence in the face of oppression, flight from the world, and the collapse of hope for salvation in history. With Jesus, however, stilted symbolism has given way to the master image of the temple (Mark 14.58 par.; John 2.19; cf. Matt. 16.18). He not only rejected all invitations to date the future, he repudiated apocalyptic calendars as irrelevant in principle (Luke 17.20f.; cf. Mark 13.32 par.). He was not at all absorbed by political oppression (Mark 12.16f. parr.). Rather than fear or despise the world, he affirmed the whole of it as issuing from God's hand and in every least detail under his loving surveillance (Matt. 10.29 par.). He had a spontaneous, if theocentric, affectivity for nature (Matt. 6.28–30 par.) which was a constant resource of imagery in his teaching. He affirmed the root structures of social existence (Mark 10.2–9 par.; 10.14 parr.; Matt. 7.11 par.; Mark 12.17 parr.) and took for granted the essential goodness of the ordinary customs (Luke 11.5–8; Matt. 25.1–12, etc.) and daily occupations

(Mark 4 parr.; Matt. 20.1–16; 21.28–32, etc.) of his surrounding world.

The one objection to apocalyptic which holds also for Jesus is that the fulness of salvation is conceived to be post-historical. As in apocalyptic, Jesus' eschatology was 'absolute'. But so far from diminishing the life of man-in-time, this fulfilled the condition on which an entirely meaningful life of man-in-time depends. Moreover, it brought to its conclusion the biblical and especially Isaian drive to affirm divine salvation in its full perfection and majesty (*kābôd*); cf. the 'lustre and glory' of the Messiah (Isa. 4.2), the 'glory' of Zion restored (Isa. 60.13), the indefectibility of God's designs (Isa. 46.9–11), his boundless lordship over the world (Isa. 2.10f.; 5.26, etc.). Divine salvation would be nothing short of total victory over evil. Such was the *a priori* which evoked and linked the repulse of Hades, the ordeal and its resolution, the reversal of the lot of the depressed, the ransom for many, the destruction and raising of the temple, the banquet of the saved in God's reign. These themes incarnated the message that good would prevail, that the vicious circle of disorder and decline would be broken. In conclusion and in sum, the tie with 'apocalyptic' offers no evidence of human or religious ambiguity in Jesus.

But there is an ambiguity about secrecy, a still greater ambiguity about self-proclaimed Messiahs, and a baffling array of opinions in historical-Jesus research about 'the messianic secret'. Here I wish only to prevent a misunderstanding of how these matters are viewed in the present study. As applied to the Jesus of history the term 'messianic secret' is misleading, for he did not seek to keep his messianic identity unknown to Israel.[45] But the reality which the so-called secret points to is extremely significant: It was Jesus' steady refusal to set before Israel an explicit messianic claim. He would neither offer a sign (Mark 8.11f.; Matt. 12.38f. par.; 16.4; John 6.30–36) nor lay claim to a title (until the high priest evoked the title and pressed him to acknowledge or repudiate it, Mark 14.61f. parr.). The step into messianic faith would be taken only under the combined impact of his densely symbolic career and of a divine illumination disclosing its sense (Matt. 16.17; cf. Matt. 11.4 par., 25f. par.). But the whole career was a deliberate, sustained question to Israel: 'Who do you say that I am?' In this view the ambiguities referred to above are dissipated in principle. On the one hand, though 'secret' is not a misnomer, it may be misleading; on the other, Jesus did not 'proclaim' his messiahship nor did he allow his disciples to do so.

Disabused of the artificially misleading impressions occasioned by 'apocalyptic' and 'messianic secret', we are better positioned to grasp the transparence and coherence of Jesus' career: his proclamation, his teaching, his choice and sending of the twelve, his exorcisms and cures, his table following with the outcast, his demonstration at the temple, his distributing of loaf and cup at the Last Supper. It was (and is) difficult to bring into uniform focus the range of meaning carried by all these words and actions; but in itself every word, every act, was mountain water. The problem lay on the side of the observer, as Jesus was aware. Hence the cool appeal to insight in the parables, hence the riddles with their challenge to construe and twig, the sign of the twelve, the invitation to catch on to the sense of the exorcisms, of Jesus' conspicuous non-fasting (Mark 2.18f. parr.; Matt. 11.16–19 par.) and dining with the unwashed. Though his actions and the purposes that informed them were of themselves entirely out of the ordinary, they were none the less diaphanous. But if so, why were they not grasped? By some, to be sure, and in diverse measure, they *were* grasped. Where they were misconstrued they posed a mystery to the will, crossing the grain of institutions, traditions, suppositions, convictions, pretensions. It is perfectly accurate to speak of an 'at least partly deliberate "misunderstanding" '.[46]

It had many roots. Jesus stood outside every attested teaching tradition in Israel. By welcoming those whom these traditions agreed to ostracize he contradicted and in principle undermined them all. This was no mere irritant. It meant that a charismatic public figure challenged them on their *raison d'être*: on God, on the will of God, on what pleased and did not please God, hence on conversion, on Torah and *halaka*, on ritual purity, on sin, on the judgment of Israel, on the Gentiles, in short, on the whole of religion. Jesus was undeducible from, uncontainable in, the religious ecology of his time.[47] His life was pellucid but unpardonable and accordingly lent itself to many modes of misconstruction.

Does this radical contradiction of the social establishment suggest the ambiguity of the revolutionary and destroyer? Disconcerting and threatening, his particular challenge was indeed rooted in a consciousness of mission. It was a unique consciousness, for he did not understand himself to have happened onto the scene of Israel at a turning point fixed independently of him. Moment (*kairos*) and message (*kerygma*) converged by divine design. A revolutionary consciousness? In favour of a yes there is especially the radicalness of his policy toward the outcast and his wholesale repudiation of halakic casuistry. On the other hand, 'revolutionary' supposes that the faith heritage of Israel was complete and fixed, whereas its specific difference was orientation to the future as promise, prophecy, and type. This conception of Israel's unfinished past was not peculiar to Jesus but substantial to the biblical tradition. Jesus transcended both the category of reformer (in which, basically, all religious movements of the period stood) and that of revolutionary – by conceiving himself to function as fulfiller. The heritage of the past – law, promise, prophecy, and type – was the good that the fulfiller affirmed and brought to completion, not the evil that the revolutionary would uproot and tear down.

But, given the radical eschatology of Jesus, did he not invite Israel to self-destruction? to abandon the everyday world with its reassuringly dull and solid compromises and to step off history's edge into the abyss? I doubt that this was the issue historically, i.e., that Judaism, in solidifying over a period of about fifty years its historic refusal of Jesus, supposed it was choosing the sober reality of history over the illusion of history's end. The decisive issue bore rather on alternative modes – each had its logic and grandeur – of appropriating the past: as a definitive revelation and economy of religion, or as promise, prophecy, and type finding fulfilment in the person and work of the (crucified!) Messiah. Still, there is a keen edge of truth under the surface of the question. The proclamation of Jesus was a summons to self-eclipse. His eschatology was an invitation to a new selfhood – which, unrealized, unknown, presents itself in retrospect, no doubt, as an insubstantial alternative to the hard, and hard-won, reality of the Judaism which has actually survived in history. . . .

The free spirit of the unselfish man tends to overwhelm the question about his 'authenticity', to make it superfluous and absurd. The fact of historical distance, however, tends to make it indispensable. As we would pose it, it is a circular question, one framed within a circle drawn from Jesus himself as point of departure. For, as Bultmann put it over fifty years ago, the point is not to give Jesus 'good marks'. (This would imply that the historian, having a ready-made set of criteria by which to measure the subject, has closed himself off in advance from 'all things counter, original, spare, strange' which give history its power to confound and enlighten.) The alternative is to concentrate on the subject's self-epitomizing deed and to grasp it in the after-life (*Wirkungsgeschichte*) which eminent deeds generate.

We may formulate numerous historical probabilities about Jesus and his death. It is probable, owing to the nexus between 'prophet' and 'violent fate' in contemporary religious tradition (cf. Luke 13.33), that the prospect of a violent death belonged unthematically to his self-understanding from the start and that under the impact of the Baptist's execution, the deadly hostility of his critics, and the consequent threats to his life, this early became thematically conscious. It is probable that he conceived his death in sacrificial terms. It is probable that despite a powerful instinct of recoil he went willingly to his death. But what, in the end, made Jesus operate in this way, what energized his incorporating death into his mission, his facing it and going to meet it?

The range of abstractly possible answers is enormous. And unless a satisfactory answer is forthcoming the inner intention of Jesus' life does remain ambiguous. We have referred to critical studies which substantially diminish the indeterminacy of the matter.[48] But, as Kant observed of the central intention of a thinker, namely, that it comes to light slowly and reaches thematic status in the tradition he generates,[49] so it is above all in the tradition generated by Jesus that we discover what made him operate in the way he did, what made him epitomize his life in the single act of going to his death: He 'loved me and handed himself over for me' (Gal. 2.20; cf. Eph. 5.2); 'having loved his own who were in the world, he loved them to the end' (John 13.1); he 'freed us from our sins by his blood' because 'he loves us' (Rev. 1.5). If authenticity lies in the coherence between word (Mark 12.28–34 parr.[50]) and deed (Gal. 2.20; Eph. 5.2; John 13.1; Rev. 1.5), our question has found an answer.

NOTES

Chapter I Introduction

1. D. F. Strauss, *Das Leben Jesu kritisch bearbeitet*, Tübingen: Osiander 1835; Vol. 2, 1836; ET of fourth edition: *The Life of Jesus Critically Examined*, tr. George Eliot; London: Chapman 1846; reprinted with 'Foreword' by Otto Pfleiderer; London: Swan Sonnenschein 1898; and again, with an editor's introduction by P. C. Hodgson; Philadelphia: Fortress, and London: SCM Press 1972. (The page references are the same for all three editions.)

2. W. Wrede, *Das Messiasgeheimnis in den Evangelien. Zugleich ein Beitrag zum Verständnis des Markusevangeliums*, Göttingen: Vandenhoeck & Ruprecht 1901; ET, *The Messianic Secret*, tr. J. C. G. Greig; Cambridge/London: Clarke 1971.

3. V. A. Harvey, *The Historian and the Believer*, New York: Macmillan 1966; London: SCM Press 1967.

4. *The Historian* . . . 104.

5. See especially B. J. F. Lonergan, *Insight. A Study of Human Understanding*, London/New York: Longmans 1958; *Collection. Papers by Bernard Lonergan*, ed. F. E. Crowe; London: Darton, Longman & Todd, and New York: Herder and Herder 1967; *Method in Theology*, London: Darton, Longman & Todd, and New York: Herder and Herder 1972; *A Second Collection. Papers by Bernard J. F. Lonergan*, ed. W. F. J. Ryan and B. J. Tyrrell; London: Darton, Longman & Todd, and New York: Herder and Herder 1974. Henceforward these works will be cited as: *Insight, Collection, Method, Second Collection*.

6. An operation as 'intentional' makes an object present to the subject; the same operation as 'conscious' makes the subject present to himself. 'To intend' something is accordingly to focus on it, e.g., by posing a question about it, and the word will sometimes appear in this sense in the present study.

7. *Life of Jesus*, 88.

8. R. Bultmann, 'Is Exegesis Without Presuppositions Possible?', *Existence and Faith. Shorter Writings of Rudolf Bultmann*, ed. and tr. S. M. Ogden; Cleveland/New York: World (Meridian) 1960; London: Hodder & Stoughton 1961, 289-96, p. 291.

9. See C. E. Braaten, 'Martin Kähler on the Historic Biblical Christ', *The Historical Jesus and the Kerygmatic Christ. Essays on the New Quest of the Historical Jesus*, ed. and tr. C. E. Braaten and R. A. Harrisville; New York/Nashville: Abingdon

1964, 79-105, p. 86. See also Kähler's presentation of the historian's dilemma, in *The So-Called Historical Jesus and the Historic, Biblical Christ*, ed. and tr. C. E. Braaten; Philadelphia: Fortress 1964, esp. p. 53 on the inapplicability of the principle of analogy to the task of understanding and presenting a sinless man.

10. For Troeltsch's principle of analogy, see 'Über historische und dogmatische Methode' (see below, ch. VIII n. 1), esp. 730–33; also 'Historiography' in Hastings' *Encyclopedia of Religion and Ethics*, New York: Scribner's, and Edinburgh: T. & T. Clark 1914, VI, 716–23, especially pp. 716, 720.

11. See Lonergan, *Insight*, 130–39.

12. This supposes the distinction between understanding and judgment and, correlatively, between the intelligible and the true. To Bultmann, who took 'world-view' to define the boundaries of the intelligible and who did not differentiate between intelligibility and truth, it was inconceivable that one should have to grapple with the truth of a world-view.

13. R. G. Collingwood, *The Idea of History*, Oxford: Oxford University Press 1946, 240.

14. Lonergan, *Insight*, 589: 'The first condition of such an extrapolation is an adequate self-knowledge. Is he [the interpreter] sufficiently aware of the diverse elements of human experience, of the different manners in which insights accumulate, of the nature of reflection and judgment, of the various patterns of human experience and the consequent varieties of philosophic views and pre-philosophic orientations? The second condition of the extrapolation is that it is to the meaning of a man at a different stage of human development. Because it is to the meaning of a man, there must be recognized some general orientation in living, some measure of critical reflection, some insight, some flow of experience. Because it is to a meaning at a different stage of human development, there can be invoked a merging of the clear and distinct into the obscure and undifferentiated. Because all stages of development are linked genetically and dialectically, it should be possible to retrace the steps that lead from the past to the present.'

15. Alexander Pope, Preface to the 1717 edition of his poems.

16. Excluded from consideration are numerous popular books of the 1960s such as those of Runes, Berna, Schonfield, Carmichael, and of the 1970s such as those of Cox, Holl, Augstein, *et al.*

17. There are exceptions but, as Morton Smith has observed, not so conspicuous 'as to leave any considerable trace in the current reviews of the literature' (*JBL* 90, 1971, 194). Time will tell whether the theologically unconcerned effort which Smith praises will prove to have substance. In the meantime Smith's own contribution, neither theological nor open-ended toward theology, has appeared: *The Secret Gospel*, New York: Harper and Row 1973. It has not, however, changed my view as to what constitutes serious historical-Jesus research. (We leave aside consideration of such non-theological efforts as the psychological studies which continue to appear regularly.)

18. 'It is impossible to use electric light and the wireless and to avail ourselves of modern medical and surgical discoveries, and at the same time to believe in the New Testament world of spirits and miracles.' R. Bultmann, 'New Testament and Mythology', *Kerygma and Myth*, Vol. I, ed. H. W. Bartsch; tr. R. H. Fuller; London: SPCK ²1964, 1–16, p. 5; German original: 'Neues Testament und Mythologie', *Kerygma and Mythos*, ed. H. W. Bartsch; Hamburg-Volksdorf: Reich ²1951, 15–48, p. 18.

19. H. Schürmann, 'Zur aktuellen Situation der Leben-Jesu-Forschung', *GuL* 46, 1973, 300–310; see especially pp. 307f. On 'open' in the sense of 'public, social' hermeneutic, see also H. Schürmann, *Das Geheimnis Jesu. Versuche zur Jesusfrage*, Leipzig: St Benno 1972, 79, 107f.
20. See B. Lonergan, *Second Collection*, 2–6; 47–50; 91–93; 193–208.
21. N. Perrin, *The Promise of Bultmann*, Philadelphia/New York: Lippencott 1969, 39. There follows the assurance: 'This is an important point which all practicing historians recognize.'
22. R. Bultmann, *Primitive Christianity in its Contemporary Setting*, tr. R. H. Fuller; New York: Meridian, and London: Thames & Hudson 1956, 93.
23. G. Dalman, *Words* (see below, ch. VII n. 1), 137.
24. E. Fuchs, *Studies of the Historical Jesus*, tr. A. Scobie; SBT 42, 1964, 63.

Part One: Hermeneutical Issues. Introduction

1. The phrase has two senses. First, it refers to the Jesus of ancient Palestine in so far as he is intended in and by historical questions and known in and by satisfactory answers to those questions. Second, it refers simply to the answers without regard to whether or not they are satisfactory. In this second sense 'the historical Jesus' is anyone's *Jesusbild* (portrait of Jesus). I use the phrase exclusively in the first sense.
2. See Lonergan, *Method*, 235–66.

Chapter II A Review of the Quest

1. A. Lundsteen, *Hermann Samuel Reimarus und die Anfänge der Leben-Jesu-Forschung*, Copenhagen: Det kongelige Bibliotek 1939, 26, summarizing the account of conscience with which Reimarus prefaced his *Apologie oder Schutzschrift für die Vernünftigen Verehrer Gottes* (the manuscript, never published, from which Lessing culled the seven 'fragments' that appeared between 1774 and 1778).
2. D. F. Strauss, *Streitschriften* III, 57, quoted from G. Backhaus, *Kerygma und Mythos bei David Friedrich Strauss und Rudolf Bultmann*, Hamburg-Bergstedt: Reich 1956, 16f. Compare the words Strauss wrote on 12 July 1835 to the director of studies at the Tübingen Stift: 'Since the end of the last century ... philosophy, which has continually entered into a closer alliance with theology, has increasingly aimed – according to the one view – to spiritualize the positive, factual element in Christianity, according to the other view, to sublimate it; this is especially the case in the most recent publication in this field – Hegel's philosophy of religion – where this process is carried out in all the main doctrines of the Christian Faith. On the other hand, New Testament criticism has recently made unexpectedly bold progress and questioned the authenticity of several of the main New Testament writings, earlier John's Gospel and now Matthew's, and has generally pronounced the first three Gospels to be post-apostolic works of tradition. Now if these two designated directions in the present-day theology – the philosophical and the

critical – worked in this manner, hand in hand with each other, then whoever has become intimate with both, as I have, must find himself challenged to bring these two directions into association, and, supported by the philosophical conviction of the intrinsically true content of the New Testament history, to allow its historical form to be ruthlessly investigated by criticism.' Horton Harris, *David Friedrich Strauss and his Theology*, Cambridge: Cambridge University Press 1973, 59f.

3. J. Weiss, *Die Predigt Jesu vom Reiche Gottes*, Göttingen: Vandenhoeck & Ruprecht ²1900 (reissued 1964), v. Translations from Weiss are from this edition (which extends to 214 pages) and are my own. The 1892 version (of only 67 pages) is, however, available in English: *Jesus' Proclamation of the Kingdom of God*, tr. and ed. R. H. Hiers and D. L. Holland; Philadelphia: Fortress, and London: SCM Press 1971.

4. H. S. Reimarus, *Von dem Zwecke Jesu und seiner Jünger*, Braunschweig: Lessing 1778. The book was posthumously published without Reimarus's name, in pamphlet form, by Lessing, whose sub-title (*Noch ein Fragment des Wolfenbüttelschen Ungenannten*) led the reader to suppose that the 'fragment' was discovered in the library of Wolfenbüttel of which Lessing was in charge. Translations from Reimarus are my own. The essay, however, is available in two English translations: H. S. Reimarus, *The Goal of Jesus and His Disciples*. Introduction and Translation by G. W. Buchanan, Leiden: Brill, 1970, and *Reimarus: Fragments*, ed. C. H. Talbert, tr. R. S. Fraser; Philadelphia: Fortress 1970, London: SCM Press 1971.

5. Arthur Koestler, *The Sleepwalkers: A History of Man's Changing Vision of the Universe*, London: Hutchinson 1959; Pelican Books 1968, 219.

6. B. F. Meyer, *The Church in Three Tenses*, Garden City: Doubleday 1971, 113f.

7. Koestler, op.cit., 537.

8. Peter Gay, *Deism: An Anthology*, Princeton: Princeton University Press 1968, 10.

9. Reimarus, *Von dem Zwecke*, 8; ET, *Fragments*, 64.

10. The prize example: For Reimarus the triumphal entry into Jerusalem was Jesus' last throw of the dice. He may have told his disciples of apprehensions of capture and execution. 'These, however, were full of hope; they promised to stand by him and not to abandon him even if they, too, had to die with him. And so it was ventured: He mounts the ass, he allows himself to be accorded royal honour, he makes a public entry. And as this appears to succeed somewhat, he goes straight to the temple where the great council was wont to meet. He puts his meekness aside and, like one already assuming worldly power, starts a violent commotion. He overturns the tables of the money-changers, seizes a whip and drives the buyers and sellers and pigeon-dealers into the temple's outer court. He then returns to the temple, works some miracles before the people and teaches them. The next day he speaks sharply against the Pharisees and scribes seated on the chair of Moses, that is, against the high council and the Sanhedrin. He thereupon tells the people publicly that he is the Christ: He alone is their master. . . . One is your master, Christ! I am he! And you shall not see my face again until you have cried out for me as the Christ, or Messiah, who has come to you in the name of the Lord!' (*Von dem Zwecke*, 146–8; ET, *Fragments*, 146f.) This was the '*actus criticus* and *decretorius*' on which everything hinged. If it had worked, the Sanhedrin of the seventy would have become that of Jesus and his seventy disciples. But the coup failed. As he saw himself deserted by the crowd, he avoided appearances at the temple. He began to meet with his disciples outside the city and only at night.

He grew apprehensive of betrayal. 'As he saw that it could cost him his life, he began to shudder and to fear. But Judas betrayed where he was and discovered his person. So he was captured in the night before the fourteenth of Nisan, swiftly brought to trial and, before the slaughter of the paschal lambs began in the temple, was crucified. He closed his life with the words *Eli Eli lama asaphtani*: My God! My God! Why hast thou forsaken me? A confession – no other interpretation is possible without obvious violence to the sense – that God had not helped him compass his aim and object as he had hoped. It had not, then, been his aim to will his suffering and death, but rather to found a worldly kingdom and free the Jews from their bondage. And therein God had abandoned him, therein had his hope come to nothing' (*Von dem Zwecke*, 153; ET, *Fragments*, 150). As is not unusual with the psychologizing style of interpretation, the shape, colour, and force of the drama are supplied by the interpreter.

11. To Reimarus the parables of Jesus say 'nothing especially new'. The 'hundredfold' promised the disciples is a flatly literal promise of riches. The commands of secrecy are a shrewd invitation to spread the word. The so-called 'incomprehension' of the disciples is designed to cover over 'the old system' – well over a century before Wrede!

12. In Schweitzer's judgment the quest of the historical Jesus has owed much to hate. For Reimarus and Strauss it is supposed to have been the spur to insight, for an antagonist is sharp-eyed. On much the same basis Schweitzer reserved a place of honour for 'that keen critic' Bruno Bauer (whose work, however, is now generally considered worthless). Joachim Jeremias (*The Problem of the Historical Jesus*, tr. N. Perrin; Philadelphia: Fortress 1964, p. 4) drily remarked apropos of Reimarus that 'Hate is no guide to historical truth.' We touch here on the psychology of interpretation but also on a hermeneutical issue which, so far as the writer knows, has yet to receive the treatment it deserves.

13. Reimarus, *Von dem Zwecke*, 210 (not in ET).

14. *Von dem Zwecke*, 178; ET, *Fragments*, 160.

15. For an informative and illuminating account of Strauss's early development see Gotthold Müller, *Identität und Immanenz. Zur Genese der Theologie von David Friedrich Strauss*, Zürich: EVZ-Verlag, 1968.

16. Strauss, *Life of Jesus*, 88.

17. Op.cit., 78f.

18. Markan priority was proposed by C. H. Weisse, C. G. Wilke, and Carl Lachmann independently at about the same time that Strauss's *Life of Jesus* appeared. Strauss himself supposed the Griesbach hypothesis, i.e., Matthew was first, Luke was dependent on Matthew, and Mark was a compilation of Matthew and Luke. But no particular resolution of the synoptic question controls the intent and force of Strauss's work.

19. Strauss, *Life of Jesus*, 70.

20. Bruno Bauer, as Wrede was to point out (*Messiasgeheimnis* [ch. I n. 2 above] 280; ET, 281f.), was an exception.

21. Strauss, op. cit., 39–44.

22. Op.cit., 80.

23. Op.cit., 779.

24. Op.cit., 81.

25. Op.cit., 80–83.

26. Op.cit., 83–5.

27. So the later editions, specifically the fourth, of Strauss's work. In the first edition he found fault with those who, acknowledging 'historical myth' in the gospels, proceeded in the mode of naturalist critique to isolate its 'historical kernel'. It does not seem, however, that even in the first edition Strauss excluded historical myth in principle. For a slightly different interpretation see R. Slenczka, *Geschichtlichkeit und Personsein Jesu Christi*, Göttingen: Vandenhoeck & Ruprecht 1967, 54f. Backhaus (see above, n. 2), 23, is surely right to criticize Strauss's critical practice for its almost total neglect of 'historical myth'. But given Strauss's perspectives and purposes, this neglect is hardly 'astonishing' nor is it 'inconsistent'.

28. Strauss, *Life of Jesus*, 83–5.

29. Op.cit., 87.

30. Op.cit., 49.

31. Eichhorn cited by Strauss, op. cit., 49.

32. Op.cit., 69–71.

33. Op.cit., 70.

34. Op.cit., 69–75.

35. Op.cit., 87–91. These criteria were positive and negative. Negative criteria for ruling historicity out were expressed in three laws: first, the iron law of nature, or the impossibility of disturbing 'the chain of secondary causes'; second, the law of plausible historical sequence (the attraction that Jesus exercised in manhood could not have been already operative in his infancy); third, the laws of human psychology (it is psychologically incredible that the Sanhedrin could believe the declaration of the night watch, and then, instead of accusing the guards of allowing the body to be stolen, should bribe them to say that exactly this happened). Positive criteria for detecting the unhistorical related to form and substance. The historicity of a narrative was doubtful if its form was poetic; for example, if the *dramatis personae* spoke in hymns. Again, historicity was doubtful if the substance of a narrative strikingly accorded with certain ideas existing within the circle in which the narrative originated, and especially if the ideas themselves seemed to be the product of preconceived opinions rather than of practical experience. Moreover, what was credible in itself was nevertheless unhistorical when it was so intimately connected with the incredible that the latter was its indispensable foundation. Where both form and substance were incredible, the whole was unhistorical; but where only the form exhibited such characteristics, 'it is at least possible to suppose a kernel of historical fact' (p. 91).

36. Op.cit., 91f.

37. This was a misreading of the sense of *'eōs* ('until') in Matt. 1.25. (To grasp the limits of *'eōs* cf. LXX II Kings 6.23.)

38. *Life of Jesus*, 193.

39. Until Strauss the Johannine theme of eyewitness testimony weighed heavy in the scales of German criticism. Strauss's reasons for suspecting John as a source of history were basically two: The discourses were too artificial and the narratives too strictly supernatural. The discourses in particular violated the laws of verisimilitude (the Johannine Jesus has but one theme, the dignity of his person) and of memory (the Johannine type of discourse is the most difficult to retain and reproduce with accuracy). Cf. op.cit., 381f.

40. Holtzmann, *Die synoptischen Evangelien: Ihr Ursprung und geschichtlicher Charakter*, Leipzig: Engelmann 1863, 1–4.

41. Holtzmann's argument: All Old Testament citations in A were drawn exclusively from the Septuagint. Mark kept to this. He shortened two texts, however (Mark 4.12 and 10.19), whereas Matthew stayed closer to A, so that in these instances his citations have a more septuagintal ring. In one passage Mark kept the septuagintal form (Mark 12.19) whereas Matthew departed from A in favour of a reading more akin to the original Hebrew (Matt. 22.24). When on his own as a redactor, Matthew consistently preferred the Hebrew text, with one perfectly explicable exception, the citation of Isa. 7.13 in Matt. 1.23, where only the Greek text provided the required messianic sense. In the first part of the citation in 13.35, also, Matthew reflects the Septuagint. Mark's citations from the Greek admit one easily detectable exception (Mark 1.2), added by the redactor to A. Finally, Luke consistently cited the Greek text, with one exception (Luke 7.27) where he followed L, in which Old Testament citations varied between the Hebrew and Greek texts (op.cit., 259–64). As it turns out, the study of Old Testament citations, even if Holtzmann's presentation of the data were absolutely and totally accurate, is at best a reduction of data to some order, not a proof of the validity of any particular solution to the synoptic problem. The presentation of data, however, is not accurate. To restrict comment to Matthew: Holtzmann systematically reduces those texts in which the redactor cites the Septuagint independently of A to 'special' (and otherwise unverifiable) source material (e.g. 5.33–35, 38, 43); he is forced to conjecture that Matt. 9.13 and 12.7, both from the Septuagint, belonged to A and were omitted by Mark (and Luke); mistakenly supposing that Mark 4.12 abbreviates a Septuagint text, he likewise gratuitously attributes Matt. 13.14–15 to A; he fails to note that numerous redactional, non-explicit citations in Matthew derive from the Septuagint (e.g. 12.40; 21.16; 27.43); and, finally, he is compelled to acknowledge undeniable septuagintal influence in numerous redactional citations over and above 13.35.

42. Holtzmann, *Synopt. Evangelien*, 431.

43. F. C. Baur, cited by Holtzmann, op. cit., 432.

44. Holtzmann, op. cit., 385.

45. Strauss, *Life of Jesus*, 402–9.

46. Holtzmann, op. cit., 95.

47. Op.cit., 220f.

48. Baur, cited by Holtzmann, op. cit., 470.

49. See Pfleiderer's 'Foreword' to Strauss's *Life of Jesus* (see above, ch. I n. 1), xix.

50. Op.cit., xxiv.

51. Weiss, *Die Predigt Jesu*; I cite the second edition of 1900 (see n. 3 above).

52. See Weiss, op.cit., 58–60.

53. Op.cit., 40f.

54. Op.cit., 154f.

55. A. Schweitzer, *Geschichte der Leben-Jesu-Forschung*, Tübingen: Mohr 1906, 235; ET, *The Quest of the Historical Jesus. A Critical Study of its Progress from Reimarus to Wrede*, tr. W. Montgomery; London: Black [3]1954, 237. In the reprint in paperback with an Introduction by J. M. Robinson; New York: Macmillan 1968, 238.

56. Weiss, *Predigt*, 154.

57. Holtzmann, *Synopt. Evangelien*, 476.

58. Op.cit., 477, citing C. H. Weisse.

59. Op.cit., 478.

60. Weiss, op.cit., 156.
61. Op.cit., 158.
62. Op.cit., 159.
63. Ibid.
64. Ibid.
65. Op.cit., 165f.
66. Op.cit., 166.
67. Op.cit., 101.
68. Ibid.
69. Op.cit., 103.
70. Schweitzer, *Leben-Jesu-Forschung*, 355–61; ET, 1954, 357–62.
71. H. Schürmann, 'Zur Traditions- und Redaktionsgeschichte von Mt. 10, 23' *BZ* 3, 1959, 82–8, reprinted in H. Schürmann, *Traditionsgeschichtliche Untersuchungen zu den synoptischen Evangelien*, Düsseldorf: Patmos 1968, 150–56.
72. Favourably citing de Wette, Strauss wrote (*Life of Jesus*, 55): 'According to de Wette the whole natural mode of explanation is set aside by the principle that the only means of acquaintance with a history is the narrative which we possess concerning it, and that beyond this narrative the historian cannot go. In the present case this reports to us only a supernatural course of events, which we must either receive or reject: if we reject it, we determine to know nothing at all about it, and are not justified in allowing ourselves to invent a natural course of events, of which the narrative is totally silent.' Fundamentally uninterested in history, Strauss was wrong in denying that the historian can go beyond the narrative, but the positive and quite justified thrust of his complaint was against arbitrarily doing so. Wrede was to echo the complaint: 'The scientific study of the life of Jesus suffers from psychological guesswork. The number of arbitrary psychological interpretations of gospel facts, words and contexts is legion. And it is not just a question of harmless superfluities. These interpretations also form the basis of weighty constructions. And how often the critic supposes that the critical task is over and done when he has found in some datum something that 'rings a bell' psychologically.... It seems to me absolutely necessary that we get away from subjective judgments in this matter. The psychological treatment of facts is only permissible when we know they are facts; and even then we should still call a guess a guess' (*Messiasgeheimnis*, 3; ET, *Messianic Secret*, 6).
73. Wrede, *Messiasgeheimnis* (see above, ch. I n. 2).
74. Op.cit., 280; ET, 281.
75. G. Volkmar, *Die Evangelien oder Marcus und die Synopsis der kanonischen und ausserkanonischen Evangelien nach dem ältesten Text mit historisch-exegetischem Commentar*, Leipzig: Fues 1870.
76. Op.cit., 457.
77. Wrede, op.cit., 32; ET, 34.
78. Op.cit., 71–73; ET, 72–4.
79. Op.cit. 45f.; ET, 45f.
80. Op.cit., 48; ET, 50.
81. Ibid.; ET, 49f.
82. See H. D. Knigge, 'The Meaning of Mark: the Exegesis of the Second Gospel', *Int* 22, 1968, 53–70.
83. Wrede, op.cit., 131; ET, 131.
84. Op.cit., 133; ET, 133.

85. Op.cit., 131; ET, 131.

86. For a persuasive critique of Billerbeck's limitations, see now E. P. Sanders, *Paul and Palestinian Judaism. A Comparison of Patterns of Religion*, London: SCM Press, and Philadelphia: Fortress 1977, 42–60.

87. M. Kähler, *Der sogenannte historische Jesus und der geschichtliche, biblische Christus*, Leipzig: Deichert 1892, ²1896; ET, *The So-Called Historical Jesus and the Historic, Biblical Christ*, tr. and ed. C. E. Braaten; Philadelphia: Fortress 1964.

88. R. Bultmann, *Jesus*, Tübingen: Mohr 1926; Munich/Hamburg: Siebenstern Taschenbuch Verlag ³1967; ET, *Jesus and the Word*, tr. L. P. Smith and E. H. Lantero; New York: Scribner's 1934, ²1958; London: Nicholson & Watson 1935. The German text is cited from the Siebenstern paperback. Translations given here are my own.

89. Bultmann, op.cit., 21f.; ET, 25f.

90. Op.cit., 7–9; ET, 5f.

91. Op.cit., 9; ET, 6.

92. In his work, says Bultmann, attention is 'uniquely fixed on what [Jesus] *willed* and so on what can become present as the demand of [Jesus'] historic existence'; op.cit., 10; ET, 8.

93. Op.cit., 12; ET, 11f.

94. Op.cit., 14; ET, 13f.

95. Ibid.

96. Op.cit., 7; ET, 4.

97. Op.cit., 11; ET, 10.

98. Op.cit., 9; ET, 6.

99. R. Bultmann, *Jesus Christ and Mythology*, New York: Scribner's 1958; London: SCM Press 1960, 17.

100. J. M. Robinson, *A New Quest of the Historical Jesus*, SBT 25, 1959. A revised version is available in German: *Kerygma and historischer Jesus*, Zurich/Stuttgart: Zwingli Verlag ²1967.

101. G. Bornkamm, *Jesus von Nazareth*, Stuttgart: Kohlhammer 1956; ET, *Jesus of Nazareth*, tr. I. and F. McLuskey with J. M. Robinson; New York: Harper & Row, and London: Hodder & Stoughton 1960.

102. Op.cit., 18; ET, 21.

103. Bornkamm, op.cit., 138; ET, 150. Cf. R. Bultmann, *Die Geschichte der synoptischen Tradition*, FRLANT 29, 1921, 171; ET, *The History of the Synoptic Tradition*, tr. J. Marsh; Oxford: Blackwell, and New York: Harper & Row 1963, ²1968, 159.

104. Bornkamm, op.cit., 142; ET, 154.

105. Ibid.

106. Op.cit., 163; ET, 178.

107. See the review of Bornkamm's book by J. M. Robinson, *JBL* 76, 1957, 310–13.

108. J. M. Robinson, *New Quest*, 13.

109. J. Jeremias, *Neutestamentliche Theologie I. Teil: Die Verkündigung Jesu*, Gütersloh: Mohn 1971, ²1973; ET, *New Testament Theology* I: *The Proclamation of Jesus*, tr. J. S. Bowden; London: SCM Press, and New York: Scribner's 1971.

110. J. Jeremias, *Jesus als Weltvollender*, Gütersloh: Bertelsmann 1930.

111. J. Jeremias, *Die Abendmahlsworte Jesu*, Göttingen: Vandenhoeck & Ruprecht 1935, ²1952 [ET, *The Eucharistic Words of Jesus*, tr. A. Ehrhardt; Oxford: Blackwell 1955]; ³1960, ET, *The Eucharistic Words of Jesus*, tr. N. Perrin; London: SCM Press,

and New York: Scribner's 1966; quoted from the latter.
112. J. Jeremias, *Die Gleichnisse Jesu*, Zürich: Zwingli-Verlag 1947; Göttingen: Vandenhoeck & Ruprecht [2]1952; [8]1970; ET, *The Parables of Jesus*, tr. S. H. Hooke; London: SCM Press, and New York: Scribner's 1954, [2]1963, [3]1972.
113. J. Jeremias, *Jesu Verheissung für die Völker*, Stuttgart: Kohlhammer 1956; ET, *Jesus' Promise to the Nations*, tr. S. H. Hooke; SBT 24, 1958.
114. *Gleichnisse*, 5; ET, *Parables*, 9.
115. J. Jeremias, 'Der gegenwärtige Stand der Debatte um das Problem des historischen Jesus', *Wissenschaftliche Zeitschrift der Ernst Moritz Arndt-Universität Greifswald, Gesellschafts- und sprachwissenschaftliche Reihe* (Greifswald) 6, 1956/57, 165–70; ET, 'The Present Position in the Controversy Concerning the Problem of the Historical Jesus', *ExpT* 69, 1957/58, 333–9. Also: *The Problem of the Historical Jesus*, tr. N. Perrin; Philadelphia: Fortress 1964.
116. For a concise statement see the second edition of *Die Verkündigung Jesu*, 295.
117. The special character of Bultmannian docetism is epitomized, as L. Goppelt, *Theologie des Neuen Testaments. Erster Teil. Jesu Wirken in seiner theologischen Bedeutung*, ed. J. Roloff; Göttingen: Vandenhoeck & Ruprecht 1975, 35, has observed, in the protest of Heinrich Schlier: 'Der Logos wurde Fleisch und nicht Wort!' ('The Word was made flesh, not word!'), 'Eine kurze Rechenschaft', *Bekenntnis zur katholischen Kirche*, ed. K. Hardt; Würzburg: Echter-Verlag [2]1955, 169–92, p. 181; ET, *We Are Now Catholics*, ed K. Hardt; tr. N. C. Reeves; Westminster, Md.: Newman 1959, 187–215, p. 198. The docetist danger was cautiously acknowledged in the concluding paragraphs of E. Käsemann's essay on 'Das Problem des historischen Jesus', *ZThK* 51, 1954, 125–53, reprinted in *Exegetische Versuche und Besinnungen* I, Göttingen: Vandenhoeck & Ruprecht 1960, 187–214; ET, 'The Problem of the Historical Jesus', *Essays on New Testament Themes*, tr. W. J. Montague; SBT 41, 1964, 15–47. For a brief sketch of the 'new quest' as a de-docetizing effort which, in time, went beyond consideration of Jesus' words to reflection on his actions (especially in the work of E. Fuchs) and has sought to overcome or at least relieve the painfully one-sided individualism of kerygma theology, see J. Roloff, 'Auf der Suche nach einem neuen Jesusbild. Tendenzen und Aspekte der gegenwärtigen Diskussion', *TLZ* 98, 1973, 561–72, esp. col. 565–70. Existentialistic interpretation's characteristic bias in favour of individualism is a theme in H.-W. Bartsch, 'Theologie und Geschichte in der Ueberlieferung vom Leben Jesu', *EvTh* 32, 1972, 128–43. See also the short but incisive comment on the meagre results of the 'new quest' by H. Schürmann, 'Zur aktuellen Situation der Leben-Jesu-Forschung', *GuL* 46, 1973, 300–10, esp. 304f.
118. Among the striking passages in Pannenberg is the following, from his *Grundzüge der Christologie*, Gütersloh: Mohn 1964, 107; ET, *Jesus – God and Man*, tr. L. L. Wilkins and D. A. Priebe; Philadelphia: Westminster, and London: SCM Press 1968, 109: 'As long as historiography does not begin dogmatically with a narrow concept of reality according to which "dead men do not rise", it is not clear why historiography should not in principle be able to speak about Jesus' resurrection as the explanation that is best established of such events as the disciples' experiences of the appearances and the discovery of the empty tomb.' For a synthesis of Pannenberg's view, see T. Peters, 'The Use of Analogy in Historical Method', *CBQ* 35, 1973, 475–82. Also instructive: Pannenberg's account of how Gerhard von Rad met this hermeneutical problem in practice. see 'Glaube und Wirklichkeit im Denken Gerhard von Rads', *Gerhard von Rad, Seine Bedeutung für die*

Theologie. Drei Reden von H. W. Wolff, R. Rendtorff, W. Pannenberg, Munich: Kaiser 1973, 37–58.

119. P. Stuhlmacher, 'Kritische Marginalien zum gegenwärtigen Stand der Frage nach Jesus', *Fides et Communicatio. Festschrift für Martin Doerne zum 70. Geburtstag*, ed. D. Rössler, G. Voigt and F. Wintzer; Göttingen: Vandenhoeck & Ruprecht 1970, 341–61; idem, 'Neues Testament und Hermeneutik – Versuch einer Bestandsaufnahme', *ZThK* 68, 1971, 122–61; repr., idem, *Schriftauslegung auf dem Wege zur biblischen Theologie*, Göttingen: Vandenhoeck & Ruprecht 1975, 9–49.

120. J. Roloff, 'Auf der Suche ...' (see above, n. 117), 565.

121. M. Hengel, 'Historische Methoden und theologische Auslegung des Neuen Testaments', *KuD* 19, 1973, 85–90.

122. H. Schürmann, 'Zur aktuellen Situation ...', esp. p. 307.

123. L. Goppelt, *Jesu Wirken*, 25–41.

124. See the two essays of P. Stuhlmacher cited in n. 117; H. Schürmann, 'Zur aktuellen Situation ...', 306–10; *Einführung in die Methoden der biblischen Exegese*, ed. J. Schreiner; Würzburg: Echter-Verlag 1971; *Versuche mehrdimensionaler Schriftauslegung*, ed. H. Harsch and G. Voss; Stuttgart: Katholisches Bibelwerk; Munich: Kaiser 1972.

125. See especially P. Stuhlmacher, 'Neues Testament und Hermeneutik'. H. Schürmann's protest ('Zur aktuellen Situation ...', 307) against the Greek-based philosophical cosmologies which have held sway up to the present century is met by Lonergan's presentation, grounded in the simultaneous affirmation of 'classical' and statistical laws, of world process as 'emergent probability'. Schürmann's protest (ibid.) against Western absorption in the drama of the individual psyche (*Introvertiertheit*), a tradition which in theology runs from Augustine to existentialism, is met by the characteristic themes of the later Lonergan, viz., self-transcendence (see *Method*, 104–12; 237–44; *Second Collection*, 117–33; 165–87) and, as the capstone of the structure of intentionality, the transcendental notion of value (see *Method*, 34–41; 110–12; and especially *Second Collection*, 81–6, on the relevance to 'the alienated subject' of theistic affirmation of the goodness of the world).

126. On the paradigmatic case of 'miracle', see the analysis of R. G. Collingwood, *The Idea of History*, 134–41. Pertinent to the real if often unarticulated foundation of the currently widespread attack on Troeltschean analogy and its cardinal principle (*die prinzipielle Gleichartigkeit alles historischen Geschehens*) is the work of such practitioners of transcendental method as E. Coreth, 'Hermeneutik und Metaphysik', *ZkTh* 90, 1968, 422–50, and B. Lonergan on *Verstehen* (see *Method*, 208f.).

127. B. Willey, *The Seventeenth Century Background: Studies in the Thought of the Age in Relation to Poetry and Religion*, London: Chatto and Windus 1934, 4.

128. Reimarus, *Von dem Zwecke*, (see above, n. 4), 268; ET, *Fragments*, 263.

129. Cf. W. G. Kümmel, *Das Neue Testament: Geschichte der Erforschung seiner Probleme*, Munich: Alber 1958, 41; ET, *The New Testament: The History of the Investigation of its Problems*, tr. S. M. Gilmour and H. C. Kee; Nashville: Abingdon, and London: SCM Press 1972, 41.

130. B. Lonergan, 'Theology in its New Context', 34–46, p. 34, in *Theology of Renewal*. I. *Renewal of Religious Thought*, ed. L. K. Shook; New York: Herder and Herder 1968; reprinted in *Second Collection*, 55–67, p. 55.

131. L. de Grandmaison, *Jésus-Christ. Sa personne, son message, ses preuves*, 2 vols, Paris: Beauchesne 1928–31; ET, *Jesus Christ, His Person, His Message, His Credentials*,

3 vols, tr. B. Whalen, A. Lane, D. Carter; London: Sheed and Ward 1930–34.

132. J. Lebreton, *La vie et l'enseignement de Jésus-Christ notre Seigneur*, 2 vols, Paris: Beauchesne 1931; ET, *The Life and Teaching of Jesus Christ Our Lord*, tr. F. Day; London: Burns, Oates and Washbourne [3]1957.

133. A. Schweitzer, *Aus meinem Leben und Denken*, Bern 1932, 5f.; ET, *Out of My Life and Thought. An Autobiography*, tr. C. T. Campion; New York: Holt 1932, [2]1949, 6f.

134. A. Loisy, *L'Évangile et l'Église*, Paris 1902, 111; cf. idem, *Les Évangiles synoptiques* II, Ceffonds 1908, 9.

135. H. Butterfield, *The Origins of Modern Science 1300–1800*, London: Bell 1957; New York: Free Press 1965, 7.

136. Op.cit., 85.

137. Op.cit., 137.

138. P. Hazard, *La crise de la conscience européene (1680–1715)*, Paris: Boivin 1935; ET, *The European Mind 1680–1715*, tr. J. L. May; London: Hollis and Carter 1953; Peter Gay, *The Enlightenment. An Interpretation*. I *The Rise of Modern Paganism*, New York: Knopf 1966.

139. See B. Lonergan, '. . . New Context' (see n. 130) p. 37 (in *Second Collection*, p. 58).

140. R. Bultmann, *Jesus Christ and Mythology* (see n. 99 above), 17.

141. Cf. H. Groos, *Der deutsche Idealismus und das Christentum: Versuch einer vergleichenden Phänomenologie*, Munich: Reinhardt 1927, 177–209.

142. Cf. above, ch. I n. 5.

143. In the common (and, doubtless, justified) view, the quest failed in two ways: as an effort to base faith on research and as an effort to write the biography of Jesus. The reasons usually given for this double failure: the first openly contradicted and subverted Christian tradition, whereas the second proved impossible for want of data appropriate to the task.

144. H.-G. Gadamer, *Wahrheit und Methode. Grundzüge einer philosophischen Hermeneutik*, Tübingen: Mohr 1960, [3]1972, 285 and *passim* thereafter; ET of second edition, *Truth and Method*, tr. G. Barden and J. Cumming; New York: Seabury, and London: Sheed & Ward 1975, 267 and *passim* thereafter.

145. I propose this as a middle position between (and an improvement on) the two common views, namely, that which conceives the quest in isolation from the larger history of Christian theology (cf., e.g., D. Georgi, 'Leben-Jesu-Theologie', *RGG*[3] 4, 249f.) and that which conceives the theology of the life of Jesus without reference to the quest (cf. H. Rahner, 'The Theology of the Life of Jesus', 107–28, *A Theology of Proclamation*, tr. R. Dimmler *et al.*; New York: Herder and Herder 1968).

Chapter III The Gospel Literature: Data on Jesus?

1. The New Testament is for all practical purposes our only means of acquaintance with the Jesus of history, for the relevant testimonies of Jewish and Roman antiquity are neither extensive nor independent of Christian witness, and extra-

canonical testimonies are no more than supplementary.

The Jewish testimonies in question are found in the Talmud and in the work of Flavius Josephus. The Talmudic writers assumed that Jesus worked miracles and they explained this as sorcery; see e.g. Sanh. 43a, which referred originally to Jesus, the pupil of Jehosua ben Perahya, who lived long before Jesus of Nazareth (see G. Dalman, *Jesus-Jeshua. Studies in the Gospels*, tr. P. Levertoff; London: SPCK 1929; New York: KTAV 1971, 89); but in time it was referred to Jesus of Nazareth (M. Hengel, *Nachfolge und Charisma. Eine exegetisch-religionsgeschichtliche Studie zu Mt 8,21f. und Jesu Ruf in die Nachfolge*, Berlin: Topelmann 1968, 45 n. 14); Sanh. 107b; Sabb. 104b; cf. Justin Martyr, *Dial. Tryph.* 69. The charge of sorcery is the central affirmation. It is not clear that we have here anything other than the standard polemic device of accepting a supposition (Jesus worked miracles) simply to ground a retort (his miracles were sorcery). This polemic structuring is sometimes transparent. Thus, Christians professed that Jesus was born of a virgin. A retort is given in the name Jesus ben-Pantira or ben-Panthera (e.g. Aboda Zara 40d) which signified (cf. Origen, *Contra Celsum* I 32f., 69) that Jesus indeed had no Jewish father but was the son of a Roman soldier by a Jewish woman (cf. Sanh. 67a). Testimony to Jesus' miracles is perhaps no better than this. The same holds for Talmudic references to his execution; the central affirmation is that he was rightly executed.

In the *Antiquitates* (c. AD 93) of Josephus there is a Christian interpolation relating to Jesus (17.63f.) and a possibly authentic passage which mentions him as 'Jesus, surnamed the Christ' (20.200) but which deals with events long after Jesus' death.

The one significant testimony in Roman literature relating to the Jesus of history occurs in the *Annals* (XV 44) of Tacitus: 'In order to destroy the rumour [that he, Nero, was responsible for setting fire to Rome], he invented a charge of guilt and inflicted the most appalling tortures on those who were hated for their abominations and who were called Christians by the multitude. This name comes to them from Christ, whom the procurator Pontius Pilate under the rule of Tiberius had handed over to the torture. Repressed for the moment, this detestable superstition broke out anew, no longer simply in Judaea where the evil arose but at Rome into which all that is horrible and shameful in the whole world flows and finds many to support it.' Maurice Goguel argued that Tacitus, in connecting Christianity with the Christ who was crucified under Pilate, drew on a pagan rather than Jewish or Christian source. A Christian source is ruled out, according to Goguel, by the notion that in the period between the execution of Jesus and a little before the year 64 the Christian movement was dormant or extinct. (But does Tacitus say this?) A Jewish source is ruled out because it 'would never have represented Judaism as united with Christianity [in the outbreak of nationalism which provoked the Jewish revolt and to which the phrase "in Judaea" probably alludes], nor would it ever have called Jesus "the Christ" ' (M. Goguel, *La vie de Jésus*, Paris: Payot 1932, ²1950, 73; ET, *The Life of Jesus*, tr. O. Wyon; London: Allen & Unwin, and New York: Macmillan 1933 [reissued as *Jesus and the Origins of Christianity*, vol. I, New York: Harper & Row 1960], 95). But even if Goguel's argument were accepted, what ultimately independent pagan witness is imaginable? An official report of Pilate (in itself uncertain) kept in the imperial archives (probably inaccessible in any case to Tacitus)?

The so-called *agrapha* do, indeed, provide data on Jesus. But in the end: 'If we would learn about the life and message of Jesus, we shall find what we want *only* in the four canonical gospels. The lost dominical sayings may supplement our knowledge here and there in important and valuable ways, but they cannot do more than that', J. Jeremias, *Unknown Sayings of Jesus*, tr. R. H. Fuller; London: SPCK, and New York: Macmillan 1957, [2]1964, 121.

2. See C. F. Evans, 'The Kerygma', *JTS* 7, 1956, 25–41, especially p. 28.

3. It may nevertheless be described in terms of two generic tendencies. Those who accent the redactional character of the discourses consider the non-exploitation of the salvific value of the death as an omission reflecting post-Pauline theology. See e.g. P. Vielhauer, 'Zum "Paulinismus" der Apostelgeschichte', *EvTh* 10, 1950, 1–15, reprinted P. Vielhauer, *Aufsätze zum Neuen Testament*, Munich: Kaiser 1965, 9–27; ET, 'On the Paulinism of Acts', *Studies in Luke-Acts*, ed. L. E. Keck and J. L. Martyn; Nashville/New York: Abingdon, and London: SPCK 1966, 33–50. Those who stress the primitive character of the kerygma in Acts see this same phenomenon of non-exploitation as due to the polemic and apologetic preoccupations of the discourses. See e.g. D. M. Stanley, 'The Conception of Salvation in Primitive Christian Preaching', *CBQ* 18, 1956, 231–54, reprinted in D. M. Stanley, *The Apostolic Church in the New Testament*, Westminster, Md: Newman 1967, 38–66.

4. The terms 'received' and 'handed on' (*paralambanein* and *paradidonai*) are technical and correlate with the rabbinic technical terms *kibbēl min* and *māsar lᵉ*. See J. Jeremias, *Abendmahlworte* (see above, ch. II n. 111), 95; ET, *Eucharistic Words*, 101.

5. See Jeremias, *Abendmahlsworte*, 95–97; ET, *Eucharistic Words*, 102f. Idem, 'Artikelloses Christos. Zur Ursprache von I Kor., XV 3b–5', *ZNW* 57, 1966, 211–15; B. Klappert, 'Zur Frage des semitischen oder griechischen Urtextes von I Kor. XV. vv. 3–5', *NTS* 13, 1967, 168–73; J. Jeremias, 'Nochmals: Artikelloses Christos in I Kor., XV 3', *ZNW* 60, 1969, 214–19.

6. This emerges from the testimony of Paul that he 'received' the formula (see above, n. 4) – possibly at his baptism by Ananias of Damascus.

7. The Levant: Aramaic composition; the tie with Jerusalem (I Cor. 15.5); its being 'received' by Paul (I Cor.15.3). Mediterranean basin: its being handed on by Paul (I Cor. 15.3) and other missionaries (I Cor. 15.11) to their newly founded churches.

8. That the summary is an entity in itself, not merely a list of topics to be developed, is evident from parallels and its own lapidary form. That it functioned both as a faith-proclamation and a credal confession is indicated by I Cor. 15.2, 11.

9. See B. Gerhardsson, *Memory and Manuscript. Oral Tradition and Written Transmission in Rabbinic Judaism and Early Christianity*, Uppsala 1961, 299–302. J. Schmitt, 'Urkerygma und Evangelienbericht. Bestand und Wandel der neutestamentlichen Auferstehungs-tradition', *BuK* 22, 1967, 14–18.

10. Compare I Thess. 4.14, 'Jesus died and rose (*anestē*)': non-Pauline; Rom. 14.9, 'Christ died and rose (*ezēsen*)': non-Pauline. (Paul himself uses the verb *egeirein*.) The pre-Pauline character of Rom. 4.25; 8.34 is established by their formulaic structure, their christological/soteriological use of Isa. 53, and their dependence on the Aramaic or Hebrew texts of the Isaian passage.

11. Even in the bare formula 'Jesus (or Christ) died and rose' (I Thess. 4.14; Rom. 14.9) the resurrection is the point of and the key to the formulaic 'he died'.

This remains true in the more extensive formula of Rom. 4.25 (hence, from the standpoint of Paul's context at the end of ch. 4, the citation of the formula is perfectly apt). There is no doubt about Rom. 8.34; the climactic aspect is confirmed by *mellon de* ('but more') and by the following motifs of exaltation and intercession. In I Cor. 15.3–5 this fundamental semantic structure is maintained and made still more evident; see below, n. 15.

12. The first limb of the formula in Rom. 4.25, *paredothē dia ta paraptōmata 'emōn* corresponds exactly to Targ. Isa. 53.5 *'itmᵉsar ba'ᵃwāyātanā'*. See J. Jeremias, *The Servant of God*, tr. H. Knight *et al.*; SBT 20, ²1965, 89 n. 397. The second limb, modelled on the first, reflects Isa. 53.11 (Targum and Hebrew text but not LXX). In Rom. 8.34 *entygchanei 'yper 'emōn* reflects Isa. 53.12 (Targum and Hebrew text but not LXX. In the Targum see also Isa. 53.11.) In I Cor. 15.3 *'yper tōn 'amartiōn 'emōn* echoes Targ Isa. 53.5 (*ba'ᵃwāyātanā'*) or the Hebrew text (*mippᵉša'ēnû ... mē'ᵃbōnōtēnû*). It is not verbally paralleled by LXX Isa. 53.4 *peri 'emōn* (no word corresponding to *'amartiōn*), nor does it depend on LXX Isa. 53.5. The *'yper* of the formula renders the sense of Hebrew *min* (or Aramaic *b*) as does the LXX, but *against* the LXX choice of *dia*.

13. See Jeremias, *Abendmahlsworte*, 96f.; ET, *Eucharistic Words*, 102f.

14. The burial 'authenticates the really occurring death and the vision authenticates the really occurring resurrection'. A. von Harnack, 'Die Verklärungs-geschichte Jesu, der Bericht des Paulus (I Kor. 15,3ff.) und die beiden Christus-visionen des Petrus', *SBBerlin*, 1922, 64.

15. As in all such formulas, the accent here is on the resurrection. The phrase 'he was buried' does indeed witness immediately to the reality of the death; but the point of doing this is deliberately to 'set up' – to anticipate and accent – the motif 'he really rose'. 'Jesus was buried *because* he was to be restored to life', A. Schlatter, *Paulus, der Bote Jesu: eine Deutung seiner Briefe an die Korinther*, Stuttgart: Calwer 1934, ³1962 (italics mine). It likewise follows that *egegertai* comprehends the specifically corporeal dimension of the resurrection.

16. See above, n. 12. On the general topic, see E. Lohse, *Märtyrer und Gottes-knecht: Untersuchungen zur urchristlichen Verkündigung vom Sühntod Jesu Christi*, FRLANT 64, ²1963.

17. There was no need for scriptural attestation to the fact that Christ died, but rather that he 'died for our sins', as H. Conzelmann observes, 'Zur Analyse der Bekenntnisformel I. Kor. 15,3–5', *EvTh* 25, 1965, 1–11, p. 8.

18. 'According to the scriptures' may refer, for example, to numerous Psalms interpreted in a messianic sense.

19. Choice of the phrase doubtless reflects a historical datum, i.e., that the paschal experience of the disciples began on the third day after Jesus' death and burial (counted as the first day). But the inclusion of the phrase in the formula is enough to suggest that its meaning, though inclusive of the intention of factuality, still goes beyond this. For the view that the second 'in accordance with the scrip-tures' has specific reference to 'on the third day' and so alludes to LXX Hos. 6.2, see J. Dupont, 'Ressuscité "le troisième jour" ', *Bib* 40, 1959, 742–61; H. Conzel-mann, 'Bekenntnisformel', 7f.; cf. H. K. McArthur, 'On the Third Day', *NTS* 18, 1971, 81–6 (Targum Hos. 6.2); J. Wijngaards, 'Death and Resurrection in Cove-nantal Context (Hos. vi 2)', *VT* 17, 1967, 226–39, finds a covenant motif both in Hos. 6.2 and I Cor. 15.4 See also K. Lehmann, *Auferweckt am dritten Tag nach der Schrift. Früheste Christologie, Bekenntnisbildung und Schriftauslegung im Licht von 1.*

Kor. 15.3–5, Freiburg/Basel/Wien: Herder 1968, esp. 269–90 on the rabbinic material relevant to the question.

20. 'To Cephas': this event with its important witness motif and ecclesial significance is referred to in Luke 24.34; but it is remarkable that a narrative account did not take shape or did not survive in the tradition (see, however, John 21.15–18, cf. Luke 5.1–11). 'Then to the twelve': this *collective* testimony, probably integral to the formula from the start, assumed ever greater significance for Christianity with the passage of time, as the synoptics and Acts show. Since *dōdeka* is formulaic it settles nothing about the historical status of the Judas tradition.

21. The theme of testimony is not the central affirmation, but it *is* the formula's specific characteristic: the scriptures, the burial, the witness of the twelve. (On the conjunction of personal witness and scriptural witness, see Gerhardsson, *Memory and Manuscript*, 330.) The climactic feature of this specifying theme is the witness of Cephas and the twelve, a once-for-all laying of the foundations of faith.

22. As O. Cullmann, *Christus und die Zeit. Die urchristliche Zeit- und Geschichtsauffassung*, Zürich: Evangelischer Verlag 1946, 75f.; ET, *Christ and Time. The Primitive Christian Conception of Time and History* tr. F. V. Filson; Philadelphia: Westminster 1950; London: SCM Press 1951; rev. ed. 1962, 87f., has pointed out, the ground and supposition, theologically and psychologically, of the expectation of Christ's imminent return was precisely the consciousness of salvation already achieved in principle. Risen and enthroned in glory, Christ himself seemed to be proof positive that time and the world had run their course.

23. On the basis of I Cor. 15.5 numerous critics hold the not unreasonable view that Jerusalem was the place of origin of the formula. But the question of literal authorship and place of origin is secondary to the fundamental point made by formula itself: the authenticating witness was that of Cephas and the twelve. In this fundamental sense they originate the formula by originating the tradition it embodies.

24. See J. A. Fitzmyer, 'The Use of Explicit Old Testament Quotations in Qumran Literature and in the New Testament', *NTS* 7, 1961, 297–333.

25. R. Bultmann, *Theologie des Neuen Testaments*, Tübingen: Mohr [2]1954, 82; ET, *Theology of The New Testament* I, tr. K. Grobel; New York: Scribner's 1951; London: SCM Press 1952, 82 (emphasis removed).

26. Paul says that he received (*paralambanein*) these words from the Lord (*apo tou kyriou*). 'If Paul did not construe *paralambanein* ... with *para* ['from'] as elsewhere (Gal. 1.12, I Thess. 2.13; 4.1.; II Thess. 3.6), but with *apo* ['from'], this was for a good reason. *Para* indicates those who hand on the tradition [see Gal. 1.12; I Thess. 2.13; II Tim. 1.13; 2.2; 3.14]; *apo*, on the contrary, the originator of the tradition [see Bauer/Arndt/Gingrich under *apo* V,4]. Paul therefore stressed in I Cor. 11.23 with the help of the preposition *apo* that the eucharistic words cited by him out of the tradition go back to Jesus himself.' J. Jeremias, *Abendmahlsworte*, 195, ET, *Eucharistic Words*, 202f. F. Hahn, *Christologische Hoheitstitel. Ihre Geschichte im frühen Christentum*, FRLANT 83, 1963, 93: ET, *The Titles of Jesus in Christology. Their History in Early Christianity*, tr. H. Knight and G. Ogg; New York: World 1969, makes the complementary observation that ' "the Lord" is by no means only the first of a long series of transmitters of tradition. The point is that, while the authority of the earthly Lord stands behind these eucharistic words, their transmission is likewise actualized and legitimized by the Exalted One. Still, the *apo*

keeps its importance inasmuch as it is primarily a question here of a word of the earthly Jesus.'

27. On the pre-Pauline character of the hymn, see E. Lohmeyer, 'Kyrios Jesus', *SBHeidel*, 1927/1928. Some non-Pauline expressions: *morphē theou, isa theō, doulos* (applied to Christ), *kenoun, 'ypsoun, charizesthai* (applied to Christ). For the hymn's literary structure and possible Pauline additions to the text, see J. Jeremias, 'Zu Philipper 2,7: *'eauton ekenōsen'*, *NovT* 6, 1963, 182–8; reprinted in *Abba: Studien zur neutestamentlichen Theologie und Zeitgeschichte*, Göttingen: Vandenhoeck & Ruprecht 1966, 308–16. The proposed Pauline additions are thematically characteristic: Christ's death becomes 'even death on a cross'; lordship over all humanity is made cosmic ('in heaven and on earth and under the earth'); finally, the confession of the exalted Christ is resolved back 'to the glory of God the Father'.

28. First, we note the thematic comparability of the hymn and the Deutero-Isaian passage. Second, the latter is confirmed as source of the hymn by four specific literary contacts: (1) Phil. 2.7, *'eauton ekenōsen*, 'emptied himself'; cf. Heb. Isa. 53.12, *he'ĕrâ lammāwet napšô*. See Jeremias, 'Zu Philipper 2,7 ...'; (2) Phil. 2.8, *etapeinōsen 'eauton*, 'he humbled himself'; cf. Heb. Isa. 53.7 *na'ăneh*. See A. Feuillet, 'L'hymne christologique de l'Épitre aux Philippiens (II, 6–11)', *RB* 72, 1965, 325–80, p. 358; (3) Phil 2.9, *dio*, 'therefore' or 'this is why'; cf. Heb. Isa. 53.12, *lākēn*; (4) Phil. 2.9, *'yperypsōsen* 'raised (him very) high'; relate the *'yper-* to *m'od* in Heb. Isa. 52.13, *w'nissâ' w'gābâ m'od* (LXX: *'ypsōthēsetai sphodra*).

29. The motifs are inescapable on the basis of the first distich of the second strophe and of the contrast of *morphē theou* with *morphē doulou* in the first strophe.

30. See D. Georgi, 'Der vorpaulinische Hymnus Phil. 2, 6–11', *Zeit und Geschichte. Dankesgabe an Rudolf Bultmann zum 80. Geburtstag*, ed. E. Dinkler; Tübingen: Mohr 1964, 263–93, esp. 264–6.

31. See E. Schweizer, *Erniedrigung und Erhöhung bei Jesus und seinen Nachfolger*, Zurich: Theologische Verlag ²1962, 99–101; ET, *Lordship and Discipleship*, SBT 28, 1960, 101f.; cf. Georgi, *art. cit.*, passim; Feuillet, *art. cit.*, 376–80.

32. Hebrew Scriptures: see n. 28 above; Greek Scriptures: Phil. 2.10f. alludes to LXX Isa. 45.23.

33. See E. Schweizer, *Erniedrigung und Erhöhung*, 99; ET, *Lordship and Discipleship* 64: 'The affirmation of the self-abasement of the Servant of God bearing divinely imposed sufferings has here gained altogether new force through its extension to the act of the Pre-existent One.' Cf. L. Krinetzki, 'Der Einfluss von Is 52, 12–53, 12 par. auf Phil 2, 6–11', *TQ* 139, 1959, 157–93, 291–336, esp. 177. More specifically, the text 'he poured out his life to death' (Isa. 53.12) has been transposed to the realm of pre-existence and made to describe the incarnation as an emptying of self, a relinquishing of exalted status.

34. That the glorified Son of man was a key theme for the Jewish-Hellenistic wing of the earliest Christian community is indicated by Acts 7.56. On Wisdom and the Son of man in Daniel, see Feuillet, 'L'hymne christologique ...', 376–80.

35. See J. Schmitt, 'Prédication apostolique', *SDB* 8, 1967/68, 246–73, cf. 259–67.

36. See E. Lohse, *Märtyrer*, (see n. 16 above) 220–24, esp. 222f., in opposition to the views of F. Hahn, *Christologische Hoheitstitel* (see n. 26 above). A fuller critique of Hahn's view is offered by W. Thüsing, *Erhöhungsvorstellung und Parusieerwartung in der ältesten nachösterlichen Christologie*, Stuttgart: Katholisches Bibelwerk n.d. (1969?), 26–40.

37. With regard to Israel at large the purposes were kerygmatic (in the strict sense), apologetic, and polemical; with regard to the inner life of the Christian community, they were liturgical, catechetical, and theological.

38. Allusion to Deutero-Isaiah is confirmed by the fact that this is the only text in the synoptics and Acts in which *doxazein* has the sense of 'clothe in splendour, transfigure, glorify'; see J. Jeremias, *Servant*, 86 n. 380.

39. Jeremias, *Servant*, 91: ' . . . Jesus is called *'o dikaios* three times in Acts (3.14; 7.52; 22.14 . . .). Since in all three passages there is an article but no noun, we are faced by a title, most probably the messianic title 'the righteous one' known from Eth-[iopian] En[och] . . . and alluding in the latter to Isa. 53.11.'

40. If the correlation is correct, we have in Acts 2.33 a conjunction of motifs from the messianism of Ps. 110 and the glorified Servant of Deutero-Isaiah, as in the pre-Pauline formula of Rom. 8.34.

41. See J. Jeremias, *Gleichnisse*, 71, 107; ET, *Parables*, 73f., 108.

42. See B. Gärtner, '*Tly*' als Messiasbezeichnung', *SvExA* 18/19, 1953/54, 98–108.

43. On Pss. 16 and 132: the antiquity of the debate on the preservation of Jesus from corruption is not automatically impugned by the fact that LXX Ps. 16.10 (and not the Hebrew text) refers to 'corruption', *diaphthora*. See the analysis of Schmitt, 'Prédication apostolique', 260f. Ps. 2 was interpreted eschatologically at Qumran (4QFlor 18f.). In view of the observations of M. Hengel, *Der Sohn Gottes. Die Entstehung der Christologie und die jüdisch-hellenistiche Religionsgeschichte*, Tübingen: Mohr 1975, 37–39, 71–73; ET, *The Son of God. The Origin of Christology and the History of Jewish-Hellenistic Religion*, tr. J. Bowden; London: SCM Press and Philadelphia: Fortress 1976, 22f., 44–47 on Ps. 2 in Palestinian Judaism, Christian use of Ps. 2.7 may well go back to the earliest community. The 'Son of God' theme, which initially belonged to royal messianism (cf. 4QFlor on II Sam. 7.13f.), facilitated a development of the Servant theme inasmuch as *pais* was increasingly understood as 'child, son'. The *sessio ad dexteram* of Ps.110 early became a favourite motif. On the 'prophet' of Deut. 18.15–18 (cf. 1QS 9.11) see the evidence for a characteristically Palestinian focus in M. Hengel, *Nachfolge* (n. 1 above), 23–7. On the antiquity of the theme of Jesus, the judge to come, see below, n.47. The primitive formulation of baptism *epi tō onomati* of Jesus indicates the antiquity of the name theme.

44. See E. Lohmeyer, *Galiläa und Jerusalem*, FRLANT 52, 1936; W. Grundmann, 'Das Problem des hellenistischen Christentums innerhalb der Jerusalemer Urgemeinde', *ZNW* 38, 1939, 45–73, esp. 45–50; L. E. Elliott-Binns, *Galilean Christianity*, SBT 16, 1956; G. Schille, *Anfänge der Kirche. Erwägungen zur apostolischen Frühgeschichte*, Munich: Kaiser 1966. See the informed and judicious survey of G. Stemberger, 'Galilee – Land of Salvation?', Appendix IV to W. D. Davies, *The Gospel and the Land. Early Christianity and Jewish Territorial Doctrine*, Berkeley/Los Angeles/London: University of California Press 1974, 409–38.

45. See F. Hahn, *Christologische Hoheitstitel* (n. 26 above) and R. H. Fuller, *The Foundations of New Testament Christology*, New York: Scribner's, and London: Lutterworth 1965. On the elimination of the allegedly early, christologically productive 'Gentile Christian community' from the early history of the kerygma, see M. Hengel, 'Christologie und neutestamentliche Chronologie. Zu einer Aporie in der Geschichte des Urchristentums', *Neues Testament und Geschichte* (O. Cullmann Festschrift), ed. H. Baltensweiler and B. Reicke; Zurich: Theologischer Verlag; Tübingen: Mohr 1972, 43–67.

46. See n. 36 above.

47. By way of support for the present consideration, though from the more limited standpoint of literary criticism: Acts 2.22 is marked by a density of *hapax legomena* rare in Luke: *andra apodedeigmenon apo tou theou eis 'ymas, dynamesi kai terasi kai semeiois*. See Schmitt, 'Prédication apostolique' (n. 35 above), 260. In Acts 10, moreover, as Schmitt points out (264), 'verses 42 and 38c highlight among the major data of the kerygma the miracles of Jesus in favour of "demoniacs", and the future "judgment of the living and the dead". . . . However, none of these traits, basically Judaic and primitive, are specially emphasized in Luke's gospel. At the same time, the fragment corresponds in tone and tenor to what must have been the teaching dispensed to Palestinian proselytes, ill-informed of the gospel history, yet already familiar with the nascent polemic between synagogue and church.'

48. Again, from the more limited standpoint of literary criticism, an objection to the historicity of this requisite to candidacy for the place of Judas has been raised on grounds that the clause *arxamemos apo* etc. (Acts 1.22) is redactional. The clause is indeed redactional, but the historicity of the requisite is not thereby impugned. For, *arxamenos apo* etc. merely specifies with accuracy the sense of *en panti chronō 'o eiselthen kai exelthen eph' 'emas 'o kyrios Iesous*. E. Haenchen, *Die Apostelgeschichte*, Göttingen: Vandenhoeck & Ruprecht 1961, 1267, ET, Oxford: Blackwell 1971, 161 n. 8, says: 'Without v. 22a (from *arxamenos* to *'emōn*) the reference would be exclusively to the forty days in which Jesus "went in and out" (an expression taken from the LXX) among his disciples. But since Luke claims the apostles likewise as witnesses for the activity of the earthly Jesus, he has inserted the words *arxamenos* to *'emōn*, failing to note that now Jesus' going in and out among the apostles is no longer an appropriate expression.' It is not Luke, however, who is at fault here. The expression *eiselthen kai exelthen* is no equivalent of 'come and go' and thus no apt description of sporadic paschal apparitions. The idiom corresponds to *wayyēṣē wayyābō'*, which signifies life and activity either in a general sense or in a variously connotative sense. *Synelthontōn* (Acts 1.21), moreover, may well have the sense of 'eorum qui nobiscum itinera fecerunt', as proposed by F. Zorell, *Lexicon Graecum Novi Testamenti*, Paris 1931, 1272, thus specifically referring, once again, to the public life of Jesus.

49. *Didaskein* and *didachē* are occasionally used for preaching to an undifferentiated public (Acts 4.2, 18; 5.21, 28, 32). V. H. Neufeld, *The Earliest Christian Confessions*, Grand Rapids: Eerdmans 1963, 20–29, aware of the distinctions between *didaskein, paradidonai, euaggelizein, kēryssein*, etc., also traces the continuities between them.

50. Mark's gospel in particular is widely taken to be 'a broad unfolding of the kerygma'. See, for example, H. Conzelmann, *Die Mitte der Zeit. Studien sur Theologie des Lukas*, Tübingen: Mohr [5]1964, 3; ET, *The Theology of St Luke*, tr. G. Buswell; New York: Harper & Row, and London: Faber & Faber 1961, 11.

51. On the continuity of word and act see H. Schürmann, 'Das Weiterleben der Sache Jesu im nachösterlichen Herrenmahl. Die Kontinuität der Zeichen in der Diskontinuität der Zeiten', *BZ* 16, 1972, 1–23; repr. H. Schürmann, *Jesu ureigene Tod. Exegetische Besinnungen und Ausblick*, Freiburg: Herder 1975, 66–96. E. Fuchs's accent on Jesus' comportment (*Verhalten*) as the context of his words has represented a solider balance and a stronger de-docetizing thrust than most work done in the context of the 'new quest'; by way of example, see his *Jesus, Wort und Tat*, Tübingen: Mohr 1971. A desideratum of 'the newest questioning' is to test the

anticipation of a dynamic congruence among Jesus' word, deed, and fate (*Botschaft, Verhalten, Geschick*); see H. Schürmann, 'Zur aktuellen Situation . . .', 304f.; J. Roloff, 'Auf der Suche . . .', 565–70 (see ch. II n. 117 above); cf. M. Lehmann, *Synoptische Quellenanalyse und die Frage nache dem historischen Jesus. Kriterien der Jesusforschung untersucht in Auseinandersetzung mit Emanuel Hirschs Frühgeschichte des Evangeliums*, BZNW 38, 1970, 7, 144–6, 198f.

52. See J. Schmitt, 'L'Église de Jérusalem ou la "Restauration" d'Israël d'après les cinq premiers chapitres des Actes', *RevSR* 27, 1953, 209–18.

53. J. M. Robinson, *The Problem of History in Mark*, SBT 21, 1957, 21 points out that *archē* (Mark 1.1) was 'a technical term employed by the early church for defining the *kērygma* (Luke 23.5; Acts 10.37) and apostleship (Luke 1.2; Acts 1.22; John 15.27)'. Once this starting point had been defined, the concern of the church, reflected in all the gospels (including Luke), entailed distinguishing the Baptist's ministry from Judaism and Jesus' ministry from that of the Baptist.

54. Some pre-Markan formal units in token of illustration: the parables collection in ch. 4; the five pronouncement stories in 2.1–3.5 and five more in 11.27–12.37; the sequence of three miracle stories in 1.23–34 and four more in 4.35–5.34.

55. The so-called 'bread cycle' (Mark 6.31–8.26) first took shape in oral tradition as a characteristic memory device and a kind of mishnaic tractate (see Gerhardsson, *Memory and Manuscript* [n. 9 above], 337); it became a true thematic unity in the Markan redaction. The parables in Mark 4 are comparable to the bread cycle inasmuch as they were originally assembled not only on the basis of parable form but also under the rubric of 'seed'. The pronouncement stories in Mark 2.1–3.5 are likewise a thematic unit, highlighting the authority of Jesus in controversy with the religious *élite*. The eschatological discourse in Mark 13 contains a pre-Markan topical unit of sayings on the eschatological crisis. Finally, the miracle stories of Mark 1.21–34 were probably in the chronological sequence of a single day prior to the Markan redaction. A pre-redactional chronological sequence in the passion accounts is obvious.

56. Certain place-names in the primitive units of oral tradition were later exploited under the influence of missionary theology to extend the sphere of his activity to Gentile lands. On the original sense of the place-names, see A. Alt, 'Die Stätten des Wirkens Jesu in Galiläa territorialgeschichtlich betrachtet', *ZDPV* 68, 1951, 51–72, reprinted in *Kleine Schriften zur Geschichte des Volkes Israel* II, Munich: Beck 1953, 436–55.

57. Diverse word-clasps (*Stichwortkomposition*) indicate diverse histories of oral transmission on the part of Q materials as found in Matthew and Luke respectively. Cf. J. Jeremias, 'Zur Hypothese einer schriftlichen Logienquelle Q', *ZNW* 29, 1930, 147–9, reprinted in *Abba*, 90–92. It is in any case clear that the material derived from an originally single tradition. That there was a primitively fixed order in this tradition and that at least the order has been better preserved in Luke than in Matthew is shown (for the 'Sermon on the Mount' materials) by J. Dupont, *Les Béatitudes. Le problème littéraire – les deux versions du Sermon sur la montagne et des Béatitudes*, Louvain: Nauwelaerts 1958. H.-T. Wrege, *Die Ueberlieferungsgeschichte der Bergpredigt*, Tübingen: Mohr 1968, attacks the hypothesis of a common written source at the basis of the two versions of the sermon; but his argument excludes with certainty only an identical text (which Dupont likewise excluded). The Proto-Luke hypothesis (cf. B. H. Streeter, *The Four Gospels. A Study of Origins Treating of the Manuscript Tradition, Sources, Authorship, and Dates*, London: Macmillan

1924, ch. 8, 'Proto-Luke', 201–22; V. Taylor, *Behind the Third Gospel. A Study of the Proto-Luke Hypothesis*, Oxford: Clarendon Press 1926) has not been established beyond doubt; but the linguistic observations of F. Rehkopf, *Die lukanische Sonderquelle. Ihr Umfang und Sprachgebrauch*, Tübingen: Mohr 1959, appear to be a step in this direction. See, however, H. Schürmann, 'Protolukanische Spracheigentümlichkeiten? Zu Fr. Rehkopf, *Die lukanische Sonderquelle*', *BZ* 5, 1961, 266–86; reprinted in *Untersuchungen* (see above, ch. II n. 71), 209–27.

58. The argument against the primacy of Mark has thus far mainly consisted in an impressive dismantling of the formal argumentation of the classic study of Streeter (see previous note), especially by W. R. Farmer, *The Synoptic Problem. A Critical Analysis*, New York and London: Macmillan 1964, ch. 4, 'An Analysis of Streeter's Contribution to the Two-Document Hypothesis', 118–77. See also D. L. Dungan, 'Mark – the Abridgement of Matthew and Luke', in *Jesus and Man's Hope*, ed. D. G. Buttrick; Pittsburgh: Perspective 1970, 51–97. But in some instances (cf. e.g. H.-J. Held, 'Matthew as Interpreter of the Miracle Stories', 165–299, esp. 179f., 216, in G. Bornkamm, O. Barth, H.-J. Held, *Tradition and Interpretation in Matthew*, London: SCM Press and Philadelphia: Westminster Press 1963) Matthew has inherited and modified traditions indistinguishable from those we find in Mark. Even a text like Mark 10.3–9, nearly always considered secondary to the parallel text in Matt. 19.3–9, may very well be the more primitive text. See D. R. Catchpole, 'The Synoptic Divorce Material as a Traditio-Historical Problem', *BJRL* 57, 1974, 92–127.

59. W. R. Farmer, 'An Historical Essay on the Humanity of Jesus Christ', 101–26, p. 105, in W. R. Farmer, C. F. D. Moule and R. R. Niebuhr (edd.), *Christian History and Interpretation. Studies Presented to John Knox*, Cambridge: Cambridge University Press 1967.

60. See G. Lindeskog, 'Empirie und Glaube im Neuen Testament', *Verborum Veritas*, (G. Stählin Festschrift), ed. O. Böcher and H. Haacker; Wuppertal: Brockhaus 1970, 279–301, esp. 288–300.

61. See below, pp. 175–8.

62. The identification of such intentions is the aim of J. Roloff, *Das Kerygma und der irdische Jesus. Historische Motive in den Jesus-Erzählungen der Evangelien*, Göttingen: Vandenhoeck & Ruprecht 1969. G. Bornkamm, 'Formen und Gattungen im Neuen Testament', *RGG*³ 2, 999–1005, col. 1001, has noted narrative variations according as the account intends the typical as such or the 'once only' character of the event.

63. Folklore elements are found in both sayings- and narrative-material. Besides being found in authentic sayings, they have also been introduced in the course of transmission (see J. Jeremias, *Gleichnisse*, 27–29, ET, *Parables*, 32f.). Practically indisputable instances (not of folklore in the strict and proper sense but of popular motifs akin to folklore and distinct from reminiscence) in the narrative material: Matt. 14.28–33; 17.27; 27.3–10, 52f.

64. The impact of the genre midrash on the gospel literature is considerable, but 'midrashic motif' in the present context has a more limited sense. It refers to elements present in the text owing not to historical reminiscence but to a didactic interest in making the story of Jesus a focal point for grasping and harmonizing the scriptures. Matt. 2.1–12 is a narrative midrash hinging on Num. 24.17; cf. Matt. 2.13–15 (Hos. 11.1); Matt. 2.16–18 (Jer. 31.15); Matt. 2.23 (Isa. 11.1; *nazir-neṣer*, unless the reference is to Judg. 13.5–7; 16.17).

65. The scope of such reformulation first emerges when the contours of the historical Jesus' vision of the future are recovered. See below, pp. 202–6. The most striking particular instances of the shift of perspective after Easter are the parousia parables (Mark 13.33–37 par. [cf. Matt. 24.42]; Matt. 24.43f. par., 45–51 par.; 25.1–13, 14–30 par.).

66. Missionary theology impinging on sayings material: Mark 14.9 par.; Matt. 13.38; 22.1–14 par.; Luke 11.33. In narrative material the redaction of Mark 4.24–8.21 par. appears to intend a foreshadowing of the Gentile mission, though in fact the itineraries of the historical Jesus remained limited to Israel. Cf. A. Alt, art. cit. (see n. 56 above). On the explicitly universalist missionary mandate, see A. Vögtle, 'Die ekklesiologische Auftragsworte des Auferstandenen', *Sacra Pagina* II, ed. J. Coppens, A. Descamps and E. Massaux; Paris: Gabalda 1959, 280–94, cf. p. 284; reprinted in A. Vögtle, *Das Evangelium und die Evangelien. Beiträge zur Evangelienforschung*, Düsseldorf: Patmos 1971, 243–52.

67. See the remarks of D. M. Stanley, 'Response to James M. Robinson's "Kerygma and History in the New Testament"', in *The Bible in Modern Scholarship*, ed. J. P. Hyatt; New York/Nashville: Abingdon 1965, 151–9, esp. 156–9.

68. N. Perrin, *Rediscovering the Teaching of Jesus*, London: SCM Press, and New York: Harper & Row 1967, 15.

69. H. von Soden, 'Das Interesse des apostolischen Zeitalters an der evangelischen Geschichte', *Theologische Abhandlungen. Carl von Weizsäcker . . . gewidmet*, ed. A. von Harnack; Freiburg: Mohr 1892, 153.

70. R. Bultmann, *Synoptische Tradition*, 135; ET, *Synoptic Tradition*, 127f.

71. See e.g. E. Käsemann, 'Sätze heiligen Rechtes im Neuen Testament', *NTS* 1, 1954, 248–60, reprinted in *Exegetische Versuche und Besinnungen* II, Göttingen: Vandenhoeck & Ruprecht 1964, 69–82; ET, 'Sentences of Holy Law in the New Testament', *New Testament Questions of Today*, tr. W. J. Montague; London: SCM Press, and Philadelphia: Fortress 1969, 66–81.

72. F. Neugebauer, 'Geistsprüche und Jesuslogien. Erwägungen zu der von der formgeschichtlichen Betrachtungsweise R. Bultmanns angenommenen grundsätzlichen Möglichkeit einer Identität von prophetischen Geistsprüchen mit Logien des irdischen Jesus', *ZNW* 53, 1962, 218–28.

73. D. Hill, 'On the Evidence for the Creative Rôle of Christian Prophets', *NTS* 20, 1974, 262–74.

74. That one ought not to expect to find gospel narrative in the New Testament letters has often been observed. See the treatment of C. F. D. Moule, 'Jesus in New Testament Kerygma', *Verborum Veritas* (see n. 60 above), 5–26, esp. 18–23.

75. See I Cor. 3.10f. (=Matt. 7.24 par.); I Cor. 4.1–5 (=Matt. 24. 45–50 par.); I Cor. 9.7 (=Mark 12.1–12 par.); I Cor. 9.14 (=Matt. 10.10 par.). On these texts see D. M. Stanley, 'Pauline Allusions to the Sayings of Jesus', *CBQ* 23, 1961, 26–39, reprinted in *The Apostolic Church* (see n. 3 above), 352–70.

76. One point deserves particular emphasis. The attitude towards enemies and persecutors in Rom. 12.14; I Cor. 4.12f.; I Thess. 5.15 should be related to Matt. 5.10–12 par., 38–40 par., for apart from Jesus Paul has no predecessor, source, or tradition to draw on for this theme. J. A. Fitzmyer, 'The Contribution of Qumran Aramaic to the Study of the New Testament', *NTS* 20, 1974, 382–407, p. 399, has proposed as possible background an uncertain reading in 1QapGen 20. 28f. dealing with an exorcism – not a really serious candidate for the role of precedent. D. L. Dungan, *The Sayings of Jesus in the Churches of Paul. The Use of the*

Synoptic Tradition in the Regulation of Early Church Life, Philadelphia: Fortress, and Oxford: Blackwell 1971, provides a cogent treatment of two instances of Pauline dependence on the Jesus tradition for principles of discipline.

77. See Stanley, 'Pauline Allusions . . .', 34–37 (=*Apostolic Church*, 364–9).

78. Ibid.

79. 'Abba' in Rom. 8.15; Gal. 4.6 derives uniquely from Jesus. Cf. Stanley, art.cit., 30–31 (358–60); J. Jeremias, 'Das tägliche Gebet im Leben Jesu und in der ältesten Kirche', *Abba* (see n. 27 above) 67–80, esp. 78–80; ET, 'Daily Prayer in the Life of Jesus and the Primitive Church', in *The Prayers of Jesus*, SBT 2.6, 1967, 66–81, cf. esp. 78–81.

80. On II Cor. 5.16: numerous exegetes have rightly urged that the phrase *kata sarka* belongs with the verb, not with *Christon*. Paul never knew the earthly Jesus; but he did at one time regard the crucified Christ as accursed by the law. The RSV accurately translates: 'Even though we once regarded Christ from a human point of view, we regard him thus no longer.' Cf. Phil. 3.3–11.

Chapter IV   Jesus and Critical History

1. As Lonergan, *Insight*, 78, observes, it belongs to empirical science that the unknown to be known through classical (as distinct from statistical) heuristic structures is a *possible*: 'Hence, empirical science rests upon two distinct grounds. As insight grasping possibility, it is science. As verification selecting the possibilities that in fact are realized, it is empirical.'

2. Collingwood distinguished 'scissors-and-paste' history from 'scientific' history. The last phase of the era of 'scissors-and-paste' history, in Collingwood's view, was 'critical history', which, though it managed to convert 'authorities' into 'sources', was still crippled in both theory and practice by positivist confusions. (So far as the semantic decision to use the term 'critical history' in this way is concerned, I have not followed Collingwood, except to allude to his view in the sentence to which this note is appended, and would not wish my own use of the term 'critical history' to be confused with his.)

3. It may be useful to draw attention to my own technical use of the term '(historical) interpretation': It is the effort to define the intentions of historical agents. Collingwood, Lonergan, and others use the term 'interpretation' to signify the construing of data, e.g. the shaping of a hypothesis about 'what happened'.

4. History, especially as explanatory, cannot afford to accent 'thought' to the disadvantage of 'instruments'. In a boxing match the 'thought' of both boxers is the will to win, a plan to win, a state of morale, and so forth. But the sports writer must also assess reach, weight, conditioning, stamina, speed, timing, and punching power. The role of 'instruments' is especially obvious in his account of why the winner won.

5. I use the term 'verification' in a wide sense to cover both the experimental cross-checking of empirical science and the non-experimental cross-checking involved in the specializations of common sense such as history. To refer to the latter Lonergan adopted the term 'the self-correcting process of learning'. See *Second Collection*, 126; *Insight*, 174; cf. *Method*, 233f.

6. A. Fridrichsen, 'Jesus, St John and St Paul', *The Root of the Vine. Essays in*

Biblical Theology, A. Fridrichsen *et al.*; London: A. and C. Black, and New York: Philosophical Library 1953, 37–62, p. 55.

7. J. Jeremias, *Jerusalem in the Time of Jesus*, tr. F. H. and C. H. Cave; London: SCM Press, and Philadelphia: Fortress 1969, 310, summarizes the evidence on the socio-religious stigma attaching to tanners: 'To the suspicion of immorality attached to tanners was the added fact that their trade was repugnant, because of the smell. . . . "Woe to him who is a tanner!" cried Rabbi. . . . We must not overlook Acts 9.43, which says very simply, not even stressing the last word: "And he (Peter) stayed in Joppa many days and lodged with one Simon, a tanner." '

8. This is not to say that of the two catch-phrases one is as bad as the other. Lonergan, *Method*, 223: 'It was Newman who remarked, apropos of Descartes' methodic doubt, that it would be better to believe everything than to doubt everything. For universal doubt leaves one with no basis for advance, while universal belief may contain some truth that in time may gradually drive out the errors.' In the literature of the past ten years on 'criteriology' for judgments of historicity it has become common to hear complaints about 'dissimilarity' or 'discontinuity' as the single acid test failing which a given tradition must be classified as 'inauthentic'. Thus, W. Marxsen punctured the burden-of-proof balloon. The burden of proof is neither on the side of historicity nor on the side of non-historicity; it is on the side of anyone who wishes to pronounce on the matter: 'If I want to declare something to be historical, I must prove it. If I want to declare something to be unhistorical, I must prove that too' (W. Marxsen, *The Beginnings of Christology: A Study of its Problems*, tr. P. Achtemeier; Philadelphia: Fortress 1969, 8). P. Stuhlmacher, 'Kritische Marginalien . . .' (see ch. II n. 119), 346, noted ironically that the acid-test criterion of discontinuity would not allow us to entertain the possibility (nevertheless commended by the Our Father, the proclamation of the reign of God, etc.) that Jesus identified his heavenly Father with the God of the Old Testament and of Judaism. M. D. Hooker in two articles, 'On Using the Wrong Tool', *Theology* 75, 1972, 570–81, and 'Christology and Methodology', *NTS* 17, 1971, 480–7, has made several telling points. What we are looking for is what was *characteristic* of Jesus but what we get from application of the principle of dissimilarity is only what was *unique* to him. This generates, not a rounded view of Jesus, but an inevitably distorted one. The principle, moreover, presupposes a more confident knowledge of both Judaism and the earliest church than we can in fact reasonably claim. Finally, inasmuch as the principle cannot wholly predetermine its own application, the critic is necessarily guided by his own way of construing the data to which he applies it. (This is not a defect in the critic; it is simply a defect in any theorizing which fails to take account of the fact that this is how critics operate.)

9. R. H. Lightfoot 'was often to be heard lamenting: "If only they [New Testament scholars] would say 'we do not know.' " ' D. E. Nineham '. . . *et hoc genus omne*', *Christian History and Interpretation* (see ch. III n. 59 above), 199–222, p. 209; cited by M. D. Hooker, 'On Using the Wrong Tool', 570.

10. Collingwood, *The Idea of History* (see ch. I n. 13 above), 244f.

11. See above, ch. III n. 26.

12. See above, pp. 81–85.

13. Collingwood, 176f.

14. Collingwood, 236.

15. Lonergan, *Insight*, 283–7.

16. Lonergan, *Insight*, 275.

Chapter V   History and Faith

1. F. de Saussure, *Cours de linguistique générale*, ed. C. Bally, A. Sechehaye, A. Riedlinger; Paris: Payot 1922, 36–39; ET, *Course in General Linguistics*, tr. W. Baskin; New York: Philosophical Library 1959, 17–20.

2. Luther's dictum is cited by H.-G. Gadamer, *Wahrheit und Methode* (see above, ch. II n. 144), 162; ET, *Truth and Method*, 151.

3. E. Coreth, *Grundfragen der Hermeneutik. Ein philosophischer Beitrag*, Freiburg: Herder 1969, 64f. Cf. p. 97 on the early Heidegger's ' "Hinsicht" auf die Sache' and pp. 116f., 123f., 182–4, on the dialogue-structure or reciprocal mediation of *Sache* and *Sprache*.

4. B. Lonergan, *Method*, 157.

5. B. Lonergan, *ibid.*: 'The less that experience, the less cultivated that intelligence, the less formed that judgment, the greater the likelihood that the interpreter will impute to the author an opinion that the author never entertained. On the other hand, the wider the interpreter's experience, the deeper and fuller the development of his understanding, the better balanced his judgment, the greater the likelihood that he will discover just what the author meant.'

6. The Horatian tag took on this sense in the Enlightenment. Kant in *Was ist Aufklärung?* writes: '*Sapere aude!* Habe Mut, *dich* deines *eigenen* Verstandes zu bedienen!'

7. See H.-G. Gadamer, op. cit., 256–61; ET, 241–5.

8. H.-G. Gadamer, ibid.

9. *Theology* 63, 1960, p. 291.

10. F. E. Crowe, 'Christology and Contemporary Philosophy', *Commonweal* 87, 1967, 242–7, p. 242.

11. F. Schnabel, *Deutsche Geschichte im neunzehnten Jahrhundert. IV Band: Die religiöse Kräfte*, Freiburg: Herder 1936, ³1955, 499f.

12. V. A. Harvey, *The Historian* (see above, ch. I n. 3), 76.

13. B. Lonergan, *Insight*, 130.

14. B. Lonergan, *Insight*, 135.

15. See B. Lonergan, *Method*, 222.

16. Taking New Testament texts as a point of departure, the 'metamiraculous' element is personal entry into what Jewish antiquity named 'the age to come'; the miraculous element bears on the corporeal dimension of this personal entry.

17. The phrase – 'ces absences qui nous font agir' – is Rilke's, in a poem beginning 'Tous mes adieux sont faits', *Sämtliche Werke*, ed. E. Zinn; Wiesbaden: Insel-Verlag 1957, vol. II, 'Zweite Abteilung: Gedichte in französischer Sprache', p. 553.

18. The sense of the phrase 'to objectify' (=to make an object of) may be specified by defining 'object' as 'what is intended in questions' (and known through correct answers). On how 'object' in this sense (i.e., as belonging to 'the world mediated by meaning') differs from 'object' as belonging to 'the world of immediacy', see *Insight*, 250–54; *Method*, 262–5, 341–3. (On the often simplistic contemporary use of phrases such as 'the overcoming of the subject-object

schema', see the remarks of Coreth, op. cit. [n. 3 above], 104–9.)

19. On the classic conciliar process of objectifying, see B. Lonergan, 'The Dehellenization of Dogma', *TS* 28, 1967, 336–51, esp. 344–7; reprinted in *Second Collection*, 11–32; see esp. pp. 19–22.

20. In accord with the sense of the Pauline texts cited, these remarks primarily envisage, not exegetical correctness (the truth of interpretation as such), but religious affirmations (the truth of the texts themselves). Secondarily, however, they envisage interpretation, too, which is always subject to the law that 'he who does not understand the things cannot draw the sense from the words'.

21. For a sketch of the heuristic thrust of historical research on early Christianity since 1800, see L. Goppelt, *Jesu Wirken* (see above, ch. II n. 117), 27–51. Research has always depended on how one defined the New Testament 'thing', i.e., the 'scope' of primitive Christianity as 'historically mediated' and 'affecting the present' (Goppelt, 27).

22. See B. Lonergan, *Insight*, 82f., 271–4.

23. R. Bultmann, *Jesus Christ and Mythology* (see ch. II n. 99), 17.

24. D. F. Strauss, *Life of Jesus*, 40. It should be noted that the direct object of Strauss's concern here is not the narrative but 'the matters' narrated. He is, in fact, so concerned with *die Sache* that the particularities of the writers' intentions cease to represent a true exegetical goal even of limited status. Strauss did not adequately thematize the issue of non-recognitive versus recognitive exegesis.

25. The distinction corresponds to the question whether it is possible to grasp past intended meaning in its own terms, for that is precisely what 'recognitive exegesis' aims at. Is it a realistic aim? A reasonable way of settling the matter is to try it and find out. In the present context a handy test case might be Jeremias's study of the parables of Jesus. The effort is to construe the issues Jesus himself meant to illuminate by his parabolic teaching. The success of this effort is verified to the extent to which a given reconstruction meets relevant questions about the text of the parable. The proof of the pudding, in other words, is in the eating. If, in fact, one has succeeded in grasping past meaning in its own terms, theoretical reflections on the impossibility of doing so are otiose, pointless, irrelevant. It is up to the reader to question himself whether through his own interpretative efforts or those of others he has, in fact, had the experience of grasping past meaning. If so, the question is settled for him. If not, the testimony of others may at least give him pause.

26. R. Bultmann, 'Das Verhältnis der urchristlichen Christusbotschaft zum historischen Jesus', in his *Exegetica. Aufsätze zur Erforschung des Neuen Testaments*, ed. E. Dinkler; Tübingen: Mohr 1967, 445–69, p. 453; ET, 'The Primitive Christian Kerygma and the Historical Jesus', *The Historical Jesus and the Kerygmatic Christ*. tr. and ed. C. E. Braaten and R. A. Harrisville (see above, ch. I n. 9), 15–42, p. 24.

27. See J. M. Robinson, *Kerygma und historischer Jesus*, Zurich/Stuttgart: Zwingli [2]1967, 109–11. *A New Quest* (see above, ch. II n. 100), 44–46. Cf. B. Lonergan, *Method*, 318.

28. The most conspicuous corrective value of historical scholarship is, first, that it disabuses the modern believer of the illusion that it is the intention of the gospels (on the analogy of journalism or of academic history) to focus on historical factuality as such; second, that it thus forces him to try and find out what the gospels in fact focus on, what framework of meaning they set up and why.

29. See J. Jeremias, 'Das Lösegeld für Viele (Mk. 10, 45)', *Jud* 3, 1947/48,

249–64; reprinted in *Abba* (see above, ch. III n. 79), 216–29. E. Schweizer, 'Mark's Contribution to the Quest of the Historical Jesus', *NTS* 10, 1963/64, 421–32, accents the historical particularity of the death of Jesus, which 'manifests what dying for our sake really means' (432). Such gains would go by the board if one were satisfied with the bare *Dass* of Jesus' historicity. Similarly, E. Käsemann, 'Die neue Jesus-Frage', *Jésus aux origines de la christologie*, ed. J. Dupont; Gembloux: Duculot 1975, 47–57, pp. 55–57, argues in the third and best part of his essay that in so far as the concreteness of the earthly Jesus is forgotten, the result is a docetism depriving Christianity of its least dispensable thrust.

30. To mediate the immediacy of knowledge is to objectify cognitional process (see *Method*, 77). 'To objectify', in this sense is to intend (by questioning) and to know (by answering the questions correctly). The objectification of cognitional process in the work of Lonergan is called 'transcendental method'.

31. See B. Lonergan, 'Metaphysics as Horizon', *Greg* 44, 1963, 307–18; reprinted in *Collection*, 202–20.

32. See K. Rahner, *Hörer des Wortes*, Munich: Kösel 1963; ET, *Hearers of the Word*, tr. M. Richards; New York: Herder and Herder 1969.

33. See below, pp. 202–4.

34. See below, p. 247; cf. also the following note.

35. By Christ's death 'for many' (=for all), the Gentiles had been called to the banquet of salvation. But since the end which was destined to bring them to Zion to feast with the patriarchs (Matt. 8.11f. par.) had simply not come with Christ's resurrection and enthronement but rather was yet to come in the indefinite future, the Gentiles' share in salvation would have to be mediated in history by extension of the field of the missionary mandate from Israel to the whole world. This revolutionary act – the launching of a world mission – thus hinged on the intrusion of an indefinitely extended segment of time between the enthronement of the Son of man and his judgment of the world.

36. The change of view is relatively recent. On the history of its development see O. Chadwick, *From Bossuet to Newman. The Idea of Doctrinal Development*, Cambridge: Cambridge University Press 1957.

37. See H. Riedlinger, *Geschichtlichkeit und Vollendung des Wissens Christi*, Freiburg/Basel/Wien: Herder 1966.

38. See below, pp. 246–8.

39. P. Ricoeur, *The Symbolism of Evil*, tr. E. Buchanan; New York: Harper and Row 1967, 348.

Part Two: The Aims of Jesus. Introduction

1. As an example of wholesale repudiation of the principle of rational inquiry one might point to the performance of J. M. Allegro, *The Sacred Mushroom and the Cross*, London: Hodder & Stoughton, and New York: Doubleday 1970. Less flamboyant examples are legion.

Chapter VI The Judgment and Salvation of Israel

1. The Syrian mode of calendrical calculation, presumably adopted by Luke, designated as the first year of a new ruler's reign the period from his accession to power to the next New Year's day (1 October). In this system Tiberius's first regnal year fell between 19 August and 30 September AD 14; his fifteenth year, between 1 October AD 27 and 30 September AD 28. (But it is at least possible that Luke followed the common Roman computation, according to which the first year of Tiberius's reign ran from August AD 14 to August AD 15 and the fifteenth from August AD 28 to August AD 29.)

2. On the quenching of prophecy cf. I Macc. 4.46; 9.27; 14.41; Syr. Bar. 85.3; Josephus, *Contra Apionem* 1.41; Billerbeck I, 127–134; II, 128–134. On the return of prophecy as a sign of messianic salvation, cf. the identification of 'prophet' in Deut. 18.15–18 with 'Messiah' (Sifre, *ad loc.*); see also Billerbeck II, 134 t; 615f.

3. See M. Hengel, *Nachfolge und Charisma* (see above, ch. III n. 1), 39 n. 71.

4. G. Dalman *Orte und Wege Jesu*, Gütersloh: Mohn [4]1924; reprinted, Darmstadt: Wissenschaftliche Buchgesellschaft 1967, 89–107, esp. 97–9. ET, *Sacred Sites and Ways. Studies in the Topography of the Gospels*, tr. P. Levertoff; London: SPCK 1935, 81–100, esp. 89–91.

5. Hos. 2.16f. (EVV 2.14f.); 12.10 (EVV 12.9); Micah 7.15; Isa. 11.11; 48.20f. The ties between messianism and the desert are a development of the theme; see Billerbeck I, 85–8.

6. See A. Schlatter, *Der Evangelist Matthäus. Seine Sprache, sein Ziel, Seine Selbstständigkeit*, Stuttgart: Calwer 1948, 62, on Matt. 3.5.

7. See A. Schlatter, *Matthäus*, 54f., on Matt. 3.1. 'New beginning' is meant to imply not rupture and renewal of covenant but the discontinuity between history and eschaton in accordance with the *Urzeit/Endzeit* schema. Both Jesus and the earliest Christian tradition saw John as belonging to the scenario of eschatological fulfilment. Cf. below, pp. 125–8; 220f.

8. On the possibility that the Baptist preached to Samaritans as well as to Jews, see W. F. Albright, 'Some Observations Favouring the Palestinian Origin of the Gospel of John', *HTR* 17, 1924, 189–95, esp. 194. B. Bagatti, 'Ricordi di S. Giovanni Battista in Samaria', *ED* 25, 1972, 294–8, offers a more probable account of the archaeological data (tombs, place names) connecting the Baptist with Samaria. Not the Baptist himself but his disciples account for the ties. They buried their master outside the territory of Antipas and, settling there (Samaria), they named their settlements after the places where they had been with him (a practice attested for other sectarian groups in Palestine).

9. With baptism 'for repentance' compare (*a*) baptism 'of repentance for the forgiveness of sins' (Mark 1.4; Luke 3.3) and (*b*) the confession of sins that accompanied baptism (Mark 1.5; Matt. 3.6). The rite signified a twofold object: the break with sin (now) and acquittal at the judgment (soon). 'Repentance' thematizes the first; 'forgiveness', the second. That John conceived his baptism as already (sacramentally) effecting the forgiveness of sins is unlikely, for, as Schlatter, *Matthäus*, 79, argues: 'If he had had a consciousness of himself as the dispenser of forgiveness, he would not have described his relation to the coming one as one of total powerlessness.' By the same token the Baptist could hardly have understood himself as 'saviour'. This is confirmed by the exclusively future role of purification

through 'the holy Spirit and fire', as well as by the historicity of the Baptist's question to Jesus. See below, p. 295 n. 96; cf. also John 1.19–34; 5.33–35. Contrast H. Thyen, *Studien zur Sündenvergebung*, FRLANT 96, 1970, 131–45.

10. The theme of the holy Spirit relates to 'the mightier one' and may well account for the epithet. That 'the mightier one' was John's circumlocution for 'God' is practically excluded by the comparative form of the present *māšāl*. Rather, John must have belonged to an esoteric stream of Judaic tradition, comparable, perhaps, to Enoch, Baruch, II (4) Ezra and the Sibylline Oracles, which attributed the coming judgment of the world to an apocalyptic figure to come. Cf. 11QMelch 9–15. On the sense of the image: when a master arrives home, his slave removes and takes away his sandals. But John completely effaces himself. With reference to the mightier one he is not even worthy to perform a slave's service.

11. The repeated verb ('baptize') indicates that the role of the messianic judge stood in positive and essential relationship to the role of John. This is likewise indicated by 'you': The Messiah will effect the final purification of the selfsame persons John has baptized.

12. Here the judgment is conceived with exclusive reference to purification of the saved. That either phrase, 'the holy Spirit' or 'and fire', is a Christian addition is gratuitous and unlikely. The combination is distinctive and probably original with John, though each element separately finds relevant attestation elsewhere. The eschatological cleansing and life-giving role of the Spirit of Yahweh is a motif found in the Psalms and prophets, especially Ezekiel (36.26f.; 37.14). It is likewise attested with reference to eschatological judgment in Qumran, 1QS 4.21. On judgment as *refining* fire, see Isa. 1.25; Zech. 13.9; Mal. 3.2; II Bar. 48.39; I Cor. 3.13–15. The judge to come does not simply pronounce the acquittal of the repentant; his judgment is a baptism, i.e., an apocalyptic cleansing.

13. The un-eschatological description of the Baptist in Josephus (*Antiquitates* 18.116–19) is a conscious accommodation to Hellenistic categories. See P. Vielhauer, 'Johannes, der Taufer', *RGG³* 3. 804–08, col. 804.

14. See below, pp. 227–9.

15. See J. Jeremias, *Verkündigung*, 51; ET, *NT Theology* (see above, ch. II n. 109), 44: 'To answer the question what led John to administer his baptism, we shall rather have to begin from the Jewish doctrinal statement (which can be traced back to the beginning of the first century AD) that on Sinai Israel was prepared for receiving salvation by means of a bath of immersion (cf. I Cor. 10.1f.). [Cf. J. Jeremias, 'Der Ursprung der Johannestaufe', *ZNW* 28, 1929, 312–20, pp. 314f.] According to a stereotyped apocalyptic pattern of thought, the Israelites in the wilderness were regarded as a type of the eschatological community of salvation; thus the tenet of their bath of immersion included the expectation that in the end-time Israel would again be prepared for salvation by a bath of immersion.' G. Friedrich, '*prophētēs*' (NT)', *TWNT* VI, 829–58, p. 839; *TDNT* VI, 828–61, p. 838, remarks apropos of I Cor. 10.1ff. that inasmuch as use of the Moses/Messiah schema is atypical of Paul (it crosses the grain of his theology of righteousness), the connection of primitive Christian baptism with Moses 'must go back to an ancient tradition which regarded baptism as a prophetic eschatological act'. Cf. John 1.25.

16. Among those whose views converge at this point: J. Jeremias, 'Der Gedanke des 'Heiligen Restes' im Spätjudentum und in der Verkündigung Jesu', *ZNW* 42, 1949, 184–94, p. 191, reprinted in *Abba* (see above, ch. III n. 79), 121–32, p. 129; A. Oepke, *Das neue Gottesvolk in Schrifttum, bildender Kunst und Weltgestaltung*, Güters-

loh: Mohn 1950, 176; P. Nepper Christensen, *Wer hat die Kirche gestiftet?*, SBU 12, 1960, 23–35, p. 30.

17. See below, pp. 229–35.

18. See below, pp. 233f.

19. See J. Jeremias, *Verheissung* (see above, ch. II n. 113), 52 n. 195; ET, *Promise*, 60 n. 3.

20. The biblical conception has had an impact on but is nevertheless to be distinguished both from Paul's *pas Israēl sōthēsetai* (all Israel will be saved, Rom. 11.26) and from the traditional dictum *kol yiśrāʾēl yeš lāhem ḥēlek bāʿōlām habbāʾ* (all Israel has a share in the age to come, Sanh. 10.1). The first promised that, once the appointed measure of the salvation of the Gentiles had been reached, the whole empirical people Israel would enter into its historic heritage of salvation (i.e., the messianic community or church of Christ). The second asserted that every Jew (with specified exceptions) would eventually find final salvation in the age to come. The biblical conception, on the other hand, does not say who or how many will be saved but rather affirms that in the saved the ecclesial reality 'Israel' is realized. Cf. the use of 'Israel' in Gal. 6.16.

21. Historicity is established by the index of discontinuity. Jesus' baptism crossed the grain of primitive Christianity in so far as it could suggest subordination to the Baptist and need of repentance (hence the didactic dialogue of Matt. 3.14f.).

22. The *paradothē* of Matt. 4.12 (cf. *paradothēnai* in Mark 1.14; cf. Matt. 17.22; 30.18; 26.2, 45) is a 'divine passive', i.e., a circumlocution employing for reverential reasons a passive verb form rather than an active form which would require 'God' as subject. See A. Schlatter, *Matthäus*, 112. The text equivalently says that Jesus acts (goes to Galilee) not simply in reaction to the initiative of Herod but on a signal from God (cf. Luke 4.14: 'by the power of the Spirit').

23. A claim to historicity for some of the data on Jesus' career as baptizer is established by the index of discontinuity: (*a*) The career of Jesus as baptizer is suggestive of subordination to the Baptist (in John 3.26 Jesus is interpreted as a rival of John); John 4.2, designed to soften the scandal, is a late addition; see J. Jeremias, *Verkündigung*, 53; ET, *NT Theology*, 45; (*b*) details apparently quite unrelated to post-paschal Christianity are given in John 3.23, 25. R. Schnackenburg, 'Das vierte Evangelium und die Johannesjünger', *HJ* 77, 1958, 21–38, p. 23 remarks: 'The debate is ... over the question of 'purification' (*katharismos*, cf. 2.6); it is, then, an intra-Jewish controversy, but one having no follow-up [in the Fourth Gospel].' See also C. H. Dodd, *Historical Tradition in the Fourth Gospel*, Cambridge: Cambridge University Press 1965, 280f. For a trenchant critique of Bultmann's literary and historical judgment of the Johannine text, see E. Linnemann, 'Jesus und der Täufer', *Festschrift für Ernst Fuchs*, ed. G. Ebeling, E. Jüngel and G. Schunack; Tübingen: Mohr 1973, 219–36, pp. 221–3. (*c*) It does not seem possible, however, to resolve the question of the historicity of one significant datum in the Johannine account; namely, that Jesus already had followers before the arrest of John. On the one hand, a synoptic omission of all data on the ministry of Jesus as baptizer is to be inferred. But might not the Johannine representation of the first disciples (particularly the representation that they were former followers of the Baptist) simply derive from the emphatic Johannine theme of the Baptist's testimony to Jesus? A marked stylization of traditions in the narrative sequence following the Prologue (John 1.19ff.) is evident. If, however, a circle of disciples

actually did surround Jesus during his career as baptizer, this will have accorded well with the general principle laid down by Anton Fridrichsen (art. cit.; [see above, ch. IV n. 6], 55) that 'the man of God' in the ancient Orient 'is never isolated. He is always the centre of a circle taught by his words and example …' It is, moreover, likely that like Jesus himself the disciples of Jesus underwent 'the baptism of John' (cf. Acts 1.21f.) and the hypothesis of the historicity of the Johannine data on the first disciples accords well with this.

24. The contrary is, to be sure, supposed by John 4.2, a late addition (see the reference in the previous note). But Aramaic *ṭᵉbal*, to which *baptizesthai* corresponds, means, not 'to be baptized', but 'to undergo immersion, to immerse oneself'. (*Baptizein* renders the causative form of the same verb.) Nor can one argue from the Greek termination *-tēs* (plu, *-tai*) in *baptistēs* that John 'performed' a rite on others, for the *ṭôbᵉlê šᵉḥārîn* (T. Yad. 2.20), who immersed themselves, were called in Greek *hēmerobaptistai*. J. Jeremias, *Verkündigung*, 58; ET, *NT Theology*, 51, refers to Luke 3.7 D *it*, 'where it is said that those who were baptized immersed themselves *enōpion autou*, 'in the presence' of the Baptist. Accordingly, John the Baptist had the function of a witness, as in proselyte baptism.'

25. This word of the Baptist was designed to provoke a realistic facing of the issue of judgment. The symbolic rite of baptism would be empty if there were lacking the repentance and will to reform which it was meant to signify and seal. Real flight from 'the wrath about to come' consisted in repentance and the break with sin, by which one escaped liability to condemnation at the impending judgment.

26. If the one mightier than John would effect the final purification from sinfulness 'by the holy Spirit and fire', it is clear that John conceived the reform God required now as a radical orientation to the good which did not, however, suppose perfect purity from sinfulness.

27. 'The repentance of tax collectors and publicans is hard …' T. B.M. 8.26 (Zuckermandel 1875, repr. Jerusalem 1963, 390); supported by j. B.M. 11a; a *baraita* in b. B.K. 94b adds herdsmen to the list. Repentance was hard for them because they could not know all whom they had cheated and to whom they accordingly owed restitution.

28. *Anachōrein* in Matt. 4.12 implies that the journey to Galilee is temporary, a withdrawal (cf. Matt. 2.22) until the moment for return to Judaea and Jerusalem; see A. Schlatter, *Matthäus*, 113. Like the Baptist, Jesus is evidently conceived here as understanding the encounter with Israel to be peculiarly mediated by and concentrated in encounter with the capital city. (Unlike the Baptist, he would provoke the encounter on the spot, by symbol-charged public acts.)

29. The question has been clarified by considerations relevant to definition of the *Gattung* of the synoptic texts on Jesus' baptism. See F. Lentzen-Deis, *Die Taufe Jesu nach den Synoptikern. Literarkritische und gattungsgeschichtliche Untersuchungen*, Frankfurt: Knecht 1970. On the significance of these considerations for the history of Jesus, see esp. 286–9.

30. See below, pp. 240f.

31. We omit discussion of the complicated problem of the Baptist's testimony to Jesus, for, unlike the question of Jesus' stance toward the Baptist, the topic has little immediate relevance to the definition of Jesus' aims. See below, however, on the question which the Baptist posed to Jesus (p. 295 n. 96).

32. That John himself invoked the Isaian text (Isa. 40.3) to define his mission is

a probable inference. First, the traditions on the Baptist provided by the Fourth Gospel have a special claim to independence (see C. H. Dodd, *Historical Tradition*, 248–301). This has rightly inclined numerous critics to account for Johannine variations from synoptic tradition on the Baptist by positing a historical component in both the evangelist's intention and in his performance (see, for example, J. Schmitt, 'Les écrits du Nouveau Testament et les textes de Qumrân', *RevSR*, 1955, 381–401, esp. 394–7). Second, the text of John 1.23 in particular is independent of synoptic tradition (Dodd, op. cit., 31–46; 252). Finally, the likelihood of the notion that the tie between the Baptist and the Isaian text was a stroke of finely calibrated Christian inventiveness designed to give John a fully eschatological but less than messianic role collapses in the face of the Essene use of the text of Isaiah (1QS 8.12–14; 9.19f.).

33. 'To come with'='To bring' (*bō' bᵉ*). See the Lukan parallel (7.30). See also A. H. McNeile, *The Gospel According to St Matthew*, London: Macmillan 1915, 308.

34. See J. Jeremias, *Gleichnisse*, 78f.; ET, *Parables*, 80f.

35. 'To come': to appear, be there, be here. Bultmann's view (*Synoptische Tradition*, 167; ET, *Synoptic Tradition*, 155f.) to the effect that *ēlthon* of itself implies viewing the life of the one named as subject of the verb *as a totality in the past* was influential but mistaken. On the senses ('to intend', 'to will', 'to have as one's task', etc.) of *ēlthon* as rendering *bō' lᵉ* or *'ătā' le* with the infinitive, see J. Jeremias, 'Die älteste Schicht der Menschensohn-Logien', *ZNW* 58, 1967, 159–172, pp. 166f.

36. 'Then along comes'; this translates an underlying Aramaic perfect (*'ătā'*). See C. Colpe, "*o 'uios tou anthropou*', *TWNT* VIII, 434; *TDNT* VIII, 432. 'One': *'o 'uios tou anthropou* renders *bar 'ĕnāšă'*, which doubtless carried here an original indefinite sense. Cf. J. Jeremias, 'Die älteste Schicht . . .' 165.; earlier, T. W. Manson, *The Teaching of Jesus*, Cambridge: Cambridge University Press 1931, ²1935, 216–18.

37. The historicity of the text is established by a variety of indices: discontinuity (John and Jesus are placed on a par; the charge, especially 'glutton and drunkard' [cf. Deut. 21.18–21 on execution of the rebellious son] was hardly devised by the post-Easter Christian tradition); resistive form (parable; the originality of the context is peculiarly attested by the refractoriness of the image, i.e., by the *difficulty* of exactly correlating the image of the children with its application to 'this generation'); Aramaic substratum (indefinite sense of underlying *bar 'ĕnāšă'*; on retrotranslation of the children's singsong into Aramaic and into *kinā* rhythm, see J. Jeremias, *Verkündigung*, 36; ET, *NT Theology*, 26; *ekopsasthe* in Matt. 11.17 and *eklausate* of Luke 7.32 are translation variants of *'arqēdtun*); multiple and multiform attestation of some aspects of the text (see Mark 2.16; Luke 7.27f.).

38. O. Linton, 'The Parable of the Children's Game', *NTS* 22, 1976 159–179, pp. 174–7. Scriptural background on 'asocial' behaviour as a prophetic sign to the nation: Jer. 16.1–4, 5–7; Ezek. 24.15–24. Cf. M. Hengel, *Nachfolge* (see above, ch III n. 1), 13.

39. For illuminating parallels to the sequence 'royal entry-temple cleansing' see J. Jeremias, *Jesus als Weltvollender* (see above, ch. II n. 110), 35–54. This was originally followed by the question about Jesus' authority (cf. John 2.18). Literary analysis (J. Jeremias, *Abendmahlsworte*, 83–87; ET, *Eucharistic Words*, 89–93) indicates the likelihood that in early oral tradition the cleansing of the temple immediately followed the account of the royal entry into the city. (That the goal of the pilgrimage procession should have been nothing other than the temple is an infer-

ence from age-old practice. It is also explicit in the texts: Mark 11.11; Matt. 21.10; Luke 19.45.)

40. See J. Jeremias, '*El(e)ias*', *TWNT* II, 930–43, esp. 933, 938–40; *TDNT* II, 928–41, esp. 931, 936–8. Both Matthew and Mark unambiguously define the Elijah-role as one of preparation for the Messiah: cf. *sou* in Matt. 11.10 (par.)! Cf. Mark 1.2.

41. Represented as privileged witness to mysterious revelation in Mark 5.37–43 (the raising of the daughter of Jairus); 9.2ff. (the Transfiguration and the present scene); 14.33–42 (Gethsemane); and, with Andrew, 13.3ff. (eschatological discourse).

42. 'Despised': *exoudenēthē*, probably reflecting *nibzeh* of Isa. 53.3a,d. Aquila, Symmachus, and Theodotion (but not LXX) draw on the same Greek word to render *nibzeh*, in Isa. 53.3a,d. See J. Jeremias, '*Pais(Theou)* in the New Testament', W. Zimmerli, J. Jeremias, *The Servant of God*, SBT 20, ²1965, 90.

43. See J. Jeremias, "*El(e)ias*', *TWNT* II, 942; *TDNT* II, 940.

Chapter VII   Public Proclamation and Career

1. The probability of this retranslation from Greek to Aramaic depends on (*a*) parallels establishing *malkût(ā')* as the substratum of *(ʿē) basileia*, and (*b*) the priority of *ʿē basileia tou theou* (the reign of God) to *ʿē basileia tōn ouranōn* (the reign of [the] heaven[s]) in the gospel tradition. On the first point, see G. Dalman, *Die Worte Jesu mit Berücksichtigung des nachkanonischen jüdischen Schrifttums und der aramäischen Sprache erörtert*, Leipzig: Hinrichs, 1898 ²1930; repr. Darmstadt: Wissenschaftliche Buchgesellschaft 1960, 77–83; ET, *The Words of Jesus Considered in the Light of Post-Biblical Jewish Writings and the Aramaic Language*, tr. D. M. Kay; Edinburgh: T. & T. Clark 1902, 91–101. Directly relevant to the second point is the observation of J. Jeremias, *Verkündigung*, 100; ET, *NT Theology*, 97: 'the reign of heaven' appears for the first time in Jewish literature half a century after Jesus' ministry, with R. Johanan ben Zakkai, c. AD 80. The translation of *ʿe basileia/malkûtā'* as 'the reign' (not 'the kingdom') was established in the latter nineteenth century by B. Weiss, K. G. Grass, and Dalman, cf. *Worte*, 78f.; ET, *Words*, 94. R. Schnackenburg, *Gottes Herrschaft und Reich* (Freiburg: Herder, 1959) 247f.; ET, *God's Rule and Kingdom*, tr. J. Murray; New York: Herder & Herder; and London: Nelson 1963, 354f., proposes that 'kingdom' be used to render texts that speak of 'entering into' the *basileia/malkût*. But it is implausible that whenever Jesus spoke of entering the *malkût* of God the sense of the word underwent so sharply defined a change (from 'kingly reign' to 'the place over which God exercises his kingly reign') that a new word is called for to translate it. S. Aalen, ' "Reign" and "House" in the Kingdom of God in the Gospels', *NTS* 8, 1961/62, 215–40, p. 220, has wondered 'what meaning is to be conveyed by saying that a person "enters" into the reign of God'; but he himself has taken the sting out of his question by noticing that one also 'enters' into 'life' (Mark 9.43 par.), a phrase quite intelligible without our making the spatial factor explicit by rendering *ʿe zōē* as 'the sphere of life'. Aalen's own proposal (*basileia*=house) runs into more serious difficulties than does the rather abstract 'reign'. A house is built; it does not 'draw near'. Moreover, the parallel

between the *Qaddi š* and the Our Father (see below, p. 134; also p. 289 n. 34) certainly favours 'reign' over 'house'.

2. Matthew attributes proclamation of 'the reign of heaven' to the Baptist (3.2). This appears to be an editorial move designed to show that the missions of John, of Jesus (4.17), and of the disciples of Jesus (10.7) make up not only successive but interlocking moments in a single, divinely inspired movement. (Contrast Luke, for whom the thematic continuity of Baptist, Jesus, and church is traced, not through *basileia* but through *aphesis 'amartiōn* ['the taking away of sins': Luke 1.77; 3.3; 4.18; 24.47; Acts 2.38; 5.31; 10.43; 13.38; 26.18].)

3. See J. Schniewind, *EUANGELION. Ursprung und erste Gestalt des Begriffs Evangelium. Untersuchungen*, Gütersloh: Bertelsmann 1931; repr. Darmstadt: Wissenschaftliche Buchgesellschaft 1970. See also the complementary work of Schniewind's student, G. Friedrich, *'euaggelizomai . . .' TWNT* II, 705–35; *TDNT* II, 707–37.

4. 'Happy . . .': *makarioi*; Aramaic substratum: *tûbêhôn*. There is no substantial difference in this context between 'happy' and 'blessed'. In the Matthean text ('poor in spirit') the poverty (like the hunger and thirst of Matt. 5.6) is metaphorical. That the Lukan form (Luke 6.20) should represent the omission of an original 'poor in spirit' is certainly less likely than that Matthew modified an original 'poor' by adding 'in spirit'. See J. Dupont, *Les béatitudes* (see above, ch. III n. 57), 209–17.

5. The form *paraklēthēsontai* ('shall be comforted') is a 'divine passive'. The real subject was understood to be God; hence the present translation.

6. The ordinary future ('will comfort') fails to convey the intended allusion to the imminence of the eschaton.

7. The Lukan version (6.21) is preferable to the Matthean ('those who hunger and thirst for righteousness', 5.6). 'For righteousness' is transparently secondary; the evangelist (or pre-redactional tradition) probably likewise added 'the thirsty' on the basis of biblical precedent, especially in such messianic texts as Isa. 49.10; 55.1ff.; 65.13.

8. See J. Dupont, op. cit., 293: ' . . . happiness is promised to the miserable, not because by their very poverty or by their moral dispositions they fulfil certain conditions, but because *God* has decided to save them'. Cf. T. Wrege, *Bergpredigt*, (see above, ch. III n. 57), 12.

9. Jesus did not say that to block the way to the reign of God was the intention of the scribes; he simply said that this was in fact what they did. How? No doubt, by their failure to grasp the real meaning of the scriptures and to mediate this meaning to Israel. Cf. J. Jeremias, *'kleis'*, *TWNT* III, 743–753, pp. 746f.; *TDNT* III, 744–753, pp. 747f.

10. 'Above all' conveys the sense in a mild form, for the poor are the very type of the saved. Men, that is, are saved only in so far as they are assimilated to 'the poor' (namely by recognition that salvation is a pure gift). In this sense the reign of God is for the poor only. It is characteristic of Semitic idiom that the sense of 'only' is often intended and understood but left verbally unexpressed. Cf. Matt. 5.46: 'For if you love [only] those who love you, what recompense do you deserve?'

11. See below, pp. 158–60. For a summary presentation of the relevant data and its socio-religious significance, see O. Hofius, *Jesu Tischgemeinschaft mit den Sündern*, Stuttgart: Calver 1967.

12. See below, pp. 160–2.

13. *Euaggelion*, which appears especially in the Pauline epistles and in Mark

(1.1, 14f.; 8.35; 10.29; 13.9 par.; 14.9 par.; cf. Matt. 4.23; 9.35; Acts 15.7; 20.24), reflects the root *bśr* and the originally cultic (Nahum 2.1; Ps. 96.2), then eschatological, conception of the reign of God (Isa. 40.9; 41.27; 52.7; 61.1).

14. Dalman, *Worte*, 77–83; ET, *Words*, 91–101.

15. Op. cit., 87–99; ET, 106–21.

16. *Verkündigung*, 40–44; ET, *NT Theology*, 31–35. Like Jeremias, we leave aside, in the following breakdown of verbs, secondary sayings as well as sayings in which the meaning of the verb is uncertain (e.g. 'to suffer violence' and 'to take by force' in Matt. 11.12).

17. See J. Jeremias, *Jesus als Weltvollender* (see above, ch. II n. 110), 31f.

18. The theme of gratuity makes good men nervous, as the Matthean additions confirm. A comparable case is the parable of the Guest Without a Wedding Garment (Matt. 22.11–13). Its original sense was to warn the hearer to accept the gift of righteousness before it would be too late (see Jeremias, *Gleichnisse*, 186–9; ET, *Parables*, 187–9). The gospel of Matthew, however, has changed its thrust, converting it into a parenetic insistence on good works.

19. See below, pp. 159–62.

20. The discussion between R. Eli'ezer ben Hyrcanus and R. Jehoshua ben Hananya in the latter first century is indicative. Eli'ezer insists that there is to be no redemption without repentance (*t*ᵉ*šûbâ*); Jehoshua argues that redemption will come by the sovereign will of God alone. Concretely, the question is not how repentance can be required if redemption is gratuitous; it is whether repentance belongs inalienably to the decree of redemption. See *Tanhuma* (ed. Buber) *B*ᵉ*huqqotai* 5; b. Sanh. 97b; Billerbeck I, 162–4. Gratuity is a theme of one of the texts cited (Isa. 52.3) but not a theme of the discussion itself, nor does the notion of having positively to accept redemption figure in the horizons of the debate.

21. Repentance as prerequisite to forgiveness is thematized by the Baptist (Matt. 3.8 par.). This accords with the standard biblical conviction that so long as the wicked remains wicked, God shall not acquit him (Ex. 23.7c); the contrary appeared to be a perversion comparable to condemning the innocent (see CD 1.19). See below, pp. 160f.

22. J. Schniewind, *Die Freude der Busse*, Göttingen: Vandenhoeck & Ruprecht 1956.

23. G. Friedrich, '*euaggelizomai* . . .', *TWNT* II, 706f.; *TDNT* II, 708f.

24. G. Friedrich '*euaggelizomai*', 715f., citing the text from J. Schniewind, *EUANGELION* (see n. 3 above).

25. For text, translation, and commentary see J. A. Fitzmyer, 'Further Light on Melchizedek from Qumran Cave 11', *JBL* 86, 1967, 25–41, repr., J. A. Fitzmyer, *Essays on the Semitic Background of the New Testament*, London: Chapman 1971; Missoula: Scholars' Press 1974, 245–67, p. 248.

26. The concluding chapter of *Derek Ereṣ Zuta*', cited by Friedrich, loc. cit.: Great is peace, for when the king, Messiah, will reveal himself to Israel, he will begin with peace, for it is written, How beautiful on the mountains are the feet of him who brings glad tidings. . . . See Song of Songs Rab. II. 13.4: 'This is the voice of the king, the Messiah, who proclaims and says: How beautiful on the mountains are the feet of him who brings good tidings.' Lev. Rab. 9.9 declares that Isa. 52.7 ('How beautiful upon the mountains . . .') will come to fulfilment when the king, the Messiah, comes.

27. See below, p. 154.

28. See O. Linton, *Das Problem der Urkirche in der neueren Forschung. Eine kritische Darstellung*, Uppsala: Almquist and Wiksells 1932.

29. K. G. Kuhn, '*basileus C. malkut šāmayîm* in der rabbinischer Literatur'; *TWNT* I, 570–73, p. 572; *TDNT* I, 571–4, p. 573.

30. Art. cit., 571; ET, 572. The collection of texts in Billerbeck I, 178–80 seems to me to settle the matter in the opposite sense.

31. See A. Causse, *Du groupe ethnique à la communauté religieuse. Le problème sociologique de la religion d'Israël*, Paris: Alcan 1937, esp. ch. VI, 'De la nation à la communauté juive', 183–215; O. Plöger, *Theokratie und Eschatologie*, Neukirchen: Neukirchener Verlag [2]1962, esp. 41–61; ET, *Theocracy and Eschatology*, tr. S. Rudman; Richmond, Va.: Knox, and Oxford: Blackwell 1968, 29–46.

32. G. Dalman, *Worte*, 82f.; ET, *Words*, 100f.

33. J. Jeremias, *Verkündigung*, 105; ET, *NT Theology*, 102.

34. The *Qaddiš* has been expanded in the course of liturgical usage but in its original form it must date from before Jesus in view of the parallel between the *Qaddiš* and the first petitions of the Our Father. See I. Elbogen, *Der jüdische Gottesdienst in seiner geschichtlichen Entwicklung*, Frankfurt: Kaufmann [3]1931; repr. Hildesheim: Olms 1967, 93, who further notes the *terminus ante quem* from rabbinic sources, namely, the mid-second century AD. On the scriptural sources of the *Qaddiš*, see above, p. 134.

35. On the dating of the *Tᵉphillâ*, see Elbogen, *Gottesdienst*, 28–30, who sets the end-period of its development in the time of Rabban Gamaliel II (after 70 AD). Cf. K. G. Kuhn, *Achtzehngebet und Vaterunser und der Reim*, Tübingen: Mohr 1950, 10. On Ezekiel especially as a resource for the eschatology of the *Tᵉphillâ*, see Elbogen, 33.

36. See above, p. 132.

37. Most scholars take the Matthean form of the tradition to be more primitive than the Markan form on the ground that the question posed by Jesus in Mark 10.2 envisaged a problem (namely, 'Is it lawful for a man to dismiss his wife?') which no Jew of the time would have had: The legality of divorce was unambiguous and universally acknowledged (cf. Deut. 24.1–4). But counterbalancing literary and historical considerations making the Markan form plausible as original have been offered by D. R. Catchpole, 'The Synoptic Divorce Material as a Traditio-Historical Problem', *BJRL* 57, 1974, 92–127, esp. 114f.

38. Index of discontinuity: Cf. the detail that the prohibition of the dismissal of one's wife was problematic to the disciples (Mark 10.10; Matt. 19.10); note also the series of post-paschal casuistic teachings, not only Pauline but synoptic, for which this prohibition was clearly the point of departure: Mark 10.11f., (=Luke 16.18); Matt. 19.9; 5.32. D. R. Catchpole, art. cit., 113, observes that it is 'thoroughly defensible for anyone to claim that Mark x.11, Lk xvi.18 fit neatly inside the teaching of Jesus'. Though this be true, it remains likely that the formulations are post-paschal. Cf. B. Schaller, 'Die Sprüche über Ehescheidung und Wiederheirat in der synoptischen Ueberlieferung', *Der Ruf Jesu and die Antwort der Gemeinde* (J. Jeremias Festschrift), ed. E. Lohse, C. Burchard and B. Schaller; Göttingen: Vandenhoeck & Ruprecht 1970, 226–46. On the exceptive clauses in Matt. 19.9; 5.32 see also J. Bonsirven, 'Nisi fornicationis causa', *RSR* 35, 1948, 442–64; A. Vaccari, 'La clausola sul divorzio in Matteo 5.32; 19.9', *RivB* 3, 1955, 97–119; H. Baltensweiler, 'Die Ehebruchsklausel bei Matthäus', *ThZ* 15, 1959, 340–56. Index of originality: Though polygamy was attacked in Judaism

(CD 4.20f.; cf. Josephus, *Antiquitates* 17.14), divorce was generally acknowledged in accord with the Torah.

39. See J. Jeremias, '*paradeisos*', *TWNT* V, 763–71, pp. 764f.; *TDNT* V, 765–73, p. 767.

40. Ibid.

41. Ibid.

42. D. Daube, 'Concessions to Sinfulness in Jewish Law', *JJS* 10, 1959, 1–13.

43. Daube, art. cit., 9f. The *prozbul* was a legal device which Hillel I invented to circumvent the remission of debt on the sabbatical year (cf. Deut. 15.1). See Billerbeck I, 717f.

44. As Catchpole observes, art. cit., 126: 'The tactics of Jesus' argument have the effect of achieving a striking identification between his questioners and the law of Deuteronomy xxiv. 1: "What did Jesus command *you*? . . . With a view to *your* hardness of heart Moses wrote this commandment *for you*." They are firmly associated with that commandment which Jesus abrogates.' In short, Jesus is represented as fully conscious of the gap between his interlocutors and the newness both of his own eschatological word and of those who could and would receive it as authoritative.

45. T. W. Manson, *The Teaching of Jesus* (see above, ch. VI n. 36).

46. D. Daube, 'Public Retort and Private Explanation in the Gospels', *The New Testament and Rabbinic Judaism*, London: Athlone Press 1956, 141–50.

47. On the rendering of this text, see P. Joüon, *L'Évangile de Notre-Seigneur Jésus-Christ. Traduction et commentaire du texte original grec compte tenu du substrat sémitique*, Paris: Beauchesne 1930, 42: '*Pylē* in the NT is a monumental gate, ordinarily a city gate. But here another sense, equally classic and usual, is appropriate; namely, that of pass, defile, e.g., in *Pylai tēs Kilikias*, "The Gates [Mountain passes] of Cilicia." The Aramaic substratum is doubtless *tar'ā'* (Heb. *šā'ar*) . . .' The original sense was not 'Enter the narrow gate' but 'Travel by the narrow pass.' Greek Matthew understood *pylē* as gate; we infer this from the verb *eiserchomai* (go in, enter) by which he has assimilated the logion to the 'entrance sayings' (Matt. 5.20; 7.2; 19.17; 23.13; Mark 9.43, 45, 47; 10.15, 23–25; John 3.5; 10.9). The 'entry' motif disappears once 'pass' is restored to the saying. Note that in the Matthean text, because of the change of image, the original 'few' are no longer those who take the narrow pass and its hard road; they have become the 'few' that arrive at the gate that opens into life. In Jesus' original imagery there is no indication whether the saved are many or few. The warning that few take the hard road is wholly parenetic and unspeculative.

48. See J. Jeremias, *Gleichnisse*, 199; ET, *Parables*, 200f.

49. On the literary criticism of the antitheses see J. Dupont, *Les Béatitudes* (see above, ch. III n. 57), who rightly considers only the antithesis on divorce (Matt. 5.31f.) to be a redactional formulation. The frequently proposed view that the last two antitheses are also late formulations is refuted by J. Jeremias, *Verkündigung*, 240f.; ET, *NT Theology*, 251–3.

50. See P. Joüon, 'Notes philologiques sur les Évangiles', *RSR* 17, 1927, 537–40, p. 540. *Krisis* is not 'court' but 'verdict', i.e., condemnation (in context, to death).

51. See P. Joüon, *L'Évangile*, 31: 'Mais tu pourras ne pas aimer ton ennemi': 'According to Hebrew usage (*śānē'*) 'to hate' can be a simplifying expression for 'not to love' (cf. Joüon, *Grammaire de l'hébreu biblique* 113 1).' Jeremias, *Verkündigung*, 206 n. 44; ET, *NT Theology*, 213 n. 3, adds: ' . . . the Aramaic imperfect which

underlies the two Greek futures *agapēseis-misēseis* only rarely has a future significance; usually this significance is virtual. In *agapēseis* the virtual nuance is jussive ("you shall"), in *misēseis* it is permissive ("you need not"). The translation therefore must be, "You shall love your compatriot (Lev. 19.18) (but) you need not love your [personal] adversary." '

52. The antithetic pattern of Matt. 5.21–48 supposes something which Jesus had and which the early community did not have: the authority to inaugurate a new economy of religion. Failure to appreciate how conscious this was in early Christianity is what vitiates the argument of M. Jack Suggs, 'The Antitheses as Redactional Products', *Jesus Christus in Historie und Theologie* (H. Conzelmann Festschrift), ed. G. Strecker; Tübingen: Mohr 1975, 433–44.

53. See R. Bultmann, *Jesus Christ and Mythology* (see above, ch. II n. 99), 43.

54. For the disposition of the text see C. F. Burney, *The Poetry of our Lord*, Oxford: Clarendon Press 1925, 170f.

55. P. S. Minear, *Commands of Christ*, Nashville/New York: Abingdon 1972, 102f.

56. Cf. op. cit., 61f., 96.

57. Op. cit., 53.

58. Op. cit., 61.

59. W. Eichrodt, *Man in the Old Testament*, tr. K. and R. Gregor Smith; SBT 4, 1951, 48. Among the Isaian texts on adhesion to God by faith and love alone, see Isa. 7.9b; 28.16; 30.15a.

60. See below, pp. 162–6; 235–9.

61. On the linguistic evidence relating to the Aramaic substratum of Matt. 5.17, see J. Jeremias, *Verkündigung*, 86–89; ET, *NT Theology*, 82–85.

62. W. G. Kümmel, "Das Gesetz und die Propheten gehen bis Johannes" – Lukas 16,16 im Zusammenhang der heilsgeschichtlichen Theologie der Lukasschriften', *Verborum Veritas* (see above, ch. III n. 60) 89–102, pp. 94–8.

63. Two elements of the text can be shown with probability to be authentic: the command of Mark 10.21 (discontinuity: cf. Matt. 19.21a; originality: the association of dispossession of one's goods with a personal call to discipleship; multiple and multiform attestation: pattern 'go ... sell ... give ... follow' [cf. P. S. Minear, op. cit., 102f.]) and the rebuff of Mark 10.18 (discontinuity: cf. Matt. 19.17; antithetic parallelism of question and statement [cf. Mark 3.33f. par.; 8.12; 11.17; Matt. 7.3–5 par.; 12.27f. par.; Luke 12.51; 22.35] designed to pull the interlocutor up short [cf. Mark 8.12; 11.17; Matt. 12.27f. par.; Luke 12.51]).

64. For a survey of opinion in the critical period, see H. Merkel, 'Markus 7,15 – das Jesuswort über die innere Verunreinigung', *ZRG* 20, 1968, 340–63.

65. See the texts cited above which protest the sealing off of ritual observances from the moral order. The most exact parallel is Matt. 23.25f. par. See C. F. Burney, *The Aramaic Origin of the Fourth Gospel*, Oxford: Clarendon Press, 1922, 8 on the history of the transmission of v. 26. Originally Jesus said simply: 'That which is within, purify' (*dibᵉgawwā' zakkôn*).

66. The term is taken from H. Hübner, *Das Gesetz in der synoptischen Tradition. Studien zur These einer progressiven Qumranisierung und Judaisierung innerhalb der synoptischen Tradition*, Witten: Luther-Verlag 1973, 238.

67. H. Merkel, 'Markus 7,15 ...', urges that Jesus sharply broke with the ritual law and that this has been softened and obscured in the synoptic tradition.

Käsemann has presented this case in several essays, e.g., 'Begründet der neutestamentliche Kanon die Einheit der Kirche?' *Exegetische Versuche und Besinnungen* I (see above. ch. II n. 117), 214–23, p. 219; ET, 'The Canon of the New Testament and the Unity of the Church', *Essays on New Testament Themes*, 95–107, p. 101f. L. Goppelt, *Jesu Wirken* (see above, ch. II n. 117), 143f., offers a variation on the theme of Jesus the secularizer. The underlying rationale of his repudiation of the ritual law was the intention of universal sacralization (in eschatological fulfilment of texts such as Zech. 14.21). H. Hübner, *Gesetz*, has attempted to refine the excessive thesis of E. Stauffer, *Jesus, Gestalt und Geschichte*, Bern: Francke 1957; ET, *Jesus and his Story*, London: SCM Press, and New York: Knopf 1960; and *Die Botschaft Jesu, damals und heute*, Bern/München: Francke 1959, to the effect that the synoptic tradition represented a Qumranizing conservatism meant to domesticate Jesus, transforming him from a rejector into a radicalizing affirmer of the Torah. Of these works Hübner's is most detailed on the issue in question. To the extent that such texts as Matt. 5.18; 23.2f. have very slight claim to historicity, one might even speak of a certain re-tora-izing in the Matthean tradition. On the other hand, though Hübner's critique not only of Stauffer but of the secondary literature in general is balanced and nuanced, his treatment of two key texts is not entirely satisfying: Matt. 5.17, in which the case for historicity is much too quickly dismissed, and Mark 7.15 (also vv. 18, 20) in which the ambiguity of *koinōsai* ('to defile') is left unexplored and the conclusion too quickly drawn that Mark has caught what was at least implicitly the intention of the historical Jesus. (It seems far more likely to me that Mark's is an interpretative revision of tradition in a situation [Gentile Christianity] which Jesus himself never envisaged.)

68. See H. Hübner, *Gesetz*, 145–55.

69. Johanan ben Zakkai said to his disciples apropos of Num. 19, 'By your life, it is not the corpse that pollutes or water that purifies but it is an ordinance of the king of kings' (Pesiqta de Rab Kahana, 40b). This meant, I take it, that a corpse did not pollute of itself, by some intrinsic quality, but exclusively by reason of divine ordinance.

70. The antiquity of this logion is certain on the basis of linguistic considerations and its historicity gains thereby in probability. See E. Lohse, 'Jesu Worte über den Sabbat', *Judentum-Urchristentum-Kirche* (J. Jeremias Festschrift), ed. W. Eltester; BZAW 26, ²1964, 79–89, p. 87.

71. E. Lohse, 'Jesu Worte . . .', 79–81.

72. See J. Jeremias, *Verkündigung*, 239–43; ET, *NT Theology*, 250–55.

73. Op. cit., 43–5; ET, 35–7.

74. Op. cit., 65f.: ET, 59f.

75. G. Dalman, *Worte* (see n. 1 above), 232; ET, *Words*, 283.

76. G. Dalman, ibid.

77. Among recent studies, see J. Jervell, 'Die offenbarte und die verborgene Tora. Zur Vorstellung über die neue Tora im Rabbinismus', *StTh* 25, 1971, 90–108, who traces a long dispute among the rabbis as to whether the whole Torah was revealed on Sinai or part of it was reserved in heaven for revelation in the time of the Messiah. The view that the revelation on Sinai was complete and total eventually won out. P. Schäfer, 'Die Torah der messianischen Zeit', *ZNW* 65, 1974, 27–42, offers a minimalist interpretation of 'new torah' passages.

78. J. Dupont, *Les béatitudes I* (see above, ch. III n. 57), 141f., aptly remarks of Matt. 5.17, 'Taking the verse in itself, the contrast of the verbs 'destroy' and

'accomplish' would more naturally lead one to understand the second verb in the sense of 'to bring to its completion, to its full measure, to its perfection'. J. Jeremias, *Verkündigung*, 86–9; ET, *NT Theology*, 82–5, has shown that *plērōsai* here is an eschatological technical term reflecting a well attested New Testament theme and thought-form, i.e., that of the appointed measure. He has further shown that Jewish-Christian exegesis and the saying cited in b. Shab. 116b support this sense (proposing, indeed, that the latter text was the original Aramaic citation underlying Matt. 5.17).

79. Cf. M. Hengel, *Nachfolge* (see above, ch. III n. 1), 9–17.

80. Cf. *synerchesthai* in Acts 9.39; 10.23, 45; 11.12; 21.16; 25.17.

81. See M. Hengel, *Nachfolge*, 55–67.

82. Discontinuity: (*a*) That 'the twelve' existed already in the period of Jesus' public career is the uniquely plausible explanation of the tradition including Judas in this group; (*b*) the primitive community furnishes a context for the preferential status of the twelve but not for the passing over without mention of the interim between the career of Jesus and the coming of the reign of God (cf. such eschatological texts as Mark 9.1 parr.; 14.25 par., 28 par., and wherever the tribulation inaugurated by the death of Jesus is conceived as a very brief interval before the coming of the reign of God). Multiple attestation: triple tradition (Mark 3.13–19 parr.; 6.7–13 parr.); logia tradition (Matt. 19.38 par.); single traditions (Luke 8.1–3; John 6.67–71); Paul and pre-Pauline tradition (I Cor. 15.5). Multiform attestation: story, logion, faith-formula. That the *choice* of the twelve supposed an earlier, broader, fluctuating discipleship is variously supposed by the synoptists and John (Mark 3.13; Luke 10; John 6.66). In Luke 'the disciples' are all who hear and obey, see P. S. Minear, 'Jesus' Audiences, according to Luke', *NovT* 16, 1974, 81–109.

83. 1QM 1.2 by its reference to the sons of Levi (a half tribe), Judah, and Benjamin confirms the tradition distinguishing the two and a half tribes of the south and the lost nine and a half tribes of the north (II Bar. 62.5; 77.19; 78.1; II (4) Ezra 13.40 ['ten tribes', in Syr. 'nine and a half']; Asc. Isa. 3.2).

84. See Ezek. 47.13–48.29. Cf. Josephus, *Antiquitates* 11.133.

85. On condition that Judas Iscariot has his surname from *'iš qᵉrîyyôt = 'o apo Karyōtou* (John 6.71, variant reading), 'a man from Kerioth'; cf. Josh. 15.25.

86. On the make-up of the twelve, cf. H. Schürmann, 'Die Symbolhandlungen Jesu als eschatologische Erfüllungszeichen. Eine Rückfrage nach dem irdischen Jesus', in *Das Geheimnis Jesu. Versuche zur Jesusfrage*, Leipzig: St Benno 1972, 74–110, esp. pp. 88f. (This essay appeared under a slightly different title and in slightly shorter form in *BuL* 11, 1970, 29–41; 73–78; see esp. p. 37.) K. H. Rengstorf, '*mathētēs*', *TWNT* IV, 417–65, pp. 455.; *TDNT* IV, 415–60, p. 452, adds that among the twelve we find Greek as well as Semitic names. The twelve are thus 'a microcosm of the Judaism of the time'.

87. P. Gaechter, *Das Matthäus Evangelium. Ein Kommentar*, Innsbruck/Wien/München: Tyrolia 1963, 151, aptly comments, however, that in drawing on the image of Jeremiah Jesus had modified its sense. Cf. the parallel image of the harvesters in Matt. 9.37f. par.

88. Among recent discussions see esp. G. Theissen, *Urchristliche Wundergeschichten. Ein Beitrag zur formgeschichtlichen Erforschung der synoptischen Evangelien*, Gütersloh: Mohn 1974, 274–82; also, K. Kertelge, 'Die Überlieferung der Wunder Jesu und die Frage nach dem historischen Jesus', *Rückfrage nach Jesus. Zur Methodik und*

Bedeutung der Frage nach dem historischen Jesus, ed. K. Kertelge; Freiburg/Wien: Herder 1974, 174–93, esp. 179f.

89. See T. W. Manson's brilliant analysis of the meaning of the expression 'finger of God' (Luke 11.20) and its originality *vis-à-vis* 'spirit of God' (Matt. 12.28) in *Teaching* (see above, ch. VI n. 36) 82f. The submerged reference to scripture (here to Ex. 8.15, EVV 8.19) is typical of Jesus.

90. On the Old Testament conception of Satan and its development, see G. von Rad, *'diabolos'*, *TWNT* II, 71–4; *TDNT* II, 73–5; on views in Judaism and the New Testament, W. Foerster, *'diabolos'*, *TWNT* II, 74–80; *TDNT* II, 75–81. On Jesus' own view of the unity of evil under Satan, see J. Jeremias, *Verkündigung*, 96f.; ET, *NT Theology*, 93f.

91. See O. Bauernfeind, *Die Worte der Dämonen im Markusevangelium*, Stuttgart: Kohlhammer 1927; J. M. Robinson, *The Problem of History in Mark*, SBT 21, 1957.

92. See below, pp. 240f.

93. That the first genitive in the phrase 'the lost sheep of the house of Israel' (Matt. 10.6; cf. 15.24) is epexegetical ('the lost sheep that are the house of Israel') is clear from three data: The phrase is an allusion to Jer. 50.6, 'My people has become a flock of lost sheep . . .'; Matt. 9.36 describes the crowds, clearly enough representative of Israel, as 'harassed and helpless, like sheep without a shepherd'; Matt. 10.5 explicitly contrasts Gentiles and Samaritans with 'the lost sheep of the house of Israel'. The addressees of the proclamation and the beneficiaries of the miracles are accordingly Israel as such.

94. Matt. 10.8c goes with the following verses. Verses 8–10 should read:

> Cure the sick,
> raise the dead,
> cleanse lepers,
> drive out demons.
>
> You received without payment,
>   give without payment.
> Take as payment neither gold nor silver
>   nor copper change for your belts
> nor knapsack
>   nor a second tunic
> nor sandals nor staff.
>   'The labourer', however, 'deserves his food'.

This translation makes the words 'You received without payment, give without payment' completely intelligible, for it provides them with a context. It likewise makes intelligible in context the choice of the word 'food' (*trophē*) in rendering the proverb on the workman in v. 10d. Furthermore, it circumvents an oddity which would otherwise be unavoidable; namely, the twelve would be sent out on their mission barefoot. (In the hypothesis offered here they are shod, but prohibited from accepting an extra pair of sandals as recompense for their wonder-working. The confusion in the sources – contrast Luke 22.35 with Mark 6.9 – arose from failure to grasp the originally intended sense of *ktasthai*, cf. Matt. 10.9). The expression 'two tunics' will accordingly have been intended to make reference to a second tunic as 'payment'. This reading of the text (which hinges on understanding *ktasthai* in v. 9b to mean 'accept as payment, earn' [cf. A. Schlatter, *Matthäus*,

331]) is more intelligible in detail than the usual translation and recovers an original form of the theme 'the reign of God as pure gift'.

95. G. Friedrich, *'prophētēs* (NT)', *TWNT* VI, 829–58, p. 848; *TDNT* VI, 828–61, p. 847, with references to primary and secondary texts.

96. The historicity of the Baptist's question is illuminated by defining the meaning of the text. The text is meant to express the beginning of the Baptist's faith, not the beginning of doubt. (The latter view would hinge on Matt. 3.14f., but this is a redactional text.) But if this is so, the Baptist's question crosses the grain of the tendency to make John a believer in Jesus from the start (Matt. 3.14f.; John 1.26–36).

97. Isa. 26.19 refers to the raising of the dead; but as J. Jeremias, *Verkündigung*, 109 n. 29; ET, *NT Theology*, 104 n. 1, notes: '... enumeration by means of a list, which characterizes the three Isaiah texts cited above [35.5–7; 29.18f.; 61.1f.], does not appear in this passage.'

98. See the careful discussion (with references to previous studies) of K. Kertelge, 'Die Überlieferung der Wunder ...' (see n. 88 above), esp. 183–9.

99. See J. Jeremias, *Verkündigung*, 95 n. 31; ET, *NT Theology*, 91 n. 2.

100. The historicity of Luke 13.32 is commended by the combination of its comparability with other synoptic 'three days' texts and its singularity by relation to them. On both points, see J. Jeremias, 'Die Drei-Tage-Worte der Evangelien', *Tradition und Glaube. Das frühe Christentum in seiner Umwelt* (K. G. Kuhn Festschrift), ed. G. Jeremias, H.-W. Kuhn and H. Stegemann; Göttingen: Vandenhoeck & Ruprecht 1971, 221–9. The historicity of the woes on the towns of Galilee (Matt. 11.21–24 par.) is commended by the distinctive thematic connection of 'wonders' with 'imminence of eschaton', and of the place-names with the rejection of Jesus. Moreover, the two-panel rhetorical schema is typical of Jesus (see T. W. Manson, *Teaching*, 55).

101. See L. Sabourin, ' "Miracles" hellénistiques et rabbiniques', *BTB* 2, 1972, 284–302.

102. On the early rabbinic interpretation of Ex. 14.15 and its connection with the accreditation of apocalyptic prophets and zealot leaders, see M. Hengel, *Nachfolge* (see above, ch. III n. 1), 24–6.

103. See M. Hengel, ibid.

104. Mark 2.15 fits so awkwardly with what follows that it is more likely borrowed from tradition than devised by the redactor. J. Jeremias, *Gleichnisse*, 225 n. 1; ET, *Parables*, 227 n. 92, may be correct in conjecturing that it originally introduced an independent story and was set in its present place on the basis of a catchword (*telōnēs*, v. 16). If so, the original sense of 2.15 indicates Jesus' reception of 'many publicans and sinners' in his own house.

105. The point of the question, as well as its tone, is definable on the basis of socio-religious context, i.e., the continuum which made the master and his disciples somehow responsible for one another. J. Jeremias, *Gleichnisse*, 132; ET, *Parables*, 132, comments: 'When the Pharisees and scribes asked why Jesus accepted such people as table companions, they were not expressing surprise but disapproval; they were implying that he was an irreligious man, and warning his followers not to associate with him'. In *Verkündigung*, 119f.; ET, *NT Theology*, 118, Jeremias draws up a 'scale of rejection' from synoptic data: 'incomprehension (Luke 15.29f.); dismay (Luke 15.2; 19.7; Matt. 20.11); abuse (Matt. 11.19 par. Luke 7.34); charge of blasphemy (Mark 2.7); invitation to the disciples to part

company with this corruptor (Mark 2.16).' With the exception of the charge of blasphemy, every text adduced in this scale goes back to the issue of Jesus' scandalous dining with sinners!

106. J. Jeremias, *Abendmahlsworte*, 224; ET, *Eucharistic Words*, 232.

107. See O. Böcher, *Dämonenfurcht und Dämonenabwehr. Ein Beitrag zur Vorgeschichte der christlichen Taufe*, Stuttgart: Kohlhammer 1970, 144f.

108. J. Jeremias, *Verkündigung*, 113; ET, *NT Theology*, 111.

109. In attempting to recover the socio-religious situation in Palestine of the time of Jesus we should neither identify notorious sinners (the '*amartōloi* of Mark 2.15 parr., 16 parr., 17 parr., etc.) with the ordinary run of men nor disregard the continuity which the religious *élite* considered to exist between them (cf. '*oi loipoi tōn anthrōpōn* whom the Pharisee of Luke 18.11 depreciates and condemns; cf. John 7.49).

110. The precise contrast intended here is not between justification as acquittal (Ex. 23.7; Nahum 1.3) and as transformation (Rom. 4.5), but between the supposition that man's repentance is prior to God's acquittal (Ex. 23.7; Nahum 1.3) and the affirmation of the priority of God's (transformative) acquittal (Rom. 4.5).

111. See J. Jeremias, *Gleichnisse*, 124–35; ET, *Parables*, 124–36.

112. *Egeneto* in the clause *to sabbaton dia ton anthrōpon egeneto* (Mark 2.27) is circumlocutory for the divine act of creation; cf. *ginesthai* in Mark 4.11; 6.2; Matt. 11.21 (bis), 23 (bis), Luke 4.25; 11.30; 15.10; 19.9.

113. Contrast the externally similar rabbinic saying of the second century: 'The sabbath is delivered to you, you are not delivered to the sabbath', Mek. Ex. on 31.13f. (109b; cf. Billerbeck II, 5) which, as E. Lohse, 'Jesu Worte . . .' (see n. 70 above), 85, remarks, was meant to relax the law of the sabbath in emergency situations in which life was in danger.

114. See below, pp. 235–9.

115. For the first point see Manson, *Teaching*, 133 n. 1; for the second, see Jeremias *Gleichnisse* 146; ET, *Parables*, 147.

116. *Gleichnisse*, 148; ET, *Parables*, 149.

117. In Luke 15.7 *chara* is the joy of finding what had been lost; *en tō ouranō* is a circumlocution for God; *estai* is an eschatological future referring to the judgment; *metanoounti*, reflecting an atemporal Aramaic participle, has a past sense here. Luke 15.10 should be rendered accordingly.

118. In Matt. 21.31 *proagousin* reflects an atemporal Aramaic participle which would have a future sense here. The occasion for entry whether into 'darkness' or into the reign of God is the judgment (cf. the three judgment parables of Matt. 25). The Aramaic substratum ('af'el participle of *qᵉdam*) would have the sense of exclusive preference rather than that of mere precedence. For attestation of this sense, see J. Jeremias, *Gleichnisse*, 126 n. 2; ET, *Parables*, 125 n. 48.

119. See J. Jeremias, 'Die älteste Schicht der Menschensohn-Logien', *ZNW* 58, 1967, 159–72, p. 167. Contrast E. Käsemann, 'Die Anfänge christlicher Theologie', *ZTK* 57, 1690, 162–85, reprinted in *Exegetische Versuche und Besinnungen* II (see above, ch. III n. 71), ²1965, 83–104, see 96; ET, 'The Beginnings of Christian Theology', *New Testament Questions of Today*, 82–107, p. 97, who combined Bultmann's views on *ēlthon* (see above, ch. VI n. 35) with Bultmann's supposition (*Synoptische Tradition*, 135; ET, *Synoptic Tradition*, 127f.) that early Christian prophets produced dominical sayings. J. A. Bühner, 'Zur Form, Tradition und Bedeutung der *ēlthon*-Sprüche', *Das Institutum Judaicum der Universität Tübingen*

1971/72, 45–68, defines the *Sitz im Leben* of *ēlthon* sayings as the arrival and self-presentation of the herald. W. Grimm, *Weil ich dich liebe. Die Verkündigung Jesu und Deuterojesaja*, Frankfurt: P. Lang; Bern: H. Lang 1976, 85f., argues that the point of departure of the *ēlthon*-sayings of the gospels was Isa. 61.1. See also E. Arens, *The ELTHON-Sayings in the Synoptic Tradition. A Historical-Critical Investigation*, Göttingen: Vandenhoeck & Ruprecht 1976.

120. E. Lohmeyer, 'Das Abendmahl in der Urgemeinde', *JBL* 56, 1937, 217–52, pp. 221–8.

121. J. Jeremias, *Abendmahlsworte*, 196–9; ET, *Eucharistic Words*, 204–7.

122. 'The Son of Man' is secondary here. See J. Jeremias, 'Die älteste Schicht . . .', 166.

123. Matthew combines 'the law and the prophets' four times (5.17; 7.12; 11.13; 22.40). In one of these instances (11.13) the phrase is paralleled in Luke (16.16). In two of the other three instances (Matt. 7.12 and 22.40) Luke offers parallel texts without the law and prophets formula. Though Luke 16.16 attests the phrase for the tradition independently of Matthew, it may well be (especially if b.Shab. 116b is relevant to the question) that *ē tous prophetas* in Matt. 5.17 is redactional, the addition serving to make explicit that it is Israel's whole heritage of revelation which Jesus brings to its appointed fulfilment.

124. H. Hübner, *Gesetz* (n. 66 above), 32, argues on the basis of the parallel formulation in Matt. 10.34 (contrast Luke 12.51) that *mē nomisēte 'oti ēlthon . . . ouk ēlthon . . . alla* derives from the Matthean redaction. But *ouk ēlthon . . . alla* is attested by the triple tradition (Mark 2.17 parr.; cf. Mark 10.45 par.). That *plēroun* 'is one of the favourite concepts of the evangelist' (Hübner, *Gesetz*, 33) is irrelevant, for in Matt. 5.17 the sense of *plēroun* is determined by antithetical *katalysai*. The relevant observation is that *plēroun* in the sense of Matt. 5.17 has one Matthean (23.32) and several non-Matthean parallels (e.g. Mark 1.15; Luke 21.24; cf. Rev 6.11; also *anaplēroun* in I Thess. 2.16 and *antanaplēroun* in Col. 1.24 as well as *plēroma* in Rom. 11.12,25; Gal. 4.4; Eph. 1.10). Positively, the saying correlates with the substance of the tradition about Jesus and the law. Having rejected the *halaka* wholesale and dared to revise the written law of Moses, he was certainly liable to attack as an antinomian. Had he 'despised the word of the Lord' (b.Sanh. 99a Bar.; Billerbeck I, 805)? The saying meets the demand for an answer and in terms appropriate to debate with the learned.

125. The particular situation in which the saying was spoken is not recoverable, but the numerous critiques of Jesus offer a wide range of possible contexts, e.g., reaction to his teaching on the dismissal of one's wife, to table fellowship with sinners, to his indifference to sabbath *halaka* and the like.

126. See above, p. 152.

127. See below, pp. 202–4.

128. See J. Jeremias, *Verheissung* (see above, ch. II n. 113), 23; ET, *Promise*, 26f. The two series (*ēlthon/'ātêt* and *apestalēn/'ištaddarît*) are parallel, so allowing transitions from the one to the other formula (though I doubt whether Luke 19.10 is simply a variant form of Matt. 15.24). Like the Johannine *egō eimi* ('I am'), these formulas become favourites in the apocryphal literature of the second and third centuries (Gospel of the Ebionites, of the Egyptians, of Philip, of Thomas, etc.).

129. This word's glaring discontinuity with the universalist mission of the church from pre-Pauline times (Acts 11.19f.) through the mid-forties, when the

Christian community of Antioch launched its mission (Acts 13.1–3), is an index to historicity.

130. If *emartyroun autō* (Aram.: *'ăshadûn 'ălôhî*) in Luke 4.22 means 'they bore witness against him' (cf. Mark 6.11; Luke 9.5; Mark 1.44 parr.), the ground and motive of this would be Jesus' deliberate omission of the theme of vengeance on the Gentiles from the text of Isa. 61.2. In Matt. 11.5f. par. the words which immediately follow Jesus' citation of salvation images from Isa. 29, 35, and 61 – namely, 'And happy the man who finds in me no stumbling block!' – refer in some way to the blockage (*skandalizesthai*) caused by disparity between standard eschatological expectations and the phenomenon of Jesus' career; but they may also have precise reference to the exclusion of 'vengeance on the Gentiles', a theme expressed in each of the Isaian texts Jesus called on (cf. Isa. 29.20; 35.4; 61.2). On both Luke 4.22 and Matt. 11.5f. par., see J. Jeremias, *Verheissung*, 38f.; ET, *Promise*, 44–6.

131. See J. Jeremias, *Verheissung*; ET, *Promise*.

132. The original nexus of entry and cleansing is variously indicated by the synoptists. Matthew has retained the sequence of the two pericopes intact. Mark, though he has separated them, has kept the temple as the goal of the entry (11.11). Luke, too, has kept the nexus intact despite inserting vv. 39–44 between entry (Luke 19.28–38) and cleansing (Luke 19.45f.). The entry terminated at the temple (Luke 19.45).

133. In Mark 4.11 *ginetai en parabolais* stands in antithetical parallelism to *mystērion dedotai*. But this structural requisite is met only if *parabolai* are not 'parables' but 'riddles': To outsiders 'all things (relating to Jesus) are (imparted) in riddles'. Both *dedotai* and *ginetai* are circumlocutions for divine revelation. See J. Jeremias, *Gleichnisse*, 12–14; ET, *Parables*, 16f.

134. See C. H. Dodd, *Historical Tradition* (see above, ch. VI n. 23), 213–16.

135. A precise indication of how Jesus conceived this situation is provided by the saying of Mark 10.30 (cf. Luke 18.30); for, as P. Joüon, *RSR* 18, 1928, 351 (*L'Évangile*, n. 47 above, 241f.) pointed out, *en tō kairō toutō* does not mean merely 'maintenant, en ce temps-ci', but rather 'déjà', and so 'dès ce temps-ci'. Thus, the distinction between 'this age' which is now, and 'the age to come' or 'the reign of God' is retained; but in Jesus, his disciples, his followers, and the beneficiaries of his cures and exorcisms, the blessings of the age to come or the reign of God are present by anticipation. This presence, the 'realized eschatology' which is the hall-mark of Jesus' career, has its distinctive force and sense from its leaving still intact the difference between now and the coming reign.

Chapter VIII The Secret of the Reign of God

1. E. Troeltsch, 'Was heisst "Wesen des Christentums"?' [1903], *Gesammelte Schriften. II. Zur religiösen Lage, Religionsphilosophie und Ethik*, Tübingen: Mohr 1922, 386–451, p. 397. Cf. idem, 'Über historische und dogmatische Methode in der Theologie' [1898], op. cit., 729–53, pp. 734f.

2. The audience of esoteric teaching is 'disciples', who need neither be limited to the twelve nor include all the twelve. Mark depicts the audience of the instruction following the messianic confession and first prediction of the passion as a wider circle of followers than the twelve. See P. S. Minear, 'Audience Criticism

and Markan Ecclesiology', *Neues Testament und Geschichte* (see above, ch. III n. 45), 79–89, pp. 82, 84f. Mark presents 'a cohesive and committed community' (art. cit., 89 n. 18) which follows Jesus and shares in at least some (not all, cf. 4.34; 8.27–33 versus 8.34ff.) of Jesus' esoteric instructions; cf. Luke 9.23. This may well reflect the historical career of Jesus in some way; the particulars, however, have not been worked out on the historical level.

    3. L. Goppelt, *Jesu Wirken* (see above, ch. II n. 117), 219.

    4. I use 'performative' and 'performatively' not in the sense given these words by linguistic analysis but simply with reference to performance which has not yet been explicitly objectified. 'Performatively messianic' accordingly refers to words and acts merely as open to messianic interpretation, not as actually so interpreted. To explain the church's proclamation by invoking the premise of Jesus' performatively messianic career is to leave out of account (*a*) the data establishing that the proclamation had in fact been motivated by this premise and (*b*) if so, the reason why.

    5. H. Conzelmann, 'Jesus Christus', *RGG*³ 3.619–653, col. 621; ET, *Jesus*, tr. J. R. Lord; Philadelphia: Fortress 1973,10.

    6. A. Schweitzer, *Von Reimarus*, 342; ET, *The Quest* (see ch. II n. 55), 345.

    7. N. A. Dahl, 'Der gekreuzigte Messias', *Der historische Jesus und der kerygmatische Christus. Beiträge zum Christusverständnis in Forschung und Verkündigung*, ed. H. Ristow, K. Matthiae; Berlin: Evangelische Verlagsanstalt 1960, 149–69, p. 161; ET, 'The Crucified Messiah', in N. A. Dahl, *The Crucified Messiah and Other Essays*, Minneapolis: Augsburg 1974, 10–36, pp. 25f.

    8. It is true that so long as we are unable to deal cogently with the Easter experience as such, a contrary dependence might be posited with at least some plausibility. H. Schürmann, 'Das Weiterleben der Sache Jesu ...' (see ch. III n. 51) 12, proposes: 'If there had not been given the kind of pre-paschal promise such as Luke 22.15–18 par. Mark 14.25 ... the appearances of the risen Jesus would hardly have been interpreted as his exaltation, much less as the beginning of the general resurrection of the dead.'

    9. This may seem ungrateful in view of the many worth-while works on the resurrection in recent years (see L. Goppelt, *Jesu Wirken*, 277f.). The point I wish to make is limited (but crucial with respect to any heuristic anticipation of the history of Jesus on the basis of the church's christology): Wrede and his followers have never shown that 'the Easter experience' could have done what they claim it must have done, nor have their opponents ever shown what the Easter experience could not have done. The unfulfilled condition of cogent argument either way is a firm historical grasp on the Easter experience. A cautious beginning has been made by A. Vögtle, 'Wie kam es zur Artikulierung des Osterglaubens?' *BuL* 14, 1973, 231–44; 15, 1974, 16–27. For background, see the discussion in *TQ* 153, 1973, 201–83 by R. Pesch and his commentators, W. Kasper, K. H. Schelkle, P. Stuhlmacher, and M. Hengel.

    10. G. Baumbach, *Jesus von Nazareth im Lichte der jüdischen Gruppenbildung*, Berlin: Evangelische Verlagsanstalt 1971, 24, gives the exact specification. To judge from Roman practice as Josephus (*Bellum Judaicum* 2) describes it, Jesus was executed as a 'Zealot leader – more exactly, as a Sicarian revolutionary'. On the historicity of 'The King of the Jews', see E. Dinkler, 'Petrusbekenntnis und Satanswort. Das Problem der Messianität Jesu', *Zeit und Geschichte* (see above, ch. III n. 30), 127–53, pp. 147f.; ET, 'Peter's Confession and the "Satan" Saying: The

Problem of Jesus' Messiahship', *The Future of our Religious Past*, ed. J. M. Robinson, tr. C. E. Carlston and R. P. Scharlemann, London: SCM Press, and New York: Harper & Row 1971, 169–202, pp. 194–6, with references to further literature.

11. H. Lietzmann, 'Der Prozess Jesu', *SBBerlin*, 1931, 313–22; idem, 'Bemerkungen zum Prozess Jesu', *ZNW* 30, 1931, 211–15; 31, 1932, 78–84. For a brief point-by-point reconsideration of Lietzmann's arguments, see J. Blinzler, *Der Prozess Jesu*, Regensburg: Pustet [4]1969, Exkurs VIII, 'Die Geschichtlichkeit der Synedrialverhandlung', 174–83. Blinzler's work can also serve as a helpful index to the literature on the questions Lietzmann raised. The latter's most important single point, in any case, touched the competence of the Sanhedrin. On this see J. Jeremias, 'Zur Geschichtlichkeit des Verhörs Jesu vor dem hohen Rat', *ZNW* 43, 1950/51, 145–50; repr. in *Abba* (see ch. III n. 27) 139–44; A. N. Sherwin-White, *Roman Society and Roman Law in the New Testament*, Oxford: Clarendon 1963, chs. 2 and 3; idem, 'The Trial of Jesus', *Historicity and Chronology in the New Testament*, ed. D. Nineham; London: SPCK 1965, 97–116.

12. P. Winter, *On the Trial of Jesus*, Berlin: De Gruyter 1961; idem, 'The Marcan Account of Jesus' Trial by the Sanhedrin', *JTS* 14, 1963, 94–102; idem, 'The Trial of Jesus and the Competence of the Sanhedrin', *NTS* 10, 1964, 494–9. By contrast (and partly in explicit opposition to Winter's work) see A. N. Sherwin-White, op. cit. and art. cit. (n. 11 above) and D. R. Catchpole, *The Trial of Jesus: A Study in the Gospels and Jewish Historiography from 1770 to the Present Day*, Leiden: Brill 1971. So far as I can judge, the case for the historicity of the trial as presented by Mark has been fundamentally strengthened by the debate. I would not, however, regard historicity as beyond question. For a concise presentation of problems see E. Lohse, '*synedrion*', *TWNT* VII, 858–69, pp. 867f.; *TDNT* VII, 860–71, pp. 869f. Some of Lohse's points are *argumenta solubilia* (for example, the alleged lack of internal connectives in Mark 14.55–65 is open to revision in the light of II Sam. 7 and the Qumran attestation of its eschatological interpretation) and others are put too apodictically (for example, it ought not to be said that the question of the high priest, inasmuch as it makes divine sonship a messianic motif, is historically 'unthinkable';) see Lohse's own later caution, *TWNT* VIII, 363 n. 181; *TDNT* VIII, 362 n. 181. Nevertheless, problems do exist and Lohse, himself sceptical of the historicity of the Sanhedrin trial, has indicated most of them.

13. See W. C. van Unnik, 'Jesus the Christ', *NTS* 8, 1962, 101–16, p. 111; N. A. Dahl, 'Eschatologie und Geschichte im Licht der Qumrantexte', *Zeit und Geschichte*, 3–18, p. 9 n. 25; ET, 'Eschatology and History in the Light of the Dead Sea Scrolls', *The Future of our Religious Past*, 9–28, p. 16 n. 25, correlates (with a 'perhaps' [ET: 'probably'!]) the oracle of Nathan with, among other texts, Mark 14.57–62 and Matt. 16.16–18. See also B. Gärtner, *The Temple and the Community in Qumran and the New Testament. A Comparative Study in the Temple Symbolism of the Qumran Texts and the New Testament*, Cambridge: Cambridge University Press 1965, 30–42.

14. O. Betz, 'Die Frage nach dem messianischen Bewusstsein Jesu', *NovT* 6, 1963, 20–48; idem, *Was wissen wir von Jesus?*, Stuttgart: Kreuz, 1965; ET, *What Do We Know About Jesus?*, tr. M. Kohl; Philadelphia: Westminster, and London: SCM Press 1968, 83–112.

15. J. Blinzler, *Prozess*, 155 and n. 61, urges this view and deals with objections to it. Such seems to have been the sense of the strange mishnaic tradition (Sanh. 93b; Billerbeck I, 641) that the rabbis put Bar Kochba to death. His claim

to messiahship was false, for he could not back it up with supernatural powers of discernment. Cf. G. Dalman, *Worte* (see above ch. VII n. 1), 257; ET, *Words*, 313.

16. The probable garbling lies in attributing to Jesus the role of *katalyōn* or destroyer, as in the Gospel of Thomas, 71: 'Jesus says: 'I will dest(roy) (this) house and no one will be able to build it (again).' The 'Christian, perhaps Markan, addition' is the antithesis *cheiropoieton/acheiropoieton* ('built with hands/not built with hands') designed to make the symbolic nature of the new temple clear.

17. Favouring historicity: the riddle form; multiple and multiform attestation; 'unfulfilled' imminence: 'within' or 'after' three days made the saying problematic to the Christian community. See below on lack of attestation in the synoptic tradition of the word on Jesus' lips; also, on the artificial comment in John 2.21 referring 'temple' in the second limb of the saying to the body of Jesus. The 'three days' motif belonged to the original scheme of Jesus' own eschatology. See J. Jeremias, 'Die Drei-Tage-Worte . . .' (see above, ch. VII n. 100), esp. 225f., 228f.

18. The Old Testament and New Testament texts cited above establish this positive possibility; its non-necessity, however, emerges from various data. The issue surfaced in an ambiguous way apropos of Herod's rebuilding of the temple (see O. Betz, 'Die Frage . . .', p. 36 n. 1). Again, God bade 'the priest, the Teacher of Righteousness . . . to build him (God) the community . . .' (4QPs37 3.16; compare and contrast 1QH 6.25–27; 4QFlor 1–13). But neither the Teacher of Righteousness himself nor his community attributed messianic status to him.

19. The Johannine explanatory comment ('But he spoke of the temple of his body', John 2.21) should not be made to refer to both limbs of the saying ('Destroy this temple' and 'I will raise it') for that would excise all reference to the Jerusalem temple – surely not John's meaning. But if the comment refers only to the second limb, the sequence of the fulfilment is the reverse of the sequence of the prophecy: The new temple is raised before the old is destroyed. This unintended inconcinnity effectively closes down the likelihood that the verse is anything other than John's own *ad hoc* explanation.

20. See below, pp. 202–4 and pp. 246–9 on the disparity between Jesus' own eschatological scheme and that of the post-paschal church.

21. K. Beyer, *Semitische Syntax im Neuen Testament. I Satzlehre. Teil I*, Göttingen: Vandenhoeck & Ruprecht 1962, 252. Earlier, P. Joüon, *L'Évangile* (see above, ch. VII n. 47), 168f., 471. In Matt. 26.61 *dynamai katalysai* ('I am able to destroy') may be an effort to distance Jesus, even when cited by his adversaries, from any intention of destroying the temple. The Aramaic substratum of 'I shall destroy' is the personal pronoun (*'ănâ*) with the present participle (*šārē'* or *sātar*) which in any case would allow the modal nuance 'to be able' (Joüon, *L'Évangile*, 169).

22. On *lᵉ* underlying *dia* and *en* ('through' and 'within'), see Joüon, *L'Évangile*, 471; but it also underlies *dia* and *meta* in the sense of 'after'; see Jeremias, 'Die Drei-Tage-Worte . . .', 221f.

23. Jeremias, 'Die Drei-Tage-Worte . . .', 226.

24. See Billerbeck I, 647, 747.

25. On this terminology see J. Gray, 'The Day of Yahweh in Cultic Experience and Eschatological Prospect', *SvExA* 39, 1974, 5–37, p. 8. In seeking to identify the original constellation of elements in 'the day of Yahweh' as well as the changes it underwent with time, this seminal article brings to light just those ties binding the reign of God, its effective imposition in judgment, the restoration of nature and society, the remnant of Israel – all of the keenest interest in the present inquiry.

26. That the stone was interpreted in Palestinian Judaism as a copestone has been shown by J. Jeremias, '*Kephalē gōnias – Akrogōniaios*', *ZNW* 29, 1930, 264–80; idem, 'Eckstein – Schlussstein', *ZNW* 38, 1939, 154–7. The stone was not, however, conceived as a keystone; see R. J. McKelvie, *The New Temple. The Church in the New Testament*, Oxford: Oxford University Press 1969, 196–8. That the stone was interpreted as the Messiah is hinted at in the LXX; messianic interpretation is explicit in the targum; and a messianic sense may even have been originally intended: see A. Feuillet, 'Isaïe', *SDB* 4, 1949, 647–729, cf. col. 668 (following O. Procksch). On the spiritual temple evoked by Isa. 28.16 and its identification as the remnant of Israel, see Feuillet, loc. cit. and S. H. Hooke, *The Siege Perilous*, London: SPCK 1956, 235–46. Compare 1QS 5.5f.; 8.4–10; 9.3–6. B Gärtner, *The Temple*, 48, remarks: 'The "remnant" idea, when it occurs in the Old Testament and late Judaism, is connected with Zion and the appearance of the eschatological Messiah; it is thus understandable that the idea of the community as the holy, circumscribed group was readily combined with the symbolism of the temple.'

27. See A. Vögtle, 'Der Spruch vom Jonaszeichen', *Synoptische Studien* (A. Wikenhauser Festschrift), ed. J. Schmid and A. Vögtle; Munich: Zink 1954, 230–77; repr. A. Vögtle, *Das Evangelium* (see above, ch. III n. 66), 103–36 (esp. 108f., 113f., 122f.). Also J. Jeremias, '*Ionas*', *TWNT* III, 410–13; *TDNT* III, 406–10, p. 409: 'For Luke 11.30 . . . Jonah became a sign to the Ninevites, obviously as one who had been delivered from the belly of the fish, and . . . Jesus will be displayed to this generation as the One who is raised up from the dead'; p. 410: 'To those who ask for a sign Jesus replies with a riddle. The sign of Jonah will be renewed with the manifestation of the Son of Man returning from the dead.'

28. First, the literary structure indicates this. The text is a triad; each of the three parts has three lines consisting of a thematic statement elucidated by an antithetically structured distich. For the division into lines (together with a proposed reconstruction of the Aramaic substratum) see C. F. Burney, *The Poetry of Our Lord* (see above, ch. VII n. 54), 117. For the stylistic analysis of each part (theme followed by an explanatory, antithetically structured distich), see J. Jeremias, '*kleis*', *TWNT* III, 743–53; p. 749; *TDNT* III, 744–53, p. 749. Second, the text exhibits an idiom which, strange to the Greco-Roman world, is entirely at home in Aramaic and does so in all three parts: (v. 17) 'Blessed are you': *Tûbāk*; 'Bar-Jona': *Bar-Yônā*'; 'flesh and blood': *biśrā' ûd°mā*'; '(my) heavenly Father': *'abbā' d°biš°mayyā*'; (v. 18) 'Peter/rock' (Gr.: *petros/petra*): *kêpā'/kêpā*'; 'the gates of Hades': *tar°e š°'ol* (cf. Targ. Isa. 38.10); (v. 19) 'the reign of heaven': *malkûtā' diš°mayyā*'; 'heaven' (Gr.: *en tois ouranois*): *š°mayyā*'; 'bind/loose': *'āsar/š°rā*'. Bar-Jona in v. 17 is a name strictly Aramaic in origin. Of itself this does not guarantee the historicity or even the Aramaic origin of the verse. But see H. Schürmann, 'Die Sprache des Christus. Sprachliche Beobachtungen an den synoptischen Herrenworten', *BZ* 2, 1958 54–84; repr. *Traditionsgeschichtliche Untersuchungen* (see above, ch. II n. 71) 83–108, p. 94: 'The addressing of Peter as *Simon Bariōna* (Matt. 16.17) or *'o 'uios Iōannou* (John 1.42) or *Simōn Iōannou* is found only on the lips of Jesus. This will not be by chance, if one notices that the bare address *Simōn* was retained exclusively in words of Jesus.' The play on words in v. 18 (*Petros/ petra=kêpā'/ kêpā'*) is flawless only in Aramaic, strong evidence of Aramaic origin. 'Heaven' in v. 19 (*en tois ouranois*) is a reverential circumlocution for God, confirmed as such by the plural and by being set in a passive construction – indications (though not strict proofs) of a Semitic, i.e., in this case Aramaic, substratum. The cumulative

linguistic and literary evidence creates a rather strong presumption in favour of unity.

29. See J. Jeremias, *Golgotha*, Leipzig: Pfeiffer 1926, 66–8.

30. *Golgotha*, 40–65. See also R. Patai, *Man and Temple in Ancient Jewish Myth and Ritual*, London: Nelson 1947, 54–139.

31. *Golgotha*, 65f. See Jeremias's further observations in *TLZ* 88, 1957, 692f.

32. Yalqut Sim'oni I: Num 23.9; Billerbeck I, 733; *Golgotha*, 73f.

33. Ex.R 15.8; Hebrew text and German translation in *Golgotha*, 74.

34. Cf. *mou* ('my') in *ta arnia mou* and *ta probata mou* ('my lambs' and 'my sheep'), John 21.15–17 (commissioning of Peter).

35. In Acts Peter is the church's primary witness to the resurrection (2.14–40; 3.12–26; 4.8–12 etc.), primary spokesman before the Sanhedrin (4.8–12, 19f.; 5.29–32), authoritative interpreter of the scriptures (1.16–22), presider over the community (5.1–10), authorized to ban from it (8.21) and to admit to it (10.47f.). In significant detail his status is comparable to that of the Essene 'Overseer' or Guardian' (*me̱baqqēr*; cf. esp. CD 13.7–19).

36. If vv. 17–19 are a unity (see n. 28), the whole must derive from a tradition bearing on the pre-paschal period, since v. 17 rules out the paschal period. A. Vögtle, who some years ago found the arguments for the unity of vv. 17–19 uncompelling (cf. 'Messiasbekenntnis und Petrusverheissung. Zur Komposition Mt 16,13–23 par', *BZ* 1,1957, 252–72; 2, 1958, 85–103, pp. 89–95; repr. *Das Evangelium*, 137–170) and argued for the separate origin of vv. 18f. (pre-Matthean tradition) and v. 17 (redactional, cf. pp. 96–99), has since offered a follow-up study: 'Zum Problem der Herkunft von Mt 16,17–19', *Orientierung an Jesus. Zur Theologie der Synoptiker* (J. Schmid Festschrift), ed. P. Hoffmann, N. Brox, W. Pesch; Freiburg: Herder 1973, 372–93. The article is most noteworthy, in my opinion, for making the point in detailed and convincing fashion that an origin of v. 17 in an Easter apparition (the proto-epiphany to Peter) is altogether unlikely. Since, as Vögtle has effectively argued, v. 17 never existed anywhere but in the Caesarea Philippi confession scene; since, as he concedes, the name Bar-Jona derives from pre-Matthean tradition (which I would add, gives the whole verse a traditional allure); and since, contrary to Vögtle, vv. 18f. form a particularly tight linguistic and stylistic unity with v. 17, it follows that the whole unit of vv. 17–19 always belonged just where it is now found and that neither it nor the scene to which it has always belonged ever intended anything but a pre-paschal event.

37. R. Bultmann, *Synoptische Tradition* (see above, ch. II n. 103), 276–278; ET, *Synoptic Tradition*, 258f., argues that a text containing Peter's confession and no response from Jesus (Mark 8.27–29; Luke 9.18–20) is fragmentary, and proposes that the original response was Matt. 16.17–19 (understood, to be sure, as retrojected from an original Easter appearance). Luke 5.1–11 exemplifies the complete form. Bultmann's argument has not been effectively countered form-critically (though numerous scholars have made good redactional sense of the Markan text as it stands – as we would expect on the supposition that Mark himself was responsible for abbreviating the confession pericope).

38. *Worte*, 217; ET, *Words*, 265.

39. See below, pp. 203f.; 209.

40. *Peter in the New Testament*, ed. R. E. Brown, K. P. Donfried and J. Reumann; Minneapolis: Augsburg and New York: Paulist 1973, 83–101. Besides these editors, participants included J. A. Burgess, M. M. Bourke, J. A. Fitzmyer, P. J.

Achtemaier, K. Froehlich, R. H. Fuller, G. Krodel, P. S. Brown.

41. *Peter*, 85f.

42. *Peter*, 85. The point is made still more emphatically by G. Strecker, *Der Weg der Gerechtigkeit. Untersuchung zur Theologie des Matthäus*, FRLANT 82, [3]1971, 201.

43. *Peter*, 85. The hypothesis that 'Peter's confession is no longer the turning point of the Gospel' (87) is based on an either/or supposition: Either Matthew would suppress all application of messianic titles to Jesus prior to Caesarea Philippi or he would not consider Caesarea Philippi as the turning point of the story. This supposition shatters on the facts. Titles are applied to Jesus prior to Caesarea Philippi. But that Caesarea Philippi is the turning point of the story is grounded on the stubborn evidence of the confession and prediction pericopes (Matt. 16.13–20; 21–23) and especially on the formulaic *apo tote ērxato 'o Iēsous* . . . ('from that time Jesus began . . .') of v. 21 (cf. Matt. 4.17). However one wishes to account for the titles appearing prior to Caesarea Philippi (Matt. 9.27; 12.23; 14.33; 15.22 – texts which are quite diverse in character and ought not to be put on a par), Matt. 16.13–23 in any case presents itself unambiguously as the turning point of the story, just as in Mark.

44. *Peter*, 86f.

45. *Peter*, 88–97.

46. See above, pp. 71f.

47. So far as we know, *Petros* ('Rock') was an entirely novel name. The existence of texts such as Mark 3.16 and Luke 6.14 would seem inexplicable except on the supposition that the sense of the name *Petros* was the common possession of the writers and their readers. The same holds for John 1.42. In the historical context no sense other than 'foundation rock' (of the eschatological temple) is genuinely plausible.

48. Probably the most important single point here is the difference between the eschatological scenarios supposed by the text (a) in its original context and (b) in the context of the Matthean redaction. In the redaction *oikodomēsō* ('I will build') and *dōsō* ('I will give') are real futures referring to the resurrection and the period following it; originally, they were modal imperfects (Aram.: *'ebnê* and *'ihab* or *'ittēn*) expressing Jesus' will to build and will to give (from that moment on). Cf. J. Jeremias, *'kleis'*, *TWNT* III, 743–53, p. 749; *TDNT* III, 744–53, p. 749. Hence in the redaction the time of the church is defined by the interval between resurrection and parousia; originally, it followed Jesus' own eschatological scheme. The time of the church was that of the ordeal to be brought to an end by the day of the Son of man (see below, pp. 202–4; 209). It is no surprise that critics allowing their interpretative efforts to be controlled by a post-paschal conception of the eschatological scenario – e.g. R. H. Fuller, 'The "Thou Art Peter" Pericope and the Easter Experiences', *McCQ* 20, 1967, 309–15; G. Bornkamm, 'Die Binde- und Lösegewalt in der Kirche des Matthäus', *Die Zeit Jesu* (H. Schlier Festschrift), ed. G. Bornkamm and K. Rahner; Freiburg: Herder 1970, 93–107, pp. 101–5 – declare themselves unable to set the text intelligibly in the framework of Jesus' career.

49. See above, p. 152.

50. The fact that Markan and proto-Lukan texts (Mark 11.25; Luke 11.13) already reflect the 'heavenly Father' idiom attests its origin prior to the Matthean redaction. In three out of four instances in which the Matthean redactor adds 'Father' to the Markan tradition, it is without the modifier 'heavenly' (cf. Matt. 20.23; 26.29, 42; contrast 12.50). See J. Jeremias, 'Abba', in *Abba* (see

above, ch. III n. 27), 15–67, p. 35; ET, 'Abba', in *The Prayers of Jesus*, SBT 2.6, 1967, 11–65, pp. 31f.

51. G. Strecker, *Der Weg der Gerechtigkeit*, 201, proposes some redactional activity in the text, but the only trait proposed as strictly redactional (*kagō* in v. 18) fails to hold up. To conclude that *kagō* betrays the hand of the redactor, it does not suffice to show that he sometimes used *kagō*; it must be shown that *kagō* is not among his inheritances from pre-redactional tradition. But this cannot be shown. It several times occurs in Matthean *Sondergut* (e.g. 11.28; 18.33); and though it seems at first sight to have been inserted in 'Markan' sections of Matthew against Markan usage (Matt. 21.24; 26.15), in one of these two instances it may be pre-redactional (it is paralleled in Luke 20.3). The final result is a *non constat*.

52. Behind *'e basileia tōn ouranōn* may have stood Jesus' *malkûtā' dē'lāhā'*; but what might have stood behind *'o pater mou 'o en tois ouranois*? We have no evidence that Jesus himself used the 'heavenly Father' idiom. If we cannot plausibly attribute to him some comparable or parallel expression, the third line of v. 17 must be post-paschal. But if so, the whole text (vv. 17–19) must have been given its present form by post-paschal tradition.

53. See H. Clavier, 'Petros kai petra', *Neutestamentliche Studien für Rudolf Bultmann*, BZNW 21, 1954, 94–109, esp. 102f.

54. The central question is this: the surname 'Rock' was given to Simon in order to signify exactly what? This question is plausibly answered only with reference to the image of the foundation rock – not the rock of refuge (in the Psalms especially this is used of God) nor the rock of stumbling, etc. But once the central question has been answered, one may consider how secondary resonances might easily and naturally have accrued to the name (cf. *skandalon* in Matt. 16.23). Thus, I have no objection to the suggestions of C. F. D. Moule, 'Some Reflections on the "Stone" *Testimonia* in Relation to the Name Peter', *NTS* 2, 1955/56, 56–8.

55. *Petros/Kēpā'* was not in the first instance a name meant to replace the name Simon. Rather, it was a cognomen or sobriquet.

56. R. Bultmann, 'Die Frage nach der Echtheit von Mt 16, 17–19', *ThBl* 20, 1941, col. 265–279; repr. in *Exegetica* (see above, ch. V n. 26), 255–77.

57. 'Echtheit', col. 270; *Exegetica*, 263.

58. See above, pp. 83f.

59. Contrary to a common misappropriation of the messianic secret, it was not Jesus' purpose to conceal his messianic identity. It was his purpose to set before Israel symbol-charged acts and words implying a persistent question: Who do you say that I am? See below, notes 119, 120 and p. 250.

60. See H.-W. Bartsch, *Jesus. Prophet und Messias aus Galiläa*, (Frankfurt: Stimme, 1970), 46–49 and, following Bartsch, R. Pesch, 'Der Anspruch Jesu', *Or* 35, 1971, 53–56; 67–70, 77–81; see esp. 53–56; also L. Goppelt, *Jesu Wirken* (see above, ch. II n. 117), 147.

61. See C. Roth, 'The Cleansing of the Temple and Zechariah XIV. 21', *NovT* 4, 1960, 174–81. Roth's reconstruction is hardly plausible, however; if we are correct in thinking that Zech. 14.21 was relevant to Jesus' act, it was simply a matter of affirming eschatological fulfilment with reference to the messianic creation of a holy Israel.

62. See J. Jeremias, *Abendmahlsworte* (see above, ch. II n. 111), 247–51; ET, *Eucharistic Words*, 256–61, on the midrash on Ps. 118.

63. See J. Jeremias, *Jesus als Weltvollender* (see above, ch. II n. 110), 35–44, esp.

41–4. See also B. Gärtner, *The Temple* (see n. 13 above), 107–111.

64. Similarly, the parable of the Wicked Husbandmen (Mark 12.1–11 parr.) may well have been part of the same postscript, as suggested by both its point (the target was the Jerusalem leadership) and its placement. I would not, of course, limit the postscript to the single occasion of the cleansing.

65. If entry, cleansing, and riddle thus belong together, the whole takes on a peculiarly Zecharian stamp. Jesus came to the temple 'lowly and riding upon an ass' (Zech. 9.9); he drove the buyers and sellers and money-changers from the courtyard, for 'on that day there shall no longer be any merchant in the house of the LORD of hosts' (Zech. 14.20); and, challenged to establish his authority by a 'sign', he answered as 'the man whose name is "the branch" ', who would 'build the temple of the LORD' (Zech. 6.12).

66. W. Weiffenbach, *Der Wiederkunftsgedanke Jesu nach den Synoptikern kritisch untersucht und dargestellt*, Leipzig: Breitkopf und Härtel 1873. Weiffenbach names as his forerunners Schleiermacher (377–9) and Weisse (380–89).

67. A. Schweitzer, *Von Reimarus* (see above, ch. II n. 55), 229; ET, *The Quest*, 1968, 232.

68. A. Schweitzer, *Von Reimarus*, 231; ET, *The Quest*, 234.

69. C. H. Dodd, *The Parables of the Kingdom*, London: Nisbet, 1935; repr., London/Glasgow: Collins (Fontana), 1961. I cite from the reprint.

70. Op. cit., 42

71. Op. cit., 55.

72. Op. cit., 56f.

73. Op. cit., 63.

74. Op. cit., 62.

75. Op. cit., 63.

76. Op. cit., 64.

77. Op. cit., 53f.

78. Op. cit., 54.

79. Op. cit., 59.

80. Op. cit., 56.

81. Op. cit., 63.

82. Op. cit., 76 n. 24.

83. Op. cit., 76.

84. Op. cit., 115–30.

85. J. Jeremias, 'Eine neue Schau der Zukunftsaussagen Jesu', *ThBl* 20, 1941, col. 216–22.

86. See the discussion in G. Dalman, *Worte* (²1930 and 1960 reprint; not included in ET, *Words*), 325f., 328f., 332f. Favouring *epiousios* = 'of (belonging to) tomorrow': J. Jeremias, *Verkündigung*, 193f.; ET, *NT Theology*, 199f. The view is considered and rejected by, among others, K. G. Kuhn, *Achtzehngebet und Vaterunser und der Reim*, Tübingen: Mohr 1950, 36.

87. 'Enthronement' here = 'transcendent exaltation conceived as messianic investiture'. A. Strobel, *Kerygma und Apokalyptik. Ein religionsgeschichtlicher und theologischer Beitrag zur Christusfrage*, Göttingen: Vandenhoeck & Ruprecht 1967, has distinguished (64–71) between assumption (*Entrückung*) conceived as God's removing someone from the sight of men and holding him in reserve for some eschatological task, and exaltation (*Erhöhung*) conceived as a transcendent investiture in an eschatological function before the eyes of the whole world. The most

significant background for the matter in question (Dan. 7.13f.) does not meet either definition perfectly but elements of both appear to be present. M. Delcor, *Le Livre de Daniel*, Paris: Gabalda 1971, 155–8, understands (in accord with T. W. Manson) the 'one like a (son of) man' to be represented as ascending with the clouds from earth to heaven. The point of this ascension (of Israel and its messianic king) is investiture in royal power over the whole world.

88. Midrash on Ps. 11.5 cited by G. Dalman, *Worte* (²1930 and 1960 reprint, not included in ET, *Words*), 345f. Cf. Pss. Sol. 3.4f.; 10.1–3; 16.1–4. But the real parallel to the disciples' experience of the eschatological distress (*ṣārâ, thlipsis*) as test (*nisyôn, peirasmos*) would be Jesus' ordeals and especially his passion.

89. J. Jeremias, *Verkündigung*, 188–96; ET, *NT Theology*, 193–203.

90. See J. Jeremias, 'Abba' (see n. 50 above), esp. 56–67; ET, *54–65*.

91. J. Jeremias, *Verkündigung*, 140; ET, *NT Theology*, 140.

92. That aspect of the so-called Markan framework which consists in making the Caesarea Philippi confession a cardinal point for the ordering of traditions was probably established very early, long before Mark and even prior to transmission in Greek. This at least is suggested by the fact that there are Son of man sayings before Caesarea Philippi, but they are sayings which either (*a*) originally bore the indefinite sense of *bar 'ĕnāšā'* ('one, someone'): Mark 2.10 (= Matt. 9.6; Luke 5.24; cf. Matt. 9.8); Mark 2.28 (=Matt. 12.8; Luke 6.5); Matt. 8.20 (=Luke 9.58); Matt. 11.19 (=Luke 7.34), or (*b*) bore the generic sense ('man'): Matt. 12.32 (=Luke 12.10; cf. Mark 3.28.), or (*c*) are redactional (Matt. 12.40; 13.37, 41), or (*d*) are redactionally preplaced (Matt. 10.23; 16.13), or (*e*) are pre-redactional but still secondary (Luke 6.22; cf. Matt. 5.11). NB, the indefinite sense may be used with reference to the speaker. Hence, G. Dalman (though with a different account of the particulars), *Worte*, 212–16; ET, *Words*, 259–64, proposed with all due caution that Jesus did not refer to the Son of man prior to the confession of Peter. T. W. Manson, *Teaching* (see above, ch. VI n. 36), 24–7, proposed the same with reference to Mark.

93. The thesis, usually associated with the name of P. Vielhauer (cf. 'Gottesreich und Menschensohn', *Festschrift für Günther Dehn*, ed. W. Schneemelcher; Neukirchen: Moers 1957, 51–79, repr. P. Vielhauer, *Aufsätze zum Neuen Testament*, München: Kaiser 1965, 55–91), to the effect that 'reign of God' and 'Son of man' were not both of them affirmed by Jesus would have some probability (from the fact that there is no certainly authentic saying in which Jesus verbally associated them) only on condition that evidence were lacking for Jesus' differentiating public from esoteric teaching. Inasmuch as this condition is unfulfilled, the thesis collapses. The public teaching is dominated by the thematic of the reign of God whereas the Son of man sayings are limited to esoteric teaching until the trial before the Sanhedrin (Luke 22.69; cf. Mark 14.62 par.). The view, increasingly common since the mid-1960s, that all the Son of man sayings were creations of the early church has about it a certain *a priori* improbability. As Bruce Vawter, *This Man Jesus. An Essay Toward a New Testament Christology*, Garden City: Doubleday 1973, 106f., puts it: 'We would have to believe that a Jewish church invented a christology whose internal complexities indicate that it passed through various stages of development, which managed to saturate the gospel traditions while leaving all others strangely untouched, for some unaccountable reason restricted itself to words it put on the mouth of Jesus, then disappeared leaving hardly a trace.' The new thesis on Son of man is also improbable *a posteriori*; for, as Neufeld,

The Earliest Christian Confessions (see above, ch. III n. 49), 76, observes: 'The argument ... that the title was given to Jesus by the primitive church, is contrary to the evidence not only of the gospels but of the primitive *homologia* and confessions as well.' Nevertheless, this improbable thesis has 'caught on', supported in remote and oblique fashion by the current difficulty of locating Jesus' use of 'Son of man' in a full history of the thematic in ancient Near Eastern religion.

94. See below, pp. 224–41.

95. See J. Gray, 'The Day of Yahweh ...' (see n. 25 above), 14–21.

96. F. Kattenbusch, 'Der Quellort der Kirchenidee', *Festgabe* ... A. *von Harnack*, Tübingen: Mohr 1921, 143–72; idem, 'Die Vorstellung des Petrus and der Charakter der Urgemeinde zu Jerusalem', *Festgabe* ... *Karl Müller*, Tübingen: Mohr 1922, 322–51; idem, 'Der Spruch über Petrus und die Kirche bei Matthäus', *TSK* 94, 1922, 96–131.

97. K. L. Schmidt, 'Die Kirche des Urchristentums. Eine lexicographische und biblisch-theologische Studie', *Festgabe A. Deissmann*, Tübingen: Mohr 1927, 258–319; idem, '*ekklesia*', *TWNT* III, 502–39, pp. 522–8; *TDNT* III, 501–36, pp. 520–6.

98. G. Gloege, *Reich Gottes und Kirche im Neuen Testament*, Gütersloh: Mohn 1929; repr. Darmstadt: Wissenschaftliche Buchgesellschaft 1968, 212–9, 241–9.

99. T. W. Manson, *Teaching* (see above, ch. VI n. 36) 175–88, 227–36.

100. R. Bultmann, 'Echtheit' (see n. 56 above) esp. col. 273–5; *Exegetica*, 268–71.

101. A. Oepke, *Das neue Gottesvolk* (see above, ch. VI n. 16), 165ff.; idem, 'Der Herrnspruch über die Kirche, Matt. 16.17–19 in der neuesten Forschung', *StTh* 2, 1948–50, 110–65, p. 140.

102. W. G. Kümmel, *Kirchenbegriff und Geschichtsbewusstsein in der Urgemeinde und bei Jesus*, SBU 1, 1943; idem, 'Jesus und die Angfänge der Kirche', *StTh* 7, 1953, 1–27.

103. J. Jeremias, 'Der Gedanke des "Heiligen Restes" im Spätjudentum und in der Verkündigung Jesu', *ZNW* 42, 1949, 184–94; repr. *Abba* (see above, ch. III n. 27), 121–32; idem, *Die theologische Bedeutung der Funde am Toten Meer*, Göttingen: Vandenhoeck & Ruprecht 1962; idem, *Verkündigung*, 167–70; ET, *NT Theology*, 170–73.

104. G. Gloege, *Reich Gottes*, 244f.

105. T. W. Manson, *Teaching*, 181.

106. *Teaching*, 177. See also 249: 'But with the emergence of the individual as the religious unit, ...'

107. See above, p. 54.

108. R. Bultmann, *History and Eschatology. The Gifford Lectures 1955*, Edinburgh: University Press 1957, 31 (=*The Presence of Eternity*, New York: Harper & Bros. 1957, 31).

109. See below, pp. 223–35.

110. B. Lonergan (see above, ch. I n. 5), *Method*, 130; *Second Collection*, 66, 153.

111. Such was 'the 1880 consensus' described by O. Linton, *Urkirche* (see above, ch. VII n. 28), which despite several death-notices has never quite disappeared from Germany. (To be sure, it no longer represents a 'consensus'.)

112. R. Bultmann, *History and Eschatology*, 36.

113. Ibid.

114. See A. Vögtle, 'Exegetische Erwägungen über das Wissen and Selbstbewusstsein Jesu', *Gott in Welt* I (K. Rahner Festschrift), ed. J. B. Metz et al.;

Freiburg: Herder 1964, 608–67, p. 616; repr. A. Vögtle, *Das Evangelium* (see above, ch. III n. 66) 296–344, p. 303: 'The gesture [of shaking off the dust] is meant to signify that . . . the place is to be abandoned like a heathen place that has nothing to do with true Israel.'

115. R. Pesch, 'Anspruch', (see n. 60 above) 53–6. For a comparable view, stated with admirable precision, see W. D. Davies, *The Gospel and the Land* (see above, ch. II n. 44) 350 n. 46. Cf. Pss. Sol. 17.33f.: 'And he [the Son of David] shall purge Jerusalem, making it holy as of old, so that nations shall come from the ends of the earth to see his glory . . .'

116. H. Schürmann, *Geheimnis*, (see above, ch. VII n. 86) 110.

117. According to Jeremias, *Gleichnisse*, 89; ET, Parables, 90, the parables of the Tares and of the Dragnet were originally paired. In his interpretation of their original sense they are seen as rejection of an insistent proposal that Jesus gather 'the holy remnant' (cf. *Gleichnisse*, 221–4; ET, *Parables*, 223–7). By 'holy remnant' Jeremias means a full-fledged distinct community (e.g. the Essenes). Perhaps the original issue of these parables was the proposal that Jesus form such a community. But even should this have been the issue, the question of Jesus and the remnant of Israel is irreducible to it. Jeremias himself acknowledges that the Baptist sought to bring into being the remnant of Israel. But the Baptist did not organize the baptized into a full-fledged, distinct community.

118. See J. Jeremias, *'poimēn'*, *TWNT* VI, 484–501; p. 500 n. 20; *TDNT* VI, 485–502, p. 501 n. 20: 'The rendering of the vocative by nominative with art. (*to mikron poimnion*) is Semitic, Blass-Debrunner Para. 147,3. The words *poimnion/ eudokēsen* are linked by a pun in Aramaic (*mar'ita/ra'*) (M. Black, *An Aramaic Approach to the Gospels and Acts*, [2]1954, 126). The expression *dounai tēn basileian* (without addition to *basileia*) = 'to transfer (a share in) the royal dominion' is based on Dan. 7:27 *malkûtâ . . . yᵉhîbat*.'

119. It should go without saying that the messianic secret is also a redactional motif in Mark with specifically Markan traits and purposes. But 'secret' and 'mystery' should be distinguished; they have distinct functions in the Markan redaction and they refer to distinct aspects of the history of Jesus. On the redaction, see D. J. Hawkin, 'The Incomprehension of the Disciples in the Marcan Redaction', *JBL* 91, 1972, 491–500. As a trait of the historic career of Jesus, the so-called secret was Jesus' refusal to set an explicit messianic claim before Israel. This, however, was not designed to keep his messianic identity unknown to Israel. It simply reflected a realism about the decisive factor, the intimate personal orientation, which conditioned each man's response to revelation. Faith would not win out over unfaith if only the appeal for it were more explicit and spectacular (Luke 16.30f.). Hence Jesus' refusal of the demand for a 'sign' (Mark 8.11f.; Matt. 12.38f. par.; 16.4; John 6.30–36), the lack of public titles whether for himself (Mark 8.30 parr., etc.) or his following (Mark 4.30–32 parr., etc.), the thanksgiving for revelation to the simple (Matt. 11.25f. par.), the macarism on Peter (Matt. 16.17), the indirection of the response to the Baptist's question ('Tell John what you hear and see', Matt. 11.4 par.).

120. D. J. Hawkin, art. cit., 499f., has stressed the point in his critique of exegetes (A. Meyer, O. Cullmann) who effect a thematic merger of the two pericopes, thus doubly misconstruing the prohibition of v. 30. To them it signifies that Jesus refuses (A. Meyer) or accepts only with reservations (O. Cullmann) the confession of messiahship, and that the motive of the prohibition lies in the follow-

ing exchange between Jesus and Peter. 'On this view the incomprehension of the disciples indicates why there is a messianic secret: the disciples misunderstood the nature of Jesus' messiahship; so *a fortiori* would the crowds if it were revealed to them' (499). If, however, the relationship between the two pericopes is conceived not as a thematic merger but as a thematic progression, the rationale of 'secret' and 'mystery' are distinct redactionally (and, I would add, historically).

121. For the translation, see Joüon, 'Notes philologiques sur les Évangiles', *RSR* 18, 1928, 345–59, p. 347; *L'Évangile* (see above, ch. VII n. 47), 108.

122. The phrase, like the ideal, is Lonergan's, *Second Collection*, 144.

123. See J. Jeremias, *Verkündigung*, 263–84; ET, *NT Theology*, 276–99.

124. See H. Schürmann, 'Wie hat Jesus seinen Tod bestanden und verstanden? Eine methodenkritische Besinnung', *Orientierung an Jesus* (see n. 36 above), 325–63; repr. *Jesu ureigene Tod* (see above, ch. III n. 51), 16–65. (My citations will be taken from the former.) Schürmann here offers an incisive introduction to 'the systematic-hermeneutical question' (325–8). So far as the theory of historical criticism is concerned, his commitment to 'the critical principle of discrimination' (methodical scepticism) is incoherent, for whereas it is of the essence of this 'critical principle' that it be unique (Schürmann cites Käsemann's hard-line formulation: 'nur in einem einzigen Fall ...', 328), he also envisages possible additions to it of 'positive criteria' (332 n. 38). Though he fails to criticize or revise 'the critical principle', he is aware that, if strictly applied, it can only generate a distorted reconstruction of the past (330). In practice Schürmann's criticism is extremely exigent; but by the time he has assembled all the lines of evidence which converge on conclusions both as to how Jesus interpreted his coming death and how he underwent it, strict allegiance to the spirit and letter of 'the critical principle of discrimination' has yielded to a better (if still unformulated) principle.

125. The translation supposes (following Jeremias, *Verkündigung*, 277; ET, *NT Theology*, 292) that the *kai* after *diakonēsai* is epexegetical. The significance of this is recognized on other grounds (without reference to the grammatical point) by K. Kertelge, 'Der dienende Menschensohn (Mk. 10,45)', *Jesus und der Menschensohn* (A. Vögtle Festschrift), ed. R. Pesch, R. Schnackenburg and O. Kaiser; Freiburg: Herder 1975, 225–39. The question of historicity in the narrow sense still seems unresolvable, but Kertelge is certainly correct in observing (239 n. 62) that this logion 'discloses a basic dimension of the comportment and self-understanding of Jesus. ...'

126. O. H. Steck, *Israel und des gewaltsame Geschick der Propheten. Untersuchungen zur Ueberlieferung des deuteronomistischen Geschichtsbildes im Alten Testament, Spätjudentum und Urchristentum*, Neukirchen/Vluyn: Neukirchener Verlag, 1967. Steck has recovered the thematic complex in which the motif of the rejection and violent fate of the prophets was transmitted in Palestinian Judaism. However, in his effort to correct a too facile identification of 'prophets' with 'martyrs', he has underplayed the theme of the expiatory value of death (see IV Macc. 6.29; 17.21f.; cf. 1.11; 9.23f.) which is attested in Palestine from Tannaitic times (see J. Jeremias, *Verkündigung*, 273 and n. 47; ET, *NT Theology*, 288 and n. 8).

127. Historicity is commended by the motif of the 'unfulfilled' imminence of the reign of God and supported by a Semitic substratum (*amēn; ouketi ou mē piō ek; to genēma tēs ampelou; 'eōs tēs 'emeras ekeinēs; en tē basileia* [in temporal sense]) which in any case excludes an origin of the text as 'a Hellenistic cult legend'.

128. The sense of 'take up his cross' derives from a particular moment in the

procedure of execution by crucifixion, namely, when the condemned takes the *patibulum* or cross-piece on his shoulder and turns to face the crowd, the human community from which he is now excluded. See J. Jeremias, *Verkündigung*, 232; ET, *NT Theology*, 242.

129. H. Schürmann, 'Wie hat Jesus ...'.

130. See H. Schürmann, 'Die Symbolhandlungen Jesu ...' (see above, ch. VII n. 86), 97–103; idem, 'Das Weiterleben der Sache Jesu ...' (see above, ch. III n. 51), 1–23; idem, 'Wie hat Jesus ...', 353–6.

131. Pertinent to the historicity of the motif of vicarious expiation is the important role of this theme in Jewish antiquity as attested with reference to death by II Macc., IV Macc., Enoch, and Tannaitic as well as Amoraic texts. (Jeremias, after surveying the data: 'The sources compel the conclusion that *it is inconceivable that Jesus should not have thought of the atoning power of his death.*' *Abendmahlsworte*, 222; ET, *Eucharistic Words*, 231.) With reference to the historicity of the covenant theme, we should first of all recall (in connection with the centrality to the aims of Jesus of the remnant and restoration of Israel) that the covenant had always been the basis and essence of remnant theology, covenantal stipulations and covenantal blessings and curses providing the rationale of the judgment which the remnant was to survive. In accord with this logic the covenant was also the charter of the remnant's present and future life. Remnant theology as it emerged in the prophets was simply a parenetic dramatization of 'covenant' with the added factor of the judgment of Israel. But just as the eucharistic words on expiation are allied to but (by invoking Isa. 53) transcend the standard forms of this expiation thematic, so the words on covenant are allied to but transcend the prophets' theme of the restoration of the remnant. Rather than merely renewing the covenantal communion of old, the restoration of the messianic remnant inaugurated a new covenant. It was a fulfilment event (e.g. Jer. 31.31). Compare (and contrast!) the Essenes.

132. Immediately relevant to the historicity of the eucharistic words is the testimony of Paul that they derived 'from the Lord' (see above, ch. III n. 26). Oblique inferences of historicity are grounded in (a) the *originality* of the words (the otherwise unexampled mode of referring to bread and cup and the probably complete originality with which motifs from Isa. 53 are here actualized) and plausibly (cf. Schürmann, n. 130) the originality of the act of distributing the cup among the disciples; (b) distinctively personal idioms (cf. J. Jeremias, *Abendmahlsworte*, 194f.; ET, *Eucharistic Words*, 201f. on Mark 14.25 and Luke 22.16); (c) multiple attestation (two independent branches of tradition), the resistive form of liturgical libretto, Aramaic substratum.

133. Frequently the command is considered to be unhistorical (on the same basis as that on which the whole of the tradition is, namely, methodical scepticism: There is a *Sitz im Leben* in the Christian community for it). The question of the historicity of the command (in any case pre-Pauline) is complex. If, however, the following phrase *eis tēn emēn anamnēsin* originally expressed the archaic eschatology implied in 'that God may remember me', as proposed by Jeremias, *Abendmahlsworte*, 237–46; ET, *Eucharistic Words*, 246–55, the probability of historicity is sharply increased. Moreover, there is a consideration bearing on genre: With the *récit* on the making of the covenant goes the command bearing on covenant renewal.

Chapter IX   Confirmation and Reflection

1. See A. Causse, *Du groupe ethnique* and O. Plöger, *Theokratie*; ET, *Theocracy* (see above, ch. VII n. 31); K. Schubert, 'Die jüdischen Religionsparteien im Zeitalter Jesu', *Der historische Jesus und der Christus unseres Glaubens. Eine katholische Auseinandersetzung mit den Folgen der Entmythologisierungstheorie,* ed. K. Schubert; Wien: Herder 1962, 15–101, esp. 15–35; idem, *Die Religion des nachbiblisch-n Judentums*, Wien: Herder 1955.

2. Not 'will have pity on the remnant of Joseph', as if the sparing of a remnant were an independent, prior supposition. Cf. the use of *ḥnn* in II Kings 13.23; Deut. 7.2; 28.50.

3. See G. F. Hasel, *The Remnant. The History and Theology of the Remnant Idea from Genesis to Isaiah*, Berrien Springs, Mich.: Andrews University Press 1972, 50–134.

4. On the role of faith in Isaiah's remnant theology, see the theologically sensitive treatment of F. Dreyfus, 'La doctrine du Reste d'Israël chez le prophète Isaîe', *RSPT* 39, 1955, 361–86, esp. 372–5.

5. A. Gelin, *Les Pauvres de Yahvé*, Paris: Le Cerf 1956, 38f.

6. See N. A. Dahl, *Das Volk Gottes. Eine Untersuchung zum Kirchenbewusstsein des Urchristentums*, SNVAO, 1943; repr. Darmstadt: Wissenschaftliche Buchgesellschaft 1963, 7; F. Hauck, *"osios"*, *TWNT* V, 488–92, p. 490; *TDNT* V, 489–93, p. 491.

7. On the non-Qumran sources, see W. Bauer, 'Essener', in Pauli-Wissowa, *Realencyclopädie*, Supplementband IV, 1924, 386–430. The main Qumran sources in English: G. Vermes, *The Dead Sea Scrolls in English*, Harmondsworth: Penguin 1962, [3]1968.

8. For source materials in English (apart from the New Testament) see J. Bowker, *Jesus and the Pharisees*, Cambridge: Cambridge University Press 1973, 77–179; Billerbeck II, 494–519.

9. For analysis of the sources, see J. Le Moyne, *Les Sadducéens*, Paris: Gabalda 1972.

10. The unique source is Philo, *De vita contemplativa*.

11. See J. Thomas, *Le mouvement baptiste en Palestine et Syrie (150 av. J.-C – 300 ap. J.-C.)*, Louvain: Gembloux 1935.

12. After the calamity of AD 70, the scribes whose prescriptions for Israel had been mediated by the Pharisaic movement undertook to prescribe immediately for the nation. The Pharisaic *halaka* would henceforth have no Judaic competitor for the nation's allegiance. A single but illuminating facet of this transition has been recovered by C.-H. Hunzinger, 'Spuren pharisäischer Institutionen in der frühen rabbinischen Ueberlieferung', *Tradition und Glaube* (see above, ch. VII n. 100), 147–56.

13. R. Meyer, *'prophētēs'*, *TWNT* VI, 828; *TDNT* VI, 828.

14. The 'scribes' were scholars and by the time of the Maccabean Wars were already specialists in the interpretation of moral and ritual law. Before the exile the Torah had been the province of priests, and 'scribe' was a title of royal officials. After the time and under the impact of Ezra, called 'priest-scribe' (Ezra 7.11; Neh. 8.9; 12.26) with the accent on 'scribe', there began a laicizing of the study of the Torah and the members of the new and prestigious class of Torah scholars which resulted were called 'scribes'. In the last two centuries BC they entered the national *élite* and began to share (as well as to contest) the leadership of society

with the hereditary nobility and clergy. By the end of the first century the term had disappeared in favour of 'sages' (*ḥăkāmîm*).

15. This would be the natural conclusion from the New Testament expression 'scribes and Pharisees'. But this expression is misleading. First, it occurs in Matthew and Luke only. (Mark 7.5 does not attest the formulaic phrase but refers back to Mark 7.1: 'The Pharisees . . . and some of the scribes that had come from Jerusalem . . .' John 8.3 is part of a non-Johannine interpolation.) Second, whereas Matthew has combined the two groups indiscriminately, the Lukan parallel to Matt. 23 (Luke 11.39–52; 20.46f.) equivalently differentiates them as the learned and the pious, each with its besetting vices. (In Luke 11.43 a confusion between the two groups has slipped into the Lukan tradition; Luke 20.46 [cf. Mark 12.38f.] puts it right.) These points have been made by J. Jeremias, '*grammateus*', *TWNT* I, 740–42; *TDNT* I 740–42. E. Rivkin, 'Defining the Pharisees: The Tannaitic Sources', *HUCA* 40, 1969, 205–49, defines them as 'scholars'. The heuristic principle of Rivkin's analysis is clear but mechanical and settles the result in advance, unless there were to be Tannaitic texts – there are none – more or less clearly specifying that those *pᵉrûšîm* who observed special norms for purity and tithing were one and the same as those *pᵉrûšîm* whose halakic prescriptions differed from those of the *ṣaddûqîm*. Over and above its being a model of clarity in conception and expression, the special value of Rivkin's essay lies in its insistence on facing the fact of variety in the Tannaitic use of the word *pᵉrûšîm*. A shortcoming of the essay (so it seems to me) is that instead of treating the texts as data for reconstruction, it treats them as sources asked to supply, ready-made, an answer to a modern question. Finally, the essay demonstrates the difficulty, if not impossibility, of defining Pharisaism from the Tannaitic sources alone, since internal reference points are lacking by which either to differentiate or identify the several sorts of *pᵉrûšîm* they describe.

16. The Lukan parallels to Matt. 23 are significant in this connection. Even in the Matthean text there are traces of the original distinction between scribes (Matt. 23.1–22, 29–36) and Pharisees (Matt. 23.23–28). 'Woe to you, scribes and Pharisees . . .' in v. 25 is followed by 'You blind Pharisee!' in v. 26. See J. Jeremias, *Jerusalem* (see above, ch. IV n. 7), 254. See also the texts cited below on ritual handwashing and on tithes.

17. The term *ḥăbûrâ* ('society, community') may refer to any sort of social group. For a swift survey of usage in rabbinic texts, see R. Meyer, 'Tradition und Neuschöpfung im antiken Judentum dargestellt an der Geschichte des Pharisaismus', *SBLeipzig* 110, 1965, 7–88, pp. 24–28. S. Lieberman, 'The Discipline in the So-called Dead Sea Manual of Discipline', *JBL* 71, 1952, 199–206, brings together information from rabbinic sources on *ḥăbērîm* who united to observe special prescriptions on purity and tithes.

18. Favouring a yes: R. Meyer, 'Tradition . . .', 23–33, in basic accord with numerous earlier scholars (e.g. Wellhausen, Schürer). E. Rivkin, 'Defining the Pharisees', sees no reason in the Tannaitic texts to relate *ḥăbērîm* and Pharisees, a conclusion which converges with that of numerous earlier scholars (e.g. L. Baeck, R. T. Herford). For a survey of secondary literature from a historical-critical standpoint (conceived positivistically), see J. Neusner, *The Rabbinic Traditions About the Pharisees Before 70*, Leiden: Brill 1971, 320–68.

19. See, for example, *Antiquitates* 13.298, 401f., 406, 408; 18.15, 17. M. Smith, 'Palestinian Judaism in the First Century', *Israel: Its Role in Civilization*, ed. M.

Davis; New York: Harper 1956, 67–81, points out that this accent was lacking in Josephus, *Bellum Judaicum*, and that the history Josephus recounts does not independently establish it. Still, this *caveat* must be balanced against the aspects of Pharisaic *halaka* intrinsically likely to win popular approval.

20. See G. F. Moore, *Judaism in the First Centuries of the Christian Era* II, Cambridge, Mass.: Harvard University Press 1927, 76, contrasting this with the 'supersacredotal' standard of the *ḥăbērîm*.

21. R. Meyer, '*Pharisaios*, A. Pharisaism in Judaism', *TWNT* IX, 12–36, p. 15; *TDNT* IX, 12–35, p. 15: 'The Law (Aram. *dāt*) as the constitution of the Jerusalem hierocracy laid down in the Pent. is a priestly law. This means that ultimately it does not refer to the people at large but only to the priests, and to the priests only when engaged in temple service. Hence, separation in the sense of sacral law is a primary quality of the priest, who during his spell of duty is to avoid all defilement if his cultic acts are to be valid ... Hence one has to ask whether and how far that which is most distinctive of Pharisaism does not really derive from the priesthood.'

22. A comment on each of three key texts (CD 2.11; 1QM 13.7f.; and 1QH 6.6–8): first, in the light of the sect's self-understanding as the reality attested and instructed by classical prophecy, as structured in accord with the scriptures (e.g. 1QS 2.19–22), and as endowed with a new covenant (e.g. CD 6.19; 1QpHab 2.3), it is inescapable that the community identified itself as the concrete embodiment in its own time of God's will to sustain a remnant of the elect in all generations (CD 2.11; cf. 1QM 14.8–10). Second, 1QM 13.7f. envisages a future moment at which the past is recalled from the covenant with the patriarchs through the time of the remnant (i.e., the community which produced this hymnic text; cf. again 1QM 14.8–10). Third, 1QH 6.6–8 in accord with a standard thanksgiving structure recalls a past moment in which God came to the help of the afflicted by giving him the assurance of imminent reversal. Part of that reversal, namely, the raising up of a remnant (1QH 6.8–12a), has already taken place prior to the point in time supposed by the hymn and, in any case, prior to the point in time at which the hymn was composed.

23. It is to be inferred from the self-understanding inherent in the sect's status as heir of prophecy and structure as biblical Israel that it in some sense (namely, that signified by the remnant theme) identified itself already in its present existence as 'the people of God'. This stands side by side with many references to empirical Israel as still 'the people (of God)' (e.g. 1QH 4.6, 11, 16, 26). Cf. Paul's use of 'Israel' for Gentile Christians in Gal. 6.16 and for as yet unconverted Jews in Rom. 11.25 (where, however, conversion is prospective and imminent).

24. See K. G. Kuhn, 'Qumran. Bedeutung für das Judentum', *RGG*³ 5, 745–51, cf. col. 748f. (CD 12.1f.).

25. *De vita contemplativa*, 74.

26. *De vita contemplativa*, 81f.

27. See J. Jeremias, 'Der Gedanke des "Heiligen Restes" ...' (see above, ch. VI n. 16), 123.

28. K. Schubert, 'A Divided Faith. Jewish Parties and Sects', *The Crucible of Christianity. Judaism, Hellenism and the Historical Background to the Christian Faith*, ed. A. Toynbee; London: Thames and Hudson 1969, 77–98, p. 88: Once 'the death of Judas Maccabaeus had eclipsed the eschatological hopes aroused by the Maccabean revolt, one group withdrew from the Assidaean catchment-area, a group which – sobered by experience – had abandoned the apocalyptic radical-dualistic

outlook. This group was the Pharisees. . . .' Schubert has worked out in full detail his conception of the Pharisees as determinedly anti-apocalyptic. See also his *Die jüdischen Religionsparteien in neutestamentlicher Zeit*, Stuttgart: Katholisches Bibelwerk 1970, 25–32, 43–7; and, earlier, 'Die jüdischen Religionsparteien . . .' (see n. 1 above), esp. 70–79; idem, 'Die Entwicklung der eschatologischen Naherwartung im Frühjudentum', *Vom Messias zum Christus. Die Fülle der Zeit in religionsgeschichtlicher und theologischer Sicht*, ed. K. Schubert; Wien: Herder 1964, 1ff. Partly at least owing to Schubert's vigorous argumentation, the history of eschatology among the Pharisees must remain an open question; it remains nevertheless unlikely that the sparse evidences of live eschatology among the Tannaites represent an increase (as Schubert maintains) rather than a decrease of eschatological belief and hope relative to the pre-70 Pharisees.

29. R. Meyer, '*Saddoukaios*', *TWNT* VII, 35–54, p. 44; *TDNT* VII, 35–54; p. 44.

30. Cf. B. F. Meyer, *Three Tenses* (see above, ch. II n. 6), 4–12.

31. The self-understanding of the earliest community (see J. Schmitt, 'L'Église de Jérusalem . . .', see above, ch. III n. 52) shows that the 'Jesus/Israel' thematic was powerful and pervasive in Christianity from the outset; this, in turn, supposes a keen and pervasive interest in the Jesus of history (which should neither be equated with nor dissociated from interest in the gospel tradition). Whether contemporary theology is headed toward a recovery of balance on this topic is not yet settled, but the mentality of Hermann von Soden, 'Das Interesse des apostolischen Zeitalters . . .' (see above, ch. III n. 69), once dominant, is increasingly challenged and undermined. Symptomatic is interest in the relation of New Testament letters to the historic figure of Jesus, e.g. D. L. Dungan, *The Sayings of Jesus* (see above, ch. III n. 76), J. Roloff, 'Der mitleidende Hohepriester. Zur Frage nach der Bedeutung des irdischen Jesus für die Christologie des Hebräerbriefes', *Jesus Christus in Historie und Theologie* (see above, ch. VII n. 52) 143–66.

32. E. Linnemann, 'Hat Jesus Naherwartung gehabt?', *Jésus aux origines de la christologie* (see above, ch. V n. 29), 103–10; eadem, 'Zeitansage und Zeitvorstellung in der Verkündigung Jesu', *Jesus Christus in Historie und Theologie* (see above, ch. VII n. 52), 237–63.

33. See above, pp. 203f.

34. R. Guardini, *Der Herr*, Würzburg: Werkbund-Verlag 1937, 51–4, 444–54; ET, *The Lord*, tr. E. C. Briefs; Chicago: Regnery 1954, 39–42, 329–36.

35. J. Jeremias, 'Die Naherwartung des Endes in den Worten Jesu', *Kerygma und Mythos VI. Aspekte der Unfehlbarkeit. Kritische Untersuchungen und Interpretationen*, ed. E. Castelli; Hamburg/Bergstedt: Reich 1975, 139–45.

36. O. Cullmann, *Christus und die Zeit*; ET, *Christ and Time* (see above, ch. III n. 22), ²1964, 148–50; idem, *Heil als Geschichte*, Tübingen: Mohr 1965, 189–93; ET, *Salvation in History*, tr. S. G. Sowers et al., London: SCM Press, and New York: Harper & Row 1967, 211–15.

37. R. Schnackenburg, *Gottes Herrschaft*, 141–8; ET, *God's Rule* (see above, ch. VII n. 1), 203–14.

38. B. Rigaux, 'La second venue', *La venue du Messie. Messianisme et eschatologie*, Bruges: Desclée De Brouwer 1962, 173–216, esp. 191–8.

39. A. Vögtle, 'Exegetische Erwägungen . . .' (see above, ch. VIII n. 114), 637–52.

40. Linnemann's arguments do show that many texts commonly considered to strike the note of imminence do not independently establish this motif. Still, the

matter seems settled by a convergence of considerations on the form, function, and content of Jesus' words. To begin with content: Imminence is expressed by: 'I tell you, soon (*ap' arti*=Aram.: *mikkā'n*) you will see the Son of man . . .' (Matt. 26.64). Compare the 'this generation' texts such as Mark 13.30 parr.: The consummation will overtake these very persons; ergo, it is coming soon. Likewise, the Markan version of the answer to the high priest lacks 'soon' but says imminence as clearly as the Matthean text. Matt. 10.23 and Mark 9.1 parr. allow no sense other than soon. Finally, Linnemann ('Naherwartung', 107) is surely on slippery ground in denying that the application in Luke 12.56 of the image in Luke 12.54f. signifies the present *kairos* precisely as the sign of imminent judgment. By considerations of 'form' I mean those urged by Rigaux (see n. 38 above) with reference to apocalyptic genre; and by considerations of function I mean that Jesus' public words aimed at the conversion of 'this generation'. It does seem almost absurd to conceive of an urgent eschatological appeal as based on the motif, not of imminent, but simply of sudden, judgment – leaving open the question whether this or some other generation will be surprised by the actual suddenness of its coming.

41. See above, pp. 43f.
42. A. Strobel, *Untersuchungen zum eschatologischen Verzögerungsproblem auf Grund der spätjüdisch-urchristlichen Geschichte von Habakuk 2,2 ff.*, Leiden/Köln: Brill 1961.
43. See above, p. 169.
44. Ibid.
45. See above, ch. VIII, nn. 119 and 120.
46. M. Hengel, *Nachfolge* (see above, ch. III n. 1), 44.
47. The negative answer to the question of G. Jeremias, *Der Lehrer der Gerechtigkeit*, Göttingen: Vandenhoeck & Ruprecht 1963, 351, whether Jesus 'belongs to late Judaism' is supported by the whole, brilliantly executed, comparison/contrast of Jesus with the Teacher of Righteousness (319–53).
48. See the studies of J. Jeremias and H. Schürmann referred to above (ch. VIII nn. 123 and 124).
49. I. Kant, *The Critique of Pure Reason*, tr. N. K. Smith; London and New York: Macmillan 1929, 310.
50. Two essays have illuminated in quite different ways the synoptic tradition of Jesus' teaching on the 'great' or 'first' commandment and on the 'second' commandment. For the early biblical background on the great commandment, see N. Lohfink, 'The Great Commandment', *The Christian Meaning of the Old Testament*, tr. R. A. Wilson; Milwaukee: Bruce 1968, 87–102. On the synoptic texts, R. H. Fuller, 'Das Doppelgebot der Liebe. Ein Testfall für die Echtheitskriterien der Worte Jesu', *Jesus Christus in Historie und Theologie* (see above, ch. VII n. 52), 317–29.

INDEX OF SUBJECTS

INDEX OF NAMES

INDEX OF REFERENCES

OLD TESTAMENT

APOCRYPHA ·& PSEUDEPIGRAPHA